Boxing's Quintuple Champions

Boxing's Quintuple Champions

DE LA HOYA, MAYWEATHER, AND PACQUIAO EDITION

Armando Paz

Copyright © 2015 Armando Paz
All rights reserved.

ISBN: 150858432X
ISBN 13: 9781508584322
Library of Congress Control Number: 2015903148
CreateSpace Independent Publishing Platform
North Charleston, South Carolina

Table of Contents

Introduction · xi

Oscar De La Hoya · 1

    Chapter 1   Prodigy out of East LA · 3

    Chapter 2   Promise Kept to Mother · 6

    Chapter 3   Joining the Big Time · 12

    Chapter 4   Adding World-Title Trinkets to Gold · · · · · · · · · · · · · · · · 19

    Chapter 5   Fighting an Idol · 30

    Chapter 6   Sweet Pea and Bazooka · 37

    Chapter 7   Unification with Tito · 56

    Chapter 8   Old Local Rival · 62

    Chapter 9   Floyd Mayweather Sr. · 66

    Chapter 10   Seeking a Fifth Crown · 69

Chapter 11 The Grudge Match · 72

Chapter 12 Yuri Boy · 77

Chapter 13 Short End of the Stick Again · 79

Chapter 14 First Sextuple Champion · 83

Chapter 15 Entering the Executioner's Lair · 86

Chapter 16 Return to the Ring · 91

Chapter 17 Challenging the New Cash Cow · 94

Chapter 18 Mandatory Retirement · 98

                 Professional Boxing Record · 105

                 Bibliography · 109

Floyd Mayweather Jr. · 111

Chapter 1 Boxing DNA · 113

Chapter 2 Fuzzy Scoring in Atlanta · 116

Chapter 3 Pretty Boy Goes Prime Time · 121

Chapter 4 Dethroning Chicanito · 135

Chapter 5 Super Featherweight King · 138

Chapter 6 Taming Diego · 148

Chapter 7 Too Close for Comfort · 158

Chapter 8	Rematch with Castillo	163
Chapter 9	Testing the Jr. Welterweight Waters	170
Chapter 10	PPV Debut with Thunder	174
Chapter 11	Fiasco in Vegas and Baldomir	180
Chapter 12	Smashing The PPV Record	187
Chapter 13	Stars and Stripes Battles Union Jacks	194
Chapter 14	WrestleMania	199
Chapter 15	Coming Back For the Throne	201
Chapter 16	Legacy Don't Pay Bills	205
Chapter 17	Accepting the Mosley Challenge	210
Chapter 18	Turmoil-Filled Vacation	215
Chapter 19	Vicious Ortiz	220
Chapter 20	Miguel Cotto	224
Chapter 21	Prison	229
Chapter 22	Ghost Busting	232
Chapter 23	Canelo	236
Chapter 24	El Chino	242
Chapter 25	Rematch with Maidana	248

Chapter 26	Securing Both Legacy and Greatest Payday	255
	Professional Boxing Record	267
	Bibliography	273

Manny Pacquiao ··· 275

Chapter 1	Discipline and Strength through Struggle	277
Chapter 2	Making the Dream Happen	280
Chapter 3	Becoming the People's Champion	288
Chapter 4	Weight Issues	292
Chapter 5	The Super Bantamweight Risk	296
Chapter 6	The Disputed Count	299
Chapter 7	Making a Name in Sin City	304
Chapter 8	Halting the Baby-Faced Assassin	313
Chapter 9	El Dinamita	317
Chapter 10	El Terrible	326
Chapter 11	Return to Glory	332
Chapter 12	Politics and Rematch with Baby Face	340
Chapter 13	Fighter of the Year 2008	345
Chapter 14	Mega Stardom	353

Chapter 15	The Icarus of Weight Divisions	357
Chapter 16	Welterweight Division and Political Triumph	361
Chapter 17	Mayweather Time Clock and Tornado Tijuana	372
Chapter 18	Sugar Shane	378
Chapter 19	Deuce with Dinamita and Desert Storm	383
Chapter 20	Bam Bam and Avenging Bradley	400
Chapter 21	A Cinderella Opponent	408
Chapter 22	He Is Going to Fight Me? Yes! Yes!	415
	Professional Boxing Record	423
	Bibliography	429

Introduction

The sport of boxing had not seen one boxing quadruple champion prior to the year 1987. This was not because the sport was void in the talent department. In fact, there were numerous combatants as far back as the bare-knuckle period who demonstrated great aptitude in defeating much larger opponents. However, many of these fighters fought in an era that had as few as eight weight divisions with only one lineal champion per division. In addition, great multidivision fighters such as Sam Langford and Harry Greb had to settle for newspaper decisions that prevented titles from changing hands. Often bouts would require a knockout for a challenger to become the new champion during the early twentieth century of professional boxing. Fighters were also weighed the day of the bout (unlike in modern boxing), which eliminated the possibility of rehydrating. Despite seventeen modern weight classes, many titles have changed hands due to the infamous "catchweight" phenomenon. Many cynics have detracted from the accomplishments of modern multiple champions due to stipulated weight clauses ("catchweights") that are blessed by the four major sanctioning bodies to get belts in the names of some of the biggest stars in the sport. It's interesting to note that a fighter like Sam Langford defeated hall of famers ranging from the lightweight to the heavyweight division. George Carpentier competed successfully in what today would be the flyweight to heavyweight division. There were numerous other examples—such as Tony Canzoneri, Mickey Walker, Barney Ross, Henry Armstrong, and Ezzard Charles—who would likely be quintuple champions if they fought today. As I write this, there are thirty-eight fighters that have now won titles in three different weight divisions as recognized by the four major sanctioning bodies (including interim titles). Before Wilfred Benitez accomplished the feat in 1981, there were only four boxers who had previously achieved such distinction. It would be unfair to equate the Henry Armstrong's accomplishment of simultaneously holding the lineal featherweight, lightweight, and welterweight titles to a modern tripleweight champion. Armstrong, as is widely known, almost became a quadruple champion when he got a draw with Filipino fighter Cerefino Garcia in 1941.

The modern weigh-in system, which allows fighters to rehydrate the day of the fight, can also aid a fighter in making lower weights, as he can rehydrate without draining to make the same-day weight. This is crucial especially when a fighter begins their career and pick up titles from lower divisions. If a modern fighter had to weigh in the same day, they might have to climb a division or two before they desired.

The fifteen-round system that was prevalent in the past may also have prevented many boxers from winning those extra divisional titles. If the current twelve-round system that is used for titles bouts were used in the past, then Sugar Ray Robinson would have won a light heavyweight by decision instead of quitting after heat exhaustion in the fourteenth against Joey Maxim. Roberto Duran would have won a fourth-divisional title as he was leading Marvin Hagler on two cards, and Alexis Arguello would have defeated Aaron Pryor and won a fourth-divisional title as he was also leading after twelve rounds.

How can you compare the accomplishments of what fighters did in the past to today? As I pondered all these questions, I tried to incorporate a book that juxtaposed the fighters from the past to the modern quintuple champions. Unfortunately, that book had competing themes, and I realized that—at nearly one thousand pages—it would be best to first focus on the modern-day quintuple champions. A major advantage of modern-day fighters is that the majority of their fight history is on tape for all to judge. Many of the fights in the first half of the twentieth century have round-by-round accounts from secondhand newspapers that were often biased toward the local fighter. For example, there was a wide range of opinion judging the second bout between Greb-Tunney, which Greb Pittsburgh supporters disputing a Tunney win and classifying it as "robbery," while Tunney partisans would declare it a correct decision.

The major titles recognized in this book are those approved by the four major sanctioning bodies—as recognized by the International Boxing Hall of Game—which are the WBA, WBC, IBF, and WBO. There will be no inclusion of minor or interim titles for these purposes. If we use a very loose concept of defining multidivisional champions, then a guy like Hector "Macho" Camacho is a septuple champion, as he won titles from seven different divisions, if we include minor titles. This book will focus on the three most recent quintuple champions, which are Oscar De La Hoya, Floyd Mayweather Jr., and Manny Pacquiao. If you read a reference book about a film director or favorite musical group, you would want a detailed review of their major works. We have numerous reference books on film, music, and history, and those are very specific in reviewing every facet of the work being dissected. This book isn't a biographical story of these fighters outside of the ring. Although there will be inclusion of some outside-of-the-ring, extracurricular activities, these will be secondary to what happened inside the ring. This isn't about sensationalism or gossip. However, some of the lifestyle decisions that fighters made are included, mainly to give a broader cultural and social context of the boxer's life.

There is more round-by-round coverage of these three fighters than any other publication available. Although at times it's economical to cover a bout in a few sentences, sometimes a closer inspection would reveal many stories that have been overlooked. For example, many remember the "ring wars" Pacquiao had with Marquez, Morales, and Barrera. However, few recall that Pacquiao was almost out on his feet in the second round against Oscar Larios and came back to drop Larios twice and win the unanimous decision. There would be other forgotten novelties, which included trainer Eddie Mustafa Muhammad telling a young Oscar De La Hoya "it's time to go to school" as he fought Floyd Mayweather's uncle Jeff Mayweather back in 1993.

I started to write about the great boxing multidivisional fighters among other boxing news, on various websites and on my own previous site ironchinboxing.com. The tagline for my site was "Coverage without the Hate." It was simply a response to all the schism created by some sites that used various tools such as race, sexual images, and controversy to increase hits and garnish attention. Although I respect opinion, even if it's critical of people, some sites deliberately attempt to throw objectivity by the wayside. I started my site and had the idea of doing a book on the greatest multiple-divisional fighters almost at on the same time. Since I was juggling various responsibilities and this project, it was difficult to keep a proper balance without one aspect suffering. However, my output was rather great, as I had published hundreds of full-length articles, with many focusing on boxing history. To show both impartiality and independence, I got no free tickets and covered live bouts at my own expense. This actually surpised a few publicists who offered tickets. One of my articles did get an honorable recognition from the Boxers Writers Association of America in 2010. The article covered the possible fallout and consequences to the sport's future due to the Top Rank versus Golden Boy feud.

Boxing or "prizefighting" has always been classified as a money-making sport, and it can be a potentially lucrative, and tantalizing endeavor for those willing to take the risk of moving up in weight. The heavier classes usually mean bigger fights and paydays.

However, it isn't only the financial reward that many seek. Many fighters also seek the glory, adulation, and, yes, the legacy of proving their pugilistic skill by overcoming insurmountable obstacles.

What I hope this book does is give a strong, detailed history of these fighters and inspire people to have more comprehensive insight of their professional career. The book will try to give an objective presentation of each fighter's career and progression as a fighter. Hopefully, the boxing fan will be able to watch dozens of fights for the first time, or perhaps even a tenth time, and pick up crucial moments of the contest.

Finally, some of the opinions expressed here are just that—opinion. I am sure many will disagree with my views on some of these contests, but varying thought is what makes these classic fights, and diverse thought is the hallmark of democracy.

The book often includes the exact time within the round in paranthesis to denote the time of the event. The time is the actual time into the round, opposed to what is left in the round. I also added a list of inducted, probable, and possible boxers that the fighter defeated. The reason I added both probable and possible is that there are fighters who are verly likely to be in the IBHOF, while there are some who are essentially in the "bubble" and may get consideration. Moreover, some fighters listed are still active, and a few wins in their résumé may get them in. The induction of Arturo Gatti may make it more subjective in determining which fighter may or may not get in.

Oscar De La Hoya

Active: 1992–2008 (39-6 30 KOs)

Major Titles Held: WBO Super Featherweight; WBO, IBF Lightweight, WBC Jr. Welterweight, WBC Welterweight, WBC Jr. Middleweight (twice), WBO Middleweight

CHAPTER 1

Prodigy out of East LA

Oscar De La Hoya was born on February 4, 1973, in Montebello, California, with a boxing pedigree inherited from both his grandfather and father. Sometimes it's the unexpected offspring that turns out to be the one who follows the footsteps. Hockey superstar Bobby Hull planned for his namesake to be the child to continue the family tradition, but it would turn out that another son, Brett Hull, would be the one who would be a future NHL All-Star and Hall of Famer. Oscar's dad had planned for Joel De La Hoya Jr. to continue the tradition, but it would be the younger Oscar who eventually showed the promise of being a future boxing champion. De La Hoya would lace on a pair of boxing gloves at the age of four and take a punch to the nose from a young relative. Despite the trauma of the incident, De La Hoya would eventually desire to learn and visit the local Ayudate gym less than a year later. Joe Minjarez would help in the development of training the young De La Hoya. Oscar's father would work as a machine operator, and his mother, Cecilia Gonzalez De La Hoya, would be responsible for raising and taking care of Oscar, his brother Joel, and his younger sister Ceci at home. De La Hoya came from working-class and humble roots that instilled a hunger to succeed. This meant having a work ethic outside of the gym, which included De La Hoya having brief stints on various odd jobs that helped make some money as he continued his quest to become a boxing star. De La Hoya's boxing idols were Alexis Arguello, Julio Cesar Chavez, and Sugar Ray Leonard. De La Hoya's size and style reminded many of Arguello, who captured his first title as a featherweight by defeating Ruben Olivares. Arguello would tell De La Hoya when they finally met, "Work hard; stay clean, and you will be OK."

De La Hoya enjoyed other hobbies, such as baseball and skateboarding, but his dad discouraged his participation in any sports that would take time away from boxing. The young De La Hoya would be removed from the field in tears if his dad caught him playing baseball. As cruel as it may have seemed, Joel De La Hoya Sr. realized that in order for his son to become a future champion, he needed to sleep, eat, and breathe boxing.

The first major step to the road of greatness was winning the National Gloves Tournament as bantamweight in 1989. De La Hoya would defeat Ivan Robinson in the 1990 Goodwill games in Seattle for the featherweight title. The win was special since it was the last major win that De La Hoya mother witnessed as she would die later that year due to cancer. De La Hoya vowed to keep his promise to win a gold medal in the 1992 Olympics in her memory. De La Hoya would routinely look up during the referee instruction prior to matches in a symbolic gesture to acknowledge his mother's spiritual presence. This ritual would continue even late in De La Hoya's professional career.

De La Hoya would add Robert Alcazar as his trainer in hopes of developing his boxing maturity to compete with professionals. The Resurrection Gym would be his new training stop as De La Hoya was closing his amateur days. He was perfecting his left hook by fighting in the Orthodox stance to set it up. As De La Hoya's fame grew around East Los Angeles, he won respect even from some of the notorious local gangs. For example, when robbers stole De La Hoya's wallet with money it, everything would later be returned as word on the street was, "This guy is off limits." De La Hoya would graduate from high school at the age of seventeen through an accelerated program so that he could focus on his amateur career.

De La Hoya would win the 1991 US Amateur Championship, but he would lose to Eric Rudolph in the World Championship in Sydney, Australia. It was a devastating loss for De La Hoya who later would have an opportunity to avenge that loss. De La Hoya would set his eye on the 1992 Barcelona Olympics in hopes to fulfill the dream of winning Olympic Gold as his mother had wanted. The first step was qualifying through the Olympic trials. Even as a teenager moving up the amateur ranks, De La Hoya was satisfied to allow his fists to do talking instead of being a trash talker. A seventeen-year-old De La Hoya would tell NBC,

"Up in the ring I can be so aggressive, and outside the ring I like to be quiet... people tend to like quiet people more than people who talk a lot." This approach would follow De La Hoya throughout his professional career. He would usually refrain from trashing opponents, even with confronted with loquacious trash talkers as Ricardo Mayorga, Floyd Mayweather Jr., and Fernando Vargas.

De La Hoya would defeat Lewis Wood, Lupe Suazo, and Anthony Christodoulou to force a box off with Patrice Brooks in the Olympic Trials. De La Hoya would showcase his stiff left jab in the trials along with his rapid-fire combinations. He would defeat Christodoulou by the lopsided score of 41–6. The final De La Hoya opponent, Patrice Brooks, was a solid amateur champion from St. Louis who could match De La Hoya's speed and size. The southpaw Brooks would start off well by using angles and landing his right jab while following with a straight left. It was apparent immediately that this would be a great challenge for De La Hoya and that he would need to utilize all his skills. As Brooks opened up to trade with De La Hoya, he would get punished by a right hand late in the first round. The ambidextrous gift of De La Hoya would allow him to hurt Brooks with either hand. Brooks was worried mainly by the left hook and circled away from it only to be greeted by straight right hands. The De La Hoya momentum would continue in the second round as he pummeled Brooks to the body.

Both fighters would go for broke in the third round, realizing it was a close match. De La Hoya would land a solid pair of left hooks that would prompt the referee to give Brooks two standing eight counts. Both were very questionable standing eight counts, and then—in another intrusive call—the referee Marco Sarfaraz would take a point away from De La Hoya for holding. The deductions would prove to be academic, as De La Hoya would win by the final score of 44–15. The win would guarantee a trip to Barcelona and a chance at the dream of capturing Olympic Gold.

CHAPTER 2
Promise Kept to Mother

De La Hoya would travel to Spain alongside his father and coaches, Pat Nappi and Robert Alcazar. Despite having proper coaches, De La Hoya's father would always be a looming presence. De La Hoya would make a conscious effort to make his dad happy with his development, but his father would always highlight any weakness or mistake to try to make him an immaculate fighter. The pursuit for perfection and desire to please his dad was a lifelong endeavor.

Oscar De La Hoya's body was still maturing, so he would compete as a lightweight in the 1992 Summer Olympics. Those Olympics would be most notably remembered as the debut of American professional basketball players to the Games. The US team would include eleven future NBA Hall of Famers and would be dubbed the "Dream Team." In the Olympic Village, everyone was looking for Michael Jordan, Magic Johnson, and Larry Bird. This in turn deflected some of the attention off De La Hoya and other athletes.

The first De La Hoya opponent in the Olympics would be Brazilian Adilson Rosa Silva. De La Hoya would send a signal to future opponents by knocking down Silva with a left uppercut thirty-five seconds into the bout. Silva was bloodied by the end of the second round due to those stiff De La Hoya left jabs. All the headgear couldn't take the power away from those blows. De La Hoya would suffer a brief scare as he would have a small cut near his left eye due to a Silva connect. Silva would receive a combination of vicious hooks and uppers near the ropes that led to a standing eight count and ultimately a stoppage with only a few seconds left in the contest. Silva was bleeding from both sides of his face and behind in all cards, which made the stoppage logical.

Nigerian Moses Odion would be De La Hoya's second opponent. He was an opponent who would actually have the rare height and reach advantage over De La Hoya. To top that off, Odion was also a southpaw. Odion kept that long right hand out both for his jab and as a measuring stick for his left hand. The first round would be problematic for De La Hoya as he couldn't get past that Odion jab and even got nailed with a few straight left hands. De La Hoya would have some success getting on the inside and using his left hook to the body and left uppercut. Odion would land a clean right hook to De La Hoya's chin, and after one round Odion was actually ahead 1–0. The pressure was on De La Hoya to come back for his struggling Olympic team and, foremost, for his mother. The comeback would be initiated with left hooks to the body in the second round. Odion would smile at De La Hoya to suggest he wasn't hurt, but it was obvious the blows had an impact. De La Hoya would open with straight rights and left hooks to the head in the middle of the round to soften up the taller opponent. After the bell De La Hoya would get hit in the head by Odion either playfully or accidentally. De La Hoya wasn't enamored by it; he felt it was deliberate. De La Hoya still dominated the round 7–0.

De La Hoya continued his dominance in the third by forcing a standing eight count and having all the momentum necessary to win by a final score of 16–4. De La Hoya would again take a knee, make the sign of the cross, and then point up to remember his mother.

Tontcho Tonthecv was a durable Bulgarian who had solid amateur experience. De La Hoya needed to rely more on boxing skill then on physical domination to defeat his quarterfinal opponent. The jab would be doubled and even tripled to help De La Hoya get the victory. Tontchev had difficulty coping with De La Hoya's reach and height advantage. The referee would also give Tontchev warnings for holding. Despite being fatigued De La Hoya would outwork Tontchev to a final score would of 16–7.

The semifinal match would see De La Hoya face South Korean Hong Sung-Sik. Hong had defeated future WBO lightweight champion Arthur Gregorian in the quarterfinals. He won a prior match against Ronald Chavez via first-round knockout. However, the Filipino delegation would file an official protest arguing that the KO punch was really a low blow. The protest was disregarded as the blow would be ruled a legal blow. Hong stood about the same height as De La Hoya and was notorious for his rough-and-tumble physicality.

Referee Sreten Yabucanin, who was from the nation formelly known as Yugoslavia, would do a notoriously poor job in keeping it a boxing match rather than a wrestling match. In the opening minute of the bout, Yabucanin would warn Hong for holding. Hong held De La Hoya then immediately struck him with a left shot to the chin as they separated. Hong would proceed to spin De La Hoya with his right hand and then nail him with the left. De La Hoya would land several left hands in the middle of the round that were not scored, and he was losing 4–2 after one round. De La Hoya appeared to sprain his left ankle in the final thirty seconds of the round when he tripped on Hong's right foot. De La Hoya would complain about his thumb hurting as he entered the second round.

Hong routinely put De La Hoya in headlocks during clinches that would result in a three-point deduction for the South Korean in the middle of the second round. The three-point penalty would give De La Hoya a 6–4 lead. The penalty wouldn't change much, as Hong would hold De La Hoya down again several more times in the round. De La Hoya would prematurely raise his arms, thinking the referee was disqualifying Hong, but each time proved to be another warning. De La Hoya entered the final round with a 8–4 lead. The De La Hoya lead would get extended to 11–6 with only a minute left. With only nine seconds left, De La Hoya would get his own three-point holding deduction, which evaporated his lead to 11–10. De La Hoya connected with a final stiff left jab, which wouldn't be scored, but he would cling to an 11–10 win. Despite the extracurricular nature of the bout, both combatants would embrace after the match.

Joel De La Hoya was a bit critical of his son's performance. "He did not box well, and I don't know why. I want to have a talk with Oscar." De La Hoya was livid in his postfight NBC interview. "It was not tough. He doesn't even know how to box. He can't even throw a jab. All he did was hold me, and I couldn't do nothing." The young Californian would give his own assessment in fighting Hong in another interview: "I know how to box a guy who's in there to box, but I don't know how to box a wrestler. Based just on his boxing, the guy was no better than a JO (Junior Olympics) boxer. My performance was terrible. I feel kind of bad, because I enjoy impressing people."

The rough tactics seemed to take De La Hoya away from his game plan of working the jab. The learning experience was crucial as it would help De La Hoya with rough and awkward future opponents such as John John Molina. There was criticism of referee Streten Yabucanin who could have disqualified Hong after he gave him a third warning for pushing De La Hoya's head down. Amateur rules and regulations require mandatory disqualification for a third similar infraction. The good news for De La Hoya was that his one-point win would put him into the finals against his nemesis, Marco Rudolph.

As De La Hoya entered the gold-medal match against Rudolph in the Pavelló Club Joventut de Badalona arena, a large banner greeted him: "Good Luck Oscar, We love you." And a smaller black banner hung from the rafters: "Go for the Gold." The banners were right below where his family was situated. De La Hoya was also aware that there was one person who was not sitting there and who he felt was watching from a place high above. That one person was his mother, to whom he had promised to win the gold medal. All those days of waking up at half past four in the morning to train and all those nonpartying weekends could be forgotten with one more win.

De La Hoya started with a furious stiff jab that pelted Marco Rudolph. Rudolph was aggressive and landed an overhand right that shook De La Hoya, but the East LA combatant wouldn't relent and kept coming forward. After the first round, the score was somehow only an even 1–1. "Get yourself off before he does, and work on your combinations," the De La Hoya corner would advise him in between rounds.

De La Hoya would batter Rudolph with the straight lefts in the second round. De La Hoya was ahead 3–2 with one round left. There would be plenty of referee warnings but no deductions. Both fighters worked feverishly in the final round, with plenty of clinching and arm punches. A left hook would send Rudolph to his knees, and both his gloves touched the canvas. Rudolph would gingerly get up as blood trickled down his nose. The knockdown would be the finishing touch De La Hoya needed to leave no doubt about victory. After the final seconds ticked, De La Hoya would raise his arm and embrace his former nemesis. The final score was 7–2, and the gold medal that he had long-promised to his mother was complete. In the post-ring celebration, De La Hoya would wave both the American and Mexican flags. This didn't sit well with everyone, including the Olympic committee. However, for future marketing strategy, it made perfect sense to consolidate both the American and Mexican audiences to have crossover appeal. As a professional De La Hoya would often sport both the American and Mexican flag on his trunks to pay homage to both the land of his birth and the land of his heritage.

De La Hoya holds up his gold medal in the 1992 Barcelona Olympics. AP Photo/Mark Duncan.

The fact that De La Hoya would be the only American boxer to win gold in the 1992 games would give him the moniker "The Golden Boy." De La Hoya, who had promised to win the gold medal for his dying mother, would visit his mother at Resurrection Cemetery—this time with the newly won gold medal with him. De La Hoya had routinely jogged pass the cemetery, when he trained in Los Angeles, as a reminder of what motivated and inspired him in trying to win the gold.

Besides De La Hoya the only American boxers to medal were Chris Byrd (silver) and Timothy Austin (bronze). It was a major disappointment for American boxing with notable future champions like Vernon Forrest, Montell Griffith, and Raul Marquez failing to medal in the games. De La Hoya, with his telegenic appearance and personable personality, would be a major marketing force in the sport. The De La Hoya phenomenon drew women to the sport in unprecedented numbers. These new audience members would be an added incentive for the sport, especially since the first few years of De La Hoya's professional career saw former boxing cash cow Mike Tyson locked up in a state penitentiary in Indiana. De La Hoya, by merging the traditional and new boxing audiences, would become the sport's top-grossing pay-per-view boxer in history. By the end of his career, the Golden Boy had sold nearly thirteen million PPV purchases for a total gross of over $600 million in the United States alone. De La Hoya would surpass the approximately $545 million record in domestic PPV sales that Mike Tyson had achieved.

De La Hoya would end his amateur career with a stellar (223-5, 163 KOs) record.

After turning professional De La Hoya would choose Robert Middleman and Steve Nelson as his managers. The two managers would help raise the money through Bob Arum—who agreed to give the money on the condition that Top Rank would promote De La Hoya. De La Hoya would get a million up front while his father, Joel De La Hoya, was promised $1,000 per week, and Middleman and Nelson would earn 11 percent of the share. As an added bonus, De La Hoya would get a brand-new Acura NSX.

CHAPTER 3

Joining the Big Time

De La Hoya would make his debut at 133.5 pounds. He would make quick work of Lamar Williams at the Great Western Forum, Inglewood, California, on November 23, 1992. De La Hoya would corner Williams near the northeastern corner ropes and send him down with a barrage of left hands in the opening round. The Golden Boy would unleash a furious set of combinations that would send Williams down a second time in the middle of the round. When Williams would be dropped a third time with a left hook to the chin, the fight would be waved off by the referee Marty Denkin. De La Hoya would get paid $40,000 for less than two minutes of work. The De La Hoya professional debut was near his native Los Angeles in order to attract a local audience. This was similar to past fighters who stayed near their home to get sell-out crowds and network interest.

De La Hoya would follow up the win three weeks later with a first-round knockout of Clifford Hicks at the America West Arena, Phoenix, Arizona. Hicks would be dropped by a short left hand and then shortly later be knocked out by a straight right in the first round. As De La Hoya continued the early stages of his professional career, he continued to sport both the American and Mexican flags in his trunks. De La Hoya would face Paris Alexander, his third opponent, in Hollywood, California, on January 3, 1993. De La Hoya would drop Alexander by setting him up with a stiff left jab and would follow that with a four-punch combination that would send Alexander down (1:49) in the first round. De La Hoya would land 18 of 53 punches, opposed to Alexander landing 3 of 27 in the first round. Alexander would get dropped by a left hook one minute into the second round and then again by a right hook to the temple of the head at 1:52 of the second round. De La Hoya was now 3-0, 3 KOs.

Since the inception of his professional career, it was De La Hoya's hope to become boxing's first sextuple champion. However, he fully understood that he needed to make the lighter weights of super featherweight and lightweight to make it a reality. De La Hoya, who stood a little over five feet ten, would have major difficulty making weight for his fourth bout. The next opponent would be Curtis Strong at the Sports Arena, San Diego, California, on February 6, 1993. De La Hoya came in at 138.5 pounds, which was 4.5 pounds over the contractual limit; this was a sign that he was having problems making weight. This would make his future bouts at 130 pounds more difficult since he was drained. To complicate matters De La Hoya had minor leg surgery due to an ingrown hair a few days before the bout. Due to the bout being televised and the blowback of canceling a bout with little notice, the fight would go on as scheduled. Strong would be immediately dropped by a left uppercut within ten seconds of the bout. De La Hoya would continue to score with a left jab and left hook. Strong would be the recipient of more punishment on the ropes in the first round. There wouldn't be much room for Strong to navigate in the small ring, and he would take more blows to the body and head in the second round.

The early De La Hoya fights demonstrated that he was much stronger physically than his opponents and could essentially impose both his strength and will on them. Curtis Strong would land a left hook to De La Hoya's temple (1:21), but no damage was done. Strong would rally in the last thirty seconds of the round with combinations, but it was another dominant round for the Golden Boy. Strong would cover up his body due to the punishment he took early on. The ring physician would stop the fight at 1:45 of the fourth round due to a cut on Strong's right eye. The Chicago fighter felt it was a premature stoppage, but there was a lot of blood gushing out, and with over a minute left in the round, there would be added danger for a serious injury. However, Strong proved to be a durable challenger for De La Hoya and earned his paycheck and then some.

For the fifth De La Hoya professional bout, the decision was made to put him with an experienced opponent. De La Hoya would take his first trip to Las Vegas to face Jeff Mayweather (23-2-2, 6 KOs). Jeff Mayweather was brother to both Floyd Mayweather Sr. and Roger Mayweather. Jeff is uncle to undefeated fighter Floyd Mayweather Jr. Jeff was the most experienced fighter De La Hoya had faced up to that point. However, the goal was for De La Hoya to get more rounds under his belt, and there was not much fear of Mayweather's power. Jeff didn't have the power his brother Roger had when he was world champion. This didn't discourage the Mayweather trainer and former champion Eddie Mustapha from predicting a major upset. Eddie Mustapha would tell De La Hoya as he touched gloves before the opening bell, "It's time to go to school now." The opening round had De La Hoya box behind the jab with caution. There was no point to get careless with a veteran like Mayweather. The straight left and left hook would find holes through Mayweather's guard and earn De La Hoya the first round.

At 1:16 of the second round, Mayweather would land a straight right to the body and left hook to the head while avoiding a counter. This was a wake-up call to the young fighter who would get more aggressive by using his speed and left hook to take control of the second round. There would also be what De La Hoya called his "45" which was a half hook and half uppercut. The laser left jab would carry De La Hoya the rest of the bout. Mayweather would get dropped one minute into the fourth round with a counter left "45" after pawing with a left jab. He would get up but take more pummeling near the ropes, and referee Mitch Halperin would stop the contest at 1:37 of the fourth round. De La Hoya passed his first major test with flying colors.

By passing the Mayweather test, there were hopes that De La Hoya was closing in at world title. However, the matchmakers still wanted to get De La Hoya some more quality rounds. They would match De La Hoya with Mike Grable, who had never been knocked out in sixteen professional bouts. De La Hoya would get more national coverage on television in his next match. The match against Mike Grable (13-1-2) would be televised by the USA Network on April 6, 1993, in Rochester, New York. Grable would get cut near the left eye early, but he would last the distance. Grable was a stocky, durable fighter who had a solid guard that would catch a good portion of De La Hoya's punches. Grable would get knocked down by a left hook in the second round but come back to survive. The fight would be more technical than most of the early De La Hoya contests.

De La Hoya would need to try to score with combinations instead of looking for a one-punch knockout. This is precisely what De La Hoya did with success at 1:44 of the fourth round. He would land a five-punch combination that would stagger Grable near the ropes. Grable would miraculously not go down, but De La Hoya would throw another combination to make sure he did go down. Grable would take the kitchen sink for the next four rounds and manage to survive. It would be excellent experience for the young fighter, but he could have been awarded a TKO if it had been another referee. This is because referee Dick Pakozdi gave Grable a standing eight count instead of stopping it at 1:02 of the eighth round. This gave Grable time to sort himself out and last the final two minutes. Grable would actually go toe-to-toe in the final moments and do an edited version of the Ali shuffle, which definitely gave the live audience at the War Memorial Auditorium their money's worth. Both fighters would embrace in the center of the ring after the fight. The final scorecards were 80–69, 80–63, and 80–62. It would be the first time De La Hoya would be taken the full distance as a professional.

The next month De La Hoya would travel to Nevada to face Frank Avelar. Avelar was a compact fighter with good mobility and head movement. He was not as stationary as some of the early De La Hoya opponents. In fact, he predicted he would knock out De La Hoya after receiving news that the Golden Boy had a fight already signed with Troy Dorsey. Avelar thought that De La Hoya looking past him was a sign of disrespect. De La Hoya's speed was finally able to open up with combinations. Avelar was a recipient of several heavy left hooks to the body that seemed to hurt him in the first round. Avelar would start aggressively in the second round but get knocked down by a three-punch combination highlighted with a left hook to the chin at 1:36. The second knockdown would be a result of a delayed reaction to a left hook to Avelar's right ear, approximately a minute into the third round. After getting an additional warning for low blows, Avelar would be set up with a stiff left jab that dazed him and enabled De La Hoya to follow up with a barrage of shots that had Avelar down a third time (1:41) in the fourth round. Somehow, Avelar would beat the count, but he would take more unnecessary punishment, including the trademark De La Hoya "45" in between the guards that forced Referee Vic Drakulich to stop the contest.

De La Hoya would get HBO coverage for his next bout on June 7, 1993, with Troy Dorsey. The match would be part of the George Foreman-Tommy Morrison undercard. It was that night at the Thomas Mack center that Carlos Gonzalez also lost his WBO light-welterweight title to Zack Padilla. Padilla would also be remembered for being the only fighter to ever score an official stoppage of the durable Juan La Porte, due to an eye injury. The twenty-year-old De La Hoya couldn't legally enter the casinos to gamble, but the young fighter had much more to worry about than simply taking in the Las Vegas scene. He had an important match in front of him against Troy Dorsey. The blond, mullet-wearing Texan was far from a tune-up fighter. Dorsey had lost a split decision to Jorge Paez and had a draw with Paez in their rematch. In the first match, Dorsey actually landed 280 more punches than Paez and still lost the decision. The Texan also had taken notable champion Kevin Kelly the distance. When the match began, Dorsey came in very low and aggressive toward De La Hoya. Unfortunately, he didn't bob and weave with high guard to protect himself adequately. Initially, De La Hoya missed often, but his blurring hand speed at that weight would finally hit the mark. Dorsey would be badly cut near his right eye, and ring physician, Dr. Flip Ormansky, would examine the eye at 2:10 of the first round. The action would continue, but Dorsey's eye would not get much better. The Dorsey corner advised him, "You need to get him this round; they won't give us much time." De La Hoya would land 47 out of 113 punches in the opening stanza compared to 24 out of 66 for Dorsey. There wouldn't be another round, as referee Mitch Halpern would stop the contest after consultation with the ring physician. De La Hoya had improved to 8-0, 7 KOs. In the process De La Hoya would suffer some ligament damage to his left hand.

The hand injury had healed enough to allow De La Hoya to get in the ring two months later against Renaldo Carter. Renaldo Carter, with thirty-two professional fights, was an experienced fighter out of Detroit. Carter's decent speed and footwork made it an interesting bout. De La Hoya used an overhand right hand with more frequency, as he tried to dispel the myth that he was a one-handed fighter. The opening round saw both fighters only land about 20 percent of their blows and was an even round. De La Hoya would score with a solid right at 0:55 of the second round. A major reason De La Hoya had to use his right more often in the fight was that Carter was circling away from De La Hoya's left. De La Hoya would take Carter's jab away as he kept getting countered by De

La Hoya's right. Carter would go down in the closing moments, but the referee wouldn't score it, as it was not a direct result of a punch. The third round had De La Hoya take control with his superior speed and power; a right hook to the chin at 1:13 momentarily staggered Carter. Carter would take a knee a little over two minutes into the round due to the constant pressure. The veteran Detroit fighter would start to land hooks to De La Hoya's body in the fourth round. However, every time Carter set up his offense, he would pay for it. Carter would go down again in the middle of the fifth round in response to another De La Hoya barrage of combinations. Finally, De La Hoya would work downstairs and then come upstairs with left-right hooks that caused Carter's head to snap back. Carter would go down but would get back up again until the referee mercifully stop it at 2:10 of the sixth round.

Two week after defeating Carter, the Golden Boy went to Beverly Hills for his next match against Angelo Nunez. De La Hoya would fight at the lightweight limit of 135 pounds. Nunez would navigate around the ring forcing De La Hoya to act as a stalker for most of the first round. De La Hoya would win the opening round mainly with left hooks and due to Nunez's lack of activity. Nunez would land left jabs and a five-punch combination to start the second round. De La Hoya would dart forward and backward against Nunez when he had him in a corner and land a powerful left hook to the chin in the opening minute. Nunez would have his moments when he counterpunched and was able to land his own left. De La Hoya finished the round well to have at least made the round a draw. The left jab to the body did wonders for De La Hoya in the third round as he realized he had to break down the very mobile Nunez.

De La Hoya would get the TKO win by landing a right hand in the corner ropes that appeared to be the catalyst that cut Nunez's eye; there also would be a head collision after that. The combinations landed in the middle of the round would be problematic, as Nunez would have to fight with a cut over his left eye for the rest of the round. Due to the cut, he wouldn't answer the bell for the fifth.

De La Hoya's early bout observers would coin the phrase "spaghetti legs" to describe him, due to his tall, skinny frame. Those skinny legs may explain some of the flash knockdowns that De La Hoya suffered in his early career. Former NABF super featherweight champion Narciso Valenzuela would be the first opponent to knock down De La Hoya. Valenzuela had over fifty professional bouts when he faced De La Hoya at the America West Arena in Phoenix, Arizona, on October 30, 1993. A short right-cross to the chin would send De La Hoya to the canvas for the first time in his professional career, forty-five seconds inside the first round. Despite this being only his eleventh professional fight, De La Hoya showed ring savvy by taking a knee and taking a full eight count to sort himself out. Often fighters who find themselves on the canvas for the first time spring back up too soon without collecting themselves.

Joel De La Hoya Sr. would be watching ringside with added interest due to the knockdown. De La Hoya with an added sense of urgency would knock Valenzuela down in the middle of the round with a combination that ended with his trademark left hook. Valenzuela would go down again at 2:04 of the round near the ropes after being peppered with more flush hooks to the head. This time Valenzuela wouldn't get up, and De La Hoya would earn a first-round knockout. It would be the first major test of adversity that De La Hoya faced, and he would pass the test. The bout would give added exposure to De La Hoya since he fought in the undercard of a Michael Carbajal match. The 1988 silver medalist would defend his WBC and IBF light flyweight titles with a fifth-round knockout of Domingo Sosa.

CHAPTER 4

Adding World-Title Trinkets to Gold

There would be a bit of a weight gamble when De La Hoya would fight Jimmy Bredahl at the Grand Olympic Auditorium in Los Angeles on March 5, 1994. The champions of the division at the time were Azumah Nelson, Genaro Hernandez, and John John Molina. All three of those possible opponents had more power than Bredahl. The majority of De La Hoya fights were at around the lightweight limit, and he would now come in at 128.75 pounds to fight the undefeated Danish fighter. Bredahl defeated French fighter Daniel Londas to win the WBO Super Featherweight title. At the time, the WBO was still not widely recognized as a major world title like the WBC, WBA, and IBF. However, it was inevitable that as the WBO—which was created on 1988—got more recognition as an international sanctioning body, that it would become the fourth major international title.

One of the main reasons that De La Hoya would fight for this title was that, due to his size, he would have the opportunity to fight for more divisional titles. If De La Hoya was serious about becoming a sextuple champion, he needed to capture a super featherweight title. Bredahl (16-0, 5 KOs) a tall Danish southpaw was one of the few early De La Hoya opponents that could match him for size. Bredahl came out very aggressively against De La Hoya, snapping his right jab and straight lefts against De La Hoya. A straight right a little over a minute into the round would drop Bredahl. De La Hoya would try to come and get the quick knockout, but the Danish fighter, who was sporting his nation's flag on his trunks, was too conditioned and savvy to go out in one round. Bredahl would land 7 out of 67 punches, while De La Hoya would land 27 out of 57 punches in the first round. Bredahl would go down again after a left hook near the southwestern corner ropes in the second round. It was obvious that De La Hoya had too much power for Bredahl.

Bredahl would be more careful and land a few decent lefts while losing the next two rounds. It was difficult to surmise the Bredahl strategy as he kept backpedaling in the middle rounds. Perhaps he was trying to get the young De La Hoya into deeper waters, hoping he would gas out in the later rounds. Bredahl landed a right uppercut in the first minute of round five, but it didn't move De La Hoya at all. Any fears of his being weight drained were immediately answered after that punch. But it is important to note that Bredahl had only five knockouts in his sixteen wins, so lack of power may have been the factor that allowed De La Hoya to walk through Bredahl's punches. This gave De La Hoya the green light to stay aggressive and to bloody Bredahl's face.

Bredahl would close the distance and try inside fighting in the seventh round. Unfortunately, the plan backfired when he became a recipient of uppercuts. Bredahl landed several short right hooks to De La Hoya's body in the seventh round as well. If there was a charitable round to give Bredahl, it was the seventh round. But a De la Hoya rally at the end pretty much negated that round for the champion. Bredahl would come forward with his head and butted De la Hoya's head. There was no blood, and after a warning by the referee Lou Moret, the fight would continue. Moret would warn De la Hoya twice in the round for hitting during the clinch. De La Hoya was either irked about the head-butt or was simply upset that he had to go to the eighth round for only the second time of his career. De La Hoya would drop Bredahl again in the tenth round, and after the champion's face was consumed by blood and swelling, the ring physician stopped the fight after the tenth round. This was the first major world title for De La Hoya, despite the fact that the WBO was not yet universally recognized as one of the major sanctioning bodies along with the WBA, WBC, and IBF.

The fact that HBO would telecast the bout was important to De La Hoya. De La Hoya would develop a lifelong partnership with HBO that would produce some of the biggest PPV fights in the sports history. For HBO the signing of De La Hoya would be an important acquisition, due to the fact that Mike Tyson would sign with Showtime after coming out of prison in 1995. Showtime's brass had a working relationship with promoter Don King who also promoted Mexican star Julio Cesar Chavez, who fought under the Showtime umbrella for most of the 1990s. HBO ensured that they would be a serious player in boxing coverage for the rest of the 1990s by securing De La Hoya and adding him to the staple that already included Roy Jones Jr. and Lennox Lewis.

De La Hoya wouldn't vacate his WBO title but instead decide to actually defend it. It would have appeared calculative and contrived to simply win it and then vacate it, which many boxers do today. The danger would be that if De La Hoya was too drained at the super featherweight limit, he could risk getting knocked out. The possible answer came almost immediately against his next opponent Giorgio Campanella. The first left-hook counter by Campanella had De La Hoya in the canvas. As Joe Cortez would give the count to De La Hoya, he would briefly look toward his corner and his dad for assurance. The spaghetti legs didn't fully recover as Campanella came in like a rabid dog to finish him off. It would be the greatest adversity that De La Hoya faced up to that point as he survived the round. In between rounds trainer Alcazar would tell De La Hoya to "box this guy!" This is what De La Hoya would do in the next two rounds by fighting behind his jab and using his height and reach advantage for distance. De La Hoya would fire the left jab like a cannon, followed by a left hook to the body to start the second round. Campanella would take a knee at 2:35 of the round due to a combination. De La Hoya would hit him three times while he was down and also after the bell. Hitting a guy while he is taking a knee has been a major controversy, especially with the disqualification of Roy Jones in his first fight with Montel Griffith. A disqualification would have been excessive, but there could have been a point deduction. De La Hoya would pretty much abandon all boxing technique and come in blitzkrieg fashion and knock Campanella down twice in the opening minute of the third round. The bout would be stopped, giving De La Hoya his twelfth win.

De La Hoya would terminate both his managers Robert Mittleman and Steve Nelson shortly after the bout, due to differences in the management of his earnings and also since they had brought in Carlos Ortiz to train De

La Hoya. Carlos Ortiz, a former Puerto Rican world champion, had a more aggressive fighting style than did De La Hoya, which had drastically changed the Golden Boy's boxer-puncher approach. The Ortiz training sessions were what De La Hoya felt caused a hairline fracture that had forced him to cancel a fight with Jose Vidal Concepcion scheduled for December 9, 1993, at the Paramount Theatre, New York, New York. By eliminating Mittleman and Nelson, De La Hoya would essentially have more control of his financial and boxing decisions. De La Hoya would rely on advisors like his cousin Gerardo Salas and LA businessman Ray Garza. Many in the boxing media felt that the real reason for the Concepcion cancellation was that De La Hoya didn't want to fight under Mittleman and Nelson again. Reportedly, De La Hoya was not happy with 33 percent of his purse from each bout being given to his managers. Both De La Hoya and his managers would trade lawsuits that were eventually settled. Seeing firsthand the problems boxers have with business advisors and managers would later influence De La Hoya to create his own promotional company. De La Hoya would claim that he wanted to make sure that the fighters were the real bosses and that he put the fighters' interests before his own interest.

Now under new management, De La Hoya would fight his biggest rival up to that point.

Jorge "El Maromero" Paez (53-6-4, 35 KOs)—who was known for his outrageous antics, rooster haircut, and his elaborate ring robes—would be the next opponent. The charismatic Mexican was one of the few boxers who could do backflips in the ring that were worthy of the Olympics. There was also substance along with the antics, as he was a former IBF and WBO featherweight champion of the world. Paez would also give Pernell Whitaker—the number-one pound-for-pound fighter of the early 1990s—a game fight for the lightweight title. Paez was past his prime, but there still would be the experience factor, as we have seen many young fighters get when they are schooled by older adversaries. The WBO vacant lightweight title would be at stake.

The bout would take place at the MGM Grand, Las Vegas, on July 29, 1994. De La Hoya would share the stage with James Toney who would defend his IBF super middleweight title against Charles Williams.

The opening round saw Paez do numerous body feints and head movements as he tried to startle the young fighter. There would be a few left hooks landed for Paez as he rushed in and also an overhand right that landed. De La Hoya would not be fazed and stayed composed fighting behind the jab. Paez would get pummeled by a barrage of right-and-left hooks and be stopped at 0:39 of the second round. Paez would be badly hurt and stay down for a while as the medical team attended him. De La Hoya was now 14-0, with thirteen KOs, and held a lightweight title.

De La Hoya, who was not known for trash talking, would do some talking in the lead to his next bout. De La Hoya had promised to walk to Los Angeles if his next opponent, Carl Griffith, could hit him. The bout with Griffith would be part of the undercard of the Roy Jones-James Toney main event at the MGM Grand held on November 18, 1994. Both Jones and Toney were undefeated at the time, and it was another opportunity for De La Hoya to show his skill in front of a large audience. It took De La Hoya almost the full three minutes of the first round to send Griffith to the canvas. Griffith actually displayed some good technical skill and made De La Hoya miss often. Griffith would go down as a result of three left hands, all hooks to the head. The most entertaining part of the bout was Griffith playing possum in the final minute of round two as he pretended to be in Queer Street. A perfect left hook to the right temple would send Griffith down in the third round. Referee Mitch Halpern would stop the fight after another De La Hoya assault. After the bout De La Hoya said, "OK, I'll walk one mile. I must say he hit me with one punch. I'll walk to the Excalibur [hotel]."

Although "blood is thicker than water" is a common phrase, it wouldn't apply to the next De La Hoya contest. De La Hoya would actually fight his cousin John Avila on a match telecast by CBS on December 10, 1994, at the Olympic Auditorium, Los Angeles, California. Avila was related to De La Hoya through his father. Joel De La Hoya Sr. had a son through a previous relationship who was named Joel Avila. John was Joel's cousin. Despite being related the fight would be a brutal exchange without any punches being pulled.

Referee Raul Caiz would rule a possible De La Hoya knockdown at 0:50 of the first round as a slip. The actual De La Hoya slip happened as Avila landed a straight left to the body. It was a judgment call, but we have seen less convincing knockdowns scored. Avila would land a few clean rights in the first round. Avila was a busy fighter and showed himself to be an excellent challenger. Avila circled away from De La Hoya's left while trying to jab the body. De La Hoya would finally open with combinations in the final minute of the second round to take command of the fight. As the fight swayed to De La Hoya's direction, the swelling and blood on Avila's face increased. Gil Clancy who telecast the fight said, "De La Hoya needs to move his head more to slip punches by bobbing and weaving…If I trained him, that would be the thing I would be working the most on every day." Ironically, Clancy would co-train De La Hoya years later.

By the end of the fifth round, Avila's face looked so bad that even referee Raul Caiz would tell Avila "that looks f***** up." However, Avila was not interested in just getting a payday and quitting. Avila would come out for round six. It would be worth it, as Avila would give both the audience at the Olympic Auditorium and people watching at home a valiant effort. Avila would hurt De La Hoya with an overhand right and straight left combo to start the seventh round. De La Hoya would be forced to briefly hold and even push back the charging Avila. Fortunately, De La Hoya was able to withstand the assault and even come back to win the round. Both fighters would trash talk, and Referee Caiz would give them warnings to stop the rhetoric. De La Hoya would get a point deduction for low blows in the eighth, which was the only time in his professional career that he would get a point deduction. Mercifully, the ringside physician would stop the contest after Avila's right eye was leaking enough blood to aid a Red Cross blood drive. Avila never went down and wanted to continue. His championship heart was greater than many paper champions we see in the sport today. Avila would later win the WBO-NABO junior welterweight title.

John John Molina (36-3, 26 KOs) was the super featherweight IBF champion at the time he faced De La Hoya. He was a Puerto Rican fighter who had solid speed and aggressive ring savvy. Molina had solid head movement and knew how to work the body. He moved up in weight to capture the WBO lightweight title that De La Hoya now had. The match would take place at the MGM Grand in Las Vegas on February 18, 1995.

The first round had both fighters boxing on the inside as Molina used head feints to confuse De La Hoya. Molina would overreach with his right, and would get countered with a left hook-right hand combination that dropped him officially for the first time in his career at 1:30 of the opening round. Molina was not hurt and would land a few of his own counter rights, despite losing the round 10–8. The second round was more competitive as Molina was able to land short rights and didn't take a backward step, despite being knocked down in the first round. De La Hoya would land a few stiff left jabs and combinations that would give him the round. A powerful left hook that scored for De La Hoya would have sent a lesser opponent to sleep. A Molina left hook in the opening minute of the third round would actually buckle De La Hoya's knees. Moreover, Molina's bodywork was paying dividends in the round as it took De La Hoya off his rhythm. Molina had success in catching and parrying some of De La Hoya's shots and getting low to avoid straight punches. The fight was a very offensive affair with both fighters throwing more than 220 blows after only three rounds (De La Hoya connecting 118 of 238 and Molina 57 of 224).

The Molina fight was an important fight for De La Hoya because he would gain experience in fighting what is often classified as "an ugly fight." Molina would rough up De La Hoya in the clinches and would often lead in with his head. The concept was to frustrate De La Hoya and to take him off his rhythm, which he partially succeeded in doing. This style of fighting is similar to what De La Hoya faced in the Olympics against Hong Sung-Sik.

De La Hoya would tee off on Molina in the second half of the fourth round, and Molina would stay on his feet as a testament to his chin and durability. Lou Duva would keep telling Molina to keep working the body and to keep turning De La Hoya. The turning was something that Manny Pacquiao would do to perfection thirteen years later against De La Hoya. Duva's plan was to try to gradually breakdown De La Hoya with body punishment and to get him down the stretch. Molina would land a few powerful rights in the fifth and sixth rounds, along with some ill-advised head-butts, that could have given him both rounds on the scorecards. Molina's head movement and slipping ability made it difficult for De La Hoya to control him with his left jab as he had done with previous opponents. Referee Mills Lane would give Molina a warning for his head-butts in the seventh round. De La Hoya was frustrated in this fight by Molina's tactics. After the eighth I had scored it for De La Hoya 77–75, which was much closer than most expected. The reason that De La Hoya kept getting nailed with Molina's looping rights was the lack of head movement. This is what Gil Clancy had correctly pointed out as an inherit weakness in De La Hoya's defensive scheme.

After the ninth both combatants realized that, in this close bout, the last three rounds were the championship rounds. De La Hoya never threw any inside uppercuts to get Molina off him on the inside; it was an ugly final three rounds with numerous clinching. De La Hoya would land a few more clean punches in the final two rounds and did score the first-round knockdown, which I felt did enough to pull off the victory. The three judges had it 117–110, 116–111, 116–111, all for De La Hoya. Final punch stats had De La Hoya landing 315 of 740 and Molina 201 of 675. Interestingly, HBO's Harold Lederman thought Molina won 114–113.

De La Hoya now understood how to fight a twelve-round bout, and his maturity and conditioning passed the test. The defensive struggles De La Hoya had in the bout would convince him to add a second trainer, Jesus Rivero, to his corner. The man who would be known as the "professor" would not be added to change De La Hoya's style, but the concept was to make subtle improvements to make him more multidimensional.

In the spring of 1995, despite having won both the WBO super featherweight and lightweight titles, De La Hoya was not considered to be a champion by some boxing media and publications since the WBO was not yet universally recognized. The next De La Hoya opponent, Rafael Ruelas (43-1, 34 KOs) who held the IBF strap of the lightweight title, would give him that opportunity. De La Hoya would face Rafael Ruelas on May 6, 1995, at Caesars Palace, Las Vegas, Nevada. The match would take place a day after the Cinco de Mayo festival, which is celebrated by Mexicans. Mexicans remember the day due to their Cinderella win over French forces in the Battle of Puebla on May 5, 1862. For boxing promoters the date would be often used in highlighting Mexican and Mexican American fighters. The Ruelas fight would be a night for both tragedy and glory. Rafael Ruelas was brother to Gabriel Ruelas who fought that same night against Jimmy Garcia. Both Ruelas were champions, as Gabriel held the WBC super featherweight title and Rafael held the IBF lightweight title and was trying to unify the WBO title against De La Hoya. Gabriel would win an eleventh-round TKO over Colombian Jimmy Garcia. Sadly, Garcia would later fall into a coma and never recover consciousness. The sober news again reminds us how boxing can be both a sport of triumph and tragedy. Rafael would be following his brother that night.

Ruelas, due to his height of five feet eleven and his power, was one of the few opponents who could match De La Hoya's power and height. A left hook to the body at 1:04 would hurt Ruelas in the first round as he staggered to the ropes. De La Hoya's left jab would find holes in Ruelas's guard. Ruelas would hold and hit at the end of the round. We had seen the most agile and most mobile De La Hoya up to that point. De La Hoya trainer Alcazar would go in the middle of the ring complaining to Richard Steele about rabbit punching at the end of the round. Ruelas's trainer Joe Goosen would follow suit and go to the middle of the ring. Ruelas and De La Hoya would have a stare down as well in the center of the ring as the bell rang.

Ruelas would land two lefts early in the second round that would get acknowledged by De La Hoya. At 1:04 De La Hoya landed a short, precise left hook to Ruelas that snapped his head back and had him fall flat on the canvas. Ruelas wanted to make it a phone-booth inside fight but failed to protect himself while attempting to do that. As Ruelas took the eight count, De La Hoya looked at his corner and shrugged his eyebrows to suggest it was time to go for the finish. Ruelas would be dropped a second time by a right hand and would get up once more. De La Hoya would pepper Ruelas with powerful shot combinations against the ropes, forcing referee Steele to stop the fight as Ruelas was out on his feet and couldn't protect himself. It was a bad night for the Ruelas brothers. Gabriel would forever be plagued with the guilt of taking another man's life, and Rafael would lose his title. Roy Jones would say, "De La Hoya had dynamite power for a lightweight due to the sharpness of the punches." De La Hoya, by winning the IBF title, left no doubt in those who didn't acknowledge the WBO that he was a legitimate world champion.

De La Hoya was now becoming the young superstar of the sport, and a win over Carlos "Chicanito" Hernandez would pretty much consolidate him as the biggest Mexican-American star in the sport. Julio Cesar Chavez was clearly still the biggest Mexican star in the sport. De La Hoya had already defeated Mexican brand names such as Paez and Ruelas, but Hernandez was a native Californian.

The pound-per-pound kings of the sport were still Roy Jones Jr. and Pernell Whitaker. Mike Tyson was coming out of jail soon, and he would possibly be the biggest attraction once he came out. Tyson was convicted of rape charges back in 1991 and left the sport with a (41-1, 35 KO) record.

Genaro Hernandez (32-0-1, 16 KOs) was moving up in weight, like Molina, to challenge De La Hoya. Hernandez would get stripped of his WBA super featherweight title for fighting De La Hoya instead of defending his crown. De La Hoya also would get stripped of his IBF title for fighting Hernandez instead of mandatory IBF challenger Miguel Julio. Hernandez was by far the more recognizable name in the sport. The WBO super featherweight title would be the only title at stake for the match. De La Hoya at (18-0 16 KOs) was on the crest of superstardom. The five-feet-eleven-inch Hernandez would be an opponent that, like Ruelas and Bredahl, could match De La Hoya's size and reach. The question for each of these opponents was, could they match and handle his power? The De La Hoya-Hernandez fight would take place on September 9, 1995, at Caesars Palace, Las Vegas. Other boxing stars featured were James Toney, Johnny Tapia, Kevin Kelly, and rising star Erik Morales.

De La Hoya would be on his toes and boxing Hernandez more than his previous opponents. There was also head movement from De La Hoya, unlike the Molina fight. Hernandez would win the opening round with his left jab and straight-right combination. A timid De La Hoya would get nailed by a right as he kept his head low at 1:23 of the second round. The Golden Boy showed little offense in the first five minutes of the bout. A De La Hoya combination that scored would get Hernandez's attention in the round, but another solid right by Chicanito at 2:29 possibly gave Hernandez the opening two rounds. De La Hoya would start to open up more in the third-round fighting behind his jab. A straight right at 1:32 would snap Hernandez's head back. In the final minute of the round, De La Hoya also worked Hernandez's body with hooks when Hernandez was on the ropes. A right uppercut in the opening minute of the fourth round had Hernandez badly hurt and saw him struggle to survive the round. The fifth round was a close tactical round that could have gone to either fighter. De La Hoya would bloody Hernandez's nose in the sixth round. Hernandez would quit immediately at the end of the sixth round, which caught many by surprise—including De La Hoya. Some fighters choose to fight with a broken nose and even a broken jaw, but the damage was severe enough for Hernandez to not continue. I had De La Hoya winning only by one point after six rounds, but all the momentum was going his way. The official scorecards were 58–56, 59–55, and 59–55 for De La Hoya. De La Hoya was now starting to pile major names on his résumé: Paez, Molina, Ruelas, and now Hernandez. The next marquee name would be Jesse James Leija. Leija was the former WBC super featherweight champion who had earned both a win and a draw with Azumah Nelson. The fight with Leija would take place on December 15, 1995, in Madison Square Garden. The Latino population of New York is known more for its Puerto Rican and Dominican contingency rather than its Mexican population, but De La Hoya along with Leija were able to sell out the Garden. It was another example of how De La Hoya's crossover appeal was becoming a major marketing force in the sport.

De La Hoya had a major size advantage in both height and reach over Leija. Leija was naturally a super featherweight and had a solid record 30-1-1 with fourteen knockouts. The only blemish in his career was a loss to Gabriel Ruelas. Leija had never been knocked out. De La Hoya's footwork had improved, so he knew how to move back and get out of range. Leija never could figure out the De La Hoya distance and would often miss shots when De La Hoya would step back. A left hook at 2:09 would send Leija down to the canvas in the second round. De La Hoya would show no mercy and would batter Leija in the ropes and send Leija down for a second time with only a few seconds left in the round. Leija's corner would throw the towel in, despite Leija barely beating the count.

CHAPTER 5

Fighting an Idol

De La Hoya was 4-0 with three KOs for the year in 1995. He had defeated Molina, Ruelas, Hernandez, and Leija. This gave him the honor of being the 1995 Fighter of the Year. The only thing to conquer now was the growing pay-per-view market. This meant that De La Hoya would likely need to keep moving up in weight—and he had the frame to do it. De La Hoya would start by dispatching his next opponent in 1996, Darryl Tyson, in one round. De La Hoya would work Tyson's body in the first round and soften him up. De La Hoya out landed Tyson 22–3 in the first round. Tyson would be knocked out by hooks to the body at 2:38 of the second round, which proved De La Hoya brought plenty of power to the junior welterweight division.

BOXING'S QUINTUPLE CHAMPIONS

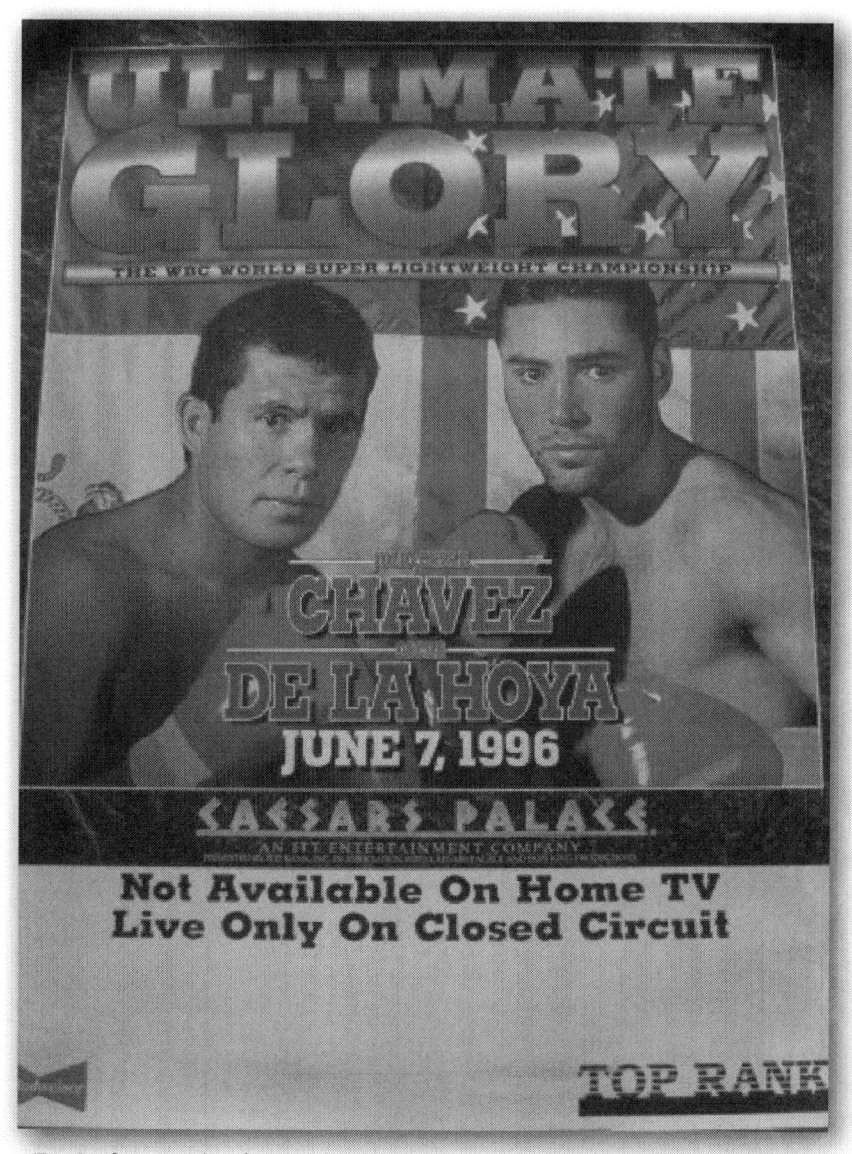

Top Rank promotional poster for the showdown between De La Hoya and Chavez.

Now it was time to face the greatest Mexican fighter of his generation. De La Hoya would state, "I am learning more about boxing and picking up things as I study older champions." De La Hoya made it clear the body shots were not trying to send a message to Chavez. When asked about fighting one of his idols,

De La Hoya said, "I always knew that fight was a possibility, and I dreamed of it—about fighting the legend and people's champion." De La Hoya had once infamously had a sparring session with Chavez in the past and was dropped by the Mexican legend. That was a teenage De La Hoya who was wearing eighteen-ounce gloves. This time, if they fought it would be a mature De La Hoya likely wearing eight-ounce gloves.

Fighting Chavez would possibly alienate some of his Mexican American and Mexican fans, since he was fighting arguably the most lionized fighter in Mexican history. De La Hoya stated that due to the volume of threats he received, he had additional security while traveling to promote the fight. The match was well publicized for most of the spring of 1996 and billed as "Ultimate Glory." The bout would get publicized with billboards and posters around major cities. It would be possibly the biggest interrivalry fight between Mexican blood since Chavez fought his local friend Jose Luis Ramirez in 1988. In reality this was not the same Chavez who dominated boxing between the mid-1980s and the early 1990s. In the eyes of many, he had lost to Pernell Whitaker and had already had an official loss to Frankie Randall. The rematch with Randall was a controversial technical-decision win that easily could have gone either way. In fact, the bout was stopped due to a cut, and we've seen worse cuts be overlooked in a world-title bout.

A prime Chavez dominated opponents by systematically breaking them down by chopping off the foundation that kept the whole body together. Despite age and accumulation of ring war mileage the fact remained that Chavez was an intelligent fighter who knew how to set up his punches and take the air out of opponents by implementing a body attack with surgical precision. There was no way that De La Hoya could take even an older Chavez too lightly, even if he was the two-to-one favorite. Despite it being a major event, the bout was on closed-circuit television and not on pay-per-view. This was due to the widespread problem of "black boxes," which gave cable companies trepidation in putting up guaranteed promotional money in an event that could be watched via cable piracy.

The match would take place on June 7, 1996, at Caesars Palace, Las Vegas, Nevada, in front of 15,283 spectators. The card would feature boxing's future stars Erik Morales, Diego Corrales, and Johnny Tapia, who held the WBO super-flyweight title at the time. The WBC light-welterweight title that Chavez held was on the line. De La Hoya would again sport both the Mexican and American flags on his trunks to pay homage to his dual heritage. The young challenger would establish his left jab in the first minute of the opening round. The durable Chavez, who never had a history of major cuts, would have the unthinkable happen: a serious cut from his left eye. The blood was spurting out like a *Friday the 13th* horror flick. Joe Cortez would have the ringside physician examine the cut two minutes into the round. The doctor would allow the bout to continue as George Foreman felt confident in proclaiming, "You better believe that cut was open in training." Chavez would egg on De La Hoya by tapping his chin, but it was futile unless his corner could stop the bleeding. If the corner failed to stop the cut, then De La Hoya would win since the cut was a result of a punch and not a head-butt. If it were a head-butt, then the bout could be declared a "no contest" if it didn't go four rounds. De La Hoya would feint with his left jab, but would follow it up with his right cross that landed solidly. When Chavez got aggressive and came forward, then De La Hoya would pepper him with Double-left jabs. The crowd would chant "Mexico" despite the fact that Chavez was fighting a boxer with a mutual Mexican heritage. However, De La Hoya was a Mexican American who had fought for the US Olympic team—and he would never be lionized and idolized as a native son. The blood was still a factor as it kept coming down Chavez's left eye. After two rounds De La Hoya out landed Chavez (41–17), more importantly the Chavez cut was not controlled. Chavez couldn't get on the inside and make it a vintage Chavez match where he wore down opponents with body shots.

De La Hoya was too quick and strong to be run over by the Culiacan veteran. Chavez needed to get a little lower and bob and weave to avoid those De La Hoya jabs. At 1:48 of the third round, both fighters got tangled up, and De La Hoya would push Chavez off, which angered the veteran champion. Joe Cortez would warn De La Hoya, "Give me a clean round." Chavez would have some success in the start of the fourth round by getting underneath De La Hoya and landing a short left hook, straight right, and would land his first major right hook to the body. Chavez would land his best left hook to De La Hoya's chin at 1:28 of the fourth. There was definitely a sense of urgency due to the cut. De La Hoya would answer back with combinations that would reopen the cut and derail the Chavez charge. There would be over two dozen De La Hoya punches that would go unanswered as Chavez's face looked like a bloody mask. Cortez would again halt the action, and this time Dr. Flip Homansky would stop the contest at 2:37 of the fourth. De La Hoya's handlers would raise him up in the air in his greatest victory. The Golden Boy was now a three-divisional champion and four-time world champion.

What would follow wouldn't be exactly the reception he had anticipated. After the bout Chavez would claim that his young son, Julio Chavez Jr., had injured him before the bout by inadvertently hitting him in the head as his son jumped up and down while playing with him. Marc Ratner, who was the executive director of the Nevada State Athletic Commission at the time, claimed that there was no cut found on Chavez at the prefight medical examination. Nonetheless, it was the first official stoppage loss on Chavez's record after ninety-nine bouts. The bad taste left in De La Hoya's mouth after Chavez failed to acknowledge losing would mandate that the men meet again.

The next De La Hoya opponent would be Miguel Gonzalez (41-0, 31 KOs) on January 18, 1997, at the Thomas & Mack Center, Las Vegas, Nevada. De La Hoya would share the stage with other boxing stars that night including Michael Carbajal, Kostya Tszyu, and Floyd Mayweather Jr. This was De La Hoya's first title defense for the junior welterweight strap, and it was not going to be a stroll in the park. He was challenging Miguel Angel Gonzalez, a former ten-time defending lightweight champion of the world. Gonzalez was a fundamentally sound Mexican fighter trained by the legendary trainer Emmanuel Steward. The referee would be Mills Lane, a former Nevada judge.

De La Hoya couldn't miss with his laser, stiff left jab and left hook early in the contest.

The Golden Boy would out land Gonzalez (37–9) in the first round. Gonzalez would get his offense going in the second round with a more sustained body assault. His own jab was also landing. The Mexican challenger would even drop his gloves after tasting some De La Hoya shots to demonstrate that De La Hoya couldn't hurt him. The Golden Boy would be on his toes, moving side to side, and punished Gonzalez with his best left hook before the close of the round. There wouldn't be any trepidation from the challenger in the third round. He felt De La Hoya's power and felt he could come forward without being worried about what came his way. As a result Gonzalez came with urgency in the third round, firing his jab and connecting with overhand rights (1:18) and left hooks (1:30). The quality punching would continue in the fourth round with both fighters landing clean violent punches. This was the type of punching that could end fights early. The De La Hoya right-left hook combination (1:19) would totally snap Gonzalez's head back. Gonzalez was starting to land jabs on De La Hoya's body in the fifth round, forcing the champion to use his elbows to block those shots. Sensing he couldn't finish off Gonzalez, the champion would return to boxing and getting on his toes. This would prompt Emmanuel Steward to tell Gonzalez after the sixth round "to keep your head moving." Gonzalez wouldn't follow the advice but still landed his best right cross at 0:30 in the seventh round. Mills Lane would deduct a point from Gonzalez for rabbit punching in the same round. The deduction made a Gonzalez round now a 9–9 round. There was no quit from Gonzalez who kept chasing De La Hoya. He landed an overhand right over the low left guard of the champion. A fighter like Gonzalez (who was 41-0) has the confidence to keep plugging away since he has not tasted defeat.

De La Hoya's left eye had a mouse and a small cut by the closing minute of the ninth round due to those right hands. Gonzalez would continue that surge in the tenth round, as a reticent De La Hoya would be mainly backpedaling on his bike. Either De La Hoya was tiring or was being intimidated by Gonzalez. The challenger would greet De La Hoya in the eleventh round with an excellent right hook (0:18) to De La Hoya's chin. De La Hoya would sparingly throw his left jab in the eleventh round while Gonzalez kept stalking. It was a close round that could have been scored even. Emmanuel Steward thought the fight was close and told Gonzalez, "This round can possibly win the fight." Mills Lane would take another Gonzalez point away for holding and hitting during clinches in the final round. This pretty much made Gonzalez need a knockout to win the fight. To his credit De La Hoya took nothing for granted and aggressively stalked Gonzalez and fired some of his best combinations in a few rounds. It was easily the most arduous and strenuous fight De La Hoya had experienced up to that point. I had it 116–111 for De La Hoya. If it weren't for the deductions, it would have been closer. The key to the victory was De La Hoya landing 212 out of 319 jabs. The judges had it 117–111, 117–110, and 117–109 all for De La Hoya. De La Hoya had improved his record to 23-0, 20 KOs. He had demonstrated his ability in three different weight classes and now planned to conquer the talented and illustrious welterweight division.

CHAPTER 6

Sweet Pea and Bazooka

Top Rank and De La Hoya understood that the lucrative fights would be made in the welterweight division, and it was the right time for De La Hoya to enter the division. The East Los Angeles native was still in his prime, and he had the size to enter his fourth division. In the mid-1990s the welterweight division was blessed with its greatest talent since the late 1970s to early 1980s—in which Palomino, Benitez, Cuevas, Hearns, Duran, and Leonard were all welterweight champions at one point. That golden era had six future Hall of Famers. The welterweight division in the spring of 1997 that De La Hoya would join had three Hall-of-Fame caliber fighters who each held a title: WBC strap owner Pernell Whitaker (40-1-1, 17 KOs), IBF holder Felix Trinidad (31-0, 27 KOs), and WBA champion Ike Quartey (34-0, 32 KOs). There was also Jose Luis Lopez (38-3-1, 30 KOs) who had held the WBO title and would later vacate it. Lopez would earn a draw with Ike Quartey in October 1997. All these combatants brought something different to the table: Whitaker was the crafty southpaw and defensive specialist; Trinidad was the hard-punching Puerto Rican star; and Quartey was the Ghana warrior with his "bazooka jab." The Quartey jab was possibly the best welterweight jab since the Hearns heyday.

Having De La Hoya fight Trinidad would possibly be the most difficult, due to the checkered past between Bob Arum and Don King who promoted Trinidad. The fact that HBO had contracts with both De La Hoya and Whitaker made it an easier to fight to get done with both Top Rank and Lou Duva, who managed Whitaker. A deal would be finalized for De La Hoya to challenge Whitaker on April 12, 1997, at the Thomas & Mack Center, Las Vegas, Nevada. De La Hoya would be guaranteed $10 million (despite fighting for Whitaker's WBC welterweight title) while Whitaker was guaranteed $7 million. Whitaker felt confident he would defeat his younger opponent. "He is nothing but a young kid to me. Get your popcorn and your beverage and your seat belts, and I'll take it from here. I'm going to give him this Academy Award performance…and I'll be picking up my Oscar."

For a good portion of the 1990s, the number-one pound-for-pound race was a two-man race between Roy Jones and Pernell Whitaker. The 1984 US Olympic boxing team had many highly touted prospects, such as Evander Holyfield, Meldrick Taylor, Tyrell Biggs, and Mark Breland. It can be argued that the greatest talent among them all was a five-feet-six-inch Virginian that would go by the moniker "Sweet Pea." The story was that Whitaker handlers were calling him "Sweet Pete," and the media thought it was "Sweet Pea." Whitaker didn't have Taylor's flare, who had supersonic hand speed, nor Holyfield's warrior mentality, who would go punch for punch in attrition with opponents. What Whitaker had were great instincts, intelligence, anticipation, and great technical skill that would make him arguably the best boxer of his generation. The sweet science preaches hit without getting hit, and few practitioners embodied this like Whitaker. Whitaker could literally twist, contort, and manipulate his body in ways similar to CGI graphics that you see in films in order to evade and to slip punches at phone-booth proximity. Whitaker combined a defensive jab with excellent blocking and parrying ability. The Virginian also had great timing that would help him against fast and offensive fighters. His low center of gravity would create headaches for taller fighters as they would have no visible target, and when they did see a target, it would dipsy doodle away in the last millisecond. The Whitaker style was different from many fighters who relied on lateral movement and distance to avoid punches. His defensive style was more closely rooted to Nicolino Locche and Wilfred Benitez who relied on reflexes and slipping while remaining in the pocket.

Whitaker almost lost the big fight with De La Hoya after he was getting outscored by Diosbelys Hurtado after ten rounds. Whitaker, by knocking out Hurtado in the eleventh, guaranteed the big De La Hoya payday. De La Hoya would be the three-to-one betting favorite over Whitaker. The fight billboards would promote the event as "pound for pound," as some thought the mythical pound-for-pound title was at stake. Having two American Olympic gold medalists (Whitaker and

De La Hoya) square off added some additional intrigue. This brought back memories when three American heavyweight gold medalists—Ali, Frazier, and Foreman—would all eventually face each other in the 1970s.

When the actual fight commenced, Whitaker would start intelligently by keeping a low stance. De La Hoya would get a right jab (0:15) in the first round. The height difference would be noticeable as De La Hoya was nearly five inches taller than Whitaker, and Whitaker was fighting lower than his height. Whitaker worked his right jab while catching De La Hoya shots. There would be excessive clinching that would be broken apart by referee Mills Lane. De La Hoya would land a left uppercut (1:08) and right jab (1:10) on the veteran fighter. Whitaker would get his own double-right jab and straight left (1:32). Whitaker would look younger and better than he had in his last fight with Hurtado. The champion was carefully avoiding the powerful De La Hoya left while getting in his own right. However, a stiff De La Hoya jab in the second round would create swelling over Whitaker's right eye. De La Hoya would time Whitaker better and get his own right hand (1:18) in the second round. Whitaker would later prevent De La Hoya from following up by making him miss ten consecutive blows with his excellent defensive slipping ability in the middle of the round. However, Whitaker didn't make him pay for missing. De La Hoya would rough up Whitaker with right hands while holding. After two rounds it could have been scored one round apiece.

De La Hoya scores with the straight right against southpaw Pernell Whitaker. AP Photo/ Bob Galbraith.

Whitaker landed in more frequency with his right jabs and left cross (0:56) in the third. De La Hoya would partially score with an uppercut and combinations in the second half of the round. The fact that the crowd would go nuts on everything he threw would give the impression that he was landing. A head-butt would give De La Hoya a small cut on the right eye. Whitaker's head would collide with De La Hoya's right eye as he came forward and arose from his crouch position. The final seconds of the round would have De La Hoya land two solid lefts—an uppercut and a hook—that would tilt a close round to his direction.

De La Hoya would revert back to his toes and land his straight rights against the southpaw in the fourth. Whitaker would make De La Hoya miss a flurry at the end of the round but, again, didn't make it him pay. The fight was a tactical match, and the De La Hoya speed and reach kept him in the fight. Whitaker would land an excellent straight right-left hook combination (0:21) in the fifth round that consisted of his most solid punches up to that point. Whitaker's ring generalship and defensive ability were more apparent in the fifth. The Sweet Pea jab would solidify the fifth round. De La Hoya would switch to southpaw for moments of the sixth round in an attempt to set up his left hook, which was neutralized for the first five rounds. The southpaw position would net a strong left (1:27) that momentarily shook Whitaker. Whitaker would land his own solid left (2:45) in the round. It would be a round that could have been scored a draw.

Both fighters had a jab contest in the seventh round, which was won by Whitaker. The round also saw Whitaker fall as he threw De La Hoya to the floor. The fact that De La Hoya would hit the canvas may have perturbed him. Whitaker, being a crafty veteran, wanted to frustrate the younger fighter with his great defense and ring tactics. De La Hoya still carried the round with his solid shots while keeping his distance by utilizing his reach and speed advantage. De La Hoya would get Whitaker with a right cross (1:10) and left hook (2:21) that Whitaker would have blocked or slipped in his heyday. Whitaker's corner would tell him after the eighth, "You are losing the fight."

Whitaker would later say he felt his corner was telling him to play more aggressive and not to get lackadaisical. Whitaker would respond by nailing De La

Hoya with a left hook (2:07) to the head that forced De La Hoya's right glove to touch the canvas. De La Hoya got hit while using the southpaw stance, and that resulted in his feet getting tangled with Whitaker and also contributed (along with the blow) to the knockdown.

Whitaker would control most of the tenth round by being aggressive, taking the fight to De La Hoya, and landing his jab. De La Hoya would try to steal the round with a flurry at the end that had the crowd cheering. It would be another round that could have swung either way. What may have caused Whitaker problems with the judges was his consistent mocking and clowning around in the ring; in a close fight, that is not always the most advisable thing to do. For example, in the eleventh De La Hoya would fire a combination (1:25). After Whitaker got hit, he left the ropes pretending to be limping. Whitaker still would get in more left hands and would take the third, consecutive round on my card. De La Hoya knew the fight was close and came in with a sense of urgency in the final round. He would throw flurries from all directions (0:41–0:45) in the final round to get the judges' attention. De La Hoya would press the action for most of the round, while Whitaker would be backpedaling and occasionally going forward to land his jab. Whitaker would do dipsy doodle and contort his body to showboat. I felt that the last round gave De La Hoya a one-point win 114–113 (6-5-1).

The deduction Whitaker got for the accidental head-butt and knockdown in the ninth round would offset each other. The final scorecards from the judges were: Chuck Giampa (115–111), Jerry Roth (116–110), and Dalby Shirley (116–110) all for De La Hoya. The final punch stats would have Whitaker landing 232 out of 582 and De La Hoya landing 191 out of 557. The jab count had Whitaker landing 160 of 390 and De La Hoya 45 of 194. Final power punches had Whitaker landing 72 of 192 and De La Hoya at 146 of 363. Whitaker felt he did enough to retain his title, as did many other people. This included boxing historian Bert Sugar who would go on sports radio after the fight and say that the WBC had robbed Whitaker as they did in the Chavez fight. I do think one could have made a case for either fighter winning. However, the De La Hoya fight was not in the same class as the robberies Whitaker suffered against Chavez nor the first Ramirez contest. De La Hoya's speed, size, and power gave Whitaker some apprehension in many of the close rounds. I do think Whitaker won three of the last four rounds, and if not for the head-butt deduction, should have retained his title. What may have also swayed the judges was that Whitaker's face had much more swelling and bruising. Sometimes judges score the blood and bruising more than the actual fight.

Whitaker would say. "I felt I won the fight but did enough, at worst, to get a draw and keep my title. If there is a toll-free number, let the fans call up and vote to see who won."

Before the fight *USA Today* quoted De La Hoya as stating, "It's all politics. It's all about money. What the WBC sees is that I'm a young fighter. If I win the title, I obviously make more money than Whitaker or anybody else." HBO's Jim Lampley would confront De La Hoya with that prefight quote. De La Hoya would acknowledge the quote but felt he had done enough to win. He stated, "A fight is where two fighters go at it and see who won…Many of the Whitaker punches were ineffective blows." Whitaker would respond, "I controlled the fight and set the tempo. I moved forward and controlled him and won the fight easily or enough to get a draw and keep my title."

De La Hoya would still claim he didn't think he was the number-one pound-for-pound fighter and that he still needed to improve. He said that he called his shots, and if the negotiations were fine, he would give Whitaker a rematch. The bout did get over 700,000 pay-per-view purchases, which generated nearly $29 million in revenue. This would stamp De La Hoya as a legitimate PPV star.

Perhaps not fully enthralled with how he had won against Whitaker, the fight may have convinced De La Hoya to do a corner change again. Legendary trainer Emmanuel Steward would join the De La Hoya camp as cotrainer. Steward's methodology was to take out opponents as soon as possible. Steward was notorious for tongue lashing his fighters who failed to take out opponents early when given the opportunity. Steward felt that if you fail to finish off opponents, the braver they become—and the more likely to knock you out. Steward felt he could improve De La Hoya's offense and conserve rounds to increase his boxing longevity. Steward also wanted to improve De La Hoya's right hand to make him a more lethal fighter with both hands. The first test under the new Steward era would come on June 14, 1997, at the Alamodome in San Antonio,

Texas. De La Hoya would challenge David Kamau (28-1, 21 KOs), a solid opponent, in his first WBC title defense.

Kamau only had one loss to Julio Cesar Chavez in a bout that was much closer than the final scorecards read—and one in which Kamau dropped the Mexican legend. Kamau started off very aggressively against De La Hoya with his straight right and left jab. Kamau threw ninety-five punches in the first round, but only sixteen landed—as opposed to twelve of thirty-four for De La Hoya.

Kamau would get dropped by a left uppercut in the opening minute of the second round. De La Hoya would tee off on Kamau in the center of the ring to drop him a second time with a flurry of punches. Lawrence Cole would stop the fight with six seconds left in the second round. The left hook was the punch that staggered Kamau before the final flurry. De La Hoya would earn a two-round demolition under the tutelage of Emmanuel Steward in their first contest working together.

Steward would remain with De La Hoya for his next opponent Hector "Macho" Camacho. Camacho was coming in with a twenty-one-win streak when he was chosen as the next De La Hoya opponent. Camacho (63-3-1) suffered his first loss via split decision, due in part to a point deduction for failing to touch gloves in the final round against Greg Haugen. Camacho would avenge that defeat. His only notable losses were to Julio Cesar Chavez and Felix Trinidad. Both fights saw Camacho clinch excessively to survive. Camacho always had great hand speed, but it gradually slowed as he kept moving up in weight. As a super featherweight and lightweight, his hand speed was a sonic blur. However, he was facing a younger and stronger De La Hoya in this bout. Camacho was a southpaw, and De La Hoya—as evidenced in the Whitaker fight—was not comfortable with the different angles from which southpaws fired shots. Moreover, De La Hoya's best punch, the left hook, is easier to land on an orthodox fighter. In the later part of his career, Camacho was thought of as a fighter who didn't like to be put on his back foot and would often clinch. Camacho had promised to stop De La Hoya in four rounds and even wagered to have his ponytail cut off, while De La Hoya promised to give Camacho $200,000 extra in incentive. De La Hoya took the wager seriously and was almost immediately on the offense when he met Camacho at the Thomas & Mack Center on September 13, 1997. De La

Hoya would hurt Camacho with a left hook and force the flamboyant fighter to hold on. Camacho tried to employ a strategy of connecting with straight lefts to the body and fighting behind the right jab and then clinching. I felt Camacho won the second round by using this tactic. De La Hoya was the stronger offensive fighter, and Camacho realized that he needed to take as much time away from the clock as possible. A football team runs the ball against a great offense to keep them off the field, and holding is used to take time away from an offensive fighter and disrupt that fighter's rhythm.

De La Hoya would change things in the third round by going to the body with his left hooks and firing uppercuts on the inside. The uppercuts were a tool to discourage Camacho to hold in the inside. Camacho was not landing any combinations or really working the body. However, he did land a good one-two, right-left hook combination at 1:56 of the fourth round that De La Hoya took well. De La Hoya would answer back with a left hook to the head and body shots to close the round. De La Hoya's intensity wouldn't allow him to sit on the stool as Emanuel Steward instructed him. Camacho would avoid major danger in the opening minute of the sixth round; he was pelted with a straight right and also left hooks to the body, forcing Camacho to retreat. Camacho would land a left and immediately clinch at 1:13 to slow down the fight. This didn't change the fact that De La Hoya landed most of the power shots. The number of power punches favored De La Hoya 121 to 21 after six rounds.

The pitty-pat punches were not going to hurt De La Hoya. Camacho would show off his underrated chin by taking solid uppercuts and a hook in the seventh round and not going down. This would continue in the eighth round where, at one point, Camacho would take a four-punch combination to the chin and not blink an eye. Unfortunately, a fight is won by scoring and not durability, and with the possible exception of the second round, De La Hoya dominated the entire fight. De La Hoya would be only the second fighter to score a knockdown against Camacho when he floored him with a combination that was started with a left uppercut at 2:25 of the ninth round. He was able to do something that Rosario, Mancini, Trinidad, and Chavez couldn't do against the "Macho" man. De La Hoya desperately tried to be the first fighter to stop Camacho, but the fighter from Bayamon would survive the final three rounds by using his legs and holding when needed. At one point in the eleventh round, Camacho would grab De La Hoya's legs and tackle De La Hoya to the canvas. Camacho would also get a point deduction for excessive holding in the final round. I had it 119–107 for De La Hoya. The judges had it 120–105, 118–108, and 120–106.

Interestingly, Camacho would go on and add a few more titles to his résumé. He would be a seven-divisional champion, if you add four minor titles to his three major world titles. In addition he would end his career (79-6-3) and never get knocked out in eighty-eight professional bouts. Camacho's life would end tragically in 2012 when he died days after being shot in Bayamon, Puerto Rico.

Before his next bout, there would be another corner change in the Golden-Boy camp. Emmanuel Steward was not going to part of the next training camp. De La Hoya felt that Steward, who would work him only four days a week, was not working him hard enough. Steward always felt that many fighters would simply overtrain and then have nothing left in the ring. There was also the concern of excessive sparring sessions that could result in injuries such as cuts. The fact that De La Hoya would run out of gas and seem to fade in some of his biggest fights may lead some to conclude that the Golden Boy did overtrain for some of his bouts. Regardless of the absence of Steward, there were still good hands working with De La Hoya. Robert Alcazar was still training an undefeated fighter who was 26-0, 21 KOs. De La Hoya, for good measure, would add veteran trainer Gil Clancy for his December 6 match with Wilfredo Rivera. Clancy was known for his work with Emile Griffith, Joe Frazier, and George Foreman. Part of the arrangement was to give Clancy the security that it was not a full-time endeavor, as he would have a backing role to head trainer Robert Alcazar.

Wilfredo Rivera was a fighter from Rio Piedras, Puerto Rico, who was 28-2-1, which included two close-decision losses against Pernell Whitaker. Many felt (myself included) that Rivera deserved to win the first bout. This meant, in many eyes, that Wilfredo Rivera should have been welterweight champion on at least one occasion. Both fighters would make it a jabbing contest in the first round. De La Hoya would also get in a good left hook and several straight rights. Rivera would get in a solid straight right at 1:49 of the first round. De La Hoya would use the left jab to the body in the second round. It looked like a staccato-pace sparring session until the second half of the second round. Rivera would get in two power rights at 1:43 of the second round as De la Hoya's knees temporarily buckled. De La Hoya would answer back with a left hook to the top of the head that staggered Rivera. Rivera would receive combinations that would open up a cut near the right eye. De La Hoya's patent "45" would be the cut's culprit. The severity of the cut would have the ringside physician momentarily thinking about stopping the contest. Rivera would rally in the third round with his lead right that scored several times. In order to protect to his eye Rivera would go to southpaw briefly. De La Hoya had a good boxer in front of him and was cautious about leaving himself open with careless aggression. However, when De La Hoya took initiative as in the final minute of the fourth round he made Rivera pay. A right cross would floor Rivera at (2:33) of the fourth. The right cut would open up and become even more severe. Referee Joe Cortez would look at the eye between corners and admonished Rivera that he wouldn't let him take more punishment if he couldn't protect himself. De La Hoya would get back to bouncing on his legs and work on the cut eye with jabs in the next rounds. Despite having a wounded fighter in front of him De La Hoya didn't go for the finish in the sixth round. Rivera had no choice but to go southpaw for a good portion of the fifth and sixth round to protect the eye. As the blood continued to flow from Rivera's face the possibility of a stoppage increased. Mercifully, the ringside physician, Dr. Howard Taylor, would stop the contest with a dozen seconds left in the eighth round. Rivera would bang his glove against the ropes in frustration. De La Hoya would land 176 of 375 punches while Rivera would land 84 of 494.

De La Hoya would lose the fighter of the year award to Evander Holyfield—despite winning all five of his bouts in 1997 that included two likely future Hall of Famers. Holyfield would win the award by earning a DQ win over Tyson, who bit his ear, and by earning an eighth-round TKO of Michael Moorer. Perhaps some of the voters weren't fully convinced that De La Hoya deserved the decision against Whitaker, and their vote reflected this.

Regardless of the award, De La Hoya had more important business to settle in 1998.

Julio Cesar Chavez, who never fully conceded his loss to De La Hoya, was an anticipated rematch. Chavez wanted another crack at a fourth-divisional crown, and De La Hoya's WBC welterweight title would suffice. De La Hoya would have one tune-up before a Chavez rematch. Bob Arum understood it was important to get De La Hoya in front of a mass audience before the Chavez. The Sun Bowl in El Paso, Texas, and was easy cash in for the De La Hoya name. Texas had a large Mexican American population that would get its first opportunity to see De La Hoya live, without needing to go to Vegas or Los Angeles. What was apparent was the large female audience that gravitated to De La Hoya. The number of women De La Hoya brought into boxing was similar to what Jack Dempsey did back in his heyday. An aristocratic female audience was usually the only major female following in the sport, but this changed over time.

The next De La Hoya victim would be Patrick Charpentier. The match would be postponed as De La Hoya suffered a wrist injury. The date was moved to June 13, 1998. De La Hoya was too fast, strong, and big for Charpentier. The fight was a total mismatch. Charpentier was a former European welterweight champion but had fought no notable opponents, with the possible exception of Scottish fighter Gary Jacobs. (Jacobs would be known mainly for losing to Pernell Whitaker in 1995.)

De La Hoya dropped Charpentier with a straight right-and-left hook combination that was set up with his left jab in the third round. Charpentier would get dropped a second time by a left uppercut in the same round. A left cross would drop Charpentier a third time, compelling referee Lawrence Cole to stop the bout at 1:56 of the third round.

After the win over Charpentier, De La Hoya set his eyes back on Chavez. De La Hoya always felt that Chavez never gave him his proper due after their first encounter. It was inevitable that a rematch would eventually take place. Chavez—who was a triple-divisional champion—had once failed to become a quadruple champion when he was gifted a draw with Pernell Whitaker in 1993. The rematch would be billed as "Ultimate Revenge" because De La Hoya felt he was never given the props for his win due to the Chavez cut. Chavez, despite fighting in his eighteenth year professionally, had still retained power and good ring generalship. De La Hoya wanted to get the win to get the respect he never got from the first Chavez fight—specifically from the Mexican public. Chavez was still trying to become the first Mexican-born fighter to win titles in four weight classes, a feat already accomplished by the Mexican American De

La Hoya and Roberto Duran (who had a Mexican biological father). The De La Hoya-Chavez rematch would take place on September 18, 1998, at the Thomas & Mack Center. Richard Steele, who had worked several notable Chavez bouts, would be the referee.

The opening round saw both combatants moving around the ring without many fireworks. Chavez fought only in spurts and had difficulty with the De La Hoya size advantage. Both fighters would catch their opponent's shots with their gloves. De La Hoya would catch a Chavez lunging left hook with his glove; while Chavez would catch the De la Hoya left jabs. De La Hoya would win the opening round by sheer activity. The young champion refused to sit on the stool, which may have been a sign of adrenaline. Gil Clancy would tell De La Hoya to keep working the jab and get in for the second round. Chavez would land a left jab followed by a right hook to the body in the opening seconds of the second round. Both fighters would open the action with combinations that partially scored. Chavez would land a solid overhand right at 0:57 of the second round. (The overhand shot works well for shorter fighters when fighting taller opponents.) In the closing minute, De La Hoya would land short hooks as Chavez fired back with his lead right and his own left hook. Referee Richard Steele would warn De la Hoya for pushing. Chavez was definitely testing the De La Hoya chin and will in this contest. De La Hoya landed his own short uppercuts on the inside; it seemed that it was becoming an inside fight that would favor the veteran, Chavez. I scored the second round for Chavez as I felt he landed the cleaner blows. The possible game changer was that Chavez again had a cut on his left eye. However, this time it would be controlled and would not be a factor. The Chavez corner wanted more movement from their fighter as the De La Hoya corner would request his vintage "45."

De La Hoya would try to take control of the action with his speed in the inside, throwing punches in bunches, until derailed by a Chavez low blow. Steele would give Chavez a warning and would give De La Hoya some time to recuperate; both fighters would touch gloves when the action resumed. The artillery exchange would continue, as it became obvious that De La Hoya was going to make it a brawl instead of a boxing match. Instead of using his reach and height advantage, he would fight in close quarters, giving Chavez opportunities to show his power. Once again, there had to be a bit of the Mexican factor for De

La Hoya wanting to beat Chavez at his own game. If he danced for twelve rounds throwing flurries, he may not have won the respect that he wanted from both the Mexican public in the homeland and in the United States. At 1:30 Chavez would land a heavy left hook flush to De La Hoya's chin in the third. If this had been the skinny-leg De La Hoya at the super featherweight division, he would have probably gone down. However, at this weight De La Hoya was much stronger and could take those shots. At the same rate, Chavez fighting at this weight class lost some of that power he had as a lightweight and super featherweight. De La Hoya had a large frame, so it was easier to move up in weight.

De La Hoya would land an overhand right at 2:06 of the third that would get Chavez's attention. An animated Chavez would drop his gloves and pound his chest to suggest he could take that and then some. De La Hoya would take the round with solid left hooks and right crosses, but Chavez would land his best left hook that actually made De La Hoya temporarily lose his footing as the power of the shot would turn his body 180 degrees to the right. That punch was easily the best shot Chavez landed in seven rounds with De La Hoya and epitomized the mistake De La Hoya was making in fighting Chavez in that style. This possibly explains why, in the fourth round, De La Hoya would resort back to boxing behind his left jab that he fired to Chavez's body. This still didn't prevent Chavez from landing a thundering overhand right at 1:03 of the fourth round. The Golden Boy would retaliate with his own left hook to the chin. De La Hoya would go back to his toes and control the rest of the round by doubling or tripling his left jab. A three-punch combination to Chavez's body with less than a minute left was intended to help slow him down as well. Chavez would actually have a decent left jab going, but the vintage Chavez bodywork was not there.

Chavez's bodywork would win him numerous contests down the stretch by breaking down opponents—and then stopping them late. De La Hoya controlled the fifth round with his boxing. Chavez did score with a short left upper-and-hook combination that even got De La Hoya to nod his head in acknowledgment. The closing moments of the round had excellent toe-to-toe action with both combatants in phone-booth style.

De La Hoya, perhaps due to being fatigued, would be less mobile and have a lower guard in the sixth round. This enabled Chavez to fight in close quarters.

Chavez would land two solid body shots in the waning seconds that would get a response of a powerful left hook to Chavez's chin. It would be the second round that could have been scored for Chavez. Most importantly for Chavez, he finally got to De La Hoya's body. It was time for the young champion to step up and take the bull by the horns. He was now in a war of attrition, and he realized this when he clamped his gloves at the end of the sixth round. De La Hoya would get a second win and would get back on his toes in the seventh round and keep his distance behind his jab. When Chavez would come in close, De La Hoya would fire inside uppercuts. Chavez would again unleash a powerful overhand right at 1:58 of the seventh round on De La Hoya's chin. De La Hoya's chin again passed the test as he nodded to Chavez in recognition of the good land. The solid jab and combinations scored would make it another De La Hoya round.

The eighth round would be a defining moment for both warriors in their careers. It was a passing of the torch that should have happened in the first fight. Both warriors would trade their best shots to see who would be the last man standing as blood spurted out of both of them. De La Hoya would cap off the round with two solid left hooks that jolted Chavez's head back. Chavez felt one of the shots was after the bell and came toward De La Hoya, but Richard Steele separated them. Many were shocked that Chavez never came out for the ninth; perhaps the pride of the champion prevented him from the chance of being taken off of his feet for the first time. Chavez never suffered a knockout in the classical sense, since his TKO loss to De La Hoya in 1996 was due to cuts. However, this time around he was being punished physically, which could have resulted in Richard Steele stopping the contest.

Despite the bickering De La Hoya and Chavez would greet and embrace after the contest. De La Hoya would have major swelling under the left eye, and Chavez had a busted nose and a bloody mouth. It was the expected end for a contest of two fighters with Mexican blood. Would the public finally give De La Hoya respect? Chavez told De La Hoya, "you beat me," which seemed enough respect that De La Hoya wanted from his idol.

There were still two major welterweights that De La Hoya had to defeat in order to lay claim as the true, undisputed king of the welterweight division. These two fighters were Ike Quartey and Felix "Tito" Trinidad. The first one that

De La Hoya would tackle was Ike Quartey. Ike Quartey (34-0-1, 29 KOs) was an opponent who would be a serious threat to the Golden Boy. The Ghanaian fighter, known as "Bazooka," had one of the greatest jabs in the history of the welterweight division. Unlike Whitaker and Chavez, there would be no excuses that De La Hoya was fighting a past-prime fighter. The only blemish in Quartey's career was a draw to Jose Luis Lopez, a hard-hitting Mexican touted as a possible De La Hoya opponent at the time. Listening to critical boxing fans, we would often hear them say, "De La Hoya didn't fight Quartey, Lopez, or Trinidad yet." Of course, like many fighters, De La Hoya would have cynics point to people he didn't face instead of who he fought. This is why the Quartey fight was so important. It would open the door for the biggest fight, which was Trinidad. The match was initially scheduled for November 21, 1998, but De La Hoya suffered a cut in sparring that had the match rescheduled for February 13, 1999, at the Thomas & Mack Center, Las Vegas, Nevada. De La Hoya would say, "I think this is my first real test of my boxing career. He is a former world champion. He is unbeaten. I took this fight because I know that style wise Ike Quartey—heavy hitter, dangerous puncher—will bring out the best in me. I'm up for this fight." Quartey was confident that he would win by knockout. De La Hoya was guaranteed $9 million and Quartey $3 million.

The match began with Quartey being the active fighter early on, as he used looping left hooks and his jab to control the action. De La Hoya would work his jab, but Quartey's tight guard would block a good portion. The Golden Boy would have better success with left hooks to the body. Quartey was taking the lead in the fight with his left hand, which landed with frequency. De La Hoya, by the middle of the second round, was starting to better anticipate the Quartey left. The Golden Boy was also able to counterpunch with his straight right (1:48). Quartey was still confident and was able to score with an overhand right (2:36) that buckled De La Hoya in the second. Both fighters would raise their arms after two rounds, thinking they had won the round.

De La Hoya would have a better third round. He would be much more aggressive with left hooks (1:35, 1:48) and an overhand right (1:46). De La Hoya was getting underneath the Quartey jab and countering. After three rounds both opponents' per-punch stats showed that they had landed forty-eight punches. De La Hoya would shorten the distance and land stiff double jabs that gave him the fourth round. De La Hoya would out land Quartey twelve to eight in the fourth. De La Hoya was doing a better job catching the Quartey jab with his gloves.

The fifth would be tactical; with neither doing much, it could have been scored as even. The sixth would start with fireworks, as Quartey would get dropped by a left hook (0:08). Quartey would be fine and beat the count. This would make De La Hoya overzealous, trying to finish off the opponent and leaving himself open for a left hook (1:00) that would drop him in a reversal of fortune. Quartey would follow up with a double hook to the chin that would force De La Hoya to clinch to buy time. Due to the traded knockdowns, it would have been scored 10–10, yet Quartey would still do more damage and out landed De La Hoya 33–23, which could have given him a 10–9 round.

De La Hoya's left eye would be pretty much shut for the rest of the contest. Quartey's dominance would continue in the seventh where he controlled De La Hoya in the center of the ring. Gil Clancy instructed De La Hoya from the corner: "Your legs are stuck in mud. You have better legs than the other guy; use them." De La Hoya would revert to boxing on his toes momentarily in the round, but once again Quartey's bazooka jab would control most of the round with solid shots both upstairs and downstairs. The straight would also pay Quartey dividends. Quartey would sport a condescending smirk for most of the contest, and he smiled increasingly at De La Hoya while outclassing him. De La Hoya would have small rallies at the end of rounds, but it didn't appear enough to win the rounds. He would land short uppercuts in the opening minute of the ninth round. Quartey would answer with a powerful right hand (2:11) in return. De La Hoya would get a solid left hook (2:18). After nine rounds I thought Quartey was winning by two points.

Quartey would get stunned by a straight left (0:22) in the tenth round. This was a clear indication that the fight was long from over. De La Hoya would possibly nick the close round with left hooks (2:17) to the head and body. Quartey possibly took the eleventh with his jab. This would set up the final round in which the Golden Boy had to figure he was behind in the cards. A desperate De La Hoya would rebound by dropping Quartey with a left hook (0:12) in the twelfth round. De La Hoya would wait after the Mitch Halpern count to come seeking the knockout. He would corner Quartey near the ropes and throw everything including the kitchen sink—and still not be able to finish off Quartey. Another referee may have stopped the bout prematurely, but Quartey was fighting back, and nonstoppage was the correct move. Joel De La Hoya Sr. could be seen just about a foot and a half away yelling instructions to his son, who must have heard him. It is important to note that the ropes are what helped Quartey stay up. If he had taken those shots in the middle of the ring, he may have been dropped for a second time, giving De La Hoya a 10–7 round. After the flurry De La Hoya literally punched himself out with ample time left. Quartey would get his feet back and land his jab and a leaping left hook; De La Hoya couldn't finish off Quartey. Now the decision would be in the judges' hands.

De La Hoya would land 206 of 551 and Quartey 201 of 608. The sixth round was the key, as De La Hoya had a 10–8 round until he would get dropped and dominated for the second half of that round. That was a three-point swing in some cards. I had it for Quartey 7–5 (114–113). De La Hoya would earn a split decision via the scores of John Keane (116–113) and Ken Morita (116–112), and Larry O'Connell (114–115) who scored it for Quartey. The split decision win was the only time that De La Hoya had a losing card. Quartey would claim that he was robbed and felt that the De La Hoya superstar status and money potential prevented him from getting a win in Vegas.

The loss would be detrimental to Quartey's trust in getting a fair shake. The Ghanaian fighter would have other losses to Fernando Vargas and Vernon Forrest. The Vargas fight was close, but most observers had Vargas the winner. The Forrest bout was a much clearer Quartey victory. If you flip the two losses to Forrest and De La Hoya, then Quartey would have had a (39-2) record and would have been a slam dunk to get inducted into the Hall of Fame. De La Hoya had a rematch clause if he had lost to Quartey. There was also a rematch with Whitaker on the table if Whitaker beat Trinidad. None of this materialized as Whitaker lost to Trinidad, and De La Hoya didn't fight Quartey again.

Before getting in the ring again, De La Hoya would run through a serious allegation. An eighteen-year-old woman claimed that De La Hoya raped her in a hotel in Cabo San Lucas, Mexico, when she was fifteen years old. De La Hoya was served with a suit seeking $10 million in monetary damages for rape, battery, and emotional distress. The allegations would later be made public on December 27, 1999. The case would be officially dropped on March 2000 after the LAPD found no supporting evidence. The suit came months after Miss USA Shanna Moakler served De La Hoya with a $62.5 million paternity suit. According to De La Hoya he never denied being the father of Atiana who was born in 1999, but he never had a proper agreement regarding financial support. De La Hoya would settle the suit and get joint custody of the child.

The WBC ranked Oba Carr (48-2-1, 28 KOs) number four when De La Hoya fought him. If De La Hoya would get past him, it would set him up with a match with Felix Trinidad. Carr had recently defeated Frankie Randall, the fighter known mainly for being the first to officially defeat Julio Cesar Chavez. However, some cynics dismissed Randall's win as "academic" as Chavez had an early disqualification loss changed to a win, and a questionable draw with Pernell Whitaker, before facing Randall. Carr was far from a tune-up for Trinidad. The Michigan fighter was a crafty fighter with plenty of experience. The only man to have stopped Carr was Felix Trinidad. De La Hoya was not worried about Carr's power and came after him in the first round. He would almost floor Carr with a stiff left jab (1:17) and moments later would score the knockdown with a short left hook (1:32). Carr would beat the count and get on his feet again. It didn't look like it would be a long day in the office for the Golden Boy. Interestingly, De La Hoya didn't really try to go in for the finish in the second round. Carr was back in the fight using his left jab and straight right. Carr was able to dig De La Hoya with the left jab to the body. After being badly hurt in the opening round, Carr was able to come back to win the second round. De La Hoya started to find the mark with his left hook in the third round. Carr would simply hold on anytime he was stunned and scored with the overhand right. There would also be some great bodywork by Carr in the middle of the fourth round. Although hurt by De La Hoya in the first round, Carr was now walking through his best shots including a solid hook (2:51) in the fourth.

De La Hoya would answer with his left hooks to the body in the fifth and sixth round. Carr would again be hurt with a straight right-left hook combination (2:50) in the sixth round; this time he would clinch and not go down. Referee Richard Steele would deduct two points from Carr. The deduction was a bit excessive, especially considering that this was the same Steele who never took points away in the Leonard-Hagler fight after notable infractions. The sixth could have been a De La Hoya round (10–7) due to the two deductions.

De La Hoya now had a comfortable lead, and that only relaxed him. De La Hoya would use his legs and be on his toes the next two rounds and outbox Carr. Carr would be very active in the tenth round, sensing he wouldn't win on the cards and seeking a knockout. De La Hoya would finally finish Carr with a fully loaded left hook that landed on the lower jaw near the back of the head. Carr would get up but be in such bad shape that Steele would stop the contest (0:55) in the eleventh round. De La Hoya's final punch stats were 240 of 548 to Carr's 157 of 759. De La Hoya would complain that a "personal problem" that happened in the second round made things difficult. De La Hoya wouldn't elaborate about the personal problem but would state it made him get on his toes and forced him to use his legs more.

CHAPTER 7

Unification with Tito

It was feared that a De La Hoya-Trinidad match wouldn't get made due to the acrimony between Don King and Bob Arum. However, in the past when a big fight needed to be made, it would get done. Don King and Bob Arum would set aside any personal differences in making easily the biggest welterweight fight since Leonard-Hearns in 1981 a reality. Felix Trinidad, the powerful, punching Puerto Rican promoted by Don King, had defended his IBF welterweight title fourteen times. The fighter from Cupey Alto was the biggest Puerto Rican boxing star since the heyday of Wilfred Benitez and Wilfredo Gomez. The fact that De La Hoya was Mexican American would add cultural rivalry and more intrigue to the unification match. Interestingly, despite the nationality difference, the fact remained that both were US citizens by birth.

Felix Trinidad (35-0, 30 KOs) was the fighter that people wanted De La Hoya to fight as soon he picked up the WBC strap of the welterweight title. De La Hoya had already fought both Whitaker and Quartey, so the biggest welterweight name left was Trinidad. The match between De La Hoya and Trinidad would be billed as the "fight of the millennium." De La Hoya would be guaranteed a staggering $21 million and Trinidad $8.5 million. Both would make millions more after the final PPV numbers set a record for a nonheavyweight match with 1.4 million sales. The match would take place on September 18, 1999, at the Mandalay Bay Resort and Casino, Las Vegas, Nevada.

The first round would be delayed due to Trinidad missing both his mouthpieces. The security would need to bring the mouthpiece to the ring. Trinidad would start the round by throwing his left hand while De La Hoya was on his toes moving side to side. De La Hoya would get a straight left-right combination (1:25). It wasn't solid, but it was flashy enough. Trinidad would continually try to land the left hook while throwing the straight left. Not everything was landing, but Trinidad was the busier fighter. De La Hoya would fire five consecutive punches (2:29), which were mainly blocked but could have swayed the judges. The round was close, but I felt Trinidad won it by being busier. Trinidad threw thirty-four punches, compared to nineteen for De La Hoya, out landing him seven to six.

De La Hoya would have a more sustained effort with his left jab that was both accurate and stiff in the second stanza. Trinidad would be slightly off with his overhand right. Trinidad would land a solid straight right (2:09) and left hook (2:18) in the second. De La Hoya would come back with a straight right, jabs, left hook, and a measured right hand in the closing seconds. Trinidad's nose would be bloodied coming back to the corner. All three judges gave the second round to Trinidad, but I thought De La Hoya nicked it due to his early work with the jab and late rally.

Trinidad would still be in the fight, working his left hook (0:47), as he followed De La Hoya around the ring in the third. De La Hoya would double his jab (1:38) and push Trinidad's head back. A three-punch combination (2:18) that included an uppercut would cement the round for De La Hoya. A few more right hands while on his bike would tally the round for De La Hoya. Alcazar would tell De La Hoya to keep boxing, while Gil Clancy would urge his fighter to give a "boxing lesson."

De La Hoya would start the fourth round by employing the double jab followed by a flurry downstairs and upstairs. Trinidad's stationary head was an easy target for De La Hoya. Trinidad needed to use better head movement. Trinidad would get his best overhand right (1:04) and made De La Hoya take a step backward. Trinidad would cut the distance and finally start to get in his best shots. This was a round that could have been scored evenly.

De La Hoya would get in a straight right-left hook (2:06) in the fifth round. The round saw Trinidad as the aggressor for the most of the round. De La Hoya would try to steal the fifth with a flurry, but most of the round belonged to Trinidad. There was blood splattered on Trinidad's white trunks that could be attributed to his bloodied nose. Trinidad wouldn't be discouraged, and he kept cutting the distance and landed an overhand right (1:25) in the sixth round. There would be a scattering of boos from the audience in the last minute as they saw Trinidad chasing De La Hoya around the ring. De La Hoya would again skillfully flurry in the last twenty seconds and land a stiff left-right (2:44) to put what was a close round in his column. The sixth-round punch stats had De La Hoya out land Trinidad twenty-nine to twelve. The most important stat was that De La Hoya threw twenty-five more punches (55–30).

The left jab had De La Hoya on cruise control as he circled the ring in the seventh round. There was no point of going toe-to-toe when he had control of the fight by boxing. Trinidad was far from finished as he did land a solid left hook at 1:24. Trinidad was stalking and getting popped with left jabs as he came in. De La Hoya would rally again with combinations at the end of the round to take a close round. Trinidad would fire a straight left after the bell, prompting a warning from referee Mitch Halpern. Gil Clancy would tell De La Hoya, "You are giving him a boxing lesson as you said you would." Trinidad would nurse a bad mouse under his left eye in addition to his bloody nose. This was the most swelling seen on Trinidad's face in thirty-five fights.

We got more of the same in the eighth as De La Hoya controlled the pace of the action with his feet and combinations. Double-left jabs followed by a straight hand demonstrated the De La Hoya hand-speed advantage. However, Trinidad was pressing the action and landing with his jab and got in a solid left hook (2:38). Trinidad would get a second warning for hitting after the bell again.

There would be twists and turns in this fight as in many championship fights. The first minute of the ninth round would belong to De La Hoya as he landed his combinations in the middle of the ring. When pressed near the ropes, Trinidad was scoring with short looping and straight shots. The distance was closing, and De La Hoya would hope the sands of time would end the contest since he was ahead on the score cards. De La Hoya hurt Trinidad with two body shots in the opening minute of the round and needed to press the action and test how badly Trinidad was hurt. De La Hoya would instead be mainly inactive and allow Trinidad to chase him down with several right hands (1:16, 1:38) and a punctuating, sizzling right cross (1:52). De La Hoya would land a right hand at 2:28 that may have allowed him to make a claim for a 10–10 round. The ninth was a close round that I had even, but the momentum of the bout was starting to shift as Trinidad was clearly becoming the aggressor, and De La Hoya was increasingly becoming more inactive while navigating on his bike—despite the possibility that De La Hoya had already had seven rounds in the bank. The fight was very close on the cards after nine rounds; De La Hoya was ahead on two cards and even on one. The actual scores were Glen Hamada (87–84), Bob Logist (86–86), and Jerry Roth (86–85). De La Hoya would need to win two of the last three rounds to ensure victory. The scores seem to be an anomaly compared with the punch stats. The punch stats had De La Hoya landing 196 of 456 and Trinidad 98 of 320. Yet, as is often the case, statistics don't always tell the full story.

Trinidad came full speed ahead, with newfound momentum, in the tenth and would land a left hook-overhand right (0:28) that would make De La Hoya bend over. The tenth round demonstrated how adept Trinidad was in cutting off the ring, despite receiving criticism for his footwork. (He would sometimes be off-balance and get dropped early.) Trinidad understood how to make an opponent fight, but De La Hoya—perhaps thinking he had the fight won—didn't want to engage much. "Two more rounds and we go home," would be what trainer Alcazar would tell De La Hoya. Perhaps there should have been more urgency in the corner in making sure to win the championship rounds. George Foreman would say, "Don't try to win the fight by just saving the fight; try to win the fight."

The eleventh round again saw a fleeting De La Hoya fire a defensive jab as he was on reverse for the round as a stalking Trinidad would connect with both left hooks and looping shots on the backpedaling target. The same would continue in the final round. A booing crowd would see the Puerto Rican fighter chasing down his prey for three minutes. Both fighters would raise their hands in victory at the closing bell. De La Hoya, who got the favorable decisions against Whitaker and Quartey, was anticipating that history would repeat itself.

The entire boxing world would have a collective shock when Michael Buffert would announce the majority-decision win for Trinidad via judges' scores: Jerry Roth (115–113), Bob Logist (115–114), and Glenn Hamada (114–114). Those who disagreed with the decision pointed to the lopsided punch stats, which had De La Hoya connecting 263 of 648 and Trinidad landing 166 of 462. However, boxing is scored in rounds, and if you believe that Trinidad swept the last four rounds, then a narrow Trinidad win wasn't impossible. As a result I didn't think the robbery that many claimed was justified. I felt De La Hoya could have taken the fight away from the judges if he had pressed action in the ninth and sealed it. With all things considered, a draw may have been the most judicial verdict. This is because De La Hoya had demonstrated great boxing skills, lateral movement, and had speed to win most of the early rounds. On the reverse token, Trinidad had clearly won the last three rounds, and constant pressure with effective aggression—at minimum—earned him the right to retain his IBF welterweight title. There were various scoring combinations that could have had either fighter winning by one point or retaining titles.

De La Hoya still felt he was robbed since he landed ninety-seven more punches and carried the ring generalship. The loss to Trinidad would alter De La Hoya's fighting style, as he would sometimes be reluctant to revert to boxing instead of fighting in the future. Specifically, it may have hurt De La Hoya in his future fights with Shane Mosley and Bernard Hopkins in which he should have used his legs more instead of remaining stationary.

Despite the final verdict, De La Hoya was pleased to break the pay-per-view record for nonheavyweight fights when it was revealed the match did 1.4 million purchases, which generated over $71 million. De La Hoya was also happy that his dad would tell him he was proud of him after the loss. Per De La Hoya it was the first time his dad told him that after a match.

There would a serious attempt to organize a rematch, but it would never materialize. Trinidad would move up to junior middleweight and didn't want to go back down to welterweight. Both camps tried to make an arrangement for a match between the welterweight and junior middleweight division. The final catchweight couldn't be negotiated, as they were reportedly two pounds apart.

De La Hoya would next set his sight on Derrell Coley. Derrell Coley was not expected to go the distance with De La Hoya. De La Hoya has stated that prior to the fight he had not protected his eyes while using a tanning machine, and that gave him difficulty with his vision and delayed his training. De La Hoya would get his full vision back in time for the fight. Coley had predicted a sixth-round TKO win due to a dream he had. It wouldn't be as accurate as the dream that Sugar Ray Robinson had where he saw himself killing Jimmy Doyle in the ring. This match was not expected to go the distance.

De La Hoya would put the Trinidad defeat behind him and get back in the ring on February 26, 2000. He would face Derrell Coley at Madison Square Garden. Both fighters would box early, and De La Hoya would catch most of the Coley punches with his gloves. De La Hoya was more interested in using the left hook to finish Coley early on. He pretty much abandoned his jab in hopes of a quick knockout. Coley was on his bike, working behind his jab. De La Hoya's bodywork in the second round would help soften Coley to take his legs away. Coley would land a solid, straight right-left hook combination in the opening minute of the fourth round. This would entice the DC fighter to keep coming forward with punches to test the Golden Boy. Coley felt his natural welterweight size would be the difference in the fight. Momentarily, it appeared De La Hoya was out on his feet; he was not returning fire, and he was getting pelted with power shots. De La Hoya would answer back with a monster left hook at 1:34 in the fourth round that would stagger Coley. Coley would survive and fight back in the seesaw action.

Coley had taken too many body shots in the next two rounds and had spaghetti legs when the seventh round started. De La Hoya would KO Coley with two hooks to the body in the final moments of the seventh. Coley wouldn't beat the count, as he stayed on one knee as referee Wayne Kelly counted him out. De La Hoya improved his record to (32-1, 26 KOs).

CHAPTER 8

Old Local Rival

Shane Mosley (34-0, 32 KOs) was someone De La Hoya knew very well. They had faced each other as amateurs, and Mosley had defeated De La Hoya. Mosley dominated the lightweight division with his great combination of speed and power. Besides Pernell Whitaker there wasn't any other lightweight since the Roberto Duran heyday that was as dominant in the division as Mosley. Like Duran, Mosley would fight as a welterweight several times before taking a title shot. Mosley defeated Wilfredo Rivera and Willie Wise as a welterweight before facing De La Hoya. Those wins proved that Mosley could be successful in the new division.

Felix Trinidad had vacated his WBC welterweight title so he could move up in weight. This gave De La Hoya a chance to regain the title he felt that he never should have lost. The match between De La Hoya and Mosley would be dubbed "Destiny." De La Hoya would get a purse of $35 million guaranteed with Mosley guaranteed $15 million. It was the most that either fighter had made up to that point. The fight would showcase two fighters from southern California. The match was held at a relatively new arena called the Staples Center in Los Angeles on June 17, 2000. The Staples Center had replaced the Great Western Forum as home to the Los Angeles Lakers.

The fight would be a very engaging affair, as De La Hoya wanted to eliminate the criticism he had received for the last four rounds of the Trinidad contest. Perhaps De La Hoya thought his size was too much for Mosley. He would be proven wrong, as Mosley would be the one hurting De La Hoya with powerful overhand rights. There would be little lateral movement as both fighters would be flat-footed, coming forward for most of the contest. Mosley landed 25 of 67 and De La Hoya 9 of 49 punches for the first round.

De La Hoya would do better in the second round as he started to work on Mosley's body with hooks to the body. The goal was to take Mosley's legs away with body punishments. The stiff left jab also worked well for De La Hoya. What was interesting was that judge Lou Filippo scored the second round for Mosley. The other two judges (Marty Sammon and Pat Russell) would give it to De La Hoya. De La Hoya still would keep his left guard low and pay dearly with another powerful Mosley overhand right (0:32) in the third round. He was also not using his reach and height advantage by fighting at his distance. De La Hoya would get in his own right cross (1:21), but it was obvious that Mosley could take a punch from a legitimate welterweight. De La Hoya would work his jab and out land Mosley 23–12 in the third round. Mosley's great durability would be able to resist a solid left hook to the body (0:41) in the fourth round. Ten seconds later Mosley would answer back with his own left hook to De La Hoya's body. This was not going to be an easy fight, and De La Hoya knew it. Mosley was still landing that overhand right, and De La Hoya was not taking steps backward or catching it with his glove to stop it.

The fourth round saw De La Hoya out land Mosley 20–13 in power punches, but Mosley was the more accurate puncher in the round. It could have been scored an even round. De La Hoya would keep following Mosley around the ring in the fifth and get hit with a right uppercut (1:31). Mosley would get hurt in the final minute of the round by a left hook in the final minute. He would be forced to hold on and momentarily clinch. After five rounds De La Hoya was ahead in two of the judges' scorecards. One judge, Russell, had him ahead by three points; I had him ahead by two points.

Mosley would do better in the sixth round by landing short left jabs and short inside connects. De La Hoya would fight back and come forward with his left jabs and hooks. All three judges would give him the sixth round. After six rounds De La Hoya was ahead four points and two points on two cards, and was even on the third card. Mosley would make a stand in the seventh round by going back to that overhand right and punishing left hooks to the body and would land his best right hand (2:18) of the fight. Mosley would complain, "My back is a little tight" to his father and trainer, Jack Mosley, after the round.

De La Hoya would land a flush right hand (1:27) in the eighth round and still not faze Mosley. Mosley would still control most of the round with his leaping left and short rights that were landing more frequently. A straight right (1:38) would get through De La Hoya's guard in the eighth. Mosley was also doing a better job in avoiding the De La Hoya jab, and he would also turn southpaw. It was another round for Mosley.

The De La Hoya lead was starting to disappear on two of the three cards. De La Hoya's mouthpiece would fall off, and it would halt the action in the ninth round as he went back to his corner to put it back on. Mosley looked fresh and revitalized and was able to land his sneaky right (1:16 and 1:29) on De La Hoya when action resumed. De La Hoya would get in one of his best left hooks (1:41) that snapped Mosley's head back. Audible grunts could be heard as these fighters were fighting "mano a mano" without going backward. Mosley would again be the slightly quicker fighter and would get in the cleaner shots. De La Hoya needed to go into a technical boxing match using his height and reach to try to win the final rounds. He had to realize that Mosley was walking through his best shots and would outslug him due to his speed. De La Hoya would remain in the pocket trying to land his left jab without any movement. Mosley would get his own left jab.

De La Hoya would get his right hand in more frequently, and that possibly gave him the tenth. The left jab would do some work for De La Hoya in the eleventh round, and he would also get in his right cross (2:17) that would snap Mosley's head back. The eleventh round would possibly be the only round De La Hoya would win in the second half of the fight.

Both fighters would again grunt in the final round, as they would trade hellacious shots in the center of the ring. A wet spot would delay the action in the opening minute, and when both returned to fight, they would touch gloves and resume the war of attrition. Mosley would get the better of the fight with those fully loaded overhand rights against the stationary De La Hoya. The final round saw Mosley out land De La Hoya 45–18. On my card I had Mosley winning 115–114 (6-5-1) with the final round being the difference in the bout. The judges gave Mosley the split-decision win: Lou Fillipo (116–112) and Pat Russell (115–113) scoring it for Mosley and Marty Sammon (115–113) for De La Hoya.

The punch stats had Mosley landing 284 of 678 and De La Hoya 257 of 718. The opinion was that De La Hoya went toe-to-toe with Mosley since he felt he was too strong for the former lightweight and wanted to erase memories of the last four rounds with Trinidad. Every loss is stinging to a fighter, but by fighting Mosley the way he did, De La Hoya did win over new fans and gain respect from some detractors. Nobody could accuse De La Hoya of having tried to run with a lead.

CHAPTER 9
Floyd Mayweather Sr.

De La Hoya always had a passion for singing, and singing with his mother was a favorite pastime while growing up. De La Hoya's mother had done some professional singing, and De La Hoya would follow suit and release an album. De La Hoya developed a wide musical taste growing up. He heard traditional Mexican ranchera music but also had a passion for hard rock, due to his older brother, Joel, constantly playing it. However, De La Hoya's self-titled debut album would consist mainly of bilingual love songs. The album would get released on October 10, 2000. The bilingual album showcased De La Hoya's talents outside boxing. The record would get nominated for a Grammy the following year but would lose to Shakira's *MTV Unplugged* in the Latin Pop category. The making of the album would be De La Hoya's catalyst to meeting his future wife, Millie Corretjer. De La Hoya was working with producer Rudy Perez who put on a video of Corretjer.

De La Hoya had a new love life, but there was still something missing. That missing figure was a new trainer. De La Hoya had just suffered two defeats in his last three fights. Although some questioned the Trinidad loss, the way he finished the fight left a lot to be desired. De La Hoya decided he needed to part ways with both his promoter, Top Rank led by Bob Arum, and longtime trainer, Robert Alcazar. De La Hoya would win a court order in 2001 that essentially terminated his contract with Top Rank. However, De La Hoya would still seek Top Rank's aid in the future to promote future fights.

The situation with Alcazar had a more definitive end. De La Hoya would replace Alcazar with Floyd Mayweather Sr. Mayweather was going to help De La Hoya's defensive style so he could save his legs and stay in the pocket without getting hit. Many felt De La Hoya lost to both Trinidad and Mosley down the stretch, and the hope was that if he used less lateral movement and countered while fighting on the inside, he could retain his stamina for the later rounds. Most importantly, Mayweather was a no-nonsense trainer who wanted perfection from his fighters as he did when training his own son.

The first test with Floyd Mayweather Sr. as trainer was challenging Arturo Gatti. Mayweather Sr. hoped to improve De La Hoya's right hand and improve his defense so he could take less punishment and prolong his career. This would be useful against Gatti who was known as a throwback fighter willing to engage in back-and-forth ring wars. Although Gatti met De La Hoya before the Mickey Ward trilogy, Gatti had already established a cult following by virtue of his fights with Gabriel Ruelas, Wilson Rodriquez, and matches with Ivan Robinson. Those ring wars, and his no-quit attitude, are what gave Gatti a cult following. Gatti himself would be moving up in weight to face De La Hoya, but the payday made it worth it. De La Hoya would face Gatti on March 24, 2001, at the MGM Grand, Las Vegas, Nevada. Gatti would start the match by bobbing and weaving while using his straight left jab. He understood he needed to show different looks instead of being stationary. Gatti would be swinging for the fences but couldn't connect with those wild hooks. De La Hoya would work the jab and land solid hooks to take some of the thunder out of Gatti. Gatti would land a tremendous left hook (1:35) in the opening round, which was intended to take De La Hoya's head off. De La Hoya's ability to take such a flush shot was another exhibit of how underrated his chin was. Gatti would get lackadaisical and would keep his hands up while moving his head and would get pummeled with a De La Hoya combination that included a left hook that dropped him onto his knees with his head covered in the canvas. Gatti would survive the round but would take another combination before the bell rang and blood trickled down his face.

There wouldn't be any quit from Gatti, who came in and landed an uppercut thirty seconds into the second round that caused De La Hoya to stumble as his glove touched the canvas. Referee Jay Nady would rule it a slip as both fighters tangled feet, but it was a judgment call. De La Hoya would showcase the shoulder roll while keeping his right glove high and left glove covering his body. There was too much speed and power for the smaller Gatti to overcome in the fight. Gatti had welts under both his eyes, and his predisposition to cuts made it unlikely that the bout would last long. De La Hoya would tee off for most of the third round as Gatti tried to fight back; the ring physician would allow the contest to continue after examining Gatti's eye. De La Hoya and Gatti would trade heavy left hooks to the chin as the final seconds waned. What was startling was that after three rounds De La Hoya had connected 131 of 222 punches, which gave him nearly a 60 percent connect percentage for the fight. Gatti had connected 65 of 199 for a 33 percent connect percentage. In the beginning of the fourth round, a rejuvenated Gatti would land another left lead to De La Hoya's chin that would have taken lesser welterweights down. Gatti never quit despite being outgunned. De La Hoya was still perfecting the Mayweather defense. He still couldn't transition from defense to offense as fast as Mayweather. Obviously, he didn't have the speed that Mayweather had, but he would rarely ever fire that right hand from a defensive posture to a right counter. De La Hoya would finally end the contest by throwing unanswered combinations on the ropes that compelled the Gatti corner to throw in the towel. The bout was a transitional period for De La Hoya, who was working with a new trainer and trying to become a more complete fighter in the second half of his career. Gatti realized that he needed go back down in weight as even his best shots couldn't buckle De La Hoya, and there was too much power in the welterweight division for a fighter who is known for taking punishment due to his toe-to-toe style.

CHAPTER 10

Seeking a Fifth Crown

After Gatti, De La Hoya set out to share history with Thomas Hearns and Ray Leonard.

Thomas Hearns and Ray Leonard were the only two quintuple champions in boxing history. De La Hoya felt it was time to share history with those two past legends. The junior middleweight division included names such as Fernando Vargas, Felix Trinidad, and Ronald "Winky" Wright. In December of 2000, Trinidad defeated Vargas to capture the IBF title in the division after he had already captured the WBA portion from David Reid on March 3, 2000. A rematch with Trinidad appeared the most lucrative proposal for De La Hoya. However, another attempt in negotiations would be scratched as Trinidad was going north to the middleweight division and was scheduled to face William Joppy on May 12, 2001, for the WBA title.

De La Hoya matchmakers would choose WBC junior middleweight champion Javier Castillejo (51-4, 34 KOs) as the next opponent. De La Hoya would fight the Spaniard on June 23, 2001 in a showdown at the MGM, Las Vegas, Nevada. Despite having five title defenses, the Spaniard Castillejo wasn't really perceived as a serious threat to De La Hoya. Castillejo didn't have the size, speed, or power that would worry him. However, De La Hoya was moving up another weight class against an opponent who was accustomed to the weight.

There was also a curve ball De La Hoya faced the days leading into the bout. De La Hoya suffered a bad case of sunburn that had his legs feeling very fatigued.

Despite feeling weak De La Hoya would go on with the scheduled contest. It would be the second tanning issue De La Hoya had leading up to a fight.

De La Hoya wouldn't bother with a feel-out process with the bigger fighter. If you looked at both fighters, you could see there was no size difference. De La Hoya looked like his body had matured to a junior middleweight. He would even score with two overhand rights in the opening thirty seconds of the bout to show he had come to take the fight to Castillejo. The Spaniard would score with a left hook to De La Hoya's body (1:16). De La Hoya's plan was to keep forward with the double-left jab. De La Hoya would come forward with left shoulder high and chin tucked in. He also would use his right glove like a catcher's mitt to catch the left Castillejo jab. Moreover, we saw some excellent head movement from De La Hoya, who eluded most of Castillejo's shots upstairs. After two rounds Castillejo had landed only 17 of 130 punches, opposed to 53 of 112 for De La Hoya. Both the De La Hoya defense and offense were clicking into gear. There were no major connects for Castillejo in the preceding two rounds, and De La Hoya would continue to back up the champion. One of the few, decent Castillejo punches that landed was a straight left (2:09) in the fourth round. Castillejo needed to close the distance and make it a phone-booth fight so he could mitigate the De La Hoya speed advantage. If Castillejo worked De La Hoya's body inside, then perhaps he could get De La Hoya in the last few rounds as Mosley and Trinidad did. Castillejo finally would penetrate the De La Hoya defense with a right uppercut-left hook combination (2:00) in the fifth round that got the Golden Boy's attention. This opportunity was created when De La Hoya leaned when he fired a straight left jab. The round was still a De La Hoya round, who out landed Castillejo 31 to 5. De La Hoya would increasingly land his combinations as he got Castillejo near the ropes in the next three rounds. Castillejo didn't have the speed or power to threaten De La Hoya. So the one-sided affair would continue. This was best illustrated in the ninth round where the champion was reduced to backpedaling as De La Hoya teed off with hooks to the head.

There would be a small Castillejo rally in the tenth round when Castillejo opened the round by landing hooks upstairs and downstairs. Castillejo had finally abandoned the jab that was either blocked or slipped by De La Hoya. A right-hook left-hook combo (1:12) would land solidly on De La Hoya's temples.

If there was one round that could have gone to Castillejo, it would have been the tenth round. Both the audience and De La Hoya desired a knockout win to put the icing on the cake. De La Hoya would try to do that in the final twenty seconds of the eleventh round when he had Castillejo pinned against the northwestern corner ropes. He would fire a string of shots that were more pity-pat than power punches. De La Hoya would finally drop Castillejo in the closing seconds of the twelfth round with culminating punishment that was finalized with a left hook. Castillejo would get up, and then the closing bell rang to seal a fifth divisional title for De La Hoya. This was a dominant win with possibly only one round going to the former champion. De La Hoya would land 403 of 749, while Castillejo landed 121 out of 664. The three judges had it 119–108. De La Hoya joined both Thomas Hearns and Sugar Ray Leonard as a quintuple champion. He would win all titles from the four major sanctioning bodies without any catchweights.

CHAPTER 11
The Grudge Match

De La Hoya would officially marry Millie Corretjer in September 2001. He would also be consumed with starting up Golden Boy Promotions the same year. De La Hoya would choose business associate Richard Schaefer as his CEO. These business and personal commitments were a factor in keeping De La Hoya away from the ring. In total, De La Hoya had a fifteen-month hiatus from the ring when he fought Fernando Vargas. There would be two delays for the contest. De La Hoya had initially wanted to fight Vargas in December 2001 but would then propose May 4, 2002, which was during the Cinco de Mayo weekend. The May date would get erased as De La Hoya would injure his hand during sparring. A doctor who worked with Shaw's Main events—the company that promoted Vargas—would later independently verify this. The third date for the contest would be September 14, 2002. Vargas felt that De La Hoya's delays were signs of trepidation and fear about getting in the ring with him.

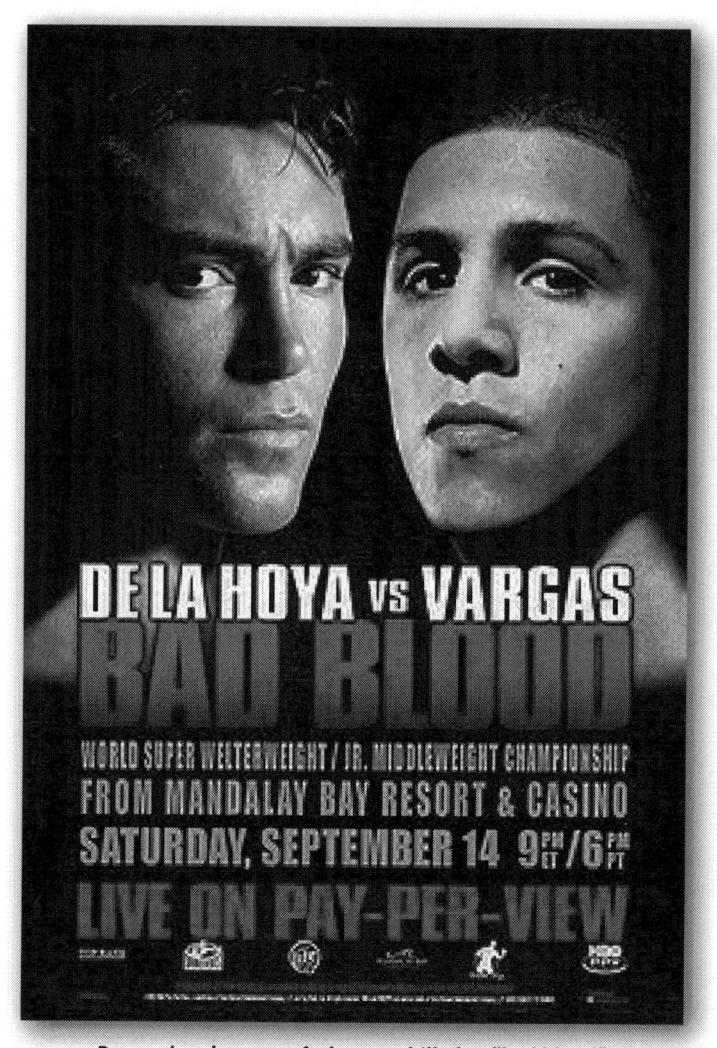

Promotional poster of what was billed as "bad blood" between De La Hoya and Vargas.

Fernando Vargas was a young phenom who had wins over fighters like Winky Wright and Ike Quartey. He took on Felix Trinidad after only twenty professional bouts and suffered his only loss up to that point. However, the fact that he recovered from early first-round knockdowns and was able to drop Trinidad in the fourth round before being stopped in the twelfth round got him some respect even in defeat.

A grudge match between De La Hoya and Vargas was in the making for years. Vargas had called out De La Hoya since he felt De La Hoya dissed him in an infamous snowbank incident. The alleged tale was that while training in Big Bear, Vargas fell into a pit, and De La Hoya allegedly refused to help him and just laughed. De La Hoya has repeatedly denied the authenticity of the story. The promotion of the fight would be simply dubbed "Bad Blood." This time the billing was accurate, as there was legitimate mutual animosity between both combatants. Since both fighters would train at Big Bear, there would be instances when they would bump into each other and start to taunt one another. Vargas felt he was the true Mexican gladiator, which got under De La Hoya's skin as it implied somehow that De La Hoya was denying his Mexican heritage. De La Hoya would make $15 million and Vargas $6 million with both getting a share of the PPV revenue. The match would finally take place on September 14, 2002, at the Mandalay Bay Resort and Casino.

De La Hoya, who usually looked up to the ceiling as a gesture he had reserved for his mother, would instead make contact with Fernando Vargas. The message was clear; he wanted to convey to Vargas that Vargas couldn't intimidate him. De La Hoya would commence the action by feinting and trying to get Vargas to commit in order to set him up for a shot. De La Hoya would score with hooks to Vargas's body. Vargas would land his first major right cross (0:49) that De La Hoya would take well. This observation would foreshadow a later revelation about what Vargas did before the fight. Vargas would be able to pin De La Hoya between the ropes in the final minute and land some solid hooks that almost dropped De La Hoya as he got between the ropes. De La Hoya would implement the Mayweather defense of curling up and protecting the vital areas while rolling with the punches. Vargas would win the round, but the De La Hoya defense would minimize the damage. De La Hoya would finally get more on his toes and use his jab both downstairs and upstairs to get back into the fight. He would also avoid the dangers of the ropes by using his feet to get out of danger. After two rounds both fighters had battle scars as Vargas had blood coming out of the nose, and De La Hoya had a bruised right cheek.

De La Hoya would be wining the boxing match in the middle of the ring in the third round until Vargas landed an overhand right (2:08) that momentarily buckled De La Hoya. Vargas would come in aggressively, firing from all cylinders, as De La Hoya shifted to a defensive posture. The Golden Boy would be more on his bike in the fourth round using a double jab and finally starting to use combinations. The hand-speed advantage was essential for De La Hoya to win the fight. He needed to land more than one punch. The fifth round would see the war break out. Vargas would land some sizzling overhand rights and combinations. De La Hoya would also get in some of his best combinations. The degree of punishment De La Hoya received was unprecedented in any of his prior fights, with perhaps the exception being the Quartey fight. This explained why De La Hoya would go back to boxing in the sixth round and be on his toes while trying to use speed and angles. De La Hoya would land a straight left-overhand-right (2:20) combination in the sixth round. The hand speed was becoming the difference. Vargas would have a cut under the left eye.

The final minute of the seventh round saw Vargas unraveling as De La Hoya would land his trademark left hook and start measuring him with overhand rights. Vargas would bang his gloves in a gesture to imply "bring it on."

The Vargas corner would admonish him for staying in the middle of the ring and fighting De La Hoya. They wanted him to take De La Hoya to the ropes; this was not easy, as De La Hoya was able to escape out of the ropes with his feet. De La Hoya had often been labeled a "one-handed fighter." The consensus was that the real damage came only from his left hand. Perhaps if these critics saw how De La Hoya pretty much dominated Vargas in the eighth round with his right hand exclusively, that perception would change. De La Hoya would repeatedly punish Vargas with overhand rights in the round that started to break down the young champion. After the round both De La Hoya's dad and Bob Arum would jubilantly clap as De La Hoya took control of the fight.

But like anything in life, things can change as if by whim. Vargas wouldn't go down without a fight and came back in the ninth round. A left hook to the body (0:30) would score for Varagas as he tried to slow De La Hoya down in the final rounds. Vargas would continue to rally with short overhand rights. The Vargas body shots had De La Hoya putting his arms down to block those shots. The seventy-six punches Vargas threw in the ninth round would be the most he threw in the fight.

Vargas would come out aggressively in the tenth, which opened up counter opportunities for De La Hoya. A three-punch combination capped off by a left hook would stagger Vargas in the closing seconds of the round. The Vargas corner would throw water all over his body in an attempt to revive him as they gave him a pep talk. Vargas was able to get his legs back, but his head wasn't fully cleared. De La Hoya would drop Vargas with a left hook (1:16) in the eleventh round. The killer instinct that was missing in the Trinidad match was resurrected. De La Hoya would pummel Vargas first in the southwestern corner ropes and then in the northwestern corner ropes until referee Joe Cortez would stop the contest. The final punch stats saw De La Hoya land 281 of 660 and Vargas 227 of 525. Shane Mosley would be grinning ear to ear as he saw the events at ringside. There was still unsettled business for both fighters, and Mosley welcomed a big payday rematch. Mosley had suffered two losses to Vernon Forrest, which had decreased his brand name. The win for De La Hoya was one of his biggest wins, as he was able to defeat a bigger opponent and one who had trashed him repeatedly.

It would later be revealed that Fernando Vargas had tested positive for stanozolol, a performance enhancement anabolic steroid. Vargas would deny knowingly taking any performance enhancement drug and release a statement: "I want everyone to understand that I would never knowingly put harmful chemicals, such as anabolic steroids, into my body…I would ask that people refrain from passing judgment until all the facts are uncovered. And I wish to make it clear that I do intend to get to the bottom of what happened and uncover the truth." The NSAC was not buying any story that he was given drugs without his knowledge and would suspend him for nine months. The revelation of Vargas's positive test made the De La Hoya win more impressive as he had defeated a "juiced" opponent.

CHAPTER 12
Yuri Boy

Veteran Yuri "Boy" Campas had eighty-five professional bouts under his belt and was considered past prime when he was selected as the next De La Hoya opponent for May 3, 2003, at the Mandalay Bay Resort and Casino. Campas was essentially a tune-up fight for the Shane Mosley rematch. The De La Hoya-Campas undercard would also feature Mexicans Jorge Arce and Erik Morales as part of the Cinco de Mayo promotion. The promotional angle used to market the match was that Campas had found the fountain of youth through a mysterious bottle. At one point in his career, Campas was 56-0 when he would suffer his first loss to Puerto Rican Felix Trinidad via a fourth-round TKO. The Mexican fighter was a former IBF light middleweight champion who defended his title three times until losing it to Fernando Vargas. Campas now had a record of 80-5, 68 KOs, yet all his loses were knockout defeats. De La Hoya was the 25–1 favorite against Campas. De La Hoya, who was just coming from his greatest win since possibly the Ike Quartey fight, was expected to make easy work of the veteran. Few people felt the bottle of youth would prevent an inevitable KO loss.

In the opening round, De La Hoya would use his feints and keep Campas at the end of his jab. There would be no rush to get the knockout, as it would come naturally. The Golden Boy looked a little more plumb and slower of foot in this contest. However, De La Hoya's hand speed was still there. De La Hoya would use his left jab to the body and follow it with a right cross upstairs. He knew that Campas would be too slow to counter. De La Hoya peppered Campas with a four-punch combination that snapped his head back in the first round. Every time Campas would try to get off, he would be met with a left jab to the face. Campas was an inside fighter who hooked on the inside. As long as De La Hoya kept it in his distance, he would have no problem. The Mexican veteran would get a good left hook to the body at (2:22) of the second round, but it didn't do much damage. The left jab followed by an overhand right would work to perfection in the third round giving De La Hoya complete control of the fight. A five-punch De La Hoya combination would knock Campas's mouthpiece off. Referee Vic Drakulich would warn Campas as it fell off a fourth time.

Campas would have his best effort in round four as he was able to dig the body with hooks and got in his own uppercuts. Despite the better round, Campas had landed only 45 of 193 punches through four rounds. This was paltry compared to De La Hoya landing 137 of 275.

De La Hoya would take command again with his combinations in the fifth round. Campos was a punching bag due to his lack of head and lateral movement. He was just following De La Hoya around to get nailed with the faster hands. The glimmer of hope came in the opening half of the sixth round when Campas had De La Hoya on the ropes and started to land solidly on a stationary target. Unfortunately, De La Hoya would turn the tables and come out of the ropes firing combinations. Drakulich would take a point away from Campas after the sixth time the Campas mouthpiece came off. The Campas corner would throw in the towel at the closing seconds of the seventh round. De La Hoya landed 264 of 498 punches, compared to 75 of 348 punches for Campas. The performance was good but not spectacular, and if Campas would have taken De La Hoya to deeper waters, he may have caught him as he got more tired. After the match De La Hoya would complain that he had a hurt left hand and stated, "I was only a seven today on a scale of one to ten." If he wanted to defeat Mosley in the rematch, he needed to be better on that scale.

CHAPTER 13

Short End of the Stick Again

Shane Mosley (38-2, 35 KOs) was not the same fighter who had defeated De La Hoya years before. Vernon Forrest dissected and exposed him on two occasions. Mosley was not a natural junior middleweight. If Floyd Mayweather Sr. was the key to the new and improved De La Hoya, it would surface in this fight. The rematch between De La Hoya and Mosley would take place on September 13, 2003, at the MGM Grand, Las Vegas, Nevada. It would be billed as "Redemption." De La Hoya would get a $12 million guarantee and Mosley $4.25 million, with a promise of additional money if he won, and also a share of the PPV.

Mayweather preached defense and would make sure that De La Hoya wouldn't be so easily victimized by overhand rights as in their first fight. De La Hoya contemplated retirement if he lost to Mosley again. It would be immediately clear that De La Hoya wouldn't fight the same way he fought Mosley in the first fight. For one, his legs were bouncing, and he also was keeping a greater distance. It was obvious he planned to outbox Mosley and not to outslug him. The Forrest blueprint used in defeating Mosley was there to study.

De La Hoya would commence the match by boxing at his distance, trying to score with his jab and right cross. The Golden Boy would still fall prey to the Mosley right hook to the body (1:37) in the first round. A three-punch combination (1:42) would partially score for the Golden Boy as he pressed the action. Mosley would buckle De La Hoya with a perfect left hook (1:52) in the opening stanza. It was a round that could have been scored for either fighter or evenly. De La Hoya would land twice as many blows (12–6), but Mosley would have the best connects in the round. The second saw De La Hoya doubling and tripling his jab with success. There were plenty of feints to keep each fighter off-balance. This time around the Mosley right hand was neutralized.

De La Hoya would also get the left hook to score in the opening seconds of the third and his own right (0:29). When Mosley would load up and try to return fire, he would see De La Hoya get out of range. After three rounds De La Hoya had out jabbed Mosley 33–5.

The fourth was a game changer. A head-butt would cause a small gash on De La Hoya's right eyebrow. Mosley was under De La Hoya and would come up causing the right side of his head to collide with the top, right side of De La Hoya's face. Ringside physician Dr. Margaret Goodman would briefly examine the cut and give the OK to Cortez for the action to continue. Both fighters would continue to jab. The cut would be a new bull's-eye for Mosley. The round was another round where De La Hoya was more active. In the fifth round, Mosley was using his right increasingly to De La Hoya's body. It was apparent that De La Hoya's cut was not controlled. There were still sprinkles of blood coming out his right eyebrow. De La Hoya would still land a solid left uppercut (2:37) in the round. Mosley would answer it with his right uppercut (2:41) in return. De La Hoya would land his stiff left jab at his distance to seemingly pull out the round.

Mosley would come out more aggressive in the sixth, trying to load up with his right hands. De La Hoya would lose his balance in an early exchange, due to slipping in the middle of the canvas. Mosley would land an overhand right (1:44) as he continually came forward behind his jab with upper-body movement.

The seventh was a close round that I scored as even. Mosley was stalking with mixed results, while De La Hoya landed straight rights (1:58 and 2:39). Jack Mosley would tell his son, Shane, "He is stealing the rounds from you; why aren't you using your legs?" "Use your toes; use your skills," would be the message to Shane as he entered the final five rounds.

Mosley still had difficulty getting off in the eighth as De La Hoya would clinch him, but he was still able to get inside right hands and a left hook in the final minute of the round. The ninth round would be the best Mosley round since the sixth round, as he landed excellent lead rights (0:41 and 1:14). Most importantly, blood was trickling again from De La Hoya's face, which could help persuade judges to favor Mosley. (Often judges score blood, and De La Hoya looked the more wounded fighter, even if the cut was a result of a head-butt.) A left hook (1:29) would land cleanly on the stationary De La Hoya who seemed to have tired. De La Hoya would fire back, but the stings seemed to be taken out of his punches. Mosley would raise his arm after the round, feeling he had come back. I had De La Hoya ahead 5-3-1 after nine. Mosley wouldn't back down in the tenth as he closed the distance and scored with double-left hooks (1:02) to the chin. De La Hoya would get on his toes again in the tenth and land a few combinations and use his right hand. It was a round that could have narrowly gone to De La Hoya. De La Hoya would out land Mosley 19–11 in the round.

Mosley would fully land left hooks and lead rights that gave him a clear eleventh round. De La Hoya would fight back and land a left uppercut (2:13) that would take Mosley's mouthpiece off. "You can believe you can win this fight…You can be the first to knock him out," Jack Mosley would tell his son in between rounds. Having the memories of Trinidad fresh in his mind, De La Hoya would come out blazing in the final round throwing combinations. It would be toe-to-toe action in the final round. This would enable Mosley (0:40) to land a perfect right hook to the chin. De La Hoya would get solid right-left crosses (0:47). I had it 115–112 for De La Hoya (7-4-1). As happens in boxing, there is no sure thing. The unanimous decision would go to Shane Mosley by a score of 115–113 on all three judges' cards.

Mosley would look genuinely shocked when he heard the announcement that he won. The final punch stats had De La Hoya landing 221 of 616 and Mosley 127 of 496. Similarly to the Trinidad contest, De La Hoya had out landed his opponent by nearly 100 punches and still came in on the short end of the stick. However, unlike the Trinidad contest where he had essentially given up the last three-and-half rounds by going on his bike, this time he fought to the last second.

Members of the press would criticize De La Hoya for wanting to file an official protest on the fight. They would even try to score the blood by saying that the blood and bruise caused by the head-butt somehow showed that Mosley won the fight. Using that same flawed logic, Duran won the third fight against Leonard. Duran looked unscathed, and Leonard was bleeding from both his eye and mouth after the fight. He needed sixty stitches. De La Hoya felt it was the second time the industry had robbed him of a decision. Those cynics who felt that De La Hoya was given gift wins against Whitaker and Quartey felt it was poetic justice.

CHAPTER 14

First Sextuple Champion

The chance to win a sixth divisional title was something that De La Hoya had always wanted to achieve since starting his professional career. It would give him an accolade that Hearns, Leonard, or Duran never achieved. Of course, this was something that had to be put into proper context with four major sanctioning bodies now present in the sport. The true lineal middleweight champion was Bernard "Executioner" Hopkins. However, if De La Hoya could beat Felix Sturm (20-0, 9 KOs) the WBO champion, he had a guaranteed mega fight with the man who broke Carlos Monzon's fourteen-consecutive middleweight-title defense streak. The match was the main event on June 5, 2004, at the MGM Grand, Las Vegas, Nevada. Bernard Hopkins would be part of the undercard as he fought Robert Allen. Hopkins would defeat Allen by lopsided unanimous decision. He then would be reduced to watching De La Hoya-Strum, hoping that De La Hoya would win to ensure his biggest payday.

De La Hoya entered the ring very warmed up and heavier than in any of his previous fights. In fact, De La Hoya would make the full 160-pound limit for the bout. Sturm came in excellent shape. It was expected that he would come in a few pounds lighter to be faster and more mobile. Sturm was not a heavy-handed puncher, and De La Hoya had a good enough chin to withstand his best shots. De La Hoya started the match at a furious pace, throwing hooks to Sturm's body. Almost immediately, Sturm was able to land that laser right jab that moved De La Hoya's upper torso back. The Sturm jab gave De La Hoya a busted nose, which still didn't prevent him from throwing 103 punches in the first round. Sturm kept a high, tight guard that protected his body with his elbows. Short straight lefts and hooks were peppering De La Hoya's face in the second round. De La Hoya's best left hooks were not doing much damage to the naturally bigger opponent. It was not ideal to stay and trade with Sturm. De La Hoya needed to get on his toes, use both head and lateral movement, and rely on his speed. The Golden Boy was leaning forward on Sturm, which gave the German fighter easy, short shots. The straight left jab (1:48) was giving De La Hoya headaches as he continued to stay in front of his opponent. De La Hoya had a swollen left eye and was bleeding from his nose after three rounds. Fortunately for the Golden Boy, he possibly took at least two of the first three rounds with his volume punching.

De La Hoya would be more cautious in the fourth round as he started to feel the impact of Sturm's punches. De La Hoya may have stolen the round with a solid flurry in the closing seconds. De La Hoya landed 19 of 81 compared to Sturm's 22 of 44 in the fourth round. The reason De La Hoya got hit often by Sturm's jab was the lack of head movement. It was a bad habit that trainer Gil Clancy tried to eliminate when he cotrained De La Hoya. De La Hoya's head was an easy target for Sturm in the fifth round with short right hooks (1:40). If Sturm had worked De La Hoya's body more, he may have been the first fighter to knock De La Hoya out. Even Sturm's left hook (2:21) was now scoring for Sturm in the fifth round. After five rounds I had this fight even (2-2-1), but the tide was going to the champion. Sturm looked fresher, and his punches had more power behind them. A short overhand right (2:49) buckled De La Hoya in the seventh round. Sturm had the major advantage with his jab out landing De La Hoya (79-44) after seven rounds. Strum would take the lead for most of the action in the middle rounds. De La Hoya would occasionally fight in spurts. It was obvious that De La Hoya understood he needed to step it up as he was behind in the fight.

The opening minute of the tenth round had the Golden-Boy fire hooks to Strum's body in frantic combinations. Sturm would come back with his jab and short punches inside. It was another close round that De La Hoya may have edged out. Sturm would momentarily turn southpaw in the eleventh round to land his straight lefts. De La Hoya was winded, and Sturm landed several notable straight lefts. De La Hoya would seemingly need two knockdowns or a knockout to win the fight in the final round.

De La Hoya would try to get it with combinations upstairs (1:56) in the twelfth, but he didn't have the power to do it. Sturm would raise his arms in the closing seconds, feeling confident he pulled out the win. The decision would go to the scorecards and so would the fate of a possible mega fight with Bernard Hopkins, slated for September of that year. Sturm would win the punch stat numbers by landing 234 of 541, compared to De La Hoya's 188 of 792. When it was announced a unanimous decision of 115–113 in all three cards, an astonished De La Hoya raised his arms, and an equally surprised Sturm walked away. De La Hoya would call Sturm an "ordinary fighter" and felt that he didn't bring his best effort into the ring. "He is a tough cookie, but I know I can do a lot better." De La Hoya would add, "It was a very close fight; let's put it that way." Felix Sturm would accept the decision stating, "I know they need to make the big De La Hoya-Hopkins fight." He was also dismissive of the chance of getting a rematch. It would also be unlikely since, to make the rematch happen, De La Hoya would need to defeat Hopkins. The De La Hoya-Sturm fight is a reminder that if you plan to have one tune-up fight before a mega fight, make sure to pick a very safe opponent. De La Hoya would later concede that he lost to Sturm and felt bad about his performance. De La Hoya understood he needed to get in much better shape if he fought Bernard Hopkins for the undisputed middleweight title of the world. The total pay-per-view sales for the match would be over 350,000, which reflected a lackluster interest in the bout.

CHAPTER 15

Entering the Executioner's Lair

Due to the poor Felix Sturm sales, it was imperative for De La Hoya to go ahead with the Hopkins bout. It would be for the undisputed middleweight title. De La Hoya was never the undisputed champion in any division, and a win against Hopkins would be a great source of motivation. The bout would be scheduled for September 18, 2004, at the MGM Grand, Las Vegas, Nevada. Bernard Hopkins defended a portion of the middleweight title eighteen times. Although he broke the Carlos Monzon record of fourteen middleweight-title defenses, some boxing purists wouldn't give Hopkins the full honor as he wasn't undisputed champion for all his defenses. Regardless of the middleweight record, there was no other middleweight since Marvelous Marvin Hagler who dominated the middleweight division as Hopkins did. Hopkins defeat of undefeated Felix "Tito" Trinidad cemented his résumé for the Boxing Hall of Fame. Hopkins would often come to the ring while Frank Sinatra's "My Way" played, this was a statement that he walked to his own tune. Hopkins enjoyed being the villain and would wear an executioner's mask during his ring entrances. The accolades and notoriety that Hopkins didn't get in his younger days were now being received in the period that, for most fighters, would be the twilight of their career. However, Hopkins was far from the twilight of his career as he developed a methodical style that gave him great success as he got closer to the age of forty. Only a few exceptions, such as George Foreman and Archie Moore, would produce the results Hopkins achieved in the latter stages of their career.

The fighter known as the "Executioner" had notable promotional disputes and learned the sport of boxing in prison. There was little that intimidated Hopkins both inside and outside of the ring. The moniker "Executioner" was a bit misleading as Hopkins was more a cryptanalyst than anything else. Hopkins didn't defeat opponents by physical brawn but by breaking down opponent strategies, and then hacking their plan, and then killing it. If boxing IQ were translated into chess, then Hopkins would be a grand master of the sport. Before Hopkins would dissect an opponent inside the ring, he would do a psych job before they met in the ring. Hopkins would notoriously make stereotypical comments about Puerto Ricans eating rice and beans only to topple that by throwing the Puerto Rican flag to the floor, which almost resulted in a riot during his promotion for the 2001 Felix Trinidad bout. Hopkins, years later, would tell Joe Calzaghe that he "couldn't lose to a white fighter." However, for the De La Hoya match, the veteran Hopkins seemed to be more complimentary than condescending. Perhaps Hopkins was appreciative that De La Hoya, who got his first major title as a super featherweight, would actually give him his biggest payday by challenging him for the undisputed middleweight title. For De La Hoya it was an opportunity to make history against an opponent who was both a thinker and had all the physical advantages. One of the few advantages that De La Hoya had was speed. The logic before the fight was that De La Hoya was going to get on his bike and use his hand speed to pick up points a la Leonard-Hagler. Although the fight with Trinidad gave Hopkins the notoriety that he never had, he had still never gotten that mega payday. Hopkins would make $10 million and De La Hoya $30 million for the match dubbed "It's History," scheduled for September 18, 2004. Both fighters were expected to make more after receiving a portion of the PPV revenue.

A few days before the bout, De La Hoya would suffer a freak injury to his hand caused by scissors that cut man Joe Chavez was using to cut off tape from his hand. There would be a V-shaped wound in the palm of his hand that required eleven stitches. Dr. Biff McCann would do the surgery and would concede that De La Hoya was given lidocaine, but the banned substance had cleared his system before the night of the fight. De La Hoya and his physician felt that the injury wouldn't have any impact on the bout. However, before the bout there was still swelling (due to an injection), and there were objections if the hand wraps would have tape over them. All of this distraction would only complicate things for De La Hoya, as Bernard "The Executioner" Hopkins would be the biggest test of De La Hoya's career.

An introduction filled with Strauss's *Also sprach Zarathustra* and Mexican ranchero music would fill the air of the Grand MGM as De La Hoya entered the ring. Hopkins looked very warmed up as he entered the ring and did his customary X and slit-throat gesture. With this win De La Hoya would pretty much elevate his name with the biggest names of the past generation: Hagler, Leonard, and Duran. Hopkins weighed in at 156 and De La Hoya at 155. They both agreed to a catchweight of 157 pounds. Hopkins, at age 39, would be the one who should have worried about being drained.

Hopkins would commence the match by landing a lead left hook in the opening minute that was partially blocked. Both fighters would be feinting and posturing rather than exchanging. De La Hoya flicked a left jab that landed but was not very stiff. An overhand right would land solidly at 1:39 of the first. The round was close, yet a stiff left jab in the final twenty seconds would tilt it to the De La Hoya scorecard. However, it is important to note that the jab was not followed by a right to the body. There were not many clean blows landed in the second round as most of the shots were either blocked or only partially landed. Hopkins would land the straight right and jabs that gave him the round. De La Hoya would try to flurry to steal the round, but it wasn't enough. Hopkins would land his best shot at 1:02 of the third round, a lead right. However, De La Hoya would land three clean shots at the last eleven seconds, which included two short hooks. In between corners, Floyd Mayweather Sr. would tell De La Hoya, "He [Hopkins] is an old man right now."

Hopkins came out more aggressively in the fourth round with his jab. At 1:05 he landed a right hook to the body, which forced De La Hoya to clinch with a tight hold. That shot would be a good prelude to the conclusion of the match. The middle of the round saw both fighters exchange combinations without anyone doing much damage. This could have been scored an even round. After four rounds the punch stat numbers were almost a wash—Hopkins 27 of 122 and De La Hoya 29 of 152. De La Hoya opened up with combinations in the fifth round. Yet it was obvious he couldn't hurt Hopkins. If De La Hoya stayed in front of Hopkins, then he risked being hurt. Hopkins was a bit busier in the fifth round with his jab, and a good portion of De La Hoya's shots missed the mark. De La Hoya would land a few double jabs and would land short combinations in the sixth round. Hopkins would land a few lead rights. It was a round that could have been scored either way. Hopkins trainer Doug Fischer will tell his fighter, "He is stealing the rounds; make him fight this round, and back him up." Hopkins would do precisely that in the seventh round. He made it into a rough inside battle where he landed clean right hands. The lead right would also land from the outside. De La Hoya needed to go to plan B, or he was risking the fight slipping away. A solid lead Hopkins right at 2:14 of the seventh round got De La Hoya's attention. Nazeem Ricahrdson, who was part of Hopkin's corner, could be heard saying, "Show me the body shot." That would come a bit later. Hopkins would use his left hook-straight left combo and force De La Hoya to take a few backward steps. All the momentum was going to the Executioner. De La Hoya needed to use lateral movement and to use his speed instead of being stationary. Hopkins was increasingly cutting the distance, and De La Hoya was paying the price with short rights and left hooks. De La Hoya would get in a left hook at the closing bell—yet it was too little, too late.

In between rounds De La Hoya would demand that his arms be stretched higher. This is possibly due to stiffness in the shoulder. Within forty seconds of the ninth round, a lead right would hurt De La Hoya, forcing him to hold on. The clinch would be long, and Kenny Bayless would be forced to give both of them warnings about keeping the fight clean. Nazeem Richardson could be heard repeating "body shot, body shot." Then, boom, at 1:24 a left hook to the liver pulverized Oscar, who grimaced to the canvas on his elbows and knees. Could he get the air back in his lungs to beat the count? Seeing De La Hoya rolling around the canvas, the answer was an obvious, *no!* The MGM Grand audience felt a collective shock when they saw the Golden Boy suffer his first KO loss in his career. De La Hoya would pound the canvas in frustration while blurting profanities. Hopkins would land 99 of 361 and De La Hoya 82 of 315. I had Hopkins winning by one point (77–76) at the time of the stoppage. The bout was a major PPV sales improvement from the Sturm match as it did close to one million sales. The judges Paul Smith (78–74) and Dave Moretti (79–73) had it for Hopkins, and Keith Macdonald (75–77) had it for De La Hoya at the time of stoppage.

After the Hopkins loss, it appeared De La Hoya wouldn't return to the sport of boxing again. He got married in 2001 and had a young family. There was also some philanthropic work that consumed De La Hoya. De La Hoya founded the Cecilia Gonzalez De La Hoya Cancer Center in 2000. He was also a father of four kids. De La Hoya would add Oscar Gabriel and Nina to his previous kids. Many fighters have difficulty away from the limelight and competitive nature of the sport, and it was inevitable that De La Hoya would return in 2006.

CHAPTER 16
Return to the Ring

Ricardo "El Matador" Mayorga was an ideal opponent for De La Hoya since all of his defensive liabilities were both exposed and exploited. Mayorga was an entertaining fighter, mainly for his caricature of a beer-chugging and cigarette-lighting boxer who stuck out his chin while brawling. Mayorga shocked the boxing world with wins over past undefeated fighters Andrew "Six Heads" Lewis and Vernon Forrest to capture the WBA and WBC welterweight titles. Don King, who took Mayorga under his wing, was able to get Mayorga the exposure that he would thrive in. Mayorga was never at a loss for words and was ridiculed for insensitive comments to fighters while promoting fights. Perhaps the worst example of Mayorga's insidious trash talk was that he vowed to "kill Corey Spinks in the ring so he can reunite with his deceased mother in heaven." Mayorga later apologized for those comments, but it was safe to say the man would do or say anything to sell a fight.

Mayorga was mainly a brawler who had great power as a welterweight but lost some of it when he moved up in weight. The fighter from Nicaragua was a deliberate caricature of the Latino machismo, stereotypical archetype. This was old-school WWF material, and Mayorga was more than happy to play the part to a tee. A good portion of this was tongue and cheek for publicity to sell his brand name. Mayorga's mannerisms were in stark contrast to the lionized former Nicaraguan champion, Alexis Arguello, who was known for his class inside and outside of the ring. Mayorga would actually be romantically linked to Arguello's daughter, Dora, for some time.

Although many disparage Mayorga's lack of technical skill, he was very durable, and his awkward style was known to confuse opponents. Mayorga had recently won the WBC junior middleweight title against Michele Piccirillo. It wouldn't be a surprise that Mayorga would try to get under De La Hoya's skin during the promotion of the fight. Mayorga would make disparaging comments about De La Hoya's wife, Millie, and even his son Gabriel. If that was not enough, Mayorga would question if De La Hoya was worthy of his ethnicity. In the press conference leading up to the fight, Mayorga (sporting a matador outfit) would exclaim: "On May sixth I'm going to make you my bitch. No one will recognize you. You remind me of an old lady past his prime sitting in a rocking chair doing nothing. This clown sitting to the right of me has disrespected me. My strongest hand is my right hand; see his eye? I'm going to use it to detach his retina… You're going to be my bitch in my bed anytime I want you. I hate bitches, and I'm going to make you my little bitch." De La Hoya would respond, "You have disrespected me, my wife, and my people, and I will knock you out."

In many ways Mayorga was as an opponent who was made to order for De La Hoya. His wide shots and lack of head movement would open up many countering opportunities. De La Hoya would face Mayorga on May 6, 2006, at the MGM Grand, Las Vegas, Nevada. Floyd Mayweather Jr.—the pound-for-pound king at that time—was ringside, hoping to get the super fight with De La Hoya. Mayorga would commence the action by lunging punches at De La Hoya from different angles but would catch mainly air in the first round. As Mayorga tried to load up with a power right, he was countered with a snapping left hook that dropped him in the opening minute of the contest. De La Hoya would glance at the fallen Mayorga with a sinister look to suggest more was on the way. Mayorga came back still throwing punches in bunches and not landing cleanly, with the exception of a few overhand rights. De La Hoya would win the rest of the round with short, precise counters. De La Hoya feinted and used his left jab to try to keep Mayorga off-balance in the second round. Mayorga would finally answer back, connecting with his overhand right and his left hook. At 1:21 of the second round, Mayorga would land a right uppercut that got De La Hoya's attention. De La Hoya would still measure Mayorga with his own right hook—a punch that became more prevalent in his repertoire with Mayweather as his trainer.

Mayorga was becoming increasingly unsteady as De La Hoya was breaking him down in the third round. De La Hoya could telegraph his punches on the rugged Mayorga style. Essentially, it was a foregone conclusion that unless Mayorga land one great haymaker, he would get knocked out. That great haymaker would land at 2:34 of the third round when a right uppercut would rock the Golden Boy and force him to take a few backward steps to retain his senses. That would be the last great opening for Mayorga. De La Hoya would feast on that Mayorga open chin as scavengers feast on a carcass; it was there for the taking. Mayorga never kept his gloves high and never tucked in his chin. De La Hoya would also work the body in the fourth round to make sure the animated Mayorga slowed down. Mayorga would resort to rabbit punching, holding, and hitting, which prompted a second warning from Jay Nady. De La Hoya would drop Mayorga the second time by landing combinations downstairs and upstairs, forcing Mayorga to take a knee (1:02) in the sixth round. Mayorga would beat the count only to get pummeled, forcing Jay Nady to stop the contest at 1:34 of the round. De La Hoya was officially back into boxing with the WBC junior middleweight title of the world. A salivating Floyd Mayweather Jr. watched in approval, as he knew his mega fight with De La Hoya in the spring of 2007 was pretty much locked. The match with Mayorga generated over 930,000 PPV domestic purchases, which resulted in over $46 million in pay-per-view alone. The numbers proved that De La Hoya was still a major attraction.

CHAPTER 17

Challenging the New Cash Cow

De La Hoya would be scheduled to face Floyd Mayweather Jr. on May 5, 2007. The date was again conveniently scheduled for the Cinco de Mayo festival. Tickets would sell out in only three hours on January 27, 2007. HBO would have a new show called 24/7 to help promote the pay-per-view event. The series largely followed reality TV that reflected the voyeuristic nature of the larger culture. The series would prove to be well suited for Mayweather's loquacious and highly inflammatory personality and would make him a megastar.

As Oscar De La Hoya was trained by Floyd Mayweather's father, it was likely that he would need a new trainer to combat Floyd Mayweather Jr. De La Hoya would hire Freddie Roach to do the job for $1.3 million. De La Hoya felt the key to the fight was his jab. (For round-by-round coverage, check the Mayweather section.) Floyd's father once told De La Hoya that the "jab neutralizes" the younger Mayweather. De La Hoya would use his jab early and be able to score, as he had Mayweather pinned against the ropes. Mayweather would control most of the action at the center of the ring with his lead rights. After eight rounds De La Hoya was ahead on two of the three scorecards.

Intense action near the ropes between De La Hoya and Mayweather in their record-setting PPV event. AP Photo/Kevork Djansezian.

De La Hoya claims he had trouble down the stretch since he had a slight tear in a rotator cup on his left shoulder. This took his jab away in the final rounds. Mayweather would win the fight by the scores—Jerry Roth (115–113), Chuck Giampa (116–112), and Tom Kaczmarek (113–115). De La Hoya would be the only fighter past or present to be on the winning side of a Floyd Mayweather Jr. scorecard.

After all the PPV revenues were tabulated to his purse, De La Hoya would earn a reported $52 million dollars, which was a record at the time for boxing purses. Mayweather would earn $25 million, which was his biggest purse up to that point. The total PPV sales would exceed 2.4 million, making it a record that stood until 2015. Total revenues would exceed $165 million, making it the most lucrative fight in boxing history at the time. Although there was a talk of a rematch, it would never take place after futile negotiation attempts. Mayweather would retire after his December 2007 match with Ricky Hatton.

For his next bout, De La Hoya wanted to go to Los Angeles and his roots on a nonpay-per-view fight. His next match would be against Steve Forbes on May 3, 2008, at the Home Depot Center, Carlson, California. The match would also feature an undercard that included Victor Ortiz and Daniel Jacobs, two young Golden Boy prospects.

Oscar De La Hoya would go back to Floyd Mayweather Sr. as his trainer for the Forbes fight. Despite the Mayweather retirement, De La Hoya was still hoping that a rematch with Mayweather Jr. would take place in September 2008. "People haven't seen the best of me; this will be a smarter and more relaxed, who will be more dangerous," De La Hoya would say before the fight. Steve Forbes would state, "We are taking on the Golden Boy and the self-proclaimed best trainer in the world, and I believe we will make our mark."

Jeff Mayweather, the third Mayweather brother in the boxing family, would train Forbes. Forbes was a fighter with decent speed and was known to have a great chin. On paper his biggest claim to fame was being the former IBF super featherweight champion of the world in 2000. He would have a win over Cornelius Bundrage, who later would be a junior middleweight champion. The fact that De La Hoya was fighting back in his hometown may have signaled that this was his swan song, and he was saying good-bye to the people who supported him from the beginning. Yet, there was no indication that De La Hoya was considering retirement, despite a young family and his commitment to Golden Boy Promotions.

Forbes's speed was able to get several combinations in on De La Hoya in the opening round. De La Hoya was still able to control the opening round with his left jab and right hooks to Forbes's midsection. Forbes would answer back with a three-punch combination (2:54) that pelted De La Hoya's face. The rally ending the round made it an even round on my card. De La Hoya would increase the pace in the second round by constantly throwing straight punches that were effective. However, Forbes would still find De La Hoya to be an easy target with the straight left. The lack of footwork is what let De La Hoya land the combinations. By the third round, Forbes was already giving De La Hoya lumps on his face. After three rounds the punch stats had De La Hoya 73 of 197 and Forbes 41 of 209.

It was a very active fight, and Forbes was hoping that De La Hoya was going to fade down the stretch. De La Hoya felt he was much more relaxed in the ring, and that was not going to happen again. The opening minute of the fourth round had Forbes land a furious pace of punches, but his lack of power couldn't really hurt De La Hoya. It also seemed the reverse was true when a three-punch combination (2:12) had Forbes tippy-toe forward in clear contempt of De La Hoya's power. Fortunately for the Golden Boy, he was able to work his left jab and combinations better than in the Mayweather fight. De La Hoya would be much more active with his punch output but had to be frustrated he couldn't KO the smaller fighter. De La Hoya looked good with his defense by catching punches, yet down the middle, he was easy to hit; this is because De La Hoya had his gloves high and wide apart.

As the rounds progressed, Forbes was finally slowing down, and his punch output decreased. This pretty much gave De La Hoya a green light to keep attacking, as there was nothing in Forbes's power to give him trepidation. Forbes, perhaps hoping De La Hoya would tire in the latter rounds, gave him a sense of urgency in the tenth round as he fired flurries and combinations. De La Hoya wouldn't fade, but he would answer back at every opportunity. The Golden Boy would win a comfortable unanimous decision after twelve rounds. The judges had it 119–109, 119–109, and 120–108. It was difficult to assess if De La Hoya would be able to compete against Mayweather or Miguel Cotto. De La Hoya at moments looked pretty sharp, but he also didn't appear to have the legs he once had. In addition, he appeared vulnerable defensively down the middle, which would give someone like Mayweather a field day. De La Hoya didn't KO Forbes or do anything to Forbes that had never been done before. On the positive side, De La Hoya's stamina looked great. The fact that De La Hoya punch stats were 253 of 810 to Forbes's 152 of 776 showed he could still keep up a high work rate.

CHAPTER 18

Mandatory Retirement

Antonio Margarito would defeat Miguel Cotto in the summer of 2008 in a bloodbath and was hoping to be the next De La Hoya opponent. Margarito, the new WBA welterweight champion, said after the Cotto win, "I hope De La Hoya keeps his promise that he would fight the winner of my match with Cotto. Hopefully, he doesn't run like other fighters as Mayweather." Perhaps the bloody gore that covered Cotto's face would persuade De La Hoya not to take the Margarito fight. (This is all before the Margarito hand-wrapping scandal that would implode on January 2009 prior to a match with Shane Mosley.) De La Hoya was forced to review other options after the failure in negotiating a rematch for the highest grossing pay-per-view boxing fight.

In the end, the next De La Hoya opponent would be Manny Pacquiao. It was a pick that seemed ludicrous on the surface. De La Hoya was a junior middleweight, and Pacquiao's last bout was as a lightweight. Pacquiao had defeated notable Mexican fighters such as Marco Antonio Barrera, Erik Morales, Oscar Larios, and Juan Manuel Marquez. De La Hoya tried to sign the Filipino star, which included a notorious episode in which a suitcase filled with $500,000 cash was given to Pacquiao. Pacquiao would sign the contract but would then sign another contract with Top Rank, who felt he was contractually obligated to them. The matter would eventually be settled by a 2007 mediation ruling by Daniel Weinstein in which Golden Boy had a 25 percent vested interest of Pacquiao promotional revenue. There were some, including Pacquiao, who felt that De La Hoya was seeking some personal retribution due to the contract dispute. In September 2010 there would be an additional lawsuit as Golden Boy would file suit against Top Rank, this time claiming that they were owed millions of dollars due to fraudulent accounting practices that were consistent with racketeering. Golden Boy would assert that Top Rank was inflating expenses while underreporting revenues gained by fight sponsors such as Tecate in several Pacquiao fights from 2008 to 2010. Top Rank would be dismissive of the claim, and this would only make business between the two promotional titans nearly impossible.

Although neither camp discussed the lawsuits or business bickering, they were all totally aware of the previous acrimony. De La Hoya would train again at Big Bear to prepare for Pacquiao. Trainer Nacho Beristain would be brought along legendary trainer Angelo Dundee to help in preparation. Dundee would serve only in an advisory role to the camp, as Beristain would be the lead trainer. Dundee was fluent in Spanish and would be able to communicate with Beristain if needed. Hall of Fame boxer Daniel Zaragoza would be the one to work the mitts with De La Hoya. Dundee would tell De La Hoya, "You can't miss a southpaw with right-hook counter." Freddie Roach would get contentious with rival trainer Nacho Beristain. "I don't like Nacho; he is an as*****." On HBO's 24/7 Roach seemed confident, as a former De La Hoya trainer, that he knew what De La Hoya's strengths and weaknesses were, and he didn't think there was anything for Pacquiao to worry about. De La Hoya would blame Roach for the Mayweather loss claiming, "It was the wrong game plan." De La Hoya also fired back at Roach, "If he thinks he knows me, then he has another thing coming." Pacquiao felt confident that his speed would be the key to the fight.

The Filipino star had been in major-title bouts in the past, but fighting De La Hoya would expose him to a mainstream audience that didn't follow boxing religiously but followed De La Hoya. Although many regarded Pacquiao as the number-one pound-per-pound fighter, he still didn't break the glass ceiling of superstardom, which could be achieved by defeating De La Hoya. On the surface, Pacquiao seemed too small for De La Hoya; however, smaller, quicker opponents gave De La Hoya difficulties (like Mosley and Mayweather). Most importantly, De La Hoya would agree to fight Pacquiao at 145 pounds, which would be his lowest weight in twelve years. The possibility of being drained was a major gamble that De La Hoya would take.

One of De La Hoya's sparring partners included Edwin Valero who was 24-0, 24 KOs at the time. Valero, like Pacquiao, was a small southpaw with a lot of power. Valero would tell the *Philippine Inquirer* that he was thrown out of Big Bear since he punished De La Hoya after eight rounds of sparring. Valero reportedly gave De La Hoya a black eye. It may have been the shiner we saw on the second episode of the 24/7 series. The Venezuelan champion claimed that De La Hoya didn't like to train and predicted a Pacquiao knockout. Valero would tell boxeomundial.com, "I was dismissed two weeks early from Big Bear…They told me Oscar needs a fighter who is less strong than you. Oscar would go four days without running, and I told him, brother, you need to run, but he didn't want to run. I told the Philippine press and maxboxing.com that Pacquiao is going to knockout De La Hoya."

Ironically, in the same interview, Valero would predict an inevitable match between him and Pacquiao in the future. Valero's untimely death in 2010, after a suspected murder and suicide, would stop the inevitable match. The Venezuelan fighter was arrested after being suspected of murdering his wife and then committed suicide by strangulation in his prison cell. Valero finished his career 27-0, 27 KOs.

De La Hoya felt confident coming to the match and felt that it would end in a knockout. The fight was scheduled for December 6, 2008, at the MGM Grand, Las Vegas, Nevada. Freddie Roach, who trained De La Hoya for the Mayweather super fight about a year and a half before, thought "De La Hoya couldn't pull the trigger anymore." When the actual fight started, he noticed De La Hoya had IV marks on his arm for rehydration and told Pacquiao "to jump on him" before the opening bell. The bout would be a one-sided pummeling for De La Hoya (round-by-round coverage in the Pacquiao section). Even the Hopkins match, which was the only De La Hoya stoppage, was fairly competitive until the KO, but this was a shutout loss for De La Hoya. The legs were gone and so was the head movement. Pacquiao ran rings around De La Hoya by landing combinations and then getting out of danger with his legs. De La Hoya was unable to establish a jab due to the Pacquiao upper body and lateral movement. De La Hoya, past his prime and drained, was not going to figure out Pacquiao's speed and various angles. After eight rounds of carnage, he would quit in his stool. A charitable judge did give De La Hoya one round. It was quite clear that De La Hoya didn't belong in the ring again with top competition.

In retrospect De La Hoya probably should have retired after the Mayweather fight since he gave a decent performance and got the biggest payday of his career. However, boxers often need to lose in brutal fashion to finally realize that they do not belong in the ring again. The actual Pacquiao fight would do over 1.2 million PPV buys, which again solidified De La Hoya as a PPV commodity. As a solace De La Hoya was guaranteed $20 million for the punishment he received. The new pound-per-pound king, Pacquiao, would get roughly $15 million, which was easily the biggest payday of his career up to that point.

De La Hoya poses outside of the Staples Center with his honorary statue.
AP Photo/Damian Dovarganes.

The De La Hoya loss to Pacquiao came on the heels of a bronze statue being erected in front of the Staples Center, alongside statues of Magic Johnson and Wayne Gretsky. Of course, the statue would garner some critics who felt that Kareem Abdul Jabbar, who won five NBA titles with the Lakers, should have been honored first. There were other great Los Angeles athletes such as Wilt Chamberlain, Jerry West, and Sandy Koufax who didn't get a statue either. Some cynics felt that since AEG (who owned the Staples Center) had an interest in Golden Boy, they did it for gratuitous reasons. However, De La Hoya won a gold medal and was easily the most commercially successful fighter to ever come out Los Angeles, and the fact that he gave back millions to his community should have at least tempered some of the criticism he faced.

De La Hoya would officially announce his retirement from the sport on April 19, 2009. "When I can't do it anymore, when I can't compete at the highest level, it's not fair to me, it's not fair to the fans, it's not fair to nobody," De La Hoya would explain in his announcement. There were rumors that he was going to fight Julio Cesar Chavez Jr. for a final hurrah, and the official announcement would put all those rumors to rest.

De La Hoya would battle some of his demons, away from the ring, after retirement. He would get treated for substance-abuse addictions to alcohol and cocaine. Cocaine is a drug of choice that has afflicted numerous boxers, including Ray Leonard, Pernell Whitaker, Aaron Pryor, Ricky Hatton, and Joe Calzaghe. The Golden Boy would finally admit that pictures taken by a model in 2007 showing him cross dressing were not photoshopped but were actually real. De La Hoya claims that he was under the influence of drugs when those pictures were taken. In an interview with Univision, he would state, "I am tired now of lying to the public and of lying to myself." De La Hoya would successfully complete a substance-abuse rehabilitation program by the fall of 2011 and has professed he has stayed sober since. De La Hoya would also face a $5 million suit filed by a woman after she accused him of "intimidating her and causing emotional distress" in a meeting that allegedly took place on March 15, 2011, in a New York City hotel. This suit would eventually be dropped.

De La Hoya has always reiterated that boxing is part of his life but not his life. Foremost, his family has been the most important driving force outside of the ring. In addition De La Hoya has been involved in both public and charitable organizations outside of the ring. In 2006 De La Hoya saw the publication of his first children's book entitled *Super Oscar*. The book written by Mark Shulman and illustrated by Lisa Kopelke and would win the 2007 award for Best Bilingual Children's Picture Book from the Latino Book Awards. De La Hoya, through Golden Boy Promotions, would be involved in many acquisitions, which included *Ring Magazine*, *World Boxing Magazine*, and equity interest in *Univision*.

De La Hoya would also contribute millions to local high schools and buy the local Resurrection Gym and convert it to the De La Hoya Youth Center. The youth center is designed to help bring education and health services to local, underprivileged people.

De La Hoya would credit his mother for influencing his philanthropic efforts. "It's my mother that had strong beliefs about education," he says. "What she really instilled in me is the fact that the more success I have, whether it's inside or outside the ring, the more I have to give back. And those words will always be with me; I'll never stop giving back to as many people as possible."

De La Hoya got in the ring with the greats, past and present. He fought possibly as many as twelve Hall of Famers that span from the 1980s to the current millennium. In the modern era where champions rarely exceed two professional bouts a year, it is more difficult to get in the ring with all the big names. In that aspect De La Hoya was a throw-back fighter by taking on all challenges, ranging from the super featherweight to middleweight division. Perhaps Winky Wright and Vernon Forrest are the only notable omissions from the De La Hoya opponent résumé. Critics would point to the close-decision wins in the Quartey, Sturm, and Whitaker fights that went his way, but there were also the Trinidad and second Mosley close decisions that went the other way. De La Hoya's presence in boxing through Golden Boy Promotions likely means he will still be a major force in the boxing industry for decades to come. De La Hoya would get inducted into the International Boxing Hall of Fame (IBHOF) in 2014.

IBHOF Members Defeated (3): Julio Cesar Chavez, Arturo Gatti, Pernell Whitaker.
Probable IBHOF Members Defeated (1): Hector Camacho.
Possible IBHOF Members Defeated (3): Miguel Angel Gonzalez, Genaro Hernandez, Ike Quartey.

Professional Boxing Record
(39-6, 30 KOs)

1992

November 23	Lamar Williams WKO 1, Great Western Forum, Inglewood, CA
December 12	Clifford Hicks WKO 1, America West Arena, Phoenix, AZ

1993

January 3	Paris Alexander WTKO 4, Hollywood Palladium, Hollywood, CA
February 6	Curtis Strong WTKO 4, Sports Arena, San Diego, CA
March 13	Jeff Mayweather WTKO 4, Hilton Hotel, Las Vegas, NV
April 6	Mike Grable WUD 8, War Memorial Auditorium, Rochester, NY
May 8	Frank Avelar WTKO 4, Caesars Tahoe, Stateline, NV
June 7	Troy Dorsey WTKO 1, Thomas & Mack Center, Las Vegas, NV
August 14	Renaldo Carter WTKO 6, Casino Magic, Bay St. Louis, MS
August 27	Angelo Nunez WTKO 4, Beverly Wilshire Hotel, Beverly Hills, CA
October 30	Narciso Valenzuela WKO 1, America West Arena, Phoenix, AZ

1994

May 3	Jimmy Bredahl WTKO 8, Olympic Auditorium, Los Angeles, CA **WBO super featherweight title**
May 27	Giorgio Campanella WTKO 3, MGM Grand, Las Vegas, NV **WBO super featherweight title**
July 29	Jorge Paez WKO 2, MGM Grand, Las Vegas, NV **vacant WBO World lightweight title**
November 18	Carl Griffith WTKO 3, MGM Grand, Las Vegas, NV **WBO World lightweight title**
December 10	John Avila WTKO 9, Olympic Auditorium, Los Angeles, CA **WBO World lightweight title**

1995

February 18	John John Molina WUD 12, MGM Grand, Las Vegas, NV
	WBO World lightweight title
May 6	Rafael Ruelas WTKO 2, Caesars Palace, Las Vegas, NV
	WBO, IBF World lightweight titles
September 9	Genaro Hernandez WTKO 6, Caesars Palace, Las Vegas, NV
	WBO World lightweight title
December 15	Jesse James Lejia WTKO 2, Madison Square Garden, NY, NY
	WBO World lightweight title

1996

February 9	Darryl Tyson WKO 2, Caesars Palace, Las Vegas, NV
June 7	Julio Cesar Chavez WTKO 4, Caesars Palace, Las Vegas, NV
	WBC World super lightweight title

1997

January 18	Miguel Angel Gonzalez WUD 12, Thomas & Mack Center, Las Vegas, NV
	WBC World super lightweight title
April 12	Pernell Whitaker WUD 12, Thomas & Mack Center, Las Vegas, NV
	WBC World welterweight title
June 14	David Kamau WKO 2, Alamodome, San Antonio, TX
	WBC World welterweight title
September 13	Hector Camacho WUD 12, Thomas & Mack Center, Las Vegas, NV
	WBC World welterweight title
December 6	Wilfredo Rivera WTKO 8, Caesars Hotel & Casino, Atlantic City, NJ
	WBC World welterweight title

1998

June 13	Patrick Charpentier WTKO 3, Sun Bowl, EL Paso, TX **WBC World welterweight title**
September 18	Julio Cesar Chavez WTKO 8, Thomas & Mack Center, Las Vegas, NV **WBC World welterweight title**

1999

February 13	Ike Quartey WSD 12, Thomas & Mack Center, Las Vegas, NV **WBC World welterweight title**
May 22	Oba Carr WTKO 11, Mandalay Bay Resort & Casino, Las Vegas, NV **WBC World welterweight title**
September 18	Felix Trinidad LMD 12, Mandalay Bay Resort & Casino, Las Vegas, NV **IBF, WBC World welterweight titles**

2000

February 26	Derrell Coley WTKO 7, Madison Square Garden, NY, NY
June 17	Shane Mosley LSD 12, MGM Grand, Las Vegas, NV **WBC World welterweight title**

2001

March 24	Arturo Gatti WTKO 5, MGM Grand, Las Vegas, NV
June 23	Javier Castillejo WUD 12, MGM Grand, Las Vegas, NV **WBC World light middleweight title**

2002

September 14	Fernando Vargas WTKO 11, MGM Grand, Las Vegas, NV **WBC, WBA World light middleweight titles**

2003

May 3	Luis R. Campas WTKO 7, Mandalay Bay Resort & Casino, Las Vegas, NV **WBC, WBA World light middleweight titles**
September 13	Shane Mosley LUD 12, MGM Grand, Las Vegas, NV **WBC, WBA World light middleweight titles**

2004

June 5	Felix Sturm WUD 12, MGM Grand, Las Vegas, NV **WBO World middleweight title**
September 18	Bernard Hopkins LKO 9, MGM Grand, Las Vegas, NV **IBF, WBA, WBC, WBO World middleweight titles (undisputed championship)**

2005

(not active)

2006

May 6	Ricardo Mayorga WTKO 6, MGM Grand, Las Vegas, NV **WBC World middleweight title**

2007

May 5	Floyd Mayweather LSD 12, MGM Grand, Las Vegas, NV **WBC World middleweight title**

2008

May 3	Steve Forbes WUD 12, Home Depot Center, Carson, CA
December 8	Manny Pacquiao LTKO 8, MGM Grand, Las Vegas, NV

BIBLIOGRAPHY

Brooks, Roger. "Oscar De La Hoya Is Good as Gold." *Success.com*, web, 4 August 2009.

Dufresne, Chris. "De La Hoya Wins, Avoids Some Road Work." *Los Angeles Times*, 19 November 1994.

Glauber, Bill. "De La Hoya Fights for Mother's Dream: A Boxing Gold Was Her Dying Wish." *The Baltimore Sun*, 27 July 1992.

Glitch. "Oscar De La Hoya: 'I Am on a Daily Fight for My Life.'" *Voxxi.com*, web, 28 August 2013.

Searcy, Jay. "Whitaker Taking Aim at De La Hoya Image, Critics Would Like to See the Younger Fighter Cut Down. 'Sweet Pea' Says He's Just the Man to Do It." *Philly Inquirer.articles.philly.com*, web, 12 April 1997.

Smith, Timothy W. "Plus: In the News—Boxing; De La Hoya Adds Clancy as Trainer." *New York Times*, 21 November 1997.

Springer, Steve. "Vargas Drug Tests Reveal Steroids." *Los Angeles Times*, web, 28 September 2002.

Front Cover De La Hoya Photo Credit: AP Photo/Laura Rauch.

Floyd Mayweather Jr.

Lifespan (1977–Present)

Active: 1996–Present (49-0, 26 KOs)

Titles Held: WBC Super Featherweight, WBC Lightweight, WBC Jr. Welterweight, WBA, WBC, WBO & IBF Welterweight, WBC & WBA Jr. Middleweight

CHAPTER 1
Boxing DNA

The Mayweather family appeared to have Boxing DNA at conception; no less than three brothers (Floyd Mayweather Sr., Roger Mayweather, and Jeff Mayweather) would have professional boxing careers. The boxing pedigree enabled Floyd Mayweather Jr. to be exposed, trained, and molded as a boxer from infancy. Mayweather would actually be born under his mother's surname, Floyd Joy Sinclair, on February 24, 1977, in Grand Rapids, Michigan. At the age of five, Mayweather's dad regularly trained him, and by the age of seven, he routinely put on fitted boxing gloves. Although a toddler, Mayweather demonstrated boxing proficiency beyond his age. Mayweather Sr. would bring the younger Mayweather to the gym so he could work on the speed bag and learn basic boxing techniques. As Mayweather Sr. was still a professional until the 1980s, the younger Mayweather would study and mimic his dad. Having a father and two uncles who could aid his growth as a fighter was a major blessing for Mayweather's progression as a pugilist. However, Mayweather's youth was far from rosy. His mother, Deborah Sinclair, was a nurse who suffered from substance-abuse problems and separated from Mayweather's dad when he was still an infant. During one notorious domestic altercation, Mayweather Sr.'s brother-in-law would shoot him in the leg with a 20-gauge shotgun while Mayweather Sr. was carrying his one-year-old son. The elder Mayweather understood the shooter wouldn't aim for his son and would shot his leg instead. The injury suffered by the wound limited his boxing abilities and hampered his attempt in becoming a world champion. Perhaps the elder Mayweather didn't have the same luck as Carlos Monzon who still retained great success after being shot in the leg. Mayweather's goal was to have his son accomplish the greatness that would elude his own career.

The younger Mayweather would often need to drift between houses as he shared time with his grandmother, mother, and his father. Mayweather credits his grandmother Bernice Sinclair as being the most stable figure in his upbringing. However, he also would acknowledge the sacrifices his mother made for him while promoting his bout with Ricky Hatton. "She made me strive harder, because I can remember days when she was working in that nursing home. There had been days when she was cleaning up old folks, and they died in her arms. She took her last money, when she took her last money for us, her last $100, and use it for my birthday. So, things like that is what make me strive hard and dedicate myself to the sport of boxing." Mayweather would also go on to say about his mother, "When nobody believed in me, she believed in me."

Despite the turmoil, the steady constant in his life was boxing. Mayweather would constantly go to the local gym and start working out on the heavier bags and learn the more technical aspects of the game. Even roadwork was not out of the question for a preadolescent Mayweather. Mayweather Sr. would be strict and, according to the younger Mayweather, would physically reprimand him when he didn't obey his father's commands. The younger Mayweather would later concede that it was analogous to child abuse, as he was whipped with an extension cord.

The Mayweather father-son relationship is likened to Joseph Jackson training the young Jacksons and Leopold Mozart teaching a young Wolfgang everything he knew. All the teaching and discipline would eventually lead to Mayweather becoming the most technically proficient fighter since the heyday of Pernell Whitaker and Ricardo Lopez. The final product would result in one of the greatest defensive fighters along with names like Jack Johnson, Willie Pep, Nicolino Locche, and Wilfred Benitez. Mayweather didn't invent the shoulder roll, as it was previously practiced by fighters such as George Benton, Nicolino Locche, and James Toney, but he perfected it.

Mayweather would get the nickname "Pretty Boy" in his amateur days since he wouldn't have a mark on his face after fighting. Having no visible scars was something that his dad demanded, as it meant ring perfection. In 2009 Mayweather would reflect on the immaculate standard his dad put on him in the ring. He would tell Jonathan Ames of interviewmagazine.com, "Well, my mother and certain other people in my life have said, 'Floyd, nobody is perfect except for God. And I always knew that; I just wanted my victories to be flawless. I didn't want to get hit at all. I wasn't gonna make any mistakes. And that's the problem with me growing up and being around a trainer that wants his fighter to be perfect." There would be notorious feuds in the love-and-hate relationship between father and son, which included moments of estrangement and reconciliation. The son resented being called "Little Floyd" while his dad was known as "Big Floyd." However, the younger Mayweather would concede when his dad returned to his corner from prison, "I know a lot of people want to see me and my father break up...but it will never happen. Because I know he is the best thing for me, and I know I got this far because all of his teaching."

At the age of sixteen, Mayweather would successfully capture the National Golden Gloves title as a light flyweight in 1993. Roger Mayweather, the former WBA super featherweight and WBC light welterweight champion of the world, was taking on more of the training role as Mayweather Sr. was facing criminal drug-trafficking charges. In 1994 Mayweather Sr. would be convicted and sentenced to five and half years in jail. While Floyd Sr. would serve time at the FCI in Milan, Michigan, his brothers Roger and Jeff would help train his son. Uncle Roger would take the lead responsibility in Floyd Mayweather's training and mentoring. Having his father removed from his life would have an emotional impact on the young Mayweather as he felt both loss and resentment not having his father by his side. However, this didn't adversely impact his boxing development. Mayweather would win both the 1994 Golden Gloves flyweight championship and the 1995 US Amateur featherweight championship. Mayweather's body would mature due to puberty, which resulted in him climbing five weight divisions in three years. In 1996 Mayweather successfully qualified for the Summer Olympics in Atlanta by defeating Augie Sanchez twice in the Olympic trials. Sanchez once defeated Mayweather as an amateur by a score of 12–11. Mayweather wanted to follow in the footsteps of previous US gold medalists such as Muhammad Ali, George Foreman, Ray Leonard, and—more recently—Oscar De La Hoya in capturing Olympic Gold.

CHAPTER 2
Fuzzy Scoring in Atlanta

The 1996 Atlanta Summer Olympics would forever be remembered for the Centennial Olympic Park bombings later tied to Eric Rudolph. Unfortunately, Richard Jewel would literally be indicted by an overzealous media who thought a "person of interest" during the early phase of an investigation meant guilty until proven innocent. Richard Jewel was pretty much castigated by the media as the main suspect after he tried to help bombing victims. Jewel's life would never be the same again. He would die in 2007, at the young age of forty-four years old. Before his death, Jewel would settle several lawsuits with media outlets as NBC, *The Atlanta Constitution*, and the *New York Post*. In these very same Olympics, there was another injustice handed out to Floyd Mayweather Jr. Mayweather would lose a semifinal match to the infamous Olympic scoring system, which is open to corruption. Boxing in the Olympics was like a plague to American fighters as Roy Jones Jr. and Evander Holyfield both of whom fell short of Olympic Gold. Jones would suffer possibly the most egregious decision in Olympic boxing history, and Holyfield would be the recipient of a preposterous disqualification.

Mayweather would actually start on a positive note in the 1996 Summer Olympics. His first match was an early stoppage against twenty-year-old Kazak fighter Bakhtiyar Tyleganov (0:57) into the second round. Mayweather would break Tyleganov's nose in the process.

The second round match would see Mayweather challenge Armenian fighter Arthur Gevorgyan (not to be confused with Artur Grigorian, who would be a future WBO lightweight champion). Mayweather would stalk Gevorgyan behind his high guard while trying to score with overhand shots on the taller opponent. Gevorgyan would get a warning for low blows in the first round. Gevorgyan would get a standing eight count after he ate a Mayweather overhand right-and-left hook combination at (2:26) of the first round. After the first round, Mayweather was ahead 9–1 using the Olympic scoring system of clean punches landed by the white portion of the glove.

Mayweather would punish Gevorgyan in the second for keeping his gloves low with lead rights. Mayweather's elusive defense and hand speed would be too much for Gevorgyan who would lose by a final score of 16–3. The scoring seemed a bit charitable, as there were a few more clean Mayweather punches that weren't scored, such as an uppercut that got Gevorgyan's attention.

Mayweather would face his most dangerous opponent next. Lorenzo Aragon was three years older than Mayweather and was a former Cuban flyweight, bantamweight, and lightweight champion. He would also be a Cuban featherweight champion in 1996, the same division in which he would be facing Mayweather. Moreover, he was also the 1994 Pan American bantamweight champion. No American had defeated a Cuban in the Olympics since the 1976 games where Ray Leonard and Leon Spinks would accomplish that feat. Mayweather understood that if he beat Aragon in the quarterfinals, then his biggest hurdle to the gold would be out of his way. However, like many things in life, it was easier said than done. Aragon was a seasoned international veteran who understood the Olympic scoring system better than Mayweather. Many young American fighters, as in the previous 1992 Olympics, fall prey to that system. This was partly responsible for the lackluster American performance in the 1992 games. Mayweather still had the talent and innate boxing instincts taught by his dad and two uncles who were professional fighters. Mayweather would get a trial by fire as he would go down 2–0 in the scorecard to Aragon and had trouble with the Cuban pugilist movement. Aragon then would land a straight right and take a 3–0 lead on the scoring system. Finally, at 2:27 a right cross that snapped Aragon's head would be scored on the Mayweather tally. There would be five more connects counted in the final thirty seconds to give Aragon a 5–4 lead on the scoring card at the end of the first round.

Mayweather was able to anticipate and time Aragon punches better, and it gave him more confidence to be more aggressive in the second round. In addition he was able to work the body with right-left hooks on the inside. This would give the young Michigan fighter a 7–6 lead in the middle of the second round. Aragon would even the score with a left hook to Mayweather's jaw. Mayweather struck back. A left hook to Aragon's body and a rally in the final seconds of the round got him a 10–7 lead going to the final round.

Mayweather didn't sit on his lead; he would still stay in front of Aragon and engage him. At 1:28 of the third, Aragon would tackle Mayweather to the canvas. Mayweather would see his 12–7 lead reduced to 12–11, as he would continue to fight Aragon on the inside. Mayweather's mistake of not being more defensive and less offensive almost cost him the match. Conversely, the victory again showed that most of the greatest Mayweather wins weren't earned by running away, but by standing and fighting. Mayweather would now be headed to the semifinals against Serafim Todorov. Todorov, a Bulgarian fighter, who was approximately a decade older than Mayweather.

The first round was a feeling-out process with only three punches being scored, which gave Todorov a 2–1 lead going to the second round. Mayweather would be a bit more defensive in this contest, with his left shoulder up higher than his previous bouts. Todorov was mainly working the stiff left jab followed by the straight right while Mayweather was using his speed to land combinations on the inside. The counter straight hand was also effective. Mayweather, while ahead 7–6 after two rounds, was still going to need a few more points to win. As a result, he was aggressive with overhand leading shots, which were landing but not getting scored. Again, this is because the judges only counted shots that were from the white portion of the glove. Mayweather would also land two short punches on the inside that weren't scored one minute into the third, while Todorov would even the score with a left hook to the body. If you look at the action between 1:33 and 1:37 of the third round, you will see there were possibly as many as three clean Mayweather connects that weren't scored. Those blows appeared to be from the white portion of the glove. Mysteriously, not even one of those connects would be scored to tie the match. Moments later, another four-punch Mayweather combination punctuated with a straight left would only have one clean punch landed.

The one connect would make it 8–8 in the scoring with less than one minute left. Both fighters wrested on the inside with only one Todorov overhand right scoring, giving him a 9–8 lead. The judges would score another right for Todorov giving him a 10–8 lead. Todorov would be allowed to push Mayweather with impunity. He would also get several warnings for slapping but no point deductions either. In the remaining seconds, Mayweather would land several blows that, at minimum, had two punches land cleanly—yet only one would be scored, making it 10–9.

Todorov would pull out the upset. Perhaps symbolically the referee would accidentally raise Mayweather's right arm as the victor. After the mistake was corrected, Todorov would take celebratory bows in another controversial Olympic moment. This didn't equate to the injustice that Roy Jones Jr. suffered in the 1988 Olympics where he completely dominated his opponent, but future details would bring about allegations of corruption and an official American protest. Todorov would lose the gold-medal match to Thai fighter Kamsing Somluck. Three Bulgarian fighters would win gold medals, as the head of the boxing officials was Bulgarian Emil Jetchev. An official American protest would be filed, but the decision wouldn't change.

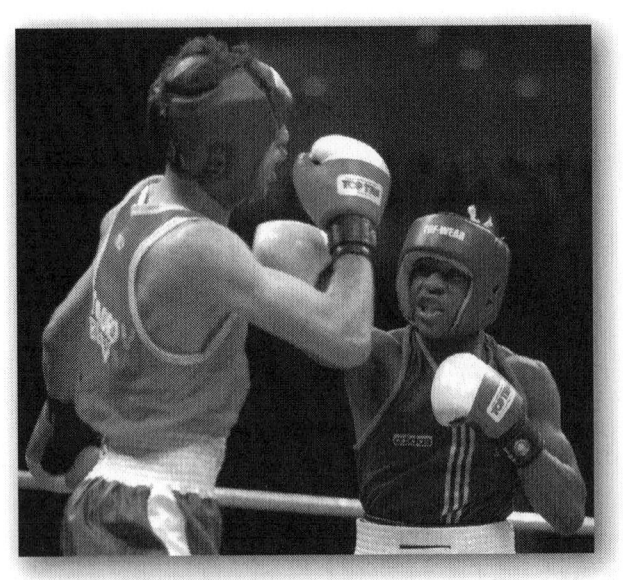

Mayweather battles Serafim Todorov in the
1996 Atlanta Olympics, an event that
ended in controversy. AP Photo/Rick Bowmer.

After the disappointment of the Atlanta Olympics, Mayweather would set his eye on turning professional. He would end his amateur career with an impressive 84–6 record. Mayweather was hoping to become another champion from Michigan as Thomas Hearns, James Toney, Joe Louis, and Stanley Ketchel had before him.

CHAPTER 3

Pretty Boy Goes Prime Time

Las Vegas would become Mayweather's permanent residence as he enjoyed the nightlife, and it was an ideal place to live and train with his uncles—who were still professional fighters. Mayweather developed a great lead right and left hook that complimented his great reflexes and defensive ability. Both of his fighting uncles—Roger and Jeff Mayweather—would be at his corner as he turned professional. Mayweather would also have experienced Argentine cut man Miguel Diaz at his side. Mayweather Jr. would make a promise to his incarcerated father, "I want to be successful so my dad won't be eating bologna sandwiches when he comes out of prison." Mayweather would tell ESPN, "The difference between fighting as a professional and amateur is that I am getting paid now." Bob Arum's Top Rank would be chiefly responsible for the business side in the early stages of Mayweather's career. In 2006 Dan Goosen would also briefly promote Mayweather who eventually would later join the Golden Boy umbrella for his mega fights starting in 2007. James Prince would also manage Mayweather before the majority of his career would see Leonard Ellerbe and Al Haymon both advise and manage him. Mayweather would buy out his contract from Top Rank at a reported $750,000 with Haymon's assistance, who would serve as Mayweather's manager for most of the new millennium. Haymon, a Harvard educated businessman, would make a major name for himself in concert promotion, including work with notable musicians such as Whitney Houston and MC Hammer. Haymon's businesses would venture to television and film, and boxing would seem a natural progression, as he was former fighter Bobby Haymon's (21-8-1, 9 KOs) brother. Sugar Ray Leonard would stop brother Bobby in three rounds in a bout that ended in bit of controversy. Leonard would drop Bobby Haymon in the third round with an overhand right-and-left hook combination near the southeastern corner ropes. Haymon would shake his head to get his senses and beat the count. However, Haymon was hurt again by another combination as the bell rung. The final left hook was clearly after the bell rang. Haymon would slump over and be left hanging between the two top ropes. Referee Harry Cecchini would try to restrain Leonard before the final two shots scored. Haymon wouldn't be able to continue, and Leonard was victorious. The Haymon corner would charge the ring feeling that Leonard hit after the bell. Haymon's manager, Dominick Polo, would say, "Leonard hit him three times after the bell, and the officials said they couldn't do anything about it." Polo felt that the hometown audience of 15,272 fans made it impossible to disqualify Leonard. Leonard and his corner felt the final blows were released as the bell rang, and a fighter must protect himself at all times. However, since Leonard had dominated the match from the opening bell, there was no outcry for a rematch.

Al Haymon would get licensed to manage fighters and work with champions such as Vernon Forrest, Paul Williams, Peter Quillen, and—most notably—Mayweather. Despite critics who accuse Haymon of skirting the line between both promoter and manager, which is prohibited by the Muhammad Ali Reform Act of 1990, there has never been a network or venue that has claimed to have directly negotiated any aspect of an event with Haymon instead of the Mayweather promoter. Haymon would prove to be effective in helping Mayweather garner major paydays while retaining maximum earnings per fight. Haymon, who was reclusive as far as media requests, would rarely be the manager who would talk to the media as this role—among other managerial functions—would be squarely on the shoulders of Leonard Ellerbee. Leonard Ellerbee would come out of Washington DC where he took up boxing to defend himself on the streets and also aspired to become a professional boxer. At the time, the DC area had seen many fighters make a name in the amateur circuit, such as Kenny Baysmore who won the 1979 National Golden Gloves Bantamweight title and Floyd Favors who won the amateur world title in the same division in 1982. Arguably the most notable fighters who fought in the DC area were New Mexico born heavy-handed puncher Bob Foster, and Maryland-born fighter Sugar Ray Leonard, who was the most direct inspiration for young fighters coming out of the area in the 1970s. For Ellerbee the dreams of a boxing career would end prematurely due to reoccurring hand injuries, and he would instead join the military after high school. However, Ellerbee's travels around the country as an amateur would introduce him to champion Roger Mayweather. Ellerbee would relocate to Las Vegas to be an assistant trainer. His passion for boxing would now be fulfilled by working directly with other boxers and helping in conditioning, training, and functioning as a bodyguard. The work with Roger Mayweather would prove to be the catalyst for introducing Ellerbee to Mayweather's nephew Floyd Mayweather Jr. Almost immediately the young Mayweather would have Ellerbee both serve as advisor and assist in fight preparation. As the years would go by, it would be Ellerbee who served the dual role of assisting in the boxing corner and also becoming the public-relations voice in front of the camera for Mayweather. There wouldn't be any issues of on-the-job training as Ellerbee would have people such as Al Haymon, Bob Arum, and, later, the people at Golden Boy to assist or function as Ellerbee's mentor. Mayweather would always make sure no stone would be unturned. This would be crucial in Mayweather marketing himself beyond the sport and getting some of the most lucrative contracts in the history of the sport.

Mayweather had many distractions but always focused in the ring. Interestingly, Mayweather would start professionally as a super featherweight instead of at the featherweight limit in which he competed in the Olympics. There was no inclination to drain himself, as De La Hoya did when he captured his first title as a super featherweight. If Mayweather had started out as a featherweight, it may have him given him a chance at becoming a sextuple champion. If Mayweather wanted to be a sextuple champion, he would eventually need to come all the way up to middleweight as De La Hoya did. Mayweather's smaller physical frame would make that an even more difficult prospect.

The nineteen-year-old Mayweather would get his professional debut on ESPN on October 11, 1996, at the Texas Station Casino, Las Vegas, Nevada. Conveniently, the bout would be held in Las Vegas, his adopted hometown, with Kenny Bayless as the referee. Mayweather would be introduced as being a silver medalist from the Olympics and by the "Pretty Boy" moniker. The introductions would prove to be not much longer than the actual contest itself.

Mayweather's professional debut was not expected to last long, and it didn't. Robert Apodaca was also making his professional debut. Mayweather, early in the contest, stuck a laser left jab and then followed it with a straight right on Apodaca. A powerful left hook in the middle of the opening round to the body would do serious damage to Apodaca. Mayweather would score a knockdown with another left hook to the body at 1:45 of the first round. A third left hook to the body at the opening moments of the second round, and Apodaca would go down again grimacing in pain at the official stoppage at 2:23 of the second round. It seemed the body shot was a prearranged strategy as Mayweather told Al Bernstein after the bout, "Mexicans could take good head shots, so I had to go to the body."

The second Mayweather opponent, Reggie Sanders, had only two professional fights. However, he was a southpaw, and few professionals would risk taking a southpaw so early in their career. For Mayweather it would be good experience to mature as a fighter. Mayweather didn't box much in the opening round, and Sanders did well early on. The left hand would find its mark on Mayweather, and the punch stats for the first round showed Sanders connecting 10 of 43 and Mayweather 12 of 41. A stiff right jab (0:50) in the second round had Mayweather take a backward step. Mayweather responded by getting more aggressive and throwing more combinations and countering to win the round. The final punch stats for the second round would have Mayweather landing 24 of 49 and Sanders 12 of 46.

Mayweather would stalk Sanders in the final two rounds, despite having a cut on his right eyebrow. Cut man Miguel Diaz would be crucial in helping to stop the bleeding. The Albuquerque crowd would initiate scattering boos due to the lack of action. Mayweather would win the unanimous decision 39–37, 40–36, and 40–36. Final punch stats were 82 of 171 for Mayweather and 59 of 178 for Sanders. The 33 percent connect rate for Sanders would be among the highest percentages connected for a Mayweather opponent early in his career.

Bob Arum's influence would help Mayweather get in the undercard of the Oscar De La Hoya and Miguel Angel Gonzalez main event. The bout would be the HBO debut for Mayweather. The bout would be held on January 18, 1997, at the Thomas & Mack Center, Las Vegas, Nevada. Mayweather's opponent would be Jerry Cooper.

Veteran ring announcer Michael Buffert would once again introduce Mayweather as the silver medalist of the 1996 Olympics. If you had left the TV to grab a sandwich or some tacos, you would have missed the action. Cooper would go down in less than thirty seconds by a straight left jab to the body. Mayweather would showboat by winding up his right hand, knowing full well this would be a quick night. A barrage of combinations would have Cooper go down on the ropes a second time. Mitch Halpern would do the count, and when asked if he wanted to continue, there would be no response, and Halpern correctly stopped the contest at 1:39 of the first round. Larry Merchant, never at a loss for words, would say, "You know when they go to Ada, Oklahoma, they are not looking for a winner." Bob Arum would immediately high-five his new boxing commodity and tell Mayweather, "Show me the money."

Despite being incarcerated, the elder Mayweather kept an "eagle eye" on his son's progress. The two often would talk on the phone. The elder Mayweather watched his son fight from prison and told him, "Don't be one-dimensional." The younger Mayweather would heed the advice against his next opponent, Edgar Ayala, two weeks after disposing Cooper. Mayweather would use more head movement to elude Ayala's jab while navigating the ring. A powerful, Mayweather left counter would floor Ayala after he was punished due to missing with his right. This fight would highlight Mayweather's speed, reflexes, and defensive ability more than his previous three fights had. Mayweather would stalk Ayala while making him miss with body twists, head movement, and slipping ability. An animated Mayweather would throw his gloves up to demand Ayala fight. The only punch of note that Ayala would land would be a left hook to the head (1:03) in the second round. However, no damage was done, and an incensed Mayweather would score with a solid left hook to the chin that had Ayala out cold, spread eagle. Referee Chuck Hassett waved off the count as Ayala wouldn't get up. The most impressive knockout of Mayweather's early career would be officially 1:39 of the second round.

Mayweather would return to his hometown of Grand Rapids, Michigan. The next Mayweather opponent, Kino Rodriquez, would be knocked out by a left hook to the body. Mayweather would actually stand near Rodriquez as he was down, in showboating fashion; the referee Frank Garza forced him to go to the neutral corner. Rodriguez would get up but choose not to fight, and Mayweather would mouth off at him for failing to continue. Mayweather would climb the ring post and demonstrate his dancing skills to the audience. Tony Paige, who broadcasted the fight, nicknamed him "Floyd Attitude Mayweather."

As Mayweather progressed in his professional career, there were some who found some of Mayweather's conduct (such as the post-Rodriquez celebration) as unsportsmanlike.

Roy Jones Jr. stated, "You have to be a sportsman and set an example since many kids will want to be like Floyd." Boxing was one of the few sports where being both vilified and despised could capture the audience. Mayweather was simply feeding off the energy that polar opposites generated.

Mayweather would next challenge Bobby Giepert on April 12, 1997, at the Thomas & Mack Center, Las Vegas, Nevada. Giepert, an electrician from Louisiana, was a part-time fighter and would not give Mayweather much of a test. Roy Jones had fought Giepert as a young amateur and when pressed would say, "The only thing I remember was that he was left-handed." The fight would be the undercard to Pernell Whitaker versus De La Hoya and would be a great setting for Top Rank to promote Mayweather to a larger boxing audience. Mayweather would send Giepert down with a straight right hand less than a minute into the fight. A four-punch combination that closed with another straight right closed the show for good. Referee Joe Cortez would waive off the count as Jim Lampley asked, "Do you think that shocked the electrician? He was electrocuted with right hands."

Mayweather would improve to (7-0) one month later after knocking out Troy Duran with one right hand. The crowd at the Orleans Hotel and Casino would have only seventy-two seconds of action. As the victories continued, so did the Mayweather notoriety. More national exposure would come again on June 14, 1997, as Mayweather would fight in another De La Hoya undercard. This time it would be the Alamadome in the De La Hoya-Kamau main event. Larry Shields (12-3-1, 5 KOs) would take Mayweather the six-round distance since he had the chin and experience to go with it. Mayweather would need to use the shoulder roll more frequently at the offensive-minded opponent. He often put his left shoulder high with right glove high. Mayweather would land clean left jabs and a few power rights, but Shields wouldn't crumble quickly as some of his easy previous opponents had. The Grand Rapids born fighter kept a more defensive posture with both gloves cradling his body as he moved forward while Shields tried to use his right jab from the outside. At 1:06 of the second round, Mayweather landed a straight right that Shields took well, unlike Duran who was knocked out. The second half of the round had both fighters exchanging their best artillery in the middle of the ring. Mayweather even had some blood come out of his lips; at the end of the round, both fighters touched gloves, knowing they could take each other's best shots. Shields would get Mayweather on the ropes and tee off while Mayweather would cover up, but most of the blows were blocked. Future opponents (such as Jose Luis Castillo and Oscar De La Hoya) would use this strategy of getting Mayweather on the ropes. Mayweather would take control in the fourth by walking Shields down while throwing three-punch combinations. There would be no point in leaving himself open while going for the knockout as Mayweather would keep coming forward while firing potshots to coast to victory in the final two rounds.

Mayweather would stick out his tongue and blow kisses to Shields as he coasted to the victory. Shields would get Mayweather on the ropes again in the sixth but not do much damage. This would be one of the few Mayweather bouts that saw him sport a bloodied nose. Mayweather would win the unanimous decision and pick up some deeper-water experience with it.

After eight professional bouts, Mayweather had received some national exposure by fighting on ESPN and HBO PPV events. However, there was no larger audience then being broadcast on one of the four major television networks at the time. Mayweather would get that opportunity when he faced Jesus Chavez on July 12, 1997, at the Grand Casino, Biloxi, Mississippi.

Floyd Mayweather would get national television exposure on the CBS boxing series. Gil Clancy and Tim Ryan would broadcast the contest. Clancy reiterated his belief that "Mayweather was the outstanding pro prospect in the entire Olympic games." This would be the first of two opponents named Jesus Chavez that Mayweather would face. Chavez would be another southpaw served up to Mayweather. The left jab would land effectively for Mayweather, and he would know how to get out of danger. Mayweather would evolve more in this fight. His offensive ability was enhanced by the use of shorter punches on the inside and more use of his left jab. Even when Chavez landed a left (as at 1:16 of the second), the blow would be partially blocked. Mayweather would check to see if he was bleeding near his left eye due to a head-butt and would blink his eye repeatedly. Feeling a sense of urgency, Mayweather would land a straight right and left hook flush with less than a minute in the round. The left jab would pepper Chavez for most of the third round, as he didn't have the feet or head movement to elude it. Chavez would motion to Mayweather to hit him and would then get punished by more straight rights.

Chavez would put his hand out to touch gloves before the fourth round, but Mayweather didn't want any part of it, for the second consecutive round. The left jab would land in more frequency, and when Chavez tried to counter, he would face Mayweather's armadillo defense that consisted of right glove up on the chin while the left arm covered the body. Mayweather would get a trivial warning for extending his arm without using it. After the warning both fighters would finally touch gloves. A right hook to the body followed by a left hook to the chin would send Chavez to the canvas for a mandatory eight count. The second knockdown would be another left hook to the chin that had Chavez so hurt that when he got up, he walked away instead of walking toward the referee. As a result, referee Paul Sita would stop the contest in the fifth round. Mayweather (9-0, 7 KOs) was now moving up the ranks in the super featherweight division.

Mayweather would utilize his left jab in his next bout with Louie Lejia two months later in El Paso, Texas. Mayweather used distance and defensive ability to frustrate Leija. A straight right hand had Leija down at 1:47 of the first round. Mayweather, facing a wounded fighter, would come in with bad intentions as he unleashed a flurry of power shots designed to get Leija out of there in the first.

Leija would go down again as either his hand touched the canvas or the referee mistakenly gave him a standing eight count. It would all be trivial as Leija would go down twice more, and the fight would be stopped as he fell near the ropes after another barrage of shots. Mayweather put an exclamation point with the win by saying, "Boxing is easy; it's not hard, just need to stay focused with my skills, will, and determination. I will keep winning."

Mayweather (10-0, 8 KOs) fully understood, as he was closing in at twenty-one years old, that if he wanted a title at super featherweight, he needed to do it within a year as his body was becoming closer to a lightweight than a super featherweight. In his next contest with Felipe Garcia in Boise, Idaho, Mayweather would come in at 133.5 pounds, which was the heaviest he had weighed as a professional. The slow-footed Garcia would be no match for Mayweather as the speed difference was apparent immediately. Garcia was very durable, and that allowed him to stay in with Mayweather for six rounds despite being outclassed in skill. Due to short height and low stance, he was a bit unorthodox, and this was solved by right hooks to the body and straight lefts to the head in the first two rounds. Garcia would continue to rush with his low stance and head coming forward, which simply couldn't penetrate the Mayweather defense. Shorter punches on the inside started to slow Garcia down, but the tenacious, experienced fighter wouldn't go down. Garcia would be only the second fighter to take Mayweather to a sixth round. This was despite Mayweather teeing off on him in the fifth round. A three-punch combination that started with a short right was highlighted by a left hook to the kisser that snapped Garcia's head back and would take the veteran out cold.

Mayweather would come back to the super featherweight limit in his next bout against Angelo Nunez at the Olympic Auditorium, Los Angeles, California. Nunez was most noted for his knockout loss to De La Hoya and a technical-decision loss to Gabriel Ruelas. Despite fighting world-class fighters, he was not considered a major threat to Mayweather. Mayweather would simply use his lead right and fire Hail Mary bombs to finish Nunez early; there wouldn't be a need for a Mayweather jab. Mayweather's speed was too much for Nunez. The only thing of substance Nunez landed was a right hook to the chin (1:31) in the second round. Mayweather would respond by landing a devastating left at 2:04 of the round, in addition to his taunts and trash talking. Referee Lou Moret would stop the fight in the third round due to a bad cut near Nunez's right eye. Like his match with De La Hoya, it would be a cut that would end the day for Nunez.

The year 1998 was the year that Mayweather expected to be a world champion. Despite having only twelve professional bouts under his belt, Mayweather expected to get a title shot toward the end of the year. As the year began, the kingpins who held title straps were Genaro Hernandez (WBC), Barry Jones (WBO), and Yong-Soo Choi (WBA), while Arturo Gatti had recently vacated the IBF. Mayweather needed to take tune-up fights with opponents who could make him go more rounds. Hector Arroyo would be that first choice for the start of the year. Mayweather would face Arroyo on January 9, 1998, at the Grand Casino, Biloxi, Mississippi. Arroyo was a Puerto Rican fighter with twenty-two professional fights. Both fighters would need warnings from the referee as they were tied up during a clinch with elbows high and refused to break. Mayweather would win the fight by landing left hooks to the body to break down Arroyo. Arroyo made it a rough and physical fight on the inside. This would be good experience as Mayweather got to learn another style of opponent. Arroyo would land an overhand right at 2:36 of the third round that Mayweather took to the chin without blinking an eye. Mayweather would score a knockdown with a four-punch combination as the bell ended the fourth.

Arroyo would get a standing eight count within a minute of the fifth round. Mayweather would get the stoppage with a left hook that sent Arroyo to the ropes. The accumulative punishment merited the stoppage. Mayweather was now (13-0, 11 KOs). When Al Bernstein asked Mayweather about showboating after the fight, Mayweather said, "They hate Camacho too. Some guys you love; some guys you hate. That is what sells tickets, and I am here to sell tickets. I am a performer and I am here to sell myself and I don't need anyone to sell me as I can sell myself." Seven weeks later Mayweather would land combinations and use his speed to dispatch his next opponent, Sam Girard. Girard would take punishment both upstairs and downstairs. The first round Girard already had a cut under his left eye and would get knocked down in the closing moments of the round. Due to Girard's reckless aggression, he would be countered with precise combinations that had him down two more times in the second round.

A final straight left at 2:34 in the second round would spell the end for Girard, who didn't beat the count.

Floyd Mayweather Sr.'s release from federal prison allowed a reunion of the Mayweather family. March 23, 1998, saw the first professional fight where both Floyd Sr. and Floyd Jr. would be reunited in the ring. It would also be a fight that showcased the chin Mayweather possessed. It would last only three rounds, but there was plenty of leather exchanged. Mayweather would put Miguel Melo on his knees with a lead right followed by two right hooks to the body in the second round. An aggressive Mayweather would come from the neutral corner and get hit with a left hook to the chin that appeared to almost snap his head off, yet he took the punch without even his knees buckling. De La Hoya, who commented on the fight, felt Mayweather needed to be patient and take his time in breaking down Melo instead of trying to take him out early. A left hook at 2:20 would seal the deal for Mayweather in the third.

As it was expected that Mayweather would get a title shot before the end of the year, it was imperative to get back in the ring soon. Less than thirty days after dispatching Melo, the young Mayweather would be back in the ring to face Gustavo Fabian Cuello. Mayweather would face Gustavo Fabian Cuello at the Olympic Stadium, Los Angeles, on April 18, 1998. Possible future Mayweather opponent Genaro Hernandez would be broadcasting the match for Telemundo Television. Cuello was an Argentinean who was the former South American super featherweight champion of the world. Cuello was expected to get Mayweather extra rounds to prepare him for his anticipated title shot. Cuello had decent movement and footwork that wouldn't allow Mayweather to control the fight with his left jab. Mayweather was able to score at times with his laser lead right and several left hooks. Cuello could never figure out Mayweather's defense and would never try to get him on the ropes. Instead, Mayweather would control the first three rounds by boxing in the middle of the ring. Cuello would miss with wild right and left hooks that Mayweather would be able to slip.

Mayweather would get a point deduction for holding and hitting Cuello with a left hook to the face toward the end of the third round. Cuello would go down to the canvas, and referee Jon Schorle would give Cuello a time-out for recovery time. That deduction would be the only thing that didn't prevent a total scoring washout for the Mayweather scorecard. Mayweather was too fast, too skilled, and too mobile for Cuello. Cuello was not adept in cutting off the ring and was foolish to take the bait and go for Mayweather's head instead of the body. Mayweather would go on his bike and win the fight by unanimous decision 99–90 in all three cards. Genaro Hernandez would observe, "Mayweather is fast and intelligent who understood if you can win fights without many exchanges, then why not do it?" Mayweather saw the bout as a learning experience. "What I learned is that you can't knock everyone out; you have ten or twelve rounds to do what you need to do to win."

Mayweather had already secured a deal to face WBC super featherweight champion Genaro Hernandez later in the year. However, Mayweather could still use a good tune-up bout. The Canadian Tony Pep (39-6, 21 KOs) would be the opponent to meet that requirement. Pep, at nearly six feet two, was the tallest opponent Mayweather would ever face. Pep felt Top Rank made a mistake putting him in the ring with Mayweather as he told ESPN, "They wanted someone to test this young man, and they got that, but this will be more of a test than they wanted." Mayweather would still be confident. "He never fought someone like Floyd Mayweather, so this will be something different for him." Pep was the former IBO lightweight champion who once fought for the WBO super featherweight title but lost to Regilio Tuur. Pep would try to work his jab against Mayweather with mixed results; however, he would get punished to the body by Mayweather. At 1:48 of the first round, Mayweather would duck a left cross with lightning reflexes. Pep's only major connect was a short left hook at 2:21 of the round.

Mayweather didn't need to go for the knockout against Pep; he just needed to outbox him. This is precisely what he did in the first round by landing 21 of 51 punches, compared to 11 of 49 for Pep.

Mayweather would work that straight left to Pep's body like a fencer worked his sword in the second round. One straight left 0:42 into the round almost had Pep's glove touch the canvas. The use of the left hand wouldn't be limited to only straight shots; Mayweather would fire some vicious left hooks to the body and head. This was a much more offensive Mayweather opposed to the

Cuello match. In the corner between rounds, Floyd Sr. told his son, "You are going to stop him; it is just a matter of time." Mayweather would land in increasing frequency in the third round, which included two dazzling hooks to the chin. Pep was durable and had an iron chin to handle the punishment. Mayweather was confident enough to fight the bigger opponent in close quarters due to his blocking and slipping ability and aided by his reflexes.

The fourth round saw Mayweather put his shoulder and guard tight to utilize an armadillo defense moving forward. Pep would have no answer and never got Mayweather on the ropes. After four rounds, Pep had thrown 88 jabs but had landed only 14, compared to 42 of 94 for Mayweather. Pep looked a bit better in the fifth as he landed a solid right hook to Mayweather's body, as well as a few jabs. Mayweather's robotic movement and elusiveness was vintage Jersey Joe Walcott. For example, Mayweather would hit Pep with a lead right then get out of the way of a counter Pep left. Pep would be more aggressive in the sixth round, but it was futile, as Mayweather would catch Pep's left hooks with his right glove or elbows. Pep would fire jabs and hooks in the seventh round that only caught air and gloves. The first seven rounds were a route for Mayweather. However, Pep was a solid opponent for his durability and experience.

If this was a sparring session, it helped Mayweather prepare for Genaro Hernandez who was his next opponent. After seven rounds Mayweather had landed 187 of 355, while Pep landed 55 of 355 for a 16 percent connect percentage.

In the last three rounds, Mayweather would continue to land combinations and pressure Pep, as he didn't believe his opponent could hurt him. Most importantly, Mayweather didn't think Pep could land anything as only 3 of 51 of the punches thrown by Pep in the eighth landed. A flush right hook would score for Pep at 1:33 in the ninth round—a testament to an opponent who was outclassed but never quit. Pep would start a rally in the tenth round that would have Mayweather answering back with his own shots. The final punch stats had Pep landing only 66 of 475 and Mayweather scoring 250 of 490. The final round I scored even, which had Mayweather winning in my card 9-0-1 or 100–91. The judges at Atlantic City would score it 99–91, 100–90, and 100–90. Mayweather told ESPN, "The main thing I wanted to do was to take his jab away and establish my jab and combinations and get the victory the best way I know how." Mayweather also predicted a victory against his scheduled bout with Genaro Hernandez, but he wouldn't say much more than that. There was a degree of respect for Hernandez that wouldn't be reserved for future Mayweather opponents. The fact was that Hernandez had never suffered a loss at the 130-pound limit, and Mayweather had only seventeen professional fights. Yet Mayweather's ring generalship and skill level were light years ahead of his experience.

CHAPTER 4
Dethroning Chicanito

On October 3, 1998, at the Las Vegas Hilton, Mayweather would fight Genaro "Chicanito" Hernandez (38-1-1, 17 KOs) for the WBC super featherweight title. Mayweather would come into the ring warmed up and loose. Mayweather would kneel on the ring post and do the sign of the cross. Hernandez would rush Mayweather in the opening bell to try to test the mental makeup of the young challenger. Mayweather peppered Hernandez with straight left jabs to the body while keeping his knees slightly buckled with a wide stance. The logic was to keep low against a taller opponent. Both fighters would trade slips that were a result of being off-balance while the opposing fighter would connect with a left. Although debatable, I don't think the punches landed cleanly, and the knockdowns were more the result of slips. I felt Jay Nady made the right calls in both instances.

Mayweather was not running away from Hernandez as he felt that he had the power and durability to stand in front of him. Mayweather would land straight rights to Hernandez's body in attempt to take the spring out of his legs. Hernandez tried to rough up Mayweather on the inside by clinching and hitting. At one point both fighters wrested each other to the canvas. Jay Nady would warn, "don't wrestle box," as he gave a warning to Hernandez for the perceived takedown. Mayweather's speed of hand and feet would systematically break down the champion. Mayweather hit Hernandez with left hooks and straight rights while being able to elude danger with a few steps or body reflexes. That being said, Mayweather didn't throw four-to-five-punch combinations as he didn't need to take such risks of staying too long. This fight strategy would often be called "potshotting." For some potshotting is essentially just out landing your opponent with a few unexpected blows. This is what Roy Jones Jr. would often implement and use to totally outclass opponents. Mayweather could land that leaping lead left sporadically without taking much risk. Hernandez's only recourse was either to get Mayweather on the ropes or to force him to fight on the inside and score with inside hooks, as he tried to do in the middle of the third round. Most importantly, he needed to have a steady jab on Mayweather's body or shoulder. After three rounds Hernandez had only landed 4 of 26 jabs, compared to 33 of 58 for Mayweather.

Hernandez had trouble with Mayweather's low posture since it removed most customary targets. What could have worked for Chicanito were right hooks to the body when Mayweather unloaded that left jab. Like the Pep fight, Mayweather would be stalking the bigger opponent for the entire contest, which dispelled the myth that Mayweather always ran from opponents. In fact, Mayweather would take the fight to Chicanito in rounds four and five and force him into the ropes. A precise, stinging right uppercut at 1:02 of the fifth round would shake the champion's foundations. Like a true champion, Hernandez would stage a rally in the final thirty seconds of the round by landing straight lefts and some quality right hooks to the solar plexus that a well-conditioned Mayweather could withstand. Mayweather Sr. would tell his son in the corner, "You keep going to the head, but you need to go downstairs to the kidney." Cut man Miguel Diaz would tell Mayweather, "Don't be fooled when you go to the ropes. He is looking for that one big counterpunch." Mayweather would totally dominate the rest of the bout by opening up with combinations as Hernandez increasingly had more trepidation in coming forward and remained on the ropes. Floyd Sr. would observe the same body language after the sixth round, "He ain't got more fight in him; he is just trying to survive." Mayweather would put on an exhibition of hand speed and ring generalship; he increased connect percentage while decreasing the frequency of getting hit. Hernandez didn't quit; he would rush Mayweather and would get in a few decent, short shots but never do any serious damage. He would make a final attempt in the final minute of the seventh round by trading exchanges with the challenger. If there was one round that could have charitably been scored for Hernandez, it could have been the seventh round. Mayweather had a small mouse under his right eye—a rarity for a Mayweather fight.

Mayweather in action with Genaro Hernandez, whom he would stop in seven rounds to capture his first world title. AP Photo/ Las Vegas Review-Journal, Craig L. Moran.

The final moments of the eighth saw the champion, perhaps in resignation, lay open in the ropes as the young challenger picked him apart. Hernandez's brother, Rudy, would stop the fight as the champion accepted fate on his stool. Hernandez was a great champion, but he had gotten in the ring with perhaps the greatest fighter in the history of that division. The new champion would sob in both happiness and relief that all the work since his youth had paid off in becoming a world champion. Mayweather kept repeating to himself, "I have done it…I have done it…I have done it!" Mayweather would out land the former champion 221–103. Despite the numbers, Hernandez did land some solid shots that would have taken a lesser opponent out, but the Mayweather chin and conditioning could take the pressure.

CHAPTER 5
Super Featherweight King

Mayweather would have one more bout in 1998. He would face Angel "El Diablo" Manfredy who was a top super featherweight with notable knockout wins over Arturo Gatti and Jorge Paez. Manfredy was a fighter of Puerto Rican heritage and originally from Gary, Indiana. Coming to the Mayweather bout, Manfredy had twenty-three consecutive wins. However, Floyd Mayweather Sr. was not impressed with Manfredy and predicted, "He is a bum, and Floyd will beat him easily." The bout would take place on December 19, 1998, in Miami, Florida. Manfredy would be escorted in the ring by Kid Rock while he held a giant-sized devil mask. Mayweather seemed eager to slay the devil in the contest almost immediately. A counter straight right would buckle Manfredy eleven seconds into the bout. The shot followed a Manfredy left jab that Mayweather eluded. Manfredy would come out stalking and tried to pin Mayweather to the ropes. Two short hooks would score for the Indiana fighter, but Mayweather controlled most of the round with his lead rights and flickering jab. A left hook-straight left combination would close the round for Mayweather. Manfredy's corner would scold him for reaching with those lead rights. This was a dangerous tactic against an excellent counterpuncher. Mayweather would out land Manfredy 16–9 in the first round.

Manfredy would land a straight right-and-left-hook combination at 1:48 of the second round as he pressured Mayweather against the ropes. Mayweather actually switched to southpaw for moments of the round as he saw that Manfredy had abandoned his left jab and tried to score with the right. An overhand right (2:22) buckled Manfredy, who was then pressured into the southeastern corner ropes. Mayweather pummeled Manfredy with powerful uppercuts and hooks that resulted in referee Frank Santore stopping the contest 2:47 into the round. Manfredy was not fighting back, and this compelled Santore to stop the contest perhaps a bit prematurely. The fact that it was so early in the contest and that Manfredy was still on his feet made it a judgment call. Many fighters don't take a knee or hold on even in danger, so a former boxer like Santore felt Manfredy was in real danger, even with only about a dozen seconds left. Santore would say after the bout, "I told Angel to fight back, and he didn't respond." "The referee never told me to fire back; this was all politics. I was composed and waiting to fire back," Manfredy would respond. Manfredy added "Gatti did more than that, and they never stopped that fight."

The controversy and public demand didn't suffice enough to merit a rematch, and the victory gave Mayweather a perfect 7-0 record for 1998. Mayweather would beat out names such as Roy Jones Jr. and Shane Mosley to win fighter-of-the-year honors from both *Ring Magzine* and *KO Magazine*. The accolades firmly established Mayweather as one of the elites of the sport. The pound-for-pound title was still firmly held by Roy Jones Jr. (39-1). The other top names of that era were Shane Mosley (32-0), Felix Trinidad (34-0), Oscar De La Hoya (30-0), and Bernard Hopkins (35-2-1). Notable fighters from the lower weight divisions included Erik Morales (31-0) and Prince Naseem Hamed (29-0).

The next bout for Mayweather would be a homecoming. Mayweather would fight in his original home, Grand Rapids, Michigan, in front of a TNT network audience. Carlos Rios (44-2-1, 29 KOs) was an experienced and durable fighter from Argentina who was expected to take Mayweather to the later rounds. Rios had fought only once for the WBC featherweight world title against Filipino fighter Luisito Espinoza but lost by a sixth-round TKO. Rios would be the most experienced opponent Mayweather would face, but it was trivial at that point. Mayweather was a world champion, and his confidence and ability were already established.

The local crowd gave Mayweather a thundering ovation as he came back with a world title around his waist. As the match commenced, it was apparent that Mayweather could anticipate Rios's punches and caught most of them with his gloves and shoulder. The Mayweather trick of catching them with his left shoulder and turning back with a right connect was utilized. Rios would come out charging in the second round, brawling and flinging wildly, but didn't do much damage. Mayweather took his time and landed hooks to the body. Both fighters would be trading shots in the closing moments of the second round, yet all of the clean shots were coming from Pretty Boy Floyd. The straight left would be Mayweather's weapon of choice in the next few rounds. He would see the opening and take advantage of it. Rios would use his own left hook to the body in the fourth round and even work Mayweather's rib cage against the ropes in the opening moments of the fifth round. Jose Luis Castillo would use the latter tactic in the future against Mayweather. Mayweather would land his own lead rights to Rios's body and start to slow him down.

An enthusiastic Mayweather would be hollering and chanting to his local fans. Rios didn't have the size or power to hurt Mayweather. This was well demonstrated when Rios landed an overhand right flush on Mayweather at 0:53 of the seventh round. If there was a punch that could have hurt Mayweather it was that, yet Mayweather took it well. Rios actually had a higher connect percentage than most Mayweather opponents as he landed 100 of 271 through eight rounds, but the power was not there. Mayweather would batter Rios around the ring in the ninth round as the Grand Rapids crowd anticipated a knockout, but it wouldn't happen.

Rios would get a long break after Mayweather would be called for a low blow in the tenth round. Mayweather would on occasion hurt Rios in the final two rounds, but Rios—with a mouse under his right eye and swelling on the left—would go the distance. It was a bit of a disappointment for Mayweather who wanted the knockout victory at home. The scorecards were 120–109, 119–108, and 120–110, all for Mayweather. The punch stats had Mayweather land 335 of 593 punches, compared to 155 of 423 for Rios. Floyd Sr. would say after the fight, "Most Argentineans are very strong, and he was a durable fighter. We tip our hat to him; he gave his best." Mayweather would promise to defend his title twenty-four more times as he wanted to break the title defense record held by Joe Louis. If Mayweather wanted to clean out the division, there were several notable names.

As Mayweather was promoted by Top Rank, which also promoted De La Hoya, it was convenient to have Mayweather fight as an undercard for De La Hoya main events.

Mayweather would be fighting in the undercard of the Oscar De La Hoya-Obe Carr bout when he faced Justin Juuko on May 22, 1999, at the Mandalay Bay Resort and Casino.

Juuko wouldn't have his trainer, Freddie Roach, who had missed a flight while working Johnny Tapia's fight. Gregario Vargas dropped out on short notice, so Juuko was the replacement. Juuko would need a lot more than Roach to have any chance against Mayweather. Juuko had been knocked out in his previous fight against Antonio Hernandez. Mayweather saw Juuko's high guard and used the left jab to the body while protecting his own. Mayweather blocked most of Juuko's shots with his gloves and shoulder. Mayweather would capitalize with the left hook to the body and lead right in the second round. It looked like a relaxed sparring session in the middle of the ring. Mayweather would simply get underneath Juuko's left jab and then counter him with those leaping rights. Juuko tried to work the body, but the blows were not clean, as they were partially blocked. The Ugandan challenger started to do better in the fourth and fifth round by landing overhand rights and left hooks on the inside.

Juuko would get warned for low blows as he tried to keep working the body. Mayweather would control the rest of the action with his right lead and straight right; for good measure, he would also throw a left hook to the body when it presented itself. Both combatants would do a little trash talking, but when the dust settled, it was Mayweather in command. Mayweather would drop Juuko with a right hook at 1:09 of the ninth round. Juuko was very dazed, and when he got up, Mitch Halperin stopped the contest. A previous right to Juuko's left ear was what took his equilibrium away. Mayweather outlanded Juuko 209–147 in the final punch stats. After the stoppage, Bernice Mayweather, Floyd Jr.'s grandmother, would fall to the canvas, ill. Ringside physicians Dr. Flip Omansky and Dr. Jan Goodman would attend her. She would be given oxygen and was able to recover. The victory was the third defense of Mayweather's super featherweight title. However, there were other claimants to the super featherweight title.

On August 7, 1999, Acelino Freitas (21-0, 21 KOs) made a big splash in the super featherweight division by becoming the WBO super featherweight with a first round knockout. Freitas was an up-and-comer who became an instant celebrity in Brazil. He defeated Antaloly Alexandrov via a first-round knockout that resulted in Alexandrov being taken out on a stretcher. Freitas had taken notice of Alexandrov's comments to the local French newspaper in which he said, "I have only heard of good football players from Brazil but no boxers." Freitas would sign a deal with Showtime, and that would complicate a unification match with Mayweather since Mayweather fought on HBO. However, matches such as Lennox Lewis and Mike Tyson demonstrated that both networks could come together when public interest and an amicable arrangement could be met. Frietas would win his first twenty-nine bouts by stoppages. The first official Freitas win would come years later to Diego Corrales, who was also a major super featherweight contender in 1999. Hard-hitting Diego Corrales (29-0, 24 KOs) would capture the IBF title in October 1999. To claim he was the best in the division, Mayweather would need to cross paths with these opponents.

Mayweather would be back in the ring on September 11, 1999, in a card he shared with Juan Manuel Marquez—who would fight Freddie Norwood for the WBA featherweight title. Carlos Gerena (34-2, 28 KOs) was a Puerto Rican fighter who had a high guard with his elbows tucked into his rib cage. He had only one title bout against Genaro Hernandez, which he lost by decision in 1998. His biggest win was Jesus Chavez, a fighter that Mayweather would meet in the future. Gerena had won his last six fights coming into the Mayweather match. Mayweather would be sporting light-blue trunks as Gerena sported the Puerto Rican flag.

Gerena tried to work Mayweather's body, but a good portion of the shots were low. Mayweather went around Gerena's guard by landing hooks to the side of the head. When Gerena opened up for a shot, Mayweather would land the straight left up the middle. An animated Gerena would demand Mayweather stand still and fight him. He would pay the price, as Mayweather would score with a counter right that staggered Gerena and then follow it up with more rights that dropped Gerena at 2:30 of the round. Gerena would get up with unsteady legs and, instead of clinching, would pound his chest and demand

Mayweather hit him again, which he did. The result would be Gerena getting dropped again by a left hook in the first round. Gerena was a stationary fighter who didn't provide the different looks or angles to confuse Mayweather.

Nonetheless, Gerena was a determined fighter who kept putting on the pressure. Gerena's coming forward without much variation allowed Mayweather to pick him up with lead left hooks. Gerena would shake his head to convince Mayweather he couldn't hurt him. There would be a few moments in the next few rounds where Gerena would take Mayweather to the ropes and get inside body shots; these were mainly rest periods for the champion. Mayweather would go back to the center of the ring and land combinations to soften up Gerena. Gerena would keep pounding his chest after each blow landed and only eat more punches.

The challenger would have his best moments in the opening minute of the fifth round when he landed a few combinations and roughed up Mayweather on the ropes. The fifth round would be the only round I scored for Gerena. Mayweather would bring back that devastating overhand right thirty-eight seconds into the sixth round, and that would swing all the momentum back to him. Unfortunately for Gerena, he got pummeled in the next two rounds, and that would force Dr. Flip Omansky to stop the contest after Mayweather landed a six-punch combination ending the seventh round. Mayweather would land 220 of 346 punches, compared to Gerena's 99 of 308. Mayweather would be asked about fighting Jose Casamayor and would say, "If I get the WBA title, then Casamayor would be a mandatory defense. I am not seeking challengers; I am seeking champions. Floyd Mayweather wants to unify titles."

Before making his next defense of his title, Mayweather would fire his father as his manager and replace him with rap mogul James Prince. Mayweather Sr.'s termination as manager would be a prelude to more things to come between father and son.

Floyd Mayweather Sr. would still train his son for the next bout scheduled with Gregario Vargas on March 18, 2000, at the MGM Grand, Las Vegas, Nevada. Vargas was the former WBC featherweight champion of the world. He would lose the title by unanimous decision in his first defense. Mayweather had been idle for six months, which was his longest hiatus from the ring. Vargas landed the best shot of the first round—a left hook upstairs. Mayweather didn't throw has patent combinations; he went one punch at a time. Vargas was the aggressor, and Mayweather was actually on his bike more than he had been in recent fights. The challenger would even counter Mayweather with an overhand after Mayweather missed with his own right. Mayweather would still win the round with his left jab and right lead, but after three rounds the match was much closer than anyone had anticipated.

Mayweather would have much better success in the fourth round. He was able to pick up Vargas one punch at a time using his speed and ring generalship. Vargas would get Mayweather in the southwestern corner ropes and get countered with straight shots. Mayweather would use his defensive ability to deflect and roll the punches when trapped in the corner. The only moment of apprehension for Mayweather would be when he slipped in the canvas in the fifth round. Vargas would have his best round since the second round, as he was able to land some hooks to Mayweather's body and rough him up on the inside. Mayweather was able to catch most of those right shots, but a good portion of those lefts got in. However, all Vargas's momentum would change when a Mayweather left hook to the body put him down with five seconds left in the round. A round that could have been 10–9 Vargas would now be 10–8 Mayweather. The punch stats after six rounds showed a closer fight than the actual scorecard as Mayweather landed 87 of 264, compared to 65 of 231 for Vargas. There would also be a brilliant exchange in the closing moments of the seventh round.

Vargas tried again to corner Mayweather on the ropes in the opening minute of the ninth round, and this time he landed both clean punches downstairs and upstairs. Mayweather would throw his own leather as they fought in a phone booth. A mouse could be seen under Mayweather's right eye, which was a rarity. The ninth may have been the first round to be scored for Vargas since the first round. Mayweather would go back to his bike and potshot Vargas; this received scattered boos from the audience. Vargas was the aggressor in the tenth and even landed his best straight left, which snapped Vargas's head back. Mayweather wouldn't take much risk and would potshot to win the last two rounds. The final punch stats had Mayweather landing 244 of 587 and Vargas 159 of 505. I had Mayweather winning 8-3-1(117–112). The official scorecards were 119–108, 118–109, and 119–108, all for Mayweather. Larry Merchant would famously state about Mayweather, "He doesn't look like a $12 million fighter to me." Mayweather would complain about his right hand being in pain for most of the second half of the fight. Issues with right hand pain would be a circumstance that Mayweather would deal with in future contests. Interestingly, Mayweather would dispel rumors of friction with his dad. "I will always love my dad and will always want him to be my trainer."

The alleged friction with his father aside, Mayweather still made the move to replace his father as trainer with his uncle Roger Mayweather. The younger Mayweather allowed his father to move in with him after his prison release, but he felt that some of his dad's old disciplinary habits were no longer suitable now that he was a grown man and father. The older Mayweather was told to leave both his son's training camp and his house. Mayweather would switch back to Uncle Roger Mayweather for his next bout with Emmanuel Burton on October 21, 2000. Emmanuel Burton would later be known as "Emmanuel Augustus." Mayweather had a seven month hiatus from the ring, which helped his hand heal and allowed him to reacclimate to trainer Roger Mayweather. Mayweather would fight on HBO's *KO Nation* in a hip-hop flavored event. Augustus had fought names such as Antonio Davis and John John Molina. The seven month delay was not apparent in this bout. Mayweather looked like a surgeon with his scalpel as his left jab landed solidly on both Burton's body and head. As Mayweather poured on solid shots, his opponent would smile and shrug his shoulders to mock the power of the shots. This only furthered Mayweather's assault of pounding hooks to the body. Burton would blow a kiss to Mayweather after the first round. None of those gimmicks really took Mayweather off his game or made him lose composure.

Burton would continue the shenanigans in the second round with exaggerated bobbing and weaving gestures while lifting his shoulders up and down. This didn't stop Mayweather from punishing him with left-hook and overhand-right combinations. The accuracy and quantity of the blows in the second round resulted in major facial swelling for Burton. Burton badly needed to get his left glove high to stop those right crosses; he was already cut under his left eye after only two rounds. The first three minutes of the third round was a frenzied assault that rivaled most barroom brawls. Both fighters exchanged indiscriminately, even including two solid right overhands by Burton. Mayweather would bloody Burton, yet it wouldn't discourage Burton from coming forward—nor did it stop him from raising his arms in contempt of Mayweather's power. Burton would keep smiling and get a few body shots on the ropes. There would be several powerful rights that had Burton seeing stars, but his will and determination had him still coming forward and smiling as he ate the punches. After four rounds Mayweather had already landed 133 of 318 punches, compared to 45 of 232 for Burton. Mayweather would pummel Burton with more right hands in the fifth round only to see more clowning around from his opponent. This time Burton would wobble his legs and torso in another possum display to shake Mayweather's confidence. This often-criticized tactic sometimes works when a fighter loses faith that he can hurt the other fighter. Burton would get Mayweather into the ropes and land more body shots. Pretty Boy Floyd was now bleeding from both his nose and mouth; he knew this was no cakewalk. Burton may have done better by using a high cross arms defense with more bobbing and weaving as he came in.

Mayweather would work the body with more intensity in the sixth round in an attempt to break down Burton. However, Burton—like a leech—was not going to be separated from Mayweather; he kept firing despite being badly hurt and outclassed. Mayweather himself had to breathe through his mouth, as his nose was broken. The tenacious Burton had no quit and was able to get a few more attempts at Mayweather's rib cage, but Mayweather himself had no threshold of pain. Mayweather would injure his right hand again and had taken many shots himself; a lesser champion may have folded under pressure. How often do we see fighters dominate an opponent only to give up under pressure? At 1:14 of the eighth round, the physician would examine Burton's ear to see if he could continue; the fighter angrily protested and was allowed to continue. Burton would make his final stand and throw the kitchen sink, but in the ninth round, his corner would throw the towel after Mayweather landed a three-power-punch combination and proceeded to use Burton's face for target practice. That would be the end of, arguably, the most action-packed Mayweather fight up to that point. Mayweather would land 287 of 669 punches, compared to 108 of 526 for Burton. Years after the contest, Mayweather would tell both ESPN and Showtime, "Emmanuel Augustus was my toughest opponent; his record didn't reflect his skill set." Some critics may point to future opponents as Jose Luis Castillo, Ricky Hatton, and—more recently—Marcos Maidana as tougher bouts. However, there was no other contest in which Mayweather's face appeared in worse shape.

CHAPTER 6
Taming Diego

Diego Corrales (33-0, 27 KOs) was seen as Mayweather's biggest test in the super featherweight division. Corrales had knocked out champions such as Roberto Garcia and Derrick Gainer, while also stopping mutual Mayweather opponent Angel Manfredy. There were still questions about how good Mayweather competition was up to that point. Many felt he didn't fight the best opponents, and—besides Chicanito Hernandez—he didn't have a big name in his résumé. The undefeated Corrales was a name that would do wonders for Mayweather's résumé. He was an undefeated fighter with power and youth who would test the abilities and skill of the Michigan fighter. Miguel Diaz, who had worked with Mayweather for years, was now working the Corrales corner with trainer Ray Woods and assistant Alex Ariza. Diaz would go to Corrales due to getting 5 percent of the purse instead of the 2 percent of the purse he got under Mayweather—a fact that Mayweather accepted without any ill will or animosity. Corrales was a mix of Mexican and Colombian blood. On July 2000 Corrales would get arrested for domestic abuse charges as he allegedly beat up his pregnant wife, Maria, after a phone argument. His wife's injuries included broken ribs and a broken collarbone. She also had a bruised spine. The matter was still an open case without a disposition being rendered. Corrales would actually get sentenced to two years in prison after the Mayweather bout and would serve fourteen months of it. Floyd Mayweather would use the domestic incident as motivation to defeat his opponent. "I will beat Corrales like a dog on behalf of all the battered women in the world." Mayweather even invited Corrales's ex-wife to watch ringside as he gave Corrales a beat down.

Corrales responded by saying, "Floyd's a guy who acts tough when he has seven or eight of his buddies around him. But this time it's going to be just him and me." Corrales also had pictures of Mayweather with the word "kill" placed on punching bags as he trained for the contest. Mayweather would receive $1.7 million and Corrales $1.4 million for their scheduled match. The money guaranteed were significant sums for a title match in the super-featherweight division, and clearly demonstrated how anticipated the match was between the two undefeated fighters.

The match would take place on January 20, 2001, at the MGM Grand, Las Vegas, Nevada. Mayweather controlled the first round mainly with his overhand left and jab to the stomach. Corrales would get in a right hook to the body and a short left hook to Mayweather's left bicep. Mayweather would be on his feet in the second and would use his great speed to create the angles to land shots on Corrales. The strategy was to land one or two punches at a time instead of standing flat-footed and going for combinations. Corrales was just following Mayweather around the ring instead of giving different looks and using his jab. Mayweather would score with a powerful left hook to the jaw at 2:10 of the second round. Floyd Mayweather Sr., watching ringside, predicted, "Tell Floyd to keep doing what he is doing, and by the seventh, eighth, and ninth round, he will be ready to go."

Corrales would land a left hook flush (0:59) on Mayweather's chin in the third round that was well taken by the champion. The left hand worked Corrales upstairs and downstairs. Corrales actually did a good job cutting off the ring but only set himself up for potshots. Mayweather would offer his glove at the end of the third round, but Corrales—perhaps discouraged—didn't notice or acknowledge it. Corrales would work his jab in the fourth round, but it didn't land frequently as Mayweather still had too much movement. Mayweather kept getting off first, and the scenario kept repeating itself. Corrales needed to double the jab to the shoulder and fire hooks to the body on the shorter opponent. After four rounds Mayweather out landed Corrales by a 3-to-1 ratio (79–26). The challenger would land two solid hooks to Mayweather's body at 1:18 of the fifth round, to try to slow down Mayweather for the later rounds.

Unfortunately, Corrales was just walking into shots, as he did at 0:36 and 2:48 of the sixth round when he walked into fully loaded left hooks to the chin. Mayweather, constantly seeing that opening, would floor Corrales with that very shot a few seconds into the seventh. Corrales would get up, only to be dropped by another lead left hook at 2:21, and this time Corrales was very hurt. Mayweather would charge Corrales and dropped him a third time, this time with a chopping right hook as Corrales was pressed against the ropes. Miguel Diaz would admonish Corrales, "If you don't throw punches, me and your dad will stop the fight." Corrales would heed the warning and land a solid left hook at 2:25 in the eighth. Mayweather would swallow the punch and smile back at Corrales. Corrales would do much better and take less punishment in possibly the only round that charitably could have been scored for him.

Mayweather wisely went back to boxing behind the left jab in the ninth. Another lead left hook to the jaw would send Corrales tumbling into the canvas at 1:25 of the tenth round. He would get up, only to receive double right hands that put him down a fifth time. Corrales would contort his torso as he barely remained on his feet Corrales's father, Ray Woods, would stop the fight against his son's wishes. Corrales's corner would console him, and even Mayweather tried to calm him down. Mayweather, who no longer used his dad as his trainer, would openly embrace him in the ring. Mayweather dominated the fight from the beginning to the conclusion. Mayweather landed 220 of 414 punches, compared to 60 of 205 for Corrales. Mayweather lamented, "Things got a little personal, but this is a business; I am here to sell myself." Mayweather wanted to fight Prince Naseem (35-0, 31 KOs) at a 128 pound catchweight or Joel Casamayor (24-0, 15 KOs). Naseem would immediately be eliminated as a future Mayweather opponent, as he would lose to Marco Antonio Barrera in the spring of 2001.

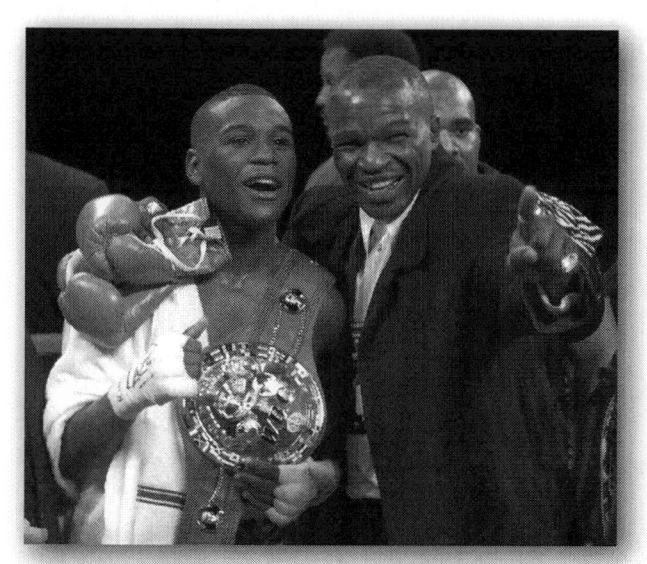

Father and son share a moment after the
Diego Corrales victory. AP Photo/Eric Risberg.

Diego Corrales would recover from the loss and have epic matches with names such as Freitas, Castillo, and Casamayor. Corrales would be the first boxer to defeat Acelino Freitas, and his win over Castillo (in their first encounter) is regarded by many as among the greatest fights in recent boxing memory. Corrales would tragically die in 2007 in a motorcycle accident.

Ironically, Mayweather wanted to punish Corrales for domestic abuse, but he himself would have a domestic incident only one month after his greatest win. The February 2001 alleged incident happened with Melissa Brim, the mother of one of his daughters. Brim claimed she was assaulted after an argument in a car in which the car door hit her jaw. A few months later, another alleged incident happened in which Brim claimed Mayweather punched her after she gave the child to a friend. There would be both criminal charges and a civil lawsuit filed. The civil lawsuit would be dropped in 2003. Mayweather would plead guilty to two counts of domestic battery and get two days of house arrest, forty-eight hours of community service, and a $3,000 fine, with a suspended six-month prison sentence.

After the Corrales win, Mayweather (25-0, 19 KOs) was now regarded among the top pound-per-pound fighters in the world, along with guys such as Roy Jones Jr., Shane Mosley, and Felix Trinidad. He would attempt an eighth defense of his WBC super featherweight title against Carlos Hernandez (33-2-1, 21 KOs). Mayweather would return to Grand Rapids for the match held May 26, 2001, at the Van Andel Arena. Hernandez would enter the ring to Carl Orff's "Carmina Burana" and would sport a black robe. Mayweather would sport Grant merchandise with a black-and-red robe. The Californian fighter had fought once for the super featherweight title but had gotten dominated by Genaro Hernandez in a one-sided, unanimous decision.

The footing would be a problem in the slippery ring, as Mayweather nearly slipped in the first round. He would shake off his shoes by appearing to do the moonwalk in the middle of the canvas. Mayweather was obviously using mainly his left hand in the first two rounds. Only the left hook and left jab were thrown consistently. It was obvious something was wrong with the right hand. Hernandez, if this tipped him off, would be wise to circle away from that left and force Mayweather to use his right. Hernandez would land an overhand right at 2:37 in the first that would be his best score in the round. Referee Dale Grable would give warnings for pushing and holding to both fighters; it would be a difficult bout to officiate. Mayweather would win the second round by landing hooks to the body and a few combinations. The third would have Hernandez get pummeled with dozens of shots—mainly left hooks. The bull moniker would be appropriate for Hernandez, as he got rocked but was able to handle the punishment. Mayweather would turn southpaw on more than one occasion to help give relief to his ailing right hand. The Hernandez corner would keep screaming to go for the body, as Hernandez had Mayweather in the ropes in the final minute of the fifth round. Hernandez's nose would already look broken by the fifth round, but no noticeable blood was trickling from it.

At 2:38 of the sixth round, Mayweather's left glove would touch the canvas in pain. It would be the only official knockdown of his career until now. The Mayweather corner would tell him to hit the body; it was obvious that the head (being made of harder tissue and bone) would cause more damage to the hand. Mayweather had no recourse but to get on his bike and try to get a point's win. He was likely four points ahead with six rounds left. Hernandez was not able to capitalize much in the seventh round, but he did out punch Mayweather 16–7, reducing the likely Mayweather lead to three points. Mayweather would use the right jab through his southpaw position.

The eighth was important to Mayweather as he turned the tide back to his favor. One punch at a time was the only way Mayweather could win the contest; he couldn't risk throwing combinations and making his hand injury worst. This is precisely what Mayweather would do for the rest of the bout, despite the collective boos from the audience. Roger Mayweather would confirm that Mayweather had hurt his right hand during training, so they realized he couldn't use the hand that much. The tenth saw a bit of a second wind for Mayweather, as his hands came back with a few more shots. The aggressor was Hernandez, and the round could have been scored even. Referee Dale Garble momentarily halted the action in the eleventh to allow the ring physician to examine Hernandez's broken nose. The action would be allowed to resume and so would Mayweather who pitty-pat punched Hernandez. Due to the injuries, the power of the punches was not there, but it was effective in scoring points. Mayweather would fall again in the wet spot in the southwestern corner ropes and do a split again. He was fortunate not to injure his legs with those gymnastic routines. Hernandez would get deducted a point for elbowing in the final round. Mayweather would land 241 of 520, while Hernandez landed 172 of 676. Mayweather would win by the scores of 119–110, 117–109, and 116–111. My score was 117–110 for Mayweather.

Mayweather would admit to having both hands hurt prior to the fight and would take shots of Novocain to both hands. It's unclear if Mayweather had confused Novocain with Xylocaine, when prompted by Larry Merchant, as the former was becoming less popular due to the higher percentage of allergic reactions. Mayweather would sometimes use Xylocaine (lidocaine) in his future bouts. Xylocaine was totally legal in Vegas but not in all state athletic commissions. Xylocaine is a fast-acting local anesthetic that causes numbness; it can be sprayed or injected. It is commonly used in minor dental procedures. Mayweather's use of Xylocaine would serve as ammunition for Mayweather detractors during the entire Pacquiao negotiation opera concerning peformance enhancement drug use. Mayweather's preference for Grant gloves over Reyes gloves can be partially explained, as the gloves gave his hands extra cushion.

Mayweather would show that he had no bone where the knuckle for his right ring finger should be.

In order to avoid getting stripped of his title, Mayweather had a mandatory defense with Jesus Chavez. Chavez (35-1, 24 KOs) who was known as "El Matador," was a tenacious, rugged fighter who would come charging his opponents like a bull. Chavez had a major life story that helped build his character in the ring. As a teenager Chavez spent two years in jail for armored robbery after being involved in a local Chicago gang. Chavez, who was originally born in Mexico, came to the United States illegally at the age of ten and would be deported back to Mexico after serving his sentence. Despite being born in Mexico, Chavez had difficulty assimilating in Mexico and was called "pocho," a disparaging term for Mexicans who grew up in the United States. Chavez would be able to come back to the United States with the help of his father, and he would move to Austin, Texas, at the age of twenty-one. He would go on to win thirty-one consecutive bouts after suffering one split-decision loss to common Mayweather opponent Carlos Gerena.

Mayweather would be scheduled to face Chavez on November 10, 2001, at the Bill Graham Civic Auditorium, San Francisco, California. A twenty-two-year-old Filipino fighter called Manny Pacquiao would be part of the undercard as he fought Agapitho Sanchez. That night would be the first time that both Mayweather and Pacquiao would ever share the stage. Mayweather would have a three-inch height advantage over Chavez, who stood five feet five inches tall. Roger Mayweather had predicted that "Chavez was going to be cooked like a chicken in a microwave for eight to twelve minutes." The Mayweather-Chavez bout would prove to be among the most thrilling bouts that Mayweather was involved in, as he was often forced into an inside phone-booth war of attrition with a relentless opponent.

Mayweather would sport red, white, and blue trunks with a small American flag—perhaps in memory of the 9/11 terror attacks that had occurred just two months earlier. There would be many Chavez fans at the Civic Auditorium; some even had signs: "Floyd is Overrated." Ronnie Shields, Chavez's trainer, had predicted the that fight was going to be "hell." The Chavez partisan crowd would yell *Cha-vez* as the Austin fighter kept charging at Mayweather in the opening stanza, throwing shots as he kept his guard high and head low. Despite Chavez's tenacity Mayweather landed the cleaner counter shots as he blocked or slipped most of the Chavez artillery.

"Bang, bang, uppercut, and keep going to the body like that," Shields would advise Chavez. Chavez would land his first solid shots in the second (0:43), which consisted of a looping left, followed by an overhand right as he pressed Mayweather on the ropes. Another overhand right (1:01) would land for Chavez as he kept throwing punches in bunches. The sheer volume of Chavez punches may have put him at risk of punching himself out in the later rounds. Mayweather was able to land some good counters toward the end of the second but not enough to steal it away from Chavez.

Chavez would commence the third round by again pressing Mayweather against the ropes while throwing short hooks to the body. Mayweather would roll with the punches as his left arm guarded his body, and the right elbow tucked in with glove high. This defense, along with the chin tucked in, took away most of Chavez's clean targets. Mayweather would respond to Chavez by using his left jab as a spear to Chavez's body while connecting with the pull counter. Chavez would use the Archie Moore crab-like defense to keep charging at Mayweather, but he would be greeted with short counter shots. At the end of the third, Mayweather would raise his glove to the crowd in a gesture that he was in command of the bout. "Keep your jabs to the chest and right hand to the body," Shields would instruct Chavez as he entered the fourth.

Mayweather would connect with a six-punch combination a minute into the fourth that included his powerful lead right. As he was teeing off on Chavez, it was expected that the challenger might back off. However, the determination of Chavez would keep his pressure steady. Mayweather's speed and reflexes would allow him to both elude and connect against Chavez as the challenger took the fight to him. Chavez would do better in the fifth, as he kept the fight in close range and was constantly in Mayweather's chest, firing short shots from different angles. After five rounds Chavez had thrown an incredible 553 punches, but he had only connected with 101 of them. Mayweather, despite throwing much less, was more productive at 106 of 261 punches landed.

In the sixth, referee Jon Schorlee would warn Chavez for rough tactics as Mayweather was pushed against the ropes. Mayweather would win the sixth by sticking and moving, which drew jeers from the audience who wanted the champion to stand and trade. Larry Merchant, who is never at a loss of words, would say, "If he wants to stink out the joint and win the fight, he can do it." Mayweather would continue hitting and moving in the seventh as he landed uppercuts and body jabs. Chavez would be able to cut off the ring better in the eighth and work Mayweather's body on the ropes. However, by the final minute of the round, it appeared fatigue was starting to set in for Chavez as the crowd gave a standing ovation for his effort. Mayweather would complain that his eye was bleeding as he came to his corner. This may have enraged Mayweather, who would engage Chavez more in the ninth and land head-snapping uppercuts and right-hand leads. Chavez fought back gallantly, but it was conspicuous that he couldn't take many more of those shots. The Chavez corner would mercifully stop the contest after the ninth.

The final punch stats saw Mayweather connect 197 of 456 and Chavez 182 of 925. Chavez averaged more than one hundred punches per round, and although it appeared Chavez had punched himself out, the reason Shields gave for the stoppage was the punishment that Chavez took. I had the bout 87–84 for Mayweather at time of stoppage. The judges had it 87–84, 88–83, and 89–82. "He is the champ, and now I am his number-one fan," Chavez would say after the contest. Mayweather's assessment was "I let him punch himself out and get tired and eventually take him to deep waters then drowned him."

Chavez would capture the WBC super featherweight title against Thai fighter Sirimongkol Singmanasak in 2003. Chavez would lose the title in a spirited fight with Erik Morales, which saw Chavez fight with a dislocated shoulder for most of the bout. Unfortunately, Chavez's second title win would end in tragedy. He would win the IBF lightweight against Leavander Johnson only to have the great moment shattered by the news that Johnson would suffer a blood clot in the brain and would need surgery to correct the hemorrhage. Unfortunately, Johnson would be put into a medically induced coma, and after organ failure the family decided to end his life. There would be a documentary made about Jesus Chavez's life called *Split Decision* and a book entitled *Standing Eight: The Inspiring Story of Jesus El Matador Chavez*. Mayweather now 27-0, 20 KOs and now planned to move to bigger fish up north in the lightweight division. He said he had difficulty making weight and planned to fight Paul Spadafora, Jose Luis Castillo, and even mentioned a future bout with Kostya Tszyu.

CHAPTER 7

Too Close for Comfort

Mayweather's introduction to the lightweight division would be against Jose Luis Castillo (45-4-1, 40 KOs). Castillo was known to be another great Mexican body puncher and had an excellent knockout rate. Although Mayweather was only moving up five pounds, the difference in power would immediately be evident in the weight class. The Mexican champion had upset Stevie Johnston to win both the WBC lightweight title and Ring's Upset of the Year honors. Castillo had defended his lightweight title three times before facing Mayweather on April 20, 2002, at the MGM Grand, Las Vegas, Nevada.

Mayweather would start the contest by greeting Castillo with a lead left hook seconds into the fight. Castillo took a couple of steps backward and then received two more straight lefts. The straight left jabs to the body made the opening round an easy round for Mayweather. Castillo didn't land anything significant as Mayweather either slipped or blocked punches. Castillo would land only three punches in the first round. In the second round (0:22), Mayweather would drop Castillo with a left hook that was not scored by referee Vic Drakulich. The actual punch landed on Castillo's gloves, and the impact made Castillo slip into the canvas. This was a judgment call; however, we have seen innocuous punches or even phantom blows scored as knockdowns as Pacquiao-Barrera I and Hagler-Roldan can attest. By not scoring the knockdown, Drakulich made a possible 10–8 round now a 10–9 Mayweather round. Mayweather would still get in a right pull counter at 1:00 of the round. A few seconds later, both fighters would clash heads. Mayweather would stay in and land a few good left jabs. Castillo got in an overhand right and a jab to the body that was partially blocked. The best Castillo connect was a straight left-overhand-right combination at 1:55 of the round. Mayweather would barely squeeze the round with a couple of solid jabs and a right cross (2:30).

Castillo would do much better in the third, as he was increasingly able to cut off the ring. He would connect partially with a left uppercut. Mayweather would nullify that by landing straight lefts-jabs for most of the round. Castillo's pressure was closing the distance, but it wouldn't suffice to be classified as effective aggression. Castillo would score with lefts both downstairs and upstairs, near the ropes. A straight right and a left to the pit of Castillo's body would give the round to Mayweather. After three rounds Mayweather out jabbed Castillo 29–5.

Mayweather started off the fourth with a left hook again to Castillo's chin. He would land the same punch at 1:48 of the round. Mayweather circled around and made Castillo miss a left uppercut (0:42) and again worked the body with the jab. Mayweather would connect with another lead right (0:48) and have control in the center of the ring. The left jab was worked to Castillo's head (1:27), and another straight right (1:35) landed on Castillo's body. Drakulich would give Castillo a warning for holding and hitting as he worked Mayweather's rib cage during a clinch. The best Castillo blow was another left uppercut (2:53) that countered a lazy left jab. Mayweather controlled the first four rounds with his jab and ring generalship.

Mayweather would score with a straight left (0:38) and left hook (0:48) that gave him the opening minute of the fifth round. Castillo would answer back with a left hook. Mayweather answered that with another solid left (1:35) to Castillo's chin. Castillo would land an excellent right hook (1:56) to Mayweather's body in the northwestern corner ropes. Castillo would partially connect with a left hook to the head as well. Mayweather would hold on, which was a sign he was hurt. Castillo would follow it up with another right body shot (2:19) and a right cross (2:34). The straight right-left hook combination (2:55) gave this round to Castillo. He finally landed some very solid shots that put Mayweather in retreat for the first time in the fight. Castillo would out land Mayweather (16–13) in the fifth round, but more importantly, he landed the more solid blows. It can be argued that the fifth was the first clear round for Castillo.

Mayweather would get back on his toes in the sixth round using lateral movement and scoring with the lead left (0:32) and straight left (1:09). Mayweather would complain to the referee about Castillo holding and hitting. Castillo would score with a devastating straight right (1:31) that snapped Mayweather's head back. Mayweather would land a straight right (1:55) that didn't do much damage. This was another Castillo round, as Mayweather threw ineffective shots that couldn't get Castillo off him. Mayweather would complain about a low blow and fall into the canvas. Castillo would out land Mayweather 24–12 in the sixth round and carry all the momentum.

The opening minute of the seventh round was won narrowly Mayweather as he landed a few jabs and right hands. Mayweather was circling away—unlike the first four rounds—but not coming back to the pocket. Castillo scored with a right hook left hook (1:09) downstairs and upstairs that landed clean. Mayweather would come back with jabs and a lead left (1:26) and a short left (1:51). As Mayweather would work the jab, the proud Mexican would demand that the challenger come toward him. A round that was almost an even round would go to Castillo with another solid right (2:52) in the closing seconds. It was possible that Castillo could have won three consecutive rounds.

Things didn't start off well for Mayweather again in the eighth as Castillo now was throwing triple-left hooks to the body (0:16). Mayweather would score with the lead left (0:27) that snapped Castillo's head back. What saved Mayweather was that his left jab came back and was the most effective since the early rounds. The round was a close round as Castillo worked the body, but Mayweather also landed the lead right (2:02). Mayweather would also get in a double jab to the face (2:35) to possibly earn him the first round since the fourth. Castillo would hit after the break and get a point deduction, which would make it a 10–8 round for Mayweather—or 9–9 if you thought Castillo won it. The deduction could have been a makeup call due to the nonscoring of the knockdown.

The ninth saw Castillo working Mayweather on the southwestern ropes; Referee Drakulich would break them up. Mayweather would take advantage of that by going to the center and landing two lead lefts (0:21). Castillo would land another left uppercut and be charging at Mayweather the entire round. It was a close round that could have been scored as even, and Drakulich could have given Mayweather a point deduction for hitting after the bell.

Perhaps feeling a sense of urgency, Mayweather would score with four right hands and a lead left in the opening thirty seconds of the tenth round. In the southwestern corner ropes, Castillo would try to work the body, but Mayweather would block the shots and come back with his own right. Lead lefts (1:48 and 1:51) would land solidly for Mayweather in the center of the ring. Castillo would pressure inside and be allowed to fight more by the referee. Mayweather would get a point deduction for throwing elbows, and the tenth round was a two-point swing depending on how you scored the round.

Mayweather came in with his left jab in the eleventh round. Castillo would score with three body shots that were in the beltline (0:22). Mayweather answered back with right hooks (0:39 and 0:47). Castillo would work Mayweather on the inside in the middle of the round, but most of the shots were blocked. Mayweather threw seven punches that would give him the edge in that exchange in the middle of the round. A right-hook left-hook combination also scored (1:58) for the challenger. Castillo would answer back with his own combination. Mayweather would land another three-punch combination (2:30). Both fighters would exchange another flurry, including an uppercut for Castillo that landed as the bell rang. It was a close round that could have gone either way, but Mayweather did most of the clean punches on the inside, and the final Castillo rally made it 10–10 on my card.

Castillo would easily win the final round and again hit close to the beltline (1:11) by being the aggressor for the most of the round. Castillo was outworking Mayweather in the center of the ring with short left hooks. The three body shots (2:09) sealed the final round for Castillo. It also should have done enough for him to retain his title. Castillo was relentless and came after Mayweather in the final seconds. Castillo showed his ability to cut off the ring and forced Mayweather to fight his fight.

The judges gave it to Mayweather by the preposterous scores of 115–111, 115–111, and 116–111. It would be difficult to think that, even if Mayweather had pulled it out, that it would have been a difference of more than one or two points. I thought the fight was a draw 5-5-2 (113–113). The final punch stats had Castillo landing 203 of 506 and Mayweather 157 of 448. Mayweather would later complain about a left shoulder injury he suffered in training and two broken ribs. There are many who felt Castillo clearly won the bout and should be regarded as the only defeat on Mayweather's résumé.

CHAPTER 8

Rematch with Castillo

Instead of ducking a rematch with Castillo, Mayweather would take him on again to leave no doubt that he was the legitimate lightweight champion of the world. The rematch would take place on December 7, 2002, at the Mandalay Bay Resort and Casino, Las Vegas, Nevada. After the first Castillo bout, some critics felt Mayweather was not among the top pound-for-pound fighters, as he moved up only five pounds and struggled with Castillo. Many of those felt Mayweather didn't deserve the win and was gifted. Mike Tyson would be in the audience and Richard Schaffer. Castillo again weighed nine pounds more than Mayweather. Both fighters traded jabs to the body; however, Mayweather was blocking Castillo's shots. Castillo again worked the body but got a warning for low blows (2:08) by Joe Cortez in the first round. A lead left (2:45) by Mayweather would seal the first round. Mayweather would control the action in the center of the ring with his lead lefts and jabs to the body. Castillo missed many shots and didn't do any damage after two rounds. Castillo was able to cut the distance a bit more in the third round and got in some body shots. The short overhand right (1:05) was becoming Mayweather's weapon of choice. Mayweather was able to get out of the ropes when Castillo tried to corner him in the middle of the round in the northwestern corner ropes. Mayweather's legs were much better in this fight; he was able to hit and run without much return fire. Castillo would get in a solid left as the bell rang, but it was still a Mayweather round. The Castillo corner would tell him to throw combinations and keep pressuring Mayweather. Mayweather would continue to get most of the action by fighting in the middle of the ring. Joe Cortez would issue a warning to Castillo for holding and hitting. Castillo would likely drop the first four rounds, as I felt he did in the first fight.

The fifth round would be the best Castillo round as he crunched two power left hooks (1:25). Castillo worked the body on the clinches and left hooks (2:30). The sixth round was close, as both fighters landed some clean shots. Castillo would land a straight left (0:44) that snapped Mayweather's head back and another left hook (0:55) to the head. In the seventh round Mayweather would start his own bodywork with left hooks (2:08) to Castillo's body. Castillo would throw a plethora of punches that were mainly blocked in the round. It would be another round in the Mayweather score column.

Castillo would dig Mayweather's body again with hooks (1:10) in the eighth round. However, Castillo was reduced to getting pelted with short left hooks (1:19) as he chased Mayweather. Castillo would land his own short left uppercut (1:40). Mayweather's lead left (2:25) would at least give him an even round. There would also be a few lead rights that didn't score, but it demonstrated Mayweather badly wanted the round.

The opening minute of the ninth round had a very aggressive Castillo using his left hook three times to the head and connecting with two short lefts to Mayweather's body. Not everything was landing cleanly, but Castillo was the more active fighter. Castillo would get in a short right counter (0:41) that got Mayweather's attention. Another short left hook (2:38) would consolidate the round for Castillo. Mayweather had to go on his bike and potshot and utilize short left hooks (1:25) and straight rights (1:45) to win the round, while keeping himself out of danger. The straight right hand (2:43) was a laser between the Castillo guard.

Castillo would be bleeding from his nose and have swelling in his right eye. The right-hand target practice would continue in the eleventh round (0:42 and 0:58). Mayweather had his gloves by his waist and his feet wide to rely on his reflexes and speed to move around. Mayweather's legs and skill were too much for Castillo in this fight. There would be plenty of clinching and potshots in the final round. Mayweather would coast with right hand leads to the final bell. The final punch stats had Mayweather land 162 of 399 punches, compared to Castillo's

137 of 604. The judges had it 115–113, 116–113, and 115–113. This time there was no controversy, as Mayweather was universally regarded as the winner and deserved the lightweight title.

Mayweather would next defend his lightweight title against Victoriana Sosa, who was 11-0-1 in his last twelve contests going into the Mayweather fight. Sosa, a Dominican fighter, fought once for the IBF lightweight title against Paul Spadafora. Sosa was able to drop Spadafora twice in the third round of that contest. Spadafora would come back to win the fight by unanimous decision. This was comforting to Mayweather, who knew he was facing an opponent who didn't finish an opponent when hurt. The bout took place on April 19, 2003, in Fresno, California, in a card that also featured Miguel Cotto facing Joel Perez.

Sosa would give a better account of himself than most anticipated. He would send a message early by landing a double-left hook to Mayweather's body and head at 0:58 of the first round. Sosa had a high, tight guard that left his rib cage exposed. This let Mayweather jab to the body while holding a wide stance. Mayweather would be able to neutralize the Sosa left jab by countering with an overhand right. The lead left hand became Mayweather's weapon of choice in the second round. Sosa was relentless and kept coming forward, which resulted in eating Mayweather counter shots. The Castillo fights probably played into the Sosa game plan. He saw an opponent impose his size and will by taking Mayweather to the ropes and punishing his rib cage. Sosa also realized early that Mayweather couldn't hurt him. It could have been a product and combination of the shoulder issues, brittle hands, or Mayweather fighting bigger opponents. Sosa was an athletic fighter with good head movement and reflexes. He would make Mayweather pay with a right cross after the champion missed his own lead right. After three rounds Sosa had actually thrown more punches but landed only 24 of 128 while Mayweather landed 59 of 119.

The fourth round saw both fighters sporadically trading counters in the middle of the ring. It was easily Sosa's best round up to that point. Sosa would land a sizzling right hook on Mayweather's jaw at 1:37 of the round. Mayweather took the punch flush on the chin and didn't even buckle—another example of the durability of Mayweather's chin. Sosa's corner would scream, "If you don't throw five or six combinations, then you won't be world champion." The corner would also motivate Sosa by reminding him that his cousin, baseball star Sammy Sosa, was watching the fight. This inspired Sosa who was more aggressive in the fifth round. Sosa would get in a solid left hook to Mayweather's temple at 1:58 of the round. Sosa's point was to keep taking the fight to Mayweather, even if a good portion of the blows were not landed cleanly or partially blocked. I felt Sosa won both rounds four and five due to his pressure and several clean connects.

Mayweather would come forward in the sixth round understanding that Sosa had taken control of the last two rounds. The laser left jabs and left hook would give Mayweather the sixth round. Mayweather would finish the round by landing a left hook and mouth off at Sosa, who would gently tap his head into Mayweather's nose. Both fighters would touch gloves in the seventh round and take a break due to a wet spot in the middle of the ring. Sosa would come back charging and fire a left hook cleanly to Mayweather's chin. Something was conspicuously wrong with Mayweather's shoulder, as he would resort mainly to defense in the seventh round. Sosa was the more productive fighter in that round due to volume and better connects. Mayweather would take back the eighth and ninth rounds by going back to the left jab. However, Sosa's upper-body movement and size did make it difficult for Mayweather to land more than one punch at a time.

The tenth round saw Mayweather rubbing his shoes to dry them after almost slipping on the wet canvas. Sosa would get short combinations to the body as he trash talked with Mayweather. The champion would still be able to connect eighteen jabs and make it, possibly, an even round. The right hand would be more active and give Mayweather the final two rounds. Mayweather, in his third consecutive fight, failed to get a KO win as a lightweight. The judges had it 118–110, 119–109, and 118–110. The result would get a scattering of boos, which was perplexing. Despite a few rounds being close, it was inconceivable to think Sosa won more than five rounds, let alone seven. Sosa threw 117 more punches but landed only 79 of 565, compared to 248 of 448 for Mayweather. The most telling sign was that Mayweather out jabbed Sosa 147–12.

As Mayweather made his name in the lightweight division, there was hope he would unify titles. The boxing public expected a unified champion by having the Spadafora and Leonard Dorin winner fight Mayweather. The two fighters would retain their titles as their contest was scored a draw. Spadafora, being a southpaw and more a boxer than puncher, would have been an intriguing matchup for Mayweather. Other possible notable opponents, such as Azumah Nelson or Joel Casamayor, never materialized. Already people were demanding that Mayweather move up in weight and challenge Kostya Tszyu. That bout would have been problematic to make, as Mayweather was an HBO fighter, and Tszyu was a Showtime fighter. However, both networks had negotiated in the past and compromised—as in 2002 when Lewis-Tyson finally materialized. Tszyu had defeated Roger Mayweather via unanimous decision in a 1995 match held in Australia. The consensus was that Floyd would want to get some revenge for Roger, who was both his uncle and trainer. However, Mayweather would concede that he wanted the larger share of purses if facing any of the major opponents mentioned.

Mayweather had some other issues to take care of outside of the ring. Due to a contractual dispute, Mayweather would end his relationship with James Prince. There were unsubstantiated reports that men came to the Top Rank gym on September 11, 2003, and a dustup ensued that resulted in Mayweather advisor Leonard Ellerbe and Thomas Summers being sent to the hospital. Mayweather was shaken up and asked for help from Top Rank's Bob Arum and Todd Dubeof. Mayweather reportedly told them, "These are bad guys, and you need to help save my family." After they suggested giving Prince a letter of credit, Mayweather was purported to respond, "James don't take no letter of credit." Top Rank reportedly helped end the dispute by buying out the contract with a $610,000 advance and giving Prince 20 percent of the $3.05 million purse for his next opponent, Phillip N'dou, who was scheduled to face Mayweather on November 1, 2003, in Grand Rapids, Michigan.

Phillip N'dou, a South African fighter, would prove his manhood as a teenager by circumcising himself instead of doing the ritual tradition of killing a lion. Former NBA player Manute Bol followed the tradition of killing a lion. Bol, who was a 7 feet 7 inch Sudanese center, was the tallest player in the NBA for years. N'dou (31-1, 30 KOs) had a strong KO record but never knocked out a notable opponent. N'dou was the number-one WBC-ranked fighter, and if Mayweather didn't fight him, he could risk being stripped of his title down the road. N'dou would enter the ring to "One Moment in Time," a song sung by Whitney Houston and written by Albert Hammond and John Bettis. Mayweather would enter the ring to 50 Cent, an artist who would be a close associate and friend for years to come.

The speed and reflexes are what allowed Mayweather to double up the left hook to N'dou's body and head. Mayweather would elude N'dou's left jab by moving his head and then coming back with his own straight right hand. This is known as a pull counter, and it would be possibly the second-most-effective punch for Mayweather, after his left hook. N'dou failed to try to go to the body instead of looking for the head. The South African fighter would do much better in the second round by roughing up Mayweather on the inside while jabbing to the shoulder instead of the head. N'dou would also score with right uppercuts to squeak out the round.

It increasingly became an inside fight in the next two rounds with Mayweather getting the best of it with hooks on the inside. There would be a few solid N'dou shots as he landed an overhand right flush at 0:58 of the fourth round. N'dou kept throwing, even if the shots missed or were partially blocked. Mayweather would land the cleaner shots, which included both straight and left hooks to the body and head. Mayweather landed twenty-two power punches compared to eleven for N'dou in the fourth round, despite N'dou throwing twenty-three more punches. The power shots would take their toll, as N'dou would start to get hurt with more frequent combinations in the fifth round. N'dou would come back, despite being hurt, and take Mayweather to the northwestern corner ropes and throw a barrage of rights and lefts that Mayweather mainly blocked or deflected. Mayweather would roll with the punches while keeping his right guard high, with elbow tucked into his rib cage, to block the left-handed shots—also keeping his left glove covering his midsection—as the left shoulder would be high to deflect right hands. The final minute of the fifth round would showcase some of the best defensive examples of Mayweather's career. N'dou would get close to punching himself out and would get dropped by an overhand right (1:16) in the sixth round. N'dou would get up, only to be stopped by three straight rights in the middle of the seventh. The N'dou corner would throw the towel against their fighter's wishes. Mayweather would out land N'dou 158–92, while throwing 156 fewer punches.

After the bout Mayweather would dispel rumors that he was ducking Casamayor, Freitas, or Lazcano. "These guys don't want to fight me, so I need to move up to bigger and better things." Mayweather would then concede, "I need to get a big piece of the money since I keep proving myself time and time again."

CHAPTER 9

Testing the Jr. Welterweight Waters

Mayweather would decide to vacate his lightweight title and move up his third weight class. He had followed the same footsteps as Paul Spadafora (34-0-1, 14 KOs) who had also vacated his WBA lightweight title in 2003 to move to the light-welterweight division. For all intents and purposes, the king of the light-welterweight division was Kostya Tszyu (30-1, 24 KOs) who became the undisputed champion when he defeated Zab Judah on November 3, 2001. Judah was dropped in the second round and, instead of taking the time to sort himself out, would immediately spring back up so wobbly that it prompted referee Jay Naday to stop the contest with only a second left in the round. The only major belt that Tszyu didn't own was the WBO, which Judah would win after defeating Demarcus Corley on July 12, 2003.

When Mayweather talked about "bigger and better things," he would demonstrate what he meant by "big piece of the money" in his next bout. In his bout with Demarcus Chop Chop Corley, Mayweather would earn $3 million to Corley's $150,000. The purse was divided up in a 20-to-1 dollar ratio in favor of Mayweather. In Corley, Mayweather would be facing a southpaw for the first time since 1997 when he faced Jesus Chavez. Corley was a DC fighter known for wearing bizarre sci-fi costumes. Mayweather's plan coming in was the no-brainer of using the straight right against the southpaw Corley. However, when the match began, Corley would have his own straight right jab land over Mayweather's shoulder in the opening round. Mayweather would answer back with his own big right to Corley's chest with less than thirty seconds left in the opening stanza. In the second Mayweather continued to come forward while working Corley's body. Corley would get in a solid left with only ten seconds left in the round. Corley had success with the overhand left. This would make Mayweather keep his right guard high more often in the third round; this wouldn't stop Corley from landing another big left. Mayweather kept his guard toward the back of the ear, which allowed Corley to score with the left. Despite this, Mayweather out landed Corley 55–31 after three rounds.

The fact that Mayweather focused on Corley's left hand made him forget the right hand. Corley would seriously hurt Mayweather with a right hook in the opening seconds of the fourth round. Mayweather would retreat to the ropes as a collective gasp from the audience could be heard. Mayweather would fight back and land pulverizing left hooks on Corley's body. Corley would get in several shots to Mayweather's head. Both fighters would be bloodied as they came back to their corners. Corley would out land Mayweather 26–23 in power shots. Roger Mayweather would scold Mayweather for fighting in this combative style. Mayweather felt he could get Corley out of there if he stuck to a disciplined game plan.

Mayweather tried to put pressure on in the next few rounds by landing to Corley's body. Corley would get Mayweather to the ropes and be unable to land anything serious in the sixth. Mayweather would fight at his distance and use his speed and reflexes in the second half of the fight. Pretty Boy saw the danger of going to the pocket and standing in front of Chop Chop. Moreover, Corley slowed down a bit due to the early body shots. Mayweather also switched to southpaw to confuse Corley and block Corley's left hand. Mayweather landed a three-punch combination at 2:00 of the eighth that slowed down Corley. Another combination of left hooks and straight right would make Corley take a knee (2:24). Mayweather would go back to the pocket and land a flurry of combinations before the closing bell.

Corley would get dropped a second time in the start of the tenth round with another flurry in the center of the ring. Mayweather tried desperately to be the first fighter to stop Corley with inside short shots, but Chop Chop was able to weather the storm. Corley would take more punishment in the last two rounds and be able to finish on his feet. Mayweather proved he could get hurt and come back to win. The judges scored it 118–108, 119–107, and 119–108 for Mayweather. Mayweather landed 283 of 600 punches, which included 230 power shots. Corley would land 157 of 657.

The Puerto Rican fighter Henry Brussels was not Kostya Tszyu, but he was a bigger opponent with power. There were no major names in Brussels's résumé besides sparring with fellow Puerto Rican Miguel Cotto. Mayweather would face Brussels on January 22, 2005, at the American Airlines Arena, Miami, Florida. It would be Mayweather's second fight in the division. Brussels was able to work Mayweather's body with hooks in the opening round. Mayweather was still able to tame Brussels with his jab and lead lefts. The pull counter and a few short hooks to the ribs would give Mayweather control of the second round. The Brussels corner would keep screaming "cuerpo" (body), as they felt Mayweather would slow down. All the momentum would go to Mayweather in the third round as his lead left hooks, pull counters, and speed were too much for Brussels. Mayweather—with his reflexes, defensive posture, and feet—would be able to elude danger, minus a few body shots.

Referee Jorge Alonso would warn Mayweather for throwing elbows on the inside in the fourth round. This was indicative that Mayweather was feeling comfortable that he could handle Brussels's power and take the war on the inside. Mayweather would fire inside and be able to slip most of Brussels's shots. When he got back to his corner, Mayweather would get anxious and ask, "Am I cut?" His corner would reassure him that he was not, in order to relax him. There wouldn't be any hurdles to overcome, as Mayweather would be on cruise control, taking advantage of his superior speed and skill. Even a right uppercut—a rare part of the Mayweather repertoire—would score at 1:53 of the sixth round. A right hook to the body (2:10) in the eighth round would have Brussels take a knee. Brussels would come back only to take more hooks to the face, compelling his corner to stop the contest at 2:55 of the eighth round.

Mayweather was part of previous pay-per-view undercards, but he had never headlined a pay-per-view. At the age of twenty-nine, and with the blessing of HBO and his management, it was time to have the entire spotlight on him. The choice of opponent and venue would be crucial in making that debut. There was a fan-favorite fighter with a cult following who happened to own a title at junior welterweight that could make it possible.

CHAPTER 10

PPV Debut with Thunder

Floyd Mayweather Jr. (33-0, 22 KOs)—despite his accomplishments—was still unknown to a good portion of the American and international audience. A pay-per-view match with Arturo Gatti would be able to help break him in with a more mainstream boxing audience. Mayweather had his eye set on Arturo Gatti (39-6, 30 KOs) for several years as a possible opponent. It wouldn't be much of a surprise that Gatti would be the first Mayweather pay-per-view event. Although Mayweather himself called Gatti a paper champion and felt indignant that some thought a fighter with six losses would beat him, the fact was that Gatti was in an upswing. Gatti was coming off five consecutive wins, and his name value was at a premium. Victories over Mickey Ward, Leonard Dorin, and Jesse James Leija had restored Gatti as a boxing commodity. Gatti had captured the WBC light welterweight title with a win over Gialunca Brano on January 24, 2004. Kostya Tszyu, the other major name in the division, was scheduled to face Ricky Hatton on June 4, 2005, in Manchester. Mayweather would sign to face Gatti on June 25 at the Boardwalk Hall, Atlantic City, New Jersey. Although Gatti was born in Italy and had lived in Montreal, his new home was Jersey City. Mayweather was essentially fighting Gatti in his hometown.

Mayweather would be guaranteed $3.1 million and proceeds of the PPV revenues. There was some anticipation that if both Mayweather and Tszyu would win, that a major unification could finally be staged between both combatants.

This possibility would be erased when Tszyu would suffer an upset at the hands of Ricky Hatton in Manchester a few weeks before Mayweather-Gatti.

The question remained how Mayweather would handle Gatti's power. On paper, it appeared that Gatti only had a puncher's chance. This had to be factored in, along with the fact that Gatti started out as a super featherweight and wasn't bigger than Mayweather who had both the slight height and reach advantage. The question should have been how Gatti would deal with Mayweather's supersonic counters after he threw wide shots. Mayweather would also have some motivation coming in to the bout, as he blamed Gatti for pleading "no contest" to a misdemeanor assault charge in Michigan after an alleged physical altercation in a Grand Rapids bar. Mayweather proclaimed his innocence and claimed he pleaded "no contest" due to part of the contract requiring Mayweather to dispose of his criminal charge to continue with the fight publicity tour. This enraged Mayweather who felt the quickest way to continue with his training and promotion was to plead no contest. Gatti and his promoter, Main Events, felt that it was just an excuse and that Mayweather and his legal advisors could have easily discharged the criminal charge in timely fashion. Nonetheless, Mayweather would use this as an inspiration to punish Gatti and tell the media, "I'm going to beat him. I'm going to talk to him while I beat him. I'm going to talk to the reporters and the announcers while I beat him, and in between rounds I want to borrow his cell phone, so I can talk to a real live Arturo Gatti fan while I beat him."

Mayweather would have the ring entrance of a king as he was hoisted on a royal chair with men dressed as Roman centurions, while Queen's "Another One Bites the Dust" rocked the speakers. Arturo Gatti would come in with a more bombastic entry, as Australian hard rock band AC/DC's "Thunderstruck" was put on high voltage, to pun one of their albums.

Two interested spectators would include Miguel Cotto and Ricky Hatton who were at ringside, hoping for a lucrative match with the winner. The best hope for Gatti would be to make a rough fight by imposing his will on Mayweather. The odds were stacked against him; he needed to attempt what Castillo did on Mayweather. Instead of trying to take Mayweather to the ropes, Gatti was trying to outbox him in the center of the ring, which was a mistake.

Mayweather was simply too fast in both hands and feet to be outmaneuvered in the center of the ring. When you add the Mayweather defense, it only complicates things for an opponent. Gatti felt that his jab to the shoulder would eventually force Mayweather to take it down and make the shoulder roll obsolete. Instead, Mayweather would catch many of those jabs with his gloves. Gatti actually slipped punches well in the first round but really didn't land anything of substance. Mayweather would also get out of the ropes when he felt endangered.

At 2:35 of the first round, referee Earl Morton would command, "stop punching." Instead, Mayweather would hit Gatti three times after the instruction. The referee usually gives the command while stepping in, but Morton didn't step in. Gatti would look at the referee after the second punch for help but only allowed himself to be hit with a left hook that floored him. Fighters are taught to protect themselves at all times, and when Mayweather hit Gatti a second time, he should have done that. Yet it is important to consider that many boxers—out of sportsmanship—wouldn't hit opponents when given a free shot, but some do, such as the infamous Dempsey-Sharkey bout. Gatti would have no problem beating the count but would utter, "That is bullshit." Trainer Buddy McGirt would tell Gatti, "Don't let that get you off your game plan." Mayweather was now up 10–8 in the scorecard and had already, with the controversy, gotten into the local fighter's head.

Mayweather would take full command of the contest in the second round. Gatti would throw a wild left and pay the price with two Mayweather counter left shots. Gatti would score notable left hook, Gatti but it wouldn't do much damage. Mayweather saw openings, and he exploited those openings with precise combinations that landed as guided missiles. Fighters like Joe Frazier and Archie Moore—who were known to be aggressive—would know how to protect themselves coming in toward a boxer with variations of a cross-arms defense while bobbing and weaving. Gatti didn't have the guard or the head movement to stay at that distance with Mayweather. He was getting picked apart with lead rights on his stationary head and body. After two rounds, Gatti had noticeable swelling in both eyes, which would usually materialize in the latter rounds in his infamous wars of attrition. The deafening ovation that Gatti received at his entrance was replaced with eerie silence that would momentarily be broken with collective oohs and aahs from the Atlantic City crowd when

Mayweather connected. Gatti was still there in the third, but—besides a couple of jabs—there was nothing landing for him. Mayweather was the fresher fighter and seemed to get stronger as the action progressed.

A six-punch combination in the middle of the fourth round would make Gatti's head appear to be a speed bag. A two-punch combination would score for Gatti in the opening minute of the fifth round. Unfortunately, this was not going to stop Mayweather who was more durable than many gave him credit for. The total domination would continue in the sixth round where Mayweather was able to choreograph combinations on Gatti mistakes. It would be a 10–8 round without even a knockdown being scored. Both of Gatti's eyes were virtually sewn shut, and the margin of Mayweather domination was increasingly one-sided. Buddy McGirt would mercifully stop the contest to save his fighter, in order to preserve his career. Mayweather had out landed Gatti 168–41 in six rounds. If it continued, that discrepancy would have increasingly tilted to Mayweather's favor. To some critics the fight had "mismatch" written all over it, and they refused to give Mayweather the credit he deserved. Cynics felt that Gatti was essentially a brawler with some boxing skill that was honed by trainer Buddy McGirt, and it wasn't a shock how much of a dominating performance that Mayweather put on.

Boxer and commentator Roy Jones would surmise, "I would never have put Gatti in the ring with Mayweather—it was the wrong fight for him—but for the fans and the payday, this is what they fight for, and they had to let it happen." The final punch stats had Mayweather connecting 168 of 295 and Gatti a paltry 41 of 245. The judges had lopsided scores of 60–52, 60–52, and 60–53 at the time of stoppage. Mayweather was now a champion in three weight classes and took what he initially called a "paper title" into his possession. The final pay-per-view numbers had 340,000 buys, which produced $15.3 million in revenue. These numbers were actually decent, since neither fighter was a mainstream PPV star at that point. There were bigger possible Mayweather pay-per-view draws in the junior welterweight division, as Miguel Cotto and Ricky Hatton were both coming off recent junior welterweight title wins. Hatton had just dethroned Kotsya Tszyu a few weeks earlier, while Cotto recently had defended the WBO strap for the third consecutive time over Muhammad Abdulaev. There was talk of Mayweather fighting Zab Judah down the road. Initially, Mayweather was not sure he would face his former US Olympic Trials teammate. Mayweather, after collecting a title at junior welterweight, decided to move up to his fourth division as a welterweight. There would be no unification match in the division.

The first Mayweather opponent in the welterweight division would be Sharmba Mitchell (56-4, 31 KOs). Mitchell was a former champion who suffered all four of his losses via knockout. However, his first KO loss to Kostya Tszyu was due to a knee injury in that junior welterweight unification bout. He would eventually face Tszyu years later in a rematch and get a TKO in three rounds. Mitchell would have an infamous wardrobe malfunction with his trunks and would never win a title again. He was more of a boxer than a puncher, and nobody felt Mitchell was going to outbox Mayweather. Moreover, Mayweather—not fearing Mitchell—would be more inclined to be more aggressive and to test Mitchell's chin. The match would take place on November 19, 2005, at the Rose Garden in Portland, Oregon. Buddy McGirt would work as the chief second behind trainer Marvin Simms in the Mitchell corner. The Air Jordan logo would be embedded in the middle of the canvas. His airiness himself (Michael Jordan) would enter the arena while the fight was in progress. Neither combatant was able to land anything of substance until Mayweather landed a straight right flush at 1:40 of the first round. It shook Mitchell, who clinched, and it was obvious that would be a punch for Mayweather to utilize in the contest. Roger Mayweather was accurate in his assessment of the fight. "Keep walking to him; the more you try to fight, the more the mother f***er is going to hold." Essentially, Roger was telling him that this was a guy who would fold under pressure.

Mitchell tried different angles and looks on Mayweather and tried to work the body with straight jabs. The best Mitchell connects were in the waning seconds when he would score with a solid right-and-left combination. Mayweather took the best Mitchell shots and didn't miss a beat. Mayweather would drop Mitchell with a straight right in the opening minute of the third round. Mitchell would beat the count and withstand a Mayweather barrage to survive. Mitchell's use of the right hand was more apparent, but Mayweather would catch most of those shots with his left shoulder. Mitchell had modest success with a right jab followed by a straight left to Mayweather's body in the fifth round. Despite a Mayweather rally in the final seconds, it was the only round that could have conceivably been scored for Mitchell. Any possibility of Mitchell taking Mayweather into deep waters was halted when one well-measured straight right to the body stopped Mitchell. There was plenty of leverage on that punch, and it could have hurt most welterweights. Mayweather out landed Mitchell 85–31, despite Mitchell throwing 51 more punches. Mitchell's 11 percent connect percentage really didn't do justice to Mitchell's effort. Mayweather had demonstrated that he could punch as a welterweight. However, cynics felt the quality of his opponent best explained his dominant performance. Mitchell wasn't regarded as a big puncher, and there were other names in the division that could punch.

At the time, the welterweight champions were Zab Judah (WBC, WBA, IBF) and Antonio Margarito (WBO). Judah was a southpaw with speed and had defeated Corey Spinks to become the undisputed welterweight champion of the world. Margarito, a tall welterweight, had captured the WBO title in 2002 in a decision win over Antonio Diaz. Margarito had successfully defended the WBO title five times, which included knockout wins over Kermit Cintron and Sebastian Luje. Margarito would be the first boxer to knock out those two opponents. He stopped Cintron by a body shot, and he stopped Lujan by almost taking his ear off. It would be difficult for Margarito to go unnoticed by Mayweather.

On February 18, 2006, Margarito had his sixth consecutive defense of this WBO title when he knocked out Manuel Gomez. Zab Judah would actually lose to Carlos Baldomir in a tune-up fight on January 7, 2006. Judah promoter Don King, and Bob Arum representing Mayweather, had a deal that would have guaranteed Mayweather $6 million and Judah $3 million. However, after the Judah defeat, the deal would be reworked to guarantee a purse of $5 million for Mayweather and $1 million for Judah. Although both Margarito and Baldomir were coming off wins, Judah would still be chosen due to his name recognition in selling a pay-per-view event.

CHAPTER 11
Fiasco in Vegas and Baldomir

Mayweather would top *Ring Magazine's* annual list for top pound-per-pound fighter for 2005. He was now seeking a fourth-divisional title in the welterweight division.

Despite their previous friendship, Mayweather's and Judah's relationship had turned sour. Perhaps this was convenient, as the pay-per-view event would be billed as "Sworn Enemies." The match would take place on April 8, 2006, at the Thomas & Mack Center, Las Vegas, Nevada, for the IBF title. Zab Judah would come out much sharper than anticipated when he faced Mayweather. Judah landed a fast straight left to Mayweather's body. He would also land a solid straight left to Mayweather's chin (1:42) in the opening stanza. Judah would also pawn the right jab to Mayweather's body. Judah would take the first round.

Both fighters neutralized each other's jabs by catching them with their gloves. At 1:01 of the second, a short Judah right made Mayweather's right glove touch the canvas. Richard Steele failed to score the first real knockdown of Mayweather's career. Judah scored with a right-hook straight-left combination. A sneaky left and another body shot would also score for Judah. Judah would win the first two rounds. Mayweather realized the best way to fight Judah was to be offensive since Judah was more comfortable when he was initiating. Mayweather would do better with left hooks to the body, and his jab started to work. Roger would tell Mayweather between rounds, "He can't fight going backward." (This is what they observed in the second half of the Baldomir fight.) Thirty seconds into the fourth round, Judah would land a straight left that momentarily stunned Mayweather. Judah would also work the right counter and jab well.

The fifth round was when the fight would change. Mayweather kept coming forward and forcing Judah on the back foot. Judah would get punished with hooks to the body and straight right shots. The bloodied Judah would start to move his arms erratically and trash talk. Judah would try to work the body again in the sixth round. Mayweather, with short right hooks, was able to control the next two rounds. Judah would start to bleed both from his mouth and nose. Mayweather's right hand was landing both more accurately and solidly on Judah. What happened in the second half of the Baldomir fight was happening again. That is to say, Judah stopped throwing punches when his opponent became more aggressive. The Mayweather corner already saw the body language and felt Judah was about to quit after the eighth round. Roger would say, "The bitch is about to quit." And Rafael Garcia would add, "He don't want anymore."

In the final seconds of the tenth round, a frustrated Judah would land a very low left hook that was south of the border and crippled Mayweather. Roger Mayweather came into the ring challenging Judah, and then Zab's father and trainer, Noel Judah, also came into the ring. The ring security and police would also come into the ring. There would be a delay before the fight resumed. The fact that a member of the Mayweather corner came inside the ring in the middle of the round could have resulted in a disqualification, as NSAC rules prohibit anyone from a corner entering the ring. However, since the action had been halted and since this rule is rarely enforced when trainers go into the ring complaining, there wouldn't be any disqualification.

Roger Mayweather would still be forced to leave the corner. After a temporary delay due to the melee, the action would later resume. The added rest would help Judah more, as he was starting to slow down. Judah would be a bit more active in the last two rounds with his jab and straight left. Mayweather would stick out his chin in the final round, demanding Judah to hit it. The final judges' scores were 116–112, 119–109, and 117–111, all for Mayweather.

With the win Mayweather was now a quadruple champion as Hearns, Leonard, Duran, Whitaker, De La Hoya, and Gamez had been before him. Mayweather landed 188 of 404 while Judah landed 82 of 444. At the postfight interview, Mayweather said he expected Judah to tire at the end. "Zab is a front-runner; he comes strong for the first six rounds then he gas out." The final pay-per-view numbers for Mayweather-Judah were 374,000 buys, which resulted in $16.8 million in revenue.

The ring fiasco would have repercussions for Roger Mayweather. The Nevada State Athletic Commission would revoke Roger's boxing license for one year and hand out a $200,000 fine. Leonard Ellerbe, who also left the corner, would get a four-month suspension and a $50,000 fine. Judah would get a one-year suspension and a $350,000 fine. This meant if Mayweather would fight as expected at the end of 2006, he would do it without his full-time trainer in his corner.

Not only did Mayweather have to worry about his corner but also about choosing his next opponent. There were really only two viable candidates: Carlos Baldomir or Antonio Margarito.

Mayweather would eventually choose Baldomir. The choice of Baldomir (43-9-6 14 KOs) has been questioned, since many people focused on the Argentinean fighter's nine losses. Yet, Baldomir was the lineal welterweight champion and had recently defeated both Gatti and Judah. Baldomir had gone twenty-one consecutive fights without a loss, and his record didn't reflect the entire picture. The nine Baldomir losses were far removed from him. Most importantly, Baldomir had called out Mayweather after both the Judah and Gatti fights. He would tell the media "I want Mayweather; he has what is mine." Baldomir was an awkward fighter who would likely come into the ring at over 160 pounds after hydrating. The Argentine boasted, "I think Mayweather would be an easier fight than Judah, since Zab has more speed and power."

Yet a strong case could definitely have been made for Margarito as the next Mayweather opponent. The fact that Margarito could bring the larger Mexican audience to the pay-per-view market did make it economically feasible compared with Baldomir.

Margarito had defended his WBO welterweight title six times, which included winning six out of his last seven bouts by knockout. The most notable wins were becoming the first fighter to earn stoppage wins over Kermit Cinton and Sebastian Andres Lujan. Margarito would stop Cinton by a vicious body shot, and Lujan would suffer his first stoppage loss after his ear was nearly taken off in a grizzly scene. Margarito, with his height of nearly six feet and relentless fighting style, would have been a major test for Mayweather. Of course, all of these events were prior to the hand-wrapping scandal that had the public putting some question marks on some of the major Margarito wins.

Top Rank promoter Bob Arum felt that Mayweather didn't want any part of a match with Margarito. "Mayweather wants no part of Margarito. If you look at Mayweather's face, that is the one guy that he doesn't want to face. And you know he doesn't have to fight him, but he should come clean and say, 'I don't want to fight Margarito because he is too dangerous'...because the offer for Margarito is the best."

The Mexican fighter wanted the big fight with Mayweather and even went so far as to corner Mayweather and demand the fight in person. The encounter between the fighters would be taped, and the video footage would be circulated around the Internet. The Mexican fighter, wearing dark shades and matching suit, would ask Mayweather to fight him next. Mayweather would, through an interpreter, advise him that "I don't duck nobody. I am making the smart business decisions by trying to get the bigger fight [De La Hoya], but when we meet down the line, the fight would be bigger." Mayweather would then tell a reporter, "Boxing fans I asked didn't know who the hell he [Margarito] is. I make the smart business decisions to move me up a level." There was reportedly $8 million on the table, which Shane Mosley said he would have taken. "I wouldn't turn down $8 million to fight Margarito. I can't understand why he turned that down. He is running, hiding, or ducking or something from somebody." Mayweather would counter critics by claiming he earned the same $8 million to fight Carlos Baldomir who was the lineal champion and had also called him out. If Mayweather had taken Margarito instead of the lineal champion, who had also called him out, then he could have expected criticism as well.

Baldomir's durability and size would create problems for Mayweather, even if Baldomir lacked speed. Mayweather had already been forced the distance by Cuello and Rios, who were both Argentineans. Names such as Carlos Monzon, Nicolino Locche, and Jorge Castro are testaments to the great chins and conditioning of Argentine fighters. Baldomir's name was not said in the same breath as theirs, but he was the defending lineal champion who hadn't lost in twenty-one fights—yet he was still described as a paper champion by many in the media. The fight would be scheduled for November 4, 2006, at the Mandalay Bay Resort and Casino.

The actual match between Mayweather and Baldomir was a one-sided, calculative boxing clinic, as Mayweather dominated the action from start to finish. Mayweather would also make a fashion statement by putting on pink gloves and matching trunks. Mayweather controlled the first round with his jab, and that resulted in Baldomir bleeding from his nose and left eye. The blood was not a major factor, as it would be controlled by the Baldomir corner for most of the fight. Mayweather would employ a strategy of circling to his left and throwing left hooks, as Baldomir would follow him around the ring in the second round. Baldomir would get in a chopping right punch (0:49) in the second round that got Mayweather's attention. Baldomir would try to follow up, but Mayweather would slip the punches and then clinch. Mayweather would resort to more potshotting than combinations in the second round, as he didn't want to give the bigger fighter a chance to land anything significant. At 2:25 Mayweather landed that lead right and then evaded Baldomir's left counter. Mayweather's reflexes and speed would prove problematic for the Santa Fe fighter.

Baldomir's plan was to make it a rough-and-tumble fight and to press Mayweather against the ropes, as he did in the opening minute of the third round. Unfortunately, Baldomir would not throw straight and accurate punches, and Mayweather would easily slip by his wide shots. Often Mayweather made him pay as at 2:35 of the third where he punished Baldomir with a right hook after missing a looping right hook. Baldomir had difficulty landing his power shots; he landed only 13 out of 105 (12 percent) after three rounds.

Mayweather would close in the distance in the next two rounds, as he was able to time Baldomir better and knew his feet could get him out of danger if needed. At 1:31 of the fifth round, Mayweather landed a perfect right hook that would have sent a lesser opponent to the canvas. "You're boxing circles around him," Ellerbe would tell Mayweather after the fifth round. Baldomir was simply winging shots around Mayweather's head without focusing up the middle with straight shots and a jab. Mayweather actually never landed those three or four punch combinations; he was potshotting with clean blows, one at a time. The final seconds of the sixth round had a minibrawl break out, with Baldomir landing a few solid punches that Mayweather took well.

Baldomir did better in the opening of the seventh round by landing two short left hooks to inside of Mayweather's body. If he had done this earlier, Baldomir may have been able to slow down the pound-for-pound king. Mayweather would still pick Baldomir with his short inside shots. Baldomir would focus more on the body and put the pressure on, but he would still not capitalize on opportunities—such as when he had Mayweather on the northeastern corner ropes in the middle of the eighth round. Mayweather was able to slip punches and use his feet to get him back into the middle of the ring and out of danger. At 2:09 both fighters would trade right punches simultaneously in the eighth, and both would stay on their feet. Baldomir would continue fruitlessly coming after Mayweather and would often get tied up and rabbit punch. Referee Jay Nady would warn Baldomir several times for the rabbit punching, as in the ninth round. Through nine rounds, Mayweather had connected 146 of 343, while Baldomir was at 58 of 467.

Scattered boos filled the arena in the tenth round as Mayweather dominated the bout without much action. The boos continued in the eleventh round as both fighters would be in the pocket but not exchanging much artillery. Mayweather would close the show by getting on his bike and landing straight lefts to the body. Baldomir would be the aggressor most of the round and landed partial connects. The final round would possibly be the only round that could go to Baldomir. The judges had it 120–108, 118–110, and 120–108. The pay-per-view bout would draw 325,000 purchases, which would generate

$16.2 million. The figures were a bit disappointing, as the Gatti and Judah numbers had done slightly better. For his effort, Mayweather had won the lineal welterweight title.

For the second consecutive year Mayweather topped *Ring Magazine's* top pound-per-pound fighter. However, the Fighter of the Year award would go to Manny Pacquiao who was now number two on the pound-per-pound list.

CHAPTER 12

Smashing The PPV Record

Larry Merchant would once famously exclaim, "Mayweather has as much chance against Oscar as Eric Morel the flyweight champ has against him." Few people thought when Mayweather was a lightweight champion that he would conceivably fight De La Hoya in the future. The logic was that Mayweather was too small to come up to junior middleweight. Mayweather was always drawn to De La Hoya simply because of notoriety. He fully understood that De La Hoya was easily the highest drawing nonheavyweight pay-per-view fighter in history. The De La Hoya-Trinidad fight was the biggest selling fight for a nonheavyweight fight. When Floyd Mayweather was in attendance for De La Hoya-Mayorga he had only thing in mind—a De La Hoya victory to ensure getting the biggest payday of his career. By facing De La Hoya he would also get a shot at a fifth divisional title and at becoming only the fourth quintuple champion in history.

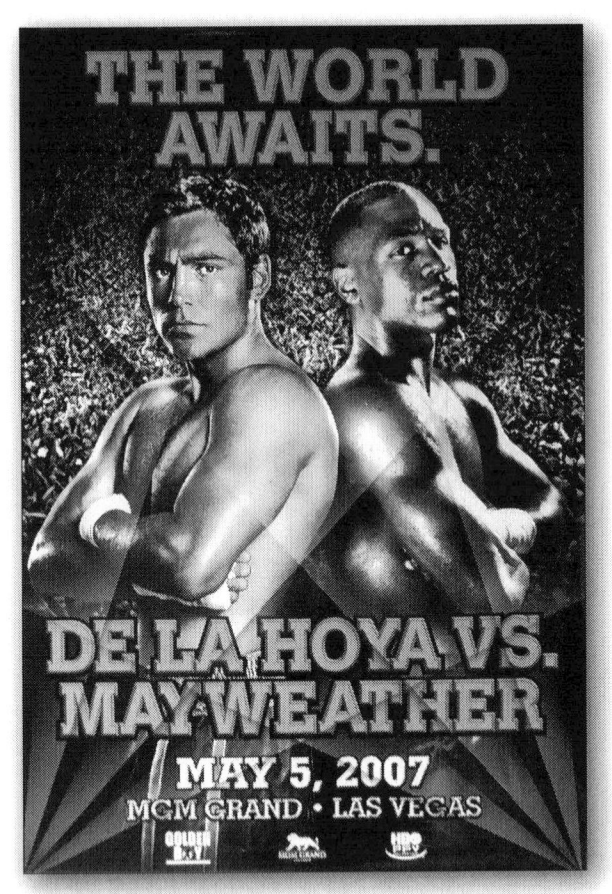

Golden Boy promotional poster for the match between De La Hoya and Mayweather.

The fight would be set for May 5, 2007, and be billed "The World Awaits." Tickets would go on sale on January 27, 2007, and be sold out within three hours. This would produce a live gate of over $19 million, which would break the previous record set by Tyson-Holyfield 2. The magnitude of the event would be captured and filmed for the new HBO series 24/7. Former HBO sports president Ross Greenburg created the idea to help boost the sales. Viewers would see parts of the fighters' training camp and some of their personal lives captured away from the ring. Boxing, like the old NBA, needed to build up stars. Due to the rise of reality TV, having a reality-based program on the day-to-day life of fighters preparing for a major match seemed a natural idea.

De La Hoya was a proven commodity, and Mayweather (37-0, 24 KOs) was a fighter who was undefeated and considered universally as the number-one pound-for-pound fighter. The fight would be promoted as the "Golden Boy vs. Pretty Boy," which was added to the "World Awaits" tagline. Mayweather would relish the opportunity to have press conferences in support of the fight. The series 24/7 would be the launch pad to introduce Mayweather to a larger audience. 24/7 was the manifestation of the growing appetite for reality TV that took viewers behind the stage of celebrity lives. Voyeurism was at a peak in American culture as more reality-based television shows were knocking out original programming. However, just like any form of entertainment, the viewer needed to be fixated on the content for it to work. In Mayweather, there was a multitude of characters that understood how to galvanize an audience. Everyone would wonder what he would say or do next. The Michigan-born fighter would relish the opportunity to become the boisterous and conceited fighter who would be both admired and despised by the audience. As the saying goes "a battery runs on both positive and negative energy." The polarizing force behind Mayweather would help consolidate both the boxing and mainstream audience to the sport. The logic was that the negative forces that hated him would pay to see him lose, and the positive forces would pay to see him win.

Some of the shenanigans in the press used to build up the fight included mocking De La Hoya by having a chicken wear a fake gold medal in one of the press conferences. "Thirty-seven have tried, and thirty-seven have failed," Mayweather would tell reporters in the buildup to the fight. De La Hoya seemed a bit irked in the promotion of the fight due to Mayweather's consistent mantra that he was the best and that he had a lot of money.

The official weights for Mayweather-De La Hoya had Mayweather come in at 150 pounds and De La Hoya at 154 pounds. The same-day weigh-in had Mayweather actually go back down to 148. Mayweather's entrance would have him sporting the Mexican national flag's colors on his robe and trunks, topped off with a sombrero. Mayweather's antic was reminiscent of his uncle Roger—also known as the "Mexican Assassin." The match commenced with Mayweather commencing the action by feinting and jabbing De La Hoya's body. A Mayweather right cross (0:31) would be the first solid punch landed in the fight. The crowd would get stirred up when De La Hoya started to fire his own left hooks (0:54), yet those shots were mainly blocked. What was surprising was how Mayweather would use his own jab in the first round. It was expected that De La Hoya would establish his jab. Mayweather understood that speed gave De La Hoya problems and that De La Hoya would slow down in the final rounds. The Golden Boy understood timing and that a great jab could neutralize speed. De La Hoya would take control of the second round by finally fighting behind his left jab and getting in a few straight right hands. Not everything landed cleanly, but De La Hoya was the much more active fighter and kept coming forward, which could help persuade the judges. De La Hoya landed 15 of 53 and Mayweather 14 of 32 in the second round.

In the corner, Roger Mayweather would tell Floyd, "Down the stretch you're going to get his ass." The analysis was not prophetic, as this is precisely what happened in several major De La Hoya bouts. Mayweather would take a more defensive stand in the third round, with the trademark right glove high and left arm wrapped around the body (perhaps a direct result of De La Hoya firing to Mayweather's rib cage with left hooks). De La Hoya would be very aggressive in the opening minute and backed up Mayweather on the ropes. Mayweather would get the action back to the center of the ring and get a short left hook (1:53) in the third round. It was obvious that Mayweather could control the fight in the center of the ring with his speed and reflexes. Freddie Roach would tell De La Hoya, "All he is using is the feint and the hook; you can block that and come back with your own shots."

De La Hoya would get his own left hook (0:15) in the fourth round and continue to pressure Mayweather. The Golden Boy would also do a good job in blocking most of Mayweather's shots. Mayweather would turn to his left hand and find some traction with it by scoring with short left hooks and a left jab. The round was almost in the Mayweather column until De La Hoya would score with nine consecutive left hooks to the body as he had Mayweather in the southwestern corner ropes. Mayweather answered by taking the fight back to the center of the ring and landing straight right hands.

Mayweather saw openings for overhand rights (0:20, 1:25, and 1:33) and punished De La Hoya with them in the fifth. The right hand would punish De La Hoya further in the final minute of the round with straight rights. A Mayweather punch at 2:41 was a result of a flat-footed De La Hoya not getting out of the way. Not only were De La Hoya's legs missing, but the head movement was also missing.

There was no way De La Hoya could fight Mayweather in the middle of the ring. The laser lead right would score for Mayweather in the sixth. De La Hoya would punish Mayweather momentarily on the ropes in the same round. However, Mayweather was in excellent condition and seemed impervious to punishment. Mayweather would bounce back and punish De La Hoya with a double-left hook that landed upstairs and downstairs (1:20). De La Hoya still retained some good slipping ability by making Mayweather miss four consecutive right hands. An overhand right (1:56) would land cleanly on Mayweather's face, yet Mayweather took the punch without blinking. De La Hoya may have narrowly captured the sixth with his clean punching and ring generalship.

De La Hoya would continue to stalk Mayweather in the seventh round and fire combinations when he had him on the ropes. Most importantly, the left jab to the shoulder would start to connect for De La Hoya. Mayweather would laugh off the punches. The center of the ring would be another rallying moment for Mayweather as he got in his combinations with his faster hands. De La Hoya would make sure to throw flurries near the ropes in the closing seconds to steal another close round. De La Hoya would land 18 of 59 to Mayweather's 17 of 31 in the seventh round. A gaping hole in De La Hoya's defense was due to both lack of head movement and also how he kept his guard wide. He kept the guard wide to improve his vision, yet those holes gave Mayweather a target. Those holes would allow Mayweather to nail him in between the gloves. This allowed Mayweather to score with a few left jabs early in the eighth round. That defensive flaw is also something that Manny Pacquiao would exploit to perfection when he faced De La Hoya in 2008.

De La Hoya would again land some clean left jabs that backed up Mayweather, this time to the northeastern ropes. Mayweather would get in powerful right hands as the fight would drift back to the center of the ring. De La Hoya looked slow and unresponsive. If Mayweather had pressed the action, he could have seriously hurt De La Hoya. It was a close round, and De La Hoya tried to steal it with another rally on the ropes. Mayweather would try to hold him, but it was futile. This was a round that could have gone either way. After eight rounds I had De La Hoya ahead by one point (4-3-1). However, the final stretch was where Roger Mayweather predicted that his nephew would take over.

The ninth round would see De La Hoya hitting a mirage, as he would flurry, but most of the shots were either blocked or slipped by Mayweather. Mayweather landed the cleaner shots and took the round. After nine rounds Mayweather out landed De La Hoya 136 to 95, despite throwing seventy-seven fewer punches. The tenth would be another Mayweather round as he took the action to the center of the ring. The left jab and straight rights would pepper De La Hoya as he tried to follow Mayweather around the ring. The momentum would completely shift to Mayweather in the final two rounds as the De La Hoya jab would be missing, and Mayweather would land his one-two combinations. De La Hoya would get a solid straight right (2:51) in the eleventh round, but it was too late to steal the round. Mayweather would look the fresher fighter in the final round as he continually beat De La Hoya to the punch. To his credit, De La Hoya didn't completely fade as in some of his bouts, like with Trinidad, Sturm, and Mosley.

In the twelfth, Mayweather would punish De La Hoya with combinations in the middle of the round. Both fighters would trade their best shots before the closing bell to end the contest. A solid right hook would land for De La Hoya but would fail to drop Mayweather. If De La Hoya had scored a late knockdown, it may have done enough to retain his title, but this wouldn't happen. Mayweather clearly won the fight down the stretch, as predicted by his trainer, Roger Mayweather. De La Hoya would land 122 of 587 and Mayweather 207 of 481. The final scorecards had a split decision. Judge Tom Kaczemarak (115–113) scored it for De La Hoya, while judges Jerry Roth (115–113) and Chuck Gampa (116–112) both had it for Mayweather. When he heard the one score for De La Hoya, we saw Mayweather mutter, "Are you serious?" Mayweather was perplexed by the split decision (as many were) and told Larry Merchant, "He threw a lot of punches, but they weren't landing. If you check the punch stats, I out punched him and outboxed. It was easy work as I told you. He was rough and tough, he suppose to fight, ten-time world champion in six weight classes, he proved himself, but he couldn't beat the best Pretty Floyd tonight." Mayweather also stated that he would retire after the fight.

De La Hoya would counter, "For some reason it was not the night of the jabs, for some reason I don't know." De La Hoya would later state he had a shoulder flare up and would then concede that he simply was past his prime and was not able to defeat someone of Mayweather's caliber. "I was done" was the explanation that De La Hoya would offer in the buildup to Mayweather-Ortiz as to why he lost to Mayweather. Mayweather was now only the fourth fighter to become a quintuple champion.

The fight would break the all-time pay-per-view record at the time with 2.4 million sales. As a result, both fighters were winners when it came to the paydays. De La Hoya made $52 million, and Mayweather made $25 million. The fight would gross over $120 million on pay-per-view revenue alone. De La Hoya certainly had to be happy that he was the only fighter in history who had at least one judge have him ahead in a final scorecard against Mayweather. De La Hoya would later help promote Mayweather bouts through Golden Boy Promotions.

Mayweather's victory over De La Hoya and the 24/7 exposure created a heightened public awareness. Mayweather's added popularity would help him get cast on ABC's *Dancing with the Stars*. He would compete with dancing partner Karina Smirnoff in the fall of 2007. Mayweather would be part of the fourth couple removed from the season. Mayweather understood he was becoming a more mainstream figure, and some people who watched the show didn't even realize he was a boxer. This was a similar experience to Black Sabbath singer and solo artist Ozzy Osbourne when people would only know him from his reality TV show.

CHAPTER 13

Stars and Stripes Battles Union Jacks

All the ingredients were on paper for an enormous blockbuster fight between Floyd Mayweather Jr. (38-0, 24 KOs) and Ricky Hatton (43-0, 31 KOs). These were two undefeated fighters; one was white and the other black, with contrasting personalities and images. Floyd Mayweather Jr. and Ricky Hatton in many ways were the caricature of the Rocky Balboa and Apollo Creed characters in the *Rocky* film. Balboa was the white guy who exceeded the natural talent given to him and came from a blue-collar working background. As Balboa would meet local friends in the bar, Hatton would shoot darts with his mates at the pub. Mayweather, as Apollo Creed, would give away and flaunt money, show off bling, and be a loquacious trash talker. The racial and personality differences worked well in promoting and selling such a fight.

When Ricky Hatton called out Mayweather after knocking out Jose Luis Castillo via a body shot on June 23, 2007, the Mayweather camp immediately accepted the challenge. Mayweather would tell advisor Leonard Ellerbe, "Make the fight f**king happen." After the Castillo bout, Hatton claimed that there was more action in the four rounds against Castillo than in an entire Mayweather bout. The bout would be scheduled for December 8, 2007, at the MGM Grand, Las Vegas, Nevada. It would simply be billed as "Undefeated."

The promotion of the fight would highlight the cultural and personality differences in order to get more interest for the fight. Mayweather didn't fully understand Ricky Hatton and would comment on 24/7, "Do you think I will train and do all those fights so I can throw darts and drink Guinness beer?" Mayweather wanted to play villain in order to build up the fight. He knew it was an opportunity to get more name recognition. Mayweather would cross the Atlantic Ocean and visit England and deliberately antagonize Hatton supporters. In reality, it was just tongue-and-cheek promotion. The conspicuous Mayweather plan was to eventually convert some of Hatton's supporters to Mayweather fans. The loyal Manchester Hatton fans would go across the Atlantic to support their local son. Hatton contrasted himself in how he treated his fans compared to Mayweather, "He doesn't talk to them. He's got five managers around everywhere he goes. I mean, what's the point of being the best fighter in the world, if everyone thinks you're a d**head?" This was contrasted to the Hatton Jack-the-lad personality. The fighter from Manchester remained approachable and enjoyed beer, darts, and having "Blue Moon" played during his ring entrance, while sporting union jacks on his trunks. Hatton, who had already fought in the states five times, fully realized that thousands of his loyal fans would once again take the trip across the Atlantic to support him.

Hatton would be fighting only a second time in the welterweight division. He had previously won the WBA welterweight title from Luis Collazo in a very close match that some felt Collazo had pulled out. Hatton did floor Collazo in the first round, but he was badly hurt in the final round against southpaw Collazo, who was not known as a heavy puncher. There was some risk involved that Hatton couldn't handle the power of a natural welterweight. Hatton would always be known for his grab-and-punch pressure style that sometimes appeared like more wrestling than boxing. However, as ugly it may have appeared to boxing purists, the fact remained that Hatton developed an effective style that resulted in an undefeated record after forty-three bouts. Hatton was excellent in neutralizing both the power and speed of his opponent by cutting off space and by using good timing.

Hatton's trainer, Billy Graham, fully expected Hatton to take Mayweather off his game by fighting him on the inside and roughing him up to neutralize his speed and boxing skills. In other words, he felt this could be a repeat of what Duran did to Leonard in their first encounter. Mayweather would come in at 147 pounds and Hatton at 145 during the weigh-in. A boisterous Hatton contingency let their presence be known during the weigh-in. On the night of the fight, part of the Hatton contingency would boo the American national anthem, which made Mayweather's choice of "Born in the USA" appropriate ring-entrance music.

Hatton's strategy was to take Mayweather off his game by doing more or less what he did to Kostya Tszyu. This was to take away space and make it an inside brawl. Hatton had the feet to cut off the ring. The question would be if he would take too many solid Mayweather counters as he attempted this plan. The first round would start well for the challenger. Hatton would land a solid right hand (1:36) and a left hook (1:38) that nearly floored Mayweather. The left hook was near the ear, which momentarily had Mayweather's equilibrium out of circuit as he stumbled and tumbled trying to get back his footing. The Hatton pressure was already making Mayweather uncomfortable. Referee Joe Cortez would give Hatton a warning for rabbit punching in the first round. Although I felt Hatton won the round, his nose was already red. The same lead left hook that got Mayweather in the first round would score again (0:39) in the second round. Mayweather would try to catch Hatton with right hands as he came barreling in, but Hatton was able to slip most of the shots—which resulted in both fighters clinching often. However, Mayweather would catch Hatton with that straight right (1:33) in the second round. Cortez would warn both fighters about dirty tactics twice in the round. It was a close round that could have gone either way, as Mayweather landed some clean shots, but Hatton was the aggressor for most of the round.

The opening minute of the third saw the same problem of excessive holding. Cortez would later receive slack for not allowing Hatton to work more during the clinches and for breaking them up too early. Mayweather would try to score a left check hook (1:05) that was slightly off the mark. That shot would be a prelude to what happened later. Mayweather would rally the last minute and cut Hatton's right eye. Mick Williamson would do an excellent job stopping the cut and allowing Hatton to continue the fight.

Mayweather was timing Hatton better as the fight progressed. He was also able to start to get off his short counter shots on the inside. The shots were becoming both more frequent and more accurate. Hatton needed to get the fight away from the center of the ring and back to the ropes. He would accomplish this for most of the fifth round, where he kept Mayweather regulated to mainly the northeastern corner ropes. Hatton would complain about Mayweather's elbows that were trying to repel him on the inside. Cortez would come to the Mayweather corner in between rounds and admonish him about those elbows. The point deduction would go to Hatton for rabbit punching, as he had Mayweather trapped around the ropes. Hatton felt it was Mayweather's fault for turning his back. The round would be a choppy and sloppy one at that, as both fighters failed to get many clean shots as they both were holding. I felt it was a 10–10 round, but with the deduction it made it 10–9 on my card. As a result, I had Mayweather ahead by one point after six.

Mayweather would commence the seventh round by retreating on his back foot from the offensive-minded Hatton. The round would be more wrestling than boxing, and it suited Hatton more. Mayweather would take control of the fight in both the eighth and ninth rounds. The combinations were finally landing with straight lefts to the body followed by hooks upstairs. Straight rights (1:01 and 2:27) in the eighth round would snap Hatton's head back violently. Hatton would withstand an onslaught on the ropes to end a round where he would receive twenty-six power shots and land only six. Mayweather would potshot Hatton with stiff left jabs in the ninth round as he moved around the ring using agile legs. "Too much skill for that mother f***er," Roger would tell Floyd before going in the tenth round.

The check hook that missed early would find the mark (1:01) in the tenth round and floor the challenger. This was a result of Hatton trying to fully load on his own left hook and being caught first. Hatton would get up on the count of eight, but his legs were not there. Despite desperately clinching to buy time, his fate was doomed. A couple more hooks on the ropes would send Hatton to the floor again, forcing Cortez to stop the contest. The total punch stats had Mayweather landing 129 of 329 and Hatton 63 of 372. Glaringly, Hatton landed only eleven jabs in the fight. He had no plan to score with the jab. If he had used a short jab to the body, it may have forced Mayweather to lower his guard.

Mayweather, who was outlandish and incendiary during the promotion, would be gracious to both Hatton and his fans. "Ricky Hatton is one tough fighter. He is still a champion in my eyes, and I'd love to see him fight again. Ricky Hatton is probably one of the toughest competitors I've faced. I hit him with some big ones, but he kept coming, and I can see why they call him the 'Hitman.'" Mayweather would explain that he wanted the knockout, as he would concede dull fights; it seems the Baldomir fight was still something he wanted to put behind him.

The final pay-per-view numbers were over 920,000, which put the Mayweather fight purse at approximately $25 million and Hatton at $10 million. Mayweather would retire from the sport immediately. With names such as Miguel Cotto and Paul Williams looming in the welterweight division, there were still hopes that Mayweather would have a short retirement and return to the ring. Mayweather would, in fact, return to a different ring.

CHAPTER 14
WrestleMania

Mayweather, who stated he was a WWF fan in his youth, would get a featured slot in WrestleMania XXVI. Mayweather would tell Larry King, "When I was a kid, I used to love to watch the WWF because, at that particular time when I was a kid, it was WWF (World Wrestling Federation) and now it is WWE (World Wrestling Entertainment)...When I watched wrestling with my grandmother, my dad used to say, 'Cut that off; wrestling is fake.'" However, Mayweather would tell King that the following incident and resulting injury with "Big Show" weren't staged, and he, in fact, broke the seven-foot wrestler's nose.

Floyd Mayweather was in the audience during a Las Vegas WWE match on February 17, 2008. The "Big Show" would come in to the arena and enter the ring. Big Show would then get out of the ring and seize an injured Rey Mysterio by the throat and take him inside the ring. Mayweather, who was ringside, would climb into the ring and challenge the Big Show. The entire Mayweather entourage would also come into the ring and separate the combatants. Big Show would get on one knee and coax Mayweather to take a free shot at him, and Mayweather would be happy to accommodate.

The WWE was officially classified as entertainment, and it was widely accepted that the feud was produced to facilitate a lucrative Big Show versus Mayweather match in the upcoming WrestleMania XXVI. Despite boxing being classified as a legitimate combat sport, recent boxing feuds and atrocious judging decisions have often made the WWE appear as the more honest form of entertainment. Vince McMahon was known as a marketing genius and understood the importance of development of characters, such as Hulk Hogan, Andre the Giant, and Randy Macho Man Savage. In Mayweather, McMahon understood he had a polarizing character that could consolidate both the WWE and boxing audiences.

The Big Show, who is seven feet and weighed in excess of 440 pounds, would be a dangerous opponent, regardless if the match was staged or not. Any miscalculation in either Mayweather's or Big Show's part could result in a serious injury. This could eliminate any possibility of Mayweather returning to the ring. Mayweather would tell CNN host Larry King that he was paid $20 million for the event. The fighter known as "Money Mayweather" brought back memories of the vintage wrestler known as "Mr. Rich Ted Diabisi" with his flashy style. Mayweather, by participating in WrestleMania XXIV, was again trying to attract a wider audience that didn't necessarily follow boxing.

The event would take place in the Citrus Bowl in Orlando, Florida, in front of a capacity audience of nearly 75,000 fans. Mayweather would wear boxing gloves to the match and would drink from a chalice provided by one of his handlers. The Big Show would eventually capture Mayweather and hoist up the canvas with one hand, but Mayweather would punch himself out of the clutch and then put a choke-hold on the Big Show. Big Show would slam Mayweather to the canvas and stomp on his left hand. There would be more stomps and maneuvers on Mayweather, who put out some excellent banshee wails that would rival any good horror-film production. After some more ruckuses, Mayweather would get the advantage by using a chair for batting practice, the aid of a kick on the family jewels, and a final right blow with brass knuckles. The accumulative punishment would lead to the Big Show getting counted out.

CHAPTER 15

Coming Back For the Throne

Perhaps by choice or by coincidence, the official announcement of Mayweather's return to the ring came at the heels of Manny Pacquiao's showdown with Ricky Hatton. Mayweather officially announced his return on May 2, 2009. Mayweather said, "When I made my decision to retire last year, I felt like it was time for me to go as I had been boxing my whole life and felt like I had done all that I could do. But after I had time to rest, enjoy life with my family and friends, I started to miss the competition and my fans. I am ready to return to boxing and give people another dose of the Mayweather experience."

Manny Pacquiao had now become the sport's pound-per-pound king—a throne that Mayweather felt he should have received by default upon his comeback. After Juan Manuel Marquez's thrilling ninth-round KO of Juan Diaz on February 28, 2009, he called out Mayweather. "I want to go up and meet Mayweather. He is a great fighter and best pound for pound. Pacquiao claims he is the best pound for pound, but he won't fight me again. I want to fight the best pound-for-pound fighter, which is Floyd Mayweather."

The scheduled fight between Mayweather and Marquez would be scheduled for July 18, 2009. However, a rib injury reported on June 14, 2009, from sparring would have the bout rescheduled to September 19, 2009. Conventional wisdom was that Marquez was a safe choice since he was perceived as a blown-up lightweight who was not going to hurt Mayweather. There would be a catchweight of 144 pounds, but Mayweather would come in at 146 and gladly pay the $600,000 penalty that was added to the $3.2 million Marquez purse. Mayweather was guaranteed $10 million, and he expected to make millions more after the pay-per-view revenue was added to his purse. HBO would again promote the event by having a 24/7 series. The highlight of the series was possibly Marquez drinking his own urine, which he claimed supplemented his training regimen.

When Marquez took the ring on the night of September 19, 2009, at the MGM Grand, it was conspicuous that his soft body didn't adjust well to the higher weight. It appeared Marquez retained a lot of water weight. At the opening bell, Mayweather used the lead left exceptionally well. Mayweather tried to jab the body. Most of Marquez's combinations were blocked or slipped as Mayweather landed his jab to the body. Mayweather would land 18 of 31 opposed to just 4 of 52 for Marquez in the first round. Marquez would continue to have problems landing his jab in the following round since Mayweather was able to take back steps and avoid the shots. An overhand right for Marquez at 1:06 in the second round would be his first major punch landed. Mayweather would laugh off the punch, as the ballooned lightweight couldn't seriously hurt him. Mayweather would answer the shot with a left hook that floored Marquez at 1:19 of the second round. Marquez would throw more haymakers that Mayweather would be able to slip. Mayweather would consistently come forward with his left shoulder high, left glove protecting his body, with right glove high to defend against the left hook.

Marquez couldn't find holes against that defense, and when opportunities would arise, they would completely close down. Marquez landed a right-hook straight-right combo at 1:55 of the fourth round but then got peppered with left jabs to make it another Mayweather round.

After four rounds, perhaps only the third round was close at all. Marquez would be bleeding from his nose already in the fifth round due to the jabs. Mayweather would exemplify the hit-and-don't-get-hit strategy at 1:28 of the sixth round by scoring with the lead right and then immediately slipping a Marquez counter left. The pull counter also worked beautifully in the sixth round. Marquez landed only 32 of 262, which gave him only a 12 percent connect rate after six rounds. Mayweather landed 113 of 190 for a 59 percent connect rate after six rounds.

Even "sí, se puede" chants in the seventh round couldn't really inspire Marquez to land anything of significance. In fact, it would be Mayweather who kept coming forward and who would stay in the pocket giving Marquez opportunities. Marquez's plan B had to be to get Mayweather on the ropes to work the body as Castillo had and to use the jab to the shoulder or body. Marquez didn't have a puncher's chance, as he didn't have the power to hurt Mayweather. A major problem for Marquez was, as a counterpuncher, he wasn't going to initiate or force the fight as Mayweather opponents such as Hatton and Castillo had.

Marquez may have nicked the eighth by landing his body shots when he had Mayweather on the ropes in the closing seconds. The eighth was possibly the only round Marquez would win. The Marquez flurry would be reversed in the ninth round, as Mayweather would start to potshot with straight rights and lefts. Marquez never clinched or closed the distance on Mayweather. He never got into his chest—something that Ricky Hatton had done well in his early rounds against Mayweather. Marquez was pockmarked with red welts on his forehead after nine rounds. Mayweather would continue the dominance in the tenth round, which was highlighted with a lead left-right combination at 2:05. Marquez would make it to the final bell, despite Mayweather trying to get the knockout in the final two rounds. The final punch stats had Marquez landing 69 of 583 for a 12 percent rate compared to 290 of 493 (59 percent) for Mayweather. I only gave Marquez the eighth and had the third a draw, which had Mayweather the winner on my card 119–109. The judges had it 119–108, 120–107, and 118–109, all for Mayweather. The only moral victory for Marquez was that he still wouldn't be knocked out in any professional fight. The bout would do 1.1 million pay-per-view buys, which would reportedly give Mayweather a total purse of $30 million. Mayweather critics would raise the issue of Mayweather failing to knock out the naturally smaller fighter. However, Marquez was never knocked out in fifty-seven professional bouts and, as a crafty veteran, knew how to survive even when hurt.

What happened after the fight would be more memorable than what happened during the fight. As Mayweather was doing an interview with HBO's Max Kellerman, he would be interrupted by Shane Mosley and Bernard Hopkins who entered the ring to call him out for a fight. Mayweather had actually called out to fight Mosley in the past, and Mosley—after defeating Fernando Vargas in 2006—was not very interested in taking that fight.

CHAPTER 16

Legacy Don't Pay Bills

Mayweather's choice of Marquez would be ridiculed in a notorious, heated exchange between the fighter and rapper R. A. the Rugged Man on October 2009 during a radio interview. The Long Island rapper would call out Mayweather not only on the choice of Marquez, but on failing to fight the top fighters in his own weight class. Mayweather would reassert his claim that he had won titles in five weight classes by moving up, and he was fighting guys naturally bigger than he was. "Legacy don't pay bills, and how can I fight p****s by winning six world titles?" an agitated Mayweather would respond. The Rugged Man was mainly correct in pointing out how "undefeated" was not necessarily an accurate barometer in a fighter's greatness. All the greats, such as Robinson, Ali, Armstrong, and Greb have losses in their column. Recently, fighters such as Joe Calzaghe, Ricardo Lopez, and Sven Otke can all boast no losses in their record. The first two mentioned are definitive Hall of Famers, yet no one believes they are greater than Robinson, Ali, or Armstrong. Undefeated fighters like Jimmy Barry and Jack McAuliffe never got the adulation that many of their defeated contemporaries received. Perhaps Rocky Marciano, due to the fact that he fought names such as Ezzard Charles, Archie Moore, Joe Walcott, and Joe Louis, got the most praise for being undefeated. In addition, Marciano often was the fighter with the smaller reach, and yet he defeated larger opponents. Nevertheless, even Marciano had his own cynics who claimed that he defeated major names that were over the hill and argued that he didn't defend his title enough to be on the elite heavyweight lists.

There is no doubt that being undefeated was an essential part of the Mayweather marketing strategy. A good portion of Mayweather's haters wanted to see him lose, which added intrigue in his matches. Moreover, Mayweather would bring more scrutiny to himself when he responded, "*I am*" when asked if he thought he was the greatest fighter of all time. The boxing media would later highly ridicule the response. Mayweather's response was reminiscent to John 8:58 when Jesus would proclaim to a dubious mob, "Before Abraham was born, I am," which was an assertion of divinity.

However, the most controversial portion of the interview was when Mayweather expressed his opinion in public that Pacquiao was taking performance-enhancement drugs. When confronted with Pacquiao's climb in weight divisions, Mayweather would claim, "The Philippines got the best enhancement drugs." His father, who had made similar statements, shared this opinion.

A few weeks after the radio interview, the new pound-per-pound king, Manny Pacquiao, defeated Miguel Cotto in a final-round stoppage. After the November 2009 bout, the audience had already made up its mind that Mayweather was Pacquiao's next logical opponent. Hearing the audience call out Mayweather certainly got back to Mayweather himself. What eventually played out would be among the most contentious negotiations in boxing history. The biggest fight in the sport (possibly since the Leonard-Hagler and Ali-Frazier fights) would bring the issue of performance-enhancement drugs front and center in the sport. Mayweather would give an interview to Adam Smith of *Sky Sports* shortly after Pacquiao defeated Cotto. He would tell *Sky Sports*, "Miguel Cotto, at one particular time, was one of the best welterweights. But him fighting Margarito took a lot out of him. He had other wars with Judah and Clottey; he's been in a lot of wars lately. So I don't think he's the same Miguel Cotto." Mayweather felt that Cotto took plenty of damage from his fight with Margarito. It was a fight where many suspected that Margarito fought with loaded gloves, as he was caught with improper hand wraps before his January 2009 bout with Shane Mosley. As for his opinion about Pacquiao's ability, Mayweather would tell *Sky Sports*, "The thing is, with Pacquiao, I don't see any versatility as a fighter with Manny Pacquiao. I see a good puncher but just one-dimensional." In the same interview, Mayweather went down the list of recent Pacquiao opponents and argued that many of them were washed up or weight drained. His opinion was that Pacquiao had defeated a De La Hoya who was weight drained against him, and Hatton was an opponent that he had knocked out before Pacquiao fought him.

The most crucial part of the interview was when he discussed the prospect of a future super fight with Pacquiao: "If the fight ever happens with me and Manny Pacquiao, and when I beat him, people are not gonna be surprised because he's been beat before. Whatever I do to Pacquiao has been done before; he's been beaten three times, and if I knock him out, I don't want the world shouting because he's been knocked out twice before. So it's nothing new." Mayweather also felt Pacquiao failed to call him out when he had a chance. "He was asked three times, 'Do you want to fight Floyd Mayweather?' 'I want to take a vacation with my family.' 'Do you want to fight Floyd Mayweather?' 'I had a tough fight with Miguel Cotto.' 'Do you want to fight Floyd Mayweather?' 'Talk to my promoter Bob Arum.' If he wants to fight Floyd Mayweather, you need to step up to the plate." Mayweather also stated that Pacquiao couldn't beat him: "absolutely not, absolutely not, easy work, easy fight." There would be formal negotiations for a March 2010 super fight between Mayweather and Pacquiao. Leonard Ellerbe and Al Haymon—along with Golden Boy Promotions—worked the Mayweather side, while Bob Arum and Top Rank—with advice from Michael Koncz—handled the Pacquiao side. As Pacquiao was running for congress in Sarangani province, a proposed date of March would be changed to May 2009. Both parities agreed on venue, weight, gloves, and purse split. Although some sources reported that Pacquiao had signed the contract, it would prove to be false.

Random blood testing would prove to be a stumbling block in getting both contracts executed. Golden Boy and Top Rank would trade press releases in the final months of 2009 explaining their position of why the fight never happened. The culmination would be a December 25, 2009, defamation lawsuit filed by Manny Pacquiao against Floyd Mayweather and Oscar De La Hoya of Golden Boy Promotions. Pacquiao's team eventually agreed to a twenty-four-day cutoff date for blood testing leading to the day of the bout. The Mayweather camp wanted a fourteen day cutoff date. The aftermath of the failed negotiations would bring open criticism to boxing for failing to make the biggest fight in the sport. MMA and UFC fans would point to this debacle as more reason why they were the top combat sport. UFC would get the biggest fights done, and unlike boxing they didn't have multiple champions per each weight class.

Various Boxing Opinions on the Failure of Mayweather-Pacquiao

James Toney would tell Fightfan.com "I grew up with Floyd Mayweather; we all grew up in the same block with Tony Tucker, Buster Mathis Jr. and the entire Mayweather family. I love Floyd, and I am glad he is doing what he is doing, but if you claim you are the best fighter in the world pound-per-pound, then fight! Don't make any excuse. If Pacquiao was on steroids, then we would have found out by now. Nevada has the strictest testing on banned substances. Pacquiao is a freak of nature like me who started at 157 and now fighting at 200. If I would wager, Pacquiao will knock out Floyd. I call them like I see them. When a guy backpedals like Floyd is like what happens to a rabbit when it has its back to a corner, it faints." (Toney would later change his opinion after watching Mayweather-Alvarez and would tell EsNewsReporting.com "it would be the same result if he fought Pacquiao due to maturity, speed, power, and ring generalship.")

Marvelous Marvin Hagler ESPN's Friday night fights:
"That is a $100 million fight, and there is nothing in the history of the sport that could make that money. It is almost like a Hagler-Leonard fight in a sense; here is a guy who wants to dictate to another person, wants to tell you what to do. I want you to take a drug test. I think Pacquiao is right. Hello, who are you? I mean, if you want to fight, then let's fight. Let's stop all this nonsense, and let's give the people what they want to see."

Michael Irvin would tell Showtime: "Stop running man. All this running is making brothers look bad. Even if you lose, it's an honorable loss. If you die, it's an honorable death"(kidding).

Kermit Cintron: "I just honestly think that he (Pacquiao) is taking something. I mean a lot of fighters who come up weight like that, forty-something pounds, and he looks ripped like nothing I seen. He looks like Bruce Lee…A lot people who go up in weight like that hold a lot of water weight, and I just believe he is taking something. He is taking something that is for sure."

Carlos Palomino would tell boxingscene.com: "I understand why they are asking questions. If this guy has nothing to hide, then why not do it? You are going to give up 30 to 40 million dollars because you don't want to take a test. I think there is a problem there." When pressed on the issue, Palomino would add: "How could a guy be at 106 at one point and now be here? We need to know if he is doing anything…I understand."

Paulie Malignaggi to The Boxing Truth: Look at what Manny is doing. He is absolutely crushing world-class killers. And here he is this little midget. He gets a broken eardrum, and yet he is walking around afterward like he was dodging spitballs. There are things (drugs?) out there that can do that. You're hiding under a rock if you can't see what I am talking about. This is a guy who was life and death with Juan Manuel Marquez at 120 pounds, and now he's got fifteen to seventeen pounds of muscle on him. Look at how short he is. He didn't get taller, did he? How can he burn eight thousand calories a day without burning himself out and have anything left in the ring?"

Juan Diaz told Houston radio's The Box:
"Man, I'll tell you, Pacquiao is on steroids. I'm just going to flat out say it. For forty million, I'll be like, 'Stick a needle in me every day if you have to.' For forty mil? C'mon now. If you're not willing to take a test for 40 mil, something's funny."

Freddie Roach: "He is a p***y (Mayweather); he is girl…man. He doesn't want to fight; he never did, never wanted the fight."

Mike Wilbon of ESPN: "He is a coward; I have been saying for months that Mayweather is scared to get in the ring with this guy. If you are afraid to lose, then that is a cowardly thing. You don't think Michael Spinks was scarred to get in the ring with Mike Tyson? He probably was, but he got in and took the shot."

Bert Sugar told Ellie Seckback of *Fanhouse*, "He is not afraid of Pacquiao. What Floyd is afraid of is losing. Here was the chance; as the price went up, the oddsmakers in Vegas favored Pacquiao 8–5, and that played on him."

CHAPTER 17
Accepting the Mosley Challenge

After the failed attempts in making the super fight with Manny Pacquiao, the obvious choice for the next opponent would be Shane Mosley. Mayweather would refute critics (who said he ducked Shane Mosley) by choosing him as his next opponent on May 1, 2010. Mosley had called out Mayweather right after the Marquez bout, and Mayweather now accepted the challenge. Mosley's last official bout was his destruction of Antonio Margarito on January 2009. This meant Mosley had a sixteen-month ring hiatus coming into the May 1, 2010, match with Mayweather. If there was any ring rust due to the hiatus, it would show itself on May 1, 2010.

Mosley was scheduled to fight Andre Berto for a (WBC, WBA) unification bout on January 30, 2010. Berto would cancel two weeks before the contest due to the emotional toll the January 12, 2010, Hatian earthquake had on him. Berto reportedly lost several relatives due to the earthquake. Due to the short notice, there wouldn't be any Berto replacement.

Both Mayweather and Mosley would agree to random drug testing for the match, which would be conducted by the US Anti-Doping Agency (USADA). Mosley had been implicated, along with Victor Conte and the Balco scandal, when he admitted to taking the "cream and clear" before fighting Oscar De La

Hoya in their 2003 rematch. In 2009, while being deposed in a defamation suit against Victor Conte, Mosley would admit that he knew that EPO was given to him. Mosley would never test positive for any PED; this would be another example of the limitations of NSAC drug testing. In one of the press conferences leading to the match, Mayweather would state in front of Mosley, "I got here with hard work and dedication—no HGH or steroids."

Mayweather would be guaranteed $22.5 million for facing Mosley, with the possibility of millions more from the pay-per-view revenues. HBO's 24/7 would feature both fighters in their everyday lives. Mayweather would differentiate between himself and Mosley. "Mosley is talented, but I am God-gifted; there is a difference between both."

Mosley would be depicted as the nice, down-to-earth Californian who signs autographs and mixes with people. Mayweather would be depicted as the flashy and arrogant fighter who would boast that he was the greatest. One memorable Mayweather quote was "Am I better than Muhammad Ali? Yep, I am better than Muhammad Ali. Am I better than Sugar Ray Robinson? Yep, I am better than Sugar Ray Robinson. I will never say there is a fighter better than me."

The USADA would also be featured on 24/7 as they did random drug tests. "There are too many fighters dying and getting brain damage, and we don't know what fighters are taking," Mayweather would explain as the reason for drug testing. Mayweather also felt that sports in general was being hypocritical by making an issue of performance-enhancement drugs in Major League Baseball (like the Barry Bonds federal indictment). He felt PEDs in boxing were more serious, as hitting a person is more dangerous than hitting a baseball.

One comical scene would have an official staying in the Mayweather house, as Mayweather couldn't provide a urine sample. The official would be at the Mayweather residence when Mayweather would berate an NBA player for missing free throws. "He gets paid too much to miss free throws." In the series Mosley would be happy to do the testing and claim that the whole Balco episode was now behind him. "They wanted to throw the stress at me for an incident that happened seven years ago," Mosley would exclaim.

Mosley was coming off possibly his greatest win since the first De La Hoya fight, but he had a long hiatus, and there might be some ring rust. However, when the match took place on May 1, 2010, at the MGM Grand, it appeared Mosley was very sharp. Mosley would use the left jab to the body and shoulder to win the first round, which was a jabbing contest. It appeared Mayweather scored a knockdown when Mosley's glove touched the canvas, but it was ruled a slip instead. Mayweather would land a solid counter overhand right, but I thought Mosley edged it out with the jab. The second round would be the most soul-searching round for Mayweather since getting hurt by Chop Chop Corley six years earlier. Mosley would land a right cross that would momentarily stun Mayweather at 0:54 of the second round. Mayweather would hold on to Mosley's right arm to buy time. Those few precious seconds of time are the difference between getting back your senses or possibly allowing yourself to get more punishment. Mosley would come in aggressively to finish off Mayweather, but the clinching and holding would help Mayweather clear his head. However, another powerful overhand right (1:46) would buckle Mayweather's knees. Mosley utilized the opening that resulted when Mayweather tried to load up with his own left, which allowed Mosley to counter above that left hand. Mayweather wouldn't go down and kept going forward. It was a testament to the Mayweather chin. Mosley tried to work Mayweather's body as he got him into the ropes. After two rounds Mosley, who shocked the world by beating Margarito, was doing the same with Mayweather. The Mayweather corner would tell their fighter "Just box that mother f***er, and don't worry about getting into exchanges."

Mayweather would come back in the third round by landing lead left hooks to Mosley's chin. The lead right would also land as Mayweather—not discouraged by the second round—was still coming forward. The patent use of the left arm to protect the body and the high right glove suggested that Mayweather was going to keep coming forward. When Mosley would fire that right, this time Maywether would take a few steps back to evade it. Mosley would land only one punch on Mayweather in the third round. It was a comeback round that Mayweather needed badly. Roger Mayweater told Floyd Jr., "Keep feinting and keep thinking." Mosley, in the next few rounds, wouldn't let his hands go, as he seem preoccupied with getting countered—or simply wasn't allowed to get off. Mayweather could stand in front of Mosley and not worry about getting hit anymore. He could step out of range, duck, or block most of Mosley's shots. Mayweather repeatedly beat Mosley to the punch as Mosley looked his age. After five rounds Mayweather had landed 66 of 162 compared to Mosley's 46 of 165. The last three rounds were clearly Mayweather rounds.

The superior Mayweather speed allowed him use a laser jab to both Mosley's body and head in the sixth round. Mayweather also utilized the punching-then-clinching tactic that Holyfied used against Mike Tyson in the first fight. A Mosley left hook to Mayweather's body would be the only connect of any substance for him. The two-punch combination of left hook followed by overhand right landed beautifully for Mayweather in the middle of the round. Mayweather would totally dominate Mosley in the last minute of the seventh round as Mosley was huffing and puffing.

The straight right hands were already taking their toll. Mosley would get a warning from Kenny Bayless for holding and throwing his shoulder at Mayweather. After the warning both fighters touched gloves, but when Mosley wanted to touch gloves for a second time, he was greeted by a Mayweather lead right. It wasn't as flagrant as many made it out to be. They are prizefighters and paid to engage with fists and not to engage with love taps. Moreover, there is plenty of time after a contest to embrace and touch gloves. There would be a war of words and trash talking after the incident. Minus a short Mosley left hook to Mayweather's body, it was another Mayweather round.

The ninth round saw Mayweather use his left jab to the body and head. He would use the shoulder roll to block punches and come back with his own right counter. The fight couldn't end fast enough for Mosley. Mayweather out landed Mosley 17–3. The camera would pan in between rounds to Shane Mosley Jr., sitting ringside; the younger Mosley couldn't make out a smile for the camera, as he was too concerned for his dad. Mayweather could have been the first to stop Mosley if he had picked up the action. Mayweather pretty much blocked or slipped by all of Mosley's blows; there was nothing of substance landing. Mosley's legs couldn't create angles to get through the Mayweather defense. Trainer Nazeem Richardson said, "I won't stand here and watch you take a beating; you have to give me something." Even when Mosley suffered losses to Forrest and Wright, his dad Jack Mosley never threatened to stop a fight. It was indicative of how badly Mosley was getting dominated. The final two rounds saw more Mosley misses, and Mayweather used his left hand the most he had in some few years. Mayweather could have easily gone on his bike to avoid any major shot, but instead he was still in the pocket with Mosley. This enabled Mosley to land two left hooks to Mayweather's body, which wasn't seen earlier. In fact, both fighters would trade on the ropes before the closing bell; nothing could change the outcome.

The final judges' scores for Mayweather were 119–109, 118–110, and 119–109. The final punch stats had Mayweather landing 208 of 477 and Mosley 92 of 452. Final pay-per-view numbers were a resounding success: 1.4 million purchases that generated over $78 million in revenue. Many felt the PPV numbers would suffer due to a backlash from the failure of the Mayweather-Pacquiao negotiations.

CHAPTER 18
Turmoil-Filled Vacation

Despite Mayweather's public persona of being narcissistic and egotistical, he has been involved in several charities. After the Mosley win, he would meet a teenage cancer patient in his gym through Make-A-Wish Foundation. The young man was fighting Hodgkin's disease, and the meeting with Mayweather showcased another side of the fighter. While many accepted that Mayweather did have a compassionate side for the plight of humanity, there were still cynics who felt Mayweather (by granting a wish in such a public way) had done it simply as a public-relations move. This was despite the fact that the teenager was okay with cameras being present. Mayweather had established the Floyd Mayweather Jr. Foundation, which helped feed the homeless and those afflicted with poverty around the community.

There wouldn't be an immediate return to the ring after the Mosley win. Mayweather decided to take the year off and went on vacation. Many boxing fans and media would find it ironic that Pacquiao was called out for wanting a vacation after the Cotto fight, but Mayweather was now on vacation instead of negotiating a fight with Pacquiao. Despite the comments about taking the year off, it was widely believed that both camps were negotiating without media knowledge, due to a gag order. It was believed that the previous negotiations were hampered due to the constant war going on with the media. In an article I wrote back in May 7, 2010, entitled "Mayweather vs. Pacquiao: It's Now or Never," my opinion was clear that if the fight was not made for the fall of 2010, that it would never be made. My opinion was that both fighters wouldn't take the risk if losing such a lucrative payday due to one losing or getting injured. Proposed bouts—like the stock market—are volatile, and unforeseeable circumstances could plummet the value of a Mayweather-Pacquiao contest. Most importantly, I felt the public eagerness would pretty much cease to exist if there was a failed second negotiation. These fighters were fighting for an undisputed pound-for-pound title, and we would expect that an egotistical desire to prove who was the best would mandate the fight. My final analysis was simple. "If two fighters couldn't compromise to make the biggest money fight in modern times, then why should the public be so enthusiastic in watching a fight that the participants failed to make?"

Unfortunately, there would be an episode that would put racism back in the forefront in boxing. Floyd Mayweather would release a racist-laced and homophobic tirade that was released on Ustream on September 2, 2010. The timing was unusual, as Pacquiao was already training to fight Antonio Margarito in November 2010. If the purpose was trash talk, it made no sense to trash a phantom opponent. In the video, Mayweather would rant:

At this particular time, I don't know if I'm gonna fight again. As of right now, I truly believe I am gonna fight again, but as of right now, I don't have the urge to get up. But when I do got the urge to get up, believe me, my Ustream and my Twitter fans will be the first to know, and when we do come back, we will kick "Poochiao" a**. So I'll let the fans know. Don't worry; we'll kick "Poochiao" a**. He's gonna take the urine and blood test. "Poochiao" got three losses and two draws and been knocked out twice. So—like I said before—once I beat him, it's going to be a cakewalk, and it's on to the next. We on vacation for about a year, then we gonna come right back and cook that little yellow chump. So the fans ain't gotta worry about me fighting the midget. Once I kick the midget a**, I don't want y'all to start jumping on my d*ck. So y'all better get on the bandwagon right now. Because once I stomp the midget, I am going to make that motherf** make me a sushi roll and cook me some rice. He better make me a shrimp tempura cut roll. You know how it is; we gonna cook that motherf** with some cats and dogs. In another excerpt Mayweather would state,

"Three losses, two draws…this is America we are built on winning… step your game up f****t."

There was plenty of outrage and demand for all sponsors to cease any affiliation with Mayweather. There would be many who felt that if Pacquiao would engage in racial or stereotypical comments about African Americans that he would lose sponsors as Nike. Pacquiao wouldn't return any trash talk in response. However, many Pacquiao fans and Mayweather detractors would take to the blogosphere and show images of the Mayweather family as gorillas, baboons, and watermelon depictions reminiscent of Jack Johnson before he fought James Jeffries. Pictures of Floyd Mayweather were posted with the KFC logo "We do chicken right." The usual fried chicken and watermelon stereotypes associated with black people were shown with Mayweather's face. There were also pictures of gorillas morphed into both Roger and Floyd Mayweather's face. One picture had a baboon with its mouth open, which was juxtaposed with a picture of Floyd Mayweather's face used in prominent boxing sites; they loved the friction created since it increased hits and advertising revenue. Trolling may not be politically correct, but it does help create schism and great interest.

The public outrage prompted Mayweather to immediately apologize in another Ustream video. This time Mayweather would appear with sunglasses and was joined by two Asian women in a remorseful attempt. In the video Mayweather would assert:

> I do want to apologize for what happened the other night. I want to apologize to everybody that felt it was a racist comment that came from me. I don't have a racist bone in my body, you know. I love everybody. Some of my guys are Muslims. Some of my guys are Jews, Puerto Ricans, Dominicans, Mexicans, Whites, it doesn't matter. There is nothing but love in my heart, you know what I'm saying. The only thing I want to say is, anybody who was offended by what I said the other day, I apologize as a man. I apologize. Forgive me for saying what I said. I was just having fun. I didn't really mean it, nothing in a bad way.

Mayweather would also use the video to send condolences to his former promoter Bob Arum who had recently lost his son due to a tragic hiking accident on Storm Mountain in Washington State. Although some accepted the Mayweather apology, there were many who felt the apology was not sincere, as he didn't specifically apologize to Manny Pacquiao who got the brunt of the hate. There were others who felt it was simply trash talking a la Ali-Frazier to build up a possible super fight with Pacquiao in 2011. Those who felt Mayweather was ducking Pacquiao proposed the theory that the whole incident was a deliberate attempt to distract Pacquiao in his training for the Margarito fight. Their belief was that Mayweather wanted Pacquiao to lose to Margarito so he could use the loss as an excuse to avoid him.

A few days after the entire Ustream incident, there would be a criminal complaint filed against Mayweather. Mayweather would get arrested for alleged domestic battery and felony charges due to an encounter with Josie Harris, the mother of three of his kids, on September 10, 2010. Per the complaint, it was alleged that he hit Harris while the kids were in the house. Harris, the complainant, alleged that she was pulled by the hair and was thrown on the ground and then punched in the head. Rapper 50 Cent, who was a close Mayweather friend, would fire back on Twitter regarding the allegations. "She's claiming he hit her but has no bruises. Floyd went to see his kids last night; if a fighter of Floyd's caliber hits u, u would b bruised."

Mayweather was accused of taking Harris's iPhone away, which explained the grand larceny charge. The alleged motive was that Mayweather went into a jealous rage as Harris exchanged texts with an NBA player that she was currently dating. Mayweather would be held at the Clark County jail on $3,000 bail. Per the complaint, Mayweather's son Koraun had alerted a security guard that his mother was getting assaulted. Years later, Josie Harris would tell *USA Today* that she felt that her son Koraun helped save her from serious injury. In the same interview, she claims that there are both hospital records and pictures that do corroborate the authenticity of her allegation.

The charges and arrest would get added scrutiny from Mayweather detractors, who would label him a "wife beater" who hit women and ducked

Pacquiao. Mayweather would settle the charges on December 21, 2011, by pleading guilty to misdemeanor battery, domestic violence, and harassment charges. He was sentenced to six months in Clark County jail, but three months of the sentence was suspended as long he complied with the rest of the conditional discharge. He was ordered to surrender to officials on January 6, 2012. Mayweather advisor Leonard Ellerbe would say, "Floyd made the best decision for his family."

CHAPTER 19

Vicious Ortiz

Mayweather's official hiatus from the ring would end on June 7, 2011, when he announced that he was returning to the ring to face Victor Ortiz the new WBC welterweight champion. Victor Ortiz was a guy who was pretty much buried by the media after his loss to Marcos Maidana. Many thought that he lacked fortitude and mental toughness after he quit in the sixth round of the Maidana fight. Ortiz would start to win again and had a barn-burner win over previously unbeaten Andre Berto that made him the WBC welterweight champion. Pacquiao was already scheduled to fight Marquez for a third time. As a result, there was no need to worry about an act three of the Mayweather-Pacquiao soap opera.

Mayweather vowed on HBO's *Face Off*, "I will not run from Ortiz, so there is nothing to worry about." Ortiz had dropped Berto twice, and not everyone was convinced that Mayweather would stay in the pocket. However, the fact remains that Mayweather was the best defensive fighter in the sport—fighting inside the pocket—since the vintage days of Pernell Whitaker.

The promotion of the fight would be known as "Star Power" since guys like Canelo Alvarez would be featured. On HBO's 24/7 a heated exchange between Mayweather and his father would be showcased. A small disagreement would escalate to a full-blown shouting match inside the Mayweather Gym. There were some who felt it was a staged stunt, consistent with the modern culture of reality TV. However, it was very revealing when Mayweather told his father, "We are undefeated and plan in staying undefeated…Get out of our way." The younger Mayweather, who was now his own man, didn't want a controlling father to dictate the way he trained or managed his boxing career. Father-and-son relationships sometimes run through the same problem in boxing when the dad is the trainer. The paternal psychological dominance that a father has over his son creates friction, and the son has the urge of independence. This contributed to Roy Jones's and Shane Mosley's decision to replace their dad as trainer. Joe Calzaghe was able to do a balancing act with his father, Enzo, and retired undefeated.

Some were taken aback by the vitriolic nature of the exchange between the Mayweathers. Many wondered how a son could demean a father by calling him a s**t fighter, while inheriting his boxing skills had made him a multiple champion. For father and son, it was just another episode in a love-and-hate relationship that went from estrangement to reconciliation. Mayweather would end the 24/7 episode by proclaiming that "Roger [his uncle] is the one who made the Mayweather name." In an interview with Bob Costas on *Costas Tonight*, Mayweather would claim that Floyd Sr. was jealous of both his son and of his brother, Roger. "I am everything in the sport of boxing he wasn't," Mayweather would tell Costas. Mayweather would also point to Roger's having becoming a world champion and having an "unbreakable" bond with his son as another source of jealousy. "By now he expected me to take a loss without him, and I have been successful with my uncle Roger. He was always jealous of his brother since he became a world champion, unlike himself." The whole incident with his dad wouldn't be a major distraction in preparation for his bout with Victor Ortiz. Mayweather was accustomed to dealing with numerous distractions in preparation of previous bouts. On September 17, 2011, there was only one job and that was to beat Ortiz. Mayweather was guaranteed $25 million and Ortiz $2 million, and both purses would go higher—contingent upon the final pay-per-view sales.

De La Hoya felt that—unlike himself—Ortiz was in his prime to fight Mayweather and would win the bout. At the weigh-in Mayweather would grab Ortiz by the throat, which was a clear sign that he had all the psychological edge coming into the contest. There wouldn't be many fireworks in the first round of Mayweather-Ortiz. Both fighters would be calculative in trying to get off with their lead rights as they pawned with their left. Mayweather would land a decent straight right (1:09) that Ortiz took well. As long as there was a technical match in the middle of the ring, Ortiz had no chance. Ortiz had to get the match toward the ropes and punish Mayweather's rib cage and body as Castillo had. There would be several wild swings that got nothing but air from Ortiz and resulted in him connecting 5 out of 42 of his punches, compared to Mayweather's 9 of 41. Yet his aggressive style did give him the first round on the Jerry Roth scorecard.

Ortiz fared better in the second round where he was able to lead with his left and get Mayweather near the northwestern corner ropes. Ortiz would also connect at 1:12 with an inside right hook. Mayweather wouldn't take a backward step and kept marching forward and landed his best straight right (1:40) up to that point. Ortiz would respond with a looping overhand right as he again got Mayweather into the northwestern corner ropes, as both were tied up inside. Joe Cortez wouldn't allow for much inside fighting, and he would break up the fighters immediately. There could have been a few more seconds allotted to see if they could separate on their own. This would follow up the criticism from the Mayweather-Hatton fight where Cortez was criticized for breaking up the fighters too fast. A referee like Steve Smogger would allow much more time for fighters to fight inside. However, this wouldn't be a factor in this contest. Ortiz may have won the second round by getting in a decent left hook to Mayweather's chin and a straight left to the body. Interestingly, all three judges had the second round for Mayweather. Ortiz, in the third round, tried to implement the strategy of using his lead to force Mayweather into the ropes again. Mayweather would instead turn the tables by coming forward and forcing Ortiz to fight on his back foot, which made him uncomfortable. A powerful Mayweather counter right in the middle of the round again demonstrated that Ortiz couldn't stay in the center of the ring. Ortiz would eat a few more of those right hands before the round ended.

Things turned bleak for Ortiz in the opening moments of the fourth round. Mayweather started to land combinations instead of one punch at a time in the middle of the ring. As Mayweather teed off on Ortiz, it would be important for Ortiz to answer back in his moment of truth. Ortiz would do that at 1:05 of the fourth round when he landed a right hook, and then followed it up with a flurry of partially connected blows on Mayweather's armadillo defense. In the closing twenty seconds of the round, Ortiz would land several clean shots while Mayweather backpedaled to the northeastern corner ropes. Then the inexplicable would happen when Ortiz head-butted Mayweather—possibly in frustration or overzealousness. Referee Joe Cortez would immediately separate the fighters and give Ortiz a warning with a point deduction. Ortiz would touch gloves with Mayweather while embracing and kissing him on the cheek. This was perplexing, as Mayweather actually had his hand on Ortiz's throat at the weigh-in. To add insult to injury, Ortiz would touch gloves again as Cortez held Ortiz while giving out the deduction instruction to the judges. When the action resumed, Ortiz tried to apologize a third time, and Mayweather responded with a half-hearted embrace followed with a left hook and straight right. Ortiz would crumple to the canvas and not be able to beat the count.

Ortiz's lack of perception and ring instincts would be his worst enemy. It was not the most sportsmanlike act, but the Ortiz head-butt was not very sportsmanlike either. The fact that Ortiz apologized for a third time was excessive; the touching of gloves once would suffice. Moreover, looking at the Mayweather-Gatti fight alone should have been ample warning for Ortiz. The final punch stats had Mayweather landing 73 of 208 and Ortiz 26 of 148. "I got hit with a dirty shot, and it's protect yourself at all times," Mayweather would emphatically tell Larry Merchant. Than Mayweather would go after Merchant, as he felt that Merchant never gave him proper due. "You never give me a fair shake. HBO needs to fire your ass." Merchant responded by telling Mayweather "If I was fifty years younger, I would kick your ass." The eighty-two-year-old former Marine was not always a man of just words. Merchant once took down a man who interrupted his interview with boxer Daniel Zaragoza. Despite the disappointment of a four-round controversial end, the match was a success. Mayweather-Ortiz had over 1.25 million pay-per-view purchases, which generated over $78 million in revenue.

CHAPTER 20
Miguel Cotto

Mayweather, in a home video released on YouTube, would emphatically state why he didn't want the bout with Pacquiao. The performance-enhancement drug controversy would again be raised. In a video by Josh Slagter, Mayweather responds to the Pacquiao questions: "Where was Manny Pacquiao in 1996? Where was he in '97? Where was he in '98 and all these years?" When Mayweather is told that he was much lighter at the 1996 Olympic, he responds:

> It took me years to get here...If you go back and look at the pictures, first is head is small...and then, all of a sudden, is head just grew. Come on, man, this is basic common sense. This man—one went from a seven and one-fourth to a eight—how you are going to tell me that is all natural? Stop this! I am going up in weight, but I am not just walking through no damn fighters. This guy is 106, all now of a sudden, he just walks through Cotto? Cotto can't knock down Mosley, but he can? Guess what? Guess what? This is how this world is, man. You got writers saying Floyd is scared. No, Floyd cares about his family; Floyd is smart. At the end of the day, Floyd is smart...My health is important...My health is more important than money. If they say, "Floyd you are going to live a healthy life as you is right now or you going to walk with a limp or you have to walk bent over, but you are going to have a lot of money," then I tell them, "You can take it all back...I am a rich, scared coward."

Mayweather made it clear that he was not going to risk his health against a fighter he felt was doping. That should have stomped any hopes that the bout with Pacquiao would ever happen. Argentine fighter Sergio Martinez, at 154 pounds, could have been an excellent opponent for either Mayweather or Pacquiao. There was also a younger Argentine fighter named Lucas Matthysse who was also a suitable opponent for both combatants. He was an excellent opponent due to his power, durability, and success against southpaws.

The next Mayweather opponent would be Miguel Cotto. It was a prospect that became more realistic after Cotto had become a free agent after an exodus from Top Rank. The third negotiation for a super bout between Mayweather and Pacquiao would end immediately. Mayweather himself called Manny Pacquiao and offered $40 million with half of it wired within seventy-two hours. The Pacquiao camp would reject the offer, as Pacquiao was guaranteed no portion of the PPV revenue. It is estimated that the PPV alone could bring in excess of $150 million. There was no way that any competent businessperson would accept such an offer. The counteroffer was either a 50–50 split or a 45–45 split, with the remaining 10 percent going to the winner.

The next viable choice for Mayweather was Miguel Cotto (37-2, 30 KOs). Cotto himself tried to get a rematch with Pacquiao, but that would fail due to differences on a catchweight. Cotto wanted to fight Pacquiao at the junior middleweight limit of 154.

Mayweather would not need to worry about prison until after fighting Cotto. The sentence would be suspended until June 1, which was after the scheduled Cotto match on May 5. It was expected that Mayweather would serve fifty-seven days, since he was given credit for three days. There would be an additional thirty days knocked off for good behavior. Many wondered how well Mayweather—known for his lavish lifestyle—would cope with prison life. However, many failed to recognize that Mayweather's early life had prepared him to live without some of the luxuries. In a teleconference before the Cotto fight, he would tell the media, "My thing is, I try to turn anything negative into something positive. That's what I do every day when I see my family, when I see my team, I see my fans come to support me every day; it's an emotional builder for me. So even, like, when I go away, you know, the only thing it can do is make me mentally strong, you know, grow mentally strong as a person."

Part of the promotional angle for Mayweather-Cotto was that there wouldn't be a catchweight. Mayweather, on HBO's *Face Off*, would tell Max Kellerman, "I see Cotto as an undefeated fighter. Margarito cheated against him, and Pacquiao had him weight drained by putting a catchweight." Cotto's stock value had increased after defeating Margarito in a rematch that took place December 2011. I covered the fight in person for my website, and was impressed with Cotto's performance. He fought with enraged discipline. His new trainer, Luis Diaz, had helped him become a more complete fighter. Two major improvements were his balance and defense. Cotto was able to fire effectively while maintaining proper footing and was able to slip punches better. However, I was not under any illusion that Cotto could successfully compete with Mayweather. I felt that Mayweather's lightning reflexes and blurring lead shots would be too much for Cotto. Although Cotto was younger, he had taken more punishment in his career than Mayweather had. After all, this was the same guy who Mayweather felt was past his prime when he fought Pacquiao due to his "ring wars."

In order for Mayweather-Cotto to have taken place, Cotto had to exit Top Rank. This was anticipated, as Cotto would become a free agent mainly because he wanted a lucrative unification match with Saul Alvarez who held the WBC junior middleweight title. If Cotto stayed with Top Rank, there was little chance in getting Mayweather or Alvarez due to the turbulent relationship between Golden Boy and Top Rank. Alvarez was still progressing, and it was expected that Golden Boy would try to "milk" the young phenom before putting him in the ring with a dangerous opponent. This possibly explained why Alvarez would fight a forty-one-year-old Mosley next, who was 0-2-1 in his last three professional bouts.

The negotiated contract between Mayweather and Cotto was a 65-35 purse in favor of Mayweather. In fact, Mayweather would be guaranteed $32 million. That amount was expected to be much higher after both PPV and movie-theater revenues were tabulated.

The promotion leading to Mayweather-Cotto was much more cordial than usual. There was a degree of respect between the fighters leading up to the May 5, 2012, match.

The actual fight would be a bit more intriguing than probably expected. Mayweather would easily win the first round with his left hand as it scored straight and as a laser jab. Cotto couldn't land anything clean and would often be tied up in clinches trying to break free. Cotto's lack of head movement would again make the Mayweather jab the weapon of choice in the second round. Cotto would pick Mayweather (0:36) off the canvas, but not throw him down as he had Clottey. Mayweather would land two fierce overhand rights (1:00) in succession. Cotto would get Mayweather with his back on the northeastern ropes and would get in some decent shots to make it a more interesting.

Cotto would add a deuce of left hook body shots (0:43) only to be countered by a vicious Mayweather combination upstairs in the third. The third round would be closer, as Cotto increased his work rate, but most of the shots were blocked, and Maywether landed the cleaner blows. The first three rounds were all Mayweather. However, Cotto did work the body, and a stiff jab bloodied Mayweather's nose. It was the most bloodied Mayweather had been in nearly a decade.

Mayweather would take full control in the fourth round with his lead right that was landed both more accurately and solidly. If those had been eight-ounce gloves instead of ten, it is possible that Cotto may have gone down as in the Pacquiao fight.

The fifth saw the best action in the first half of the fight. As both fighters fought in close quarters, Cotto would land a left hook (2:24) flush yet not make Mayweather flinch. Mayweather would rally in the final seconds with his lead right. The fifth may have been the first Cotto round. Cotto would win the sixth round more decisively with his stiff left jab. It was the same jab that had De La Hoya ahead after eight rounds in two of the three scorecards in his bout with Mayweather in May 2007.

The seventh round would be hanging in the balance until Mayweather would take control of it in the final minute of the round. The laser overhand rights would still make Cotto's body move, even if they were partially blocked. Most importantly, Mayweather would not be pressed against the ropes as he moved side to side. This would change in the eighth round when Cotto's sheer determination would force a phone-booth inside brawl going from pillar to post on the ropes. Cotto would receive some snapping uppercuts, but Cotto would still work the body and get to Mayweather's chin. Mayweather would shake his head and sneer at Cotto to make the point that he never hurt him. It could have been the third round scored for Cotto, allowing him a chance to win in the cards if he swept the final four rounds.

The pendulum would swing back to Mayweather via short inside uppercuts, as he felt a sense of urgency. Cotto would make Mayweather miss with excellent slipping ability; however, he didn't connect enough to win both the ninth and tenth rounds. Cotto would win the eleventh mainly by default as Mayweather would be springing on his legs while momentarily throwing the left jab, but Cotto was the aggressor, and even if they were partial connects, it appeared that he wanted the round more. The center of the ring would be the key to Mayweather's victory in the final round, as he would land combinations of overhand right followed by a left uppercut on two separate occasions. The left uppercut (1:53) would be possibly the most effective punch in the entire bout as it momentarily wobbled Cotto, even with Grant gloves. The icing on the cake for Mayweather was another three-punch combination in the center of the ring. This would take away the suspense of any upset.

Mayweather would win by the judges' scores of 117–111, 117–111, and 118–110. I had it 117–112 (8-3-1) for Mayweather. The final punch stats had Mayweather landing 179 of 687 and Cotto landing 105 of 506. When the final PPV numbers were released, they revealed impressive numbers. The Mayweather-Cotto contest yielded 1.5 million purchases and grossed $94 million. (This was despite the increase of illegal streaming and any backlash from the failed Pacquiao negotiations.) Cotto was easily the top-grossing Puerto Rican fighter since Felix Trinidad which helped sales.

CHAPTER 21
Prison

Mayweather would officially start his prison sentence on June 1, 2012. He was sentenced to ninety days in jail and given credit for three days served. There would also be court-ordered counseling sessions and community service. Mayweather would do the community service on behalf of Habitat for Humanity, the Las Vegas Rescue Mission, and Three Square Food Bank. The Clark County Detention Center was light years away from the lavish lifestyle Mayweather had enjoyed.

A man who lived in a twelve-thousand-square-foot house was now going to be reduced to a cell that was less than ninety-eight square feet. To make matters worse, Mayweather was going to be locked in for twenty-three hours a day. For both Mayweather's protection and the protection of other inmates, he was also going to be isolated from the prison population. How would Mayweather cope with prison life? As Mayweather was accustomed to finicky tastes, even when it came to the simplest things, it didn't start very well. Mayweather had a difficult adjustment to prison food and water. After serving only twelve days, Mayweather attorney Richard Wright made an emergency motion to have Mayweather's sentence amended. Mayweather doctor Robert Voy had provided an affidavit in support of the motion, claiming that the adverse prison conditions could threaten the fighter's career. The motion requested that Mayweather serve the remainder of his sentence under house arrest or three days each week in jail. Judge Melissa Saragosa would deny the motion. The judge determined, "The Court finds the alleged dehydration of the defendant to be self-induced as water is made available to him twenty-four hours a day. The Court further finds the estimated intake of only eight hundred calories per day is also self-induced as defendant chooses not to eat the food provided. The court finds that while the physical training areas and times provided to the defendant may not be consistent with his prior regimen, he is indeed provided sufficient space and time for physical activity if he so chooses."

Prison officials would counter that there was plenty of space in the cell to do push-ups and sit-ups. John Donahue of the Las Vegas Metro Police would also discredit the idea that Mayweather was not provided a proper diet by stating, "The nutrition part is maintained by the American Correctional Association (ACA) standards, which we're accredited by. We're required to give him a minimum of 2,800 calories a day, which he is getting. He is choosing not to eat all his food. He's picking and choosing between cookies and some other snacks that he has available to him. He's not eating the food that's being given to him."

Mayweather detractors saw the entire drama as another example of a spoiled athlete. They pointed to the fact that other prisoners had to live under similar or even harsher circumstances and didn't complain. In addition, Mayweather had faced multiple felony counts with a maximum of thirty-four years in prison, and he was sentenced to three months as part of his plea agreement. However, the fact that Mayweather was segregated from the prison population meant that he was with some of the most heinous death-row inmates. One of those segregated prisoners included an axe murderer who was in the same cellblock as Mayweather.

Mayweather would later tell Stephen Smith of ESPN, "I got through the rough situation because there was a story. It was crazy what my counselor told me about these hostages. It was like eight hostages in boxes the size of coffins. It was one individual guy who made friends with roaches. He was inside that box for over a year. I said to myself, if he could survive and not go crazy, and make friends with roaches, then I can survive in this hole."

Mayweather would miss the simple things in life such as trees and celebrating his daughter's birthday. Although he missed fiancée Shantel Jackon's birthday party, he was still able to send her diamonds. Despite the initial difficulty of assimilating to prison life, Mayweather would occupy his time by doing 1,500 push-ups a day and reading the hundreds of letters of support from fans that he received. Mayweather was also allowed two magazines or books in his cell. The question remained, would Mayweather come out mentally stronger or worse when he returned to the ring?

CHAPTER 22

Ghost Busting

Robert Guerrero defeated Andre Berto on November 24, 2012, to successfully defend his WBC welterweight interim title. Floyd Mayweather Jr. had won the regular WBC welterweight title when he defeated Victor Ortiz. This made Guerrero, who had called out Mayweather, a possible Mayweather candidate for a Cinco de Mayo bout (due to his Mexican heritage). Mayweather also had the WBA junior middleweight title after he defeated Miguel Cotto. He could have stayed at 154 pounds and tried to unify that division with fighters such as Saul Alvarez or Austin Trout. An Alvarez bout would be something that Golden Boy Promotions would want to delay for a few more bouts as they built up the young Alvarez's popularity.

Mayweather would have two major changes when he officially signed to face Robert Guerrero for a May 4, 2013, bout. He would exit HBO and sign a six-fight deal with Showtime. The deal guaranteed Mayweather $32 million for Robert Guerrero, while the Mexican American was guaranteed $3 million. The entire deal with Showtime, which included the parent CBS company, was reported to be as high as $200 million. CBS (now the number-one network in the United States) could also help promote Mayweather. Mayweather, who had over four million followers on Twitter, would be ranked number one again on the *Sports Illustrated* "Fortunate 50" top-paid athlete list for 2012 with a projected $90 million earning. What was most remarkable was that he did that with no major endorsement listed as part of the earnings. Second on the list was Lebron James who made $56 million, but $39 million of that was from endorsements.

Mayweather's other major change—besides switching networks—was that he also switched trainers. Mayweather would return to training camp with Floyd Mayweather Sr. as his trainer. As Roger Mayweather battled diabetes, the return of Mayweather Sr. in the corner would be an added help due to Roger's health issues. Mayweather would state, "There are certain things my father can see that maybe Roger can't. When you have diabetes, your vision gets bad. I can't afford for somebody's vision to be bad in a big fight like this." Showtime would have total-access episodes, which highlighted Guerrero's wife's battle with leukemia and the fighter's faith in God through the tough ordeal. In promotion of the fight, Guerrero would tell Mayweather, "You worship your money; money is your god." The remark seemed to take Mayweather off guard because he felt God had favored him to win all his bouts. Guerrero would predict: "Floyd was talking about this and that, and I'm going to be the guy to humble him. When you boast about everything, lift yourself so high, put yourself on a pedestal, the Lord will knock you of that pedestal. He will humble you in a way that's unbelievable. He will really pierce your heart, and I know the Lord's using me to do that."

In the final press conference on May 1, 2012, Ruben Guerrero (Robert's dad) would nearly brawl with Floyd Mayweather Sr. when he threw the "woman beater" tag on Mayweather. "I am...I am what I am, and I'm the real deal. And I don't talk sh**. I back it up. I back it up, baby! We're gonna beat up that woman beater—the one that beat up his wife, man...his wife in front of his kids! You guys like that shit? You like this guy? Woman beater! He must have learned that from his dad! Woman beater, baby! We're gonna beat that woman beater! See how he's gonna like it. He's gonna get it from a real man!"

Mayweather wouldn't allow the taunts to bother him, and he stayed sitting down, oblivious to what Ruben Guerrero stated. This possibly showed a more mature and disciplined side of Mayweather, coming out of prison. Mayweather was going to let his fists do the talking. Perhaps Ruben was trying to get under Mayweather's skin so he would brawl with Guerrero instead of box him. The promotion would juxtapose the different images of the fighters. Guerrero was painted as the caring husband who vacated his world title as his wife, Casey, battled cancer. Fortunately, Guerrero's wife defeated leukemia with a new bone marrow transplant that followed three lapses. Mayweather would stir some controversy when he felt that Guerrero's wife's story was getting overcooked on *Full Access*. "I think trying to gain fans by having a sympathy story every week…I don't think that's a good thing, but I'm glad that his wife was able to beat the leukemia. I don't feel nobody should go through a situation like that, but we all go through certain things. Our mothers, our fathers, our loved ones go through certain things. I just feel like…just to gain fans, you are using your wife's story; you are using a sympathy story," Mayweather would claim.

On the night of May 4, 2013, Robert Guerrero entered the arena with a black T-shirt with the inscription "God is Great" and would wear red trunks with Acts 2:38 written on the back in which the apostle Peter stated, "Repent and be baptized, every one of you, in the name of Jesus Christ for the forgiveness of your sins. And you will receive the gift of the Holy Spirit."

Mayweather, in contrast, had a TMT (The Money Team) shirt with matching baseball cap. Mayweather controlled the first round with his lead right hand. Guerrero did get in one solid body shot after he eluded a Mayweather lead right. Mayweather would also display that he still retained mongoose reflexes by slipping punches. In the second round, Guerrero tried to establish a jab on Mayweather's body, but Mayweather blocked the shots. Mayweather was able to also slip a few wild Guerrero lefts by using his legs to get out of danger. Both fighters pawned with their jab, but nothing of substance would land. A few lead rights would score for Mayweather giving him the lackluster round. The bout was becoming a technical bout as there was space between the fighters, and the action was at the center of the ring. Mayweather simply used his lead right then immediately moved out of the way to avoid counters. When needed, Mayweather would clinch with a bear hug. The bout featured some of the best Mayweather lateral movement in recent times. In addition, Mayweather's head movement, reflexes, and slipping ability made the Guerrero jab null and void. A lead right 0:47 into the fourth round had Guerrero's head snap all the way back. Unless Guerrero went to a plan B, he was going to get routed. Mayweather's constant movement would prevent him from getting trapped on the ropes.

The fifth was possibly the best Guerrero round up to that point as he was able to do some minor damage on the southeastern corner ropes and landed his best straight left in the middle of the round. Guerrero would continue to show improvement in the sixth, as the distance was cut allowing Guerrero to land a few hooks to the body. When both fighters clinched, Guerrero would keep his left hand free and hit Mayweather's body. The seventh was at times more of a wrestling match than boxing. Referee Robert Byrd had difficulty separating the fighters due to the intensity of the clinches. There were no major connects, and the round could have been scored a draw by default.

In the eighth, Mayweather would go back to using his legs to create distance while pawning his left jab and following it with rights to Guerrero's body. The lead right was starting to become target practice for Mayweather as he kept his arms low while relying on sonic reflexes to avoid the Guerrero shots. A right cross (2:38) in the eighth would move Guerrero's upper body. To complicate matters Guerrero was cut and had swelling on both eyes that impaired his vision. Mayweather would tee off on those eyes in the next two rounds.

To his credit, Guerrero wouldn't quit and kept coming forward in the eleventh round. However, he would still pay, with Mayweather landing straight rights. There would be no major fireworks in the final round as Mayweather would get on his toes and tie up Guerrero when the distance was closed. Guerrero may have charitably been given the final round as he was the aggressor and initiated most of the action. Despite being outclassed Guerrero would raise his arm after the bout. Perhaps he was glad to have lasted the full twelve rounds and to collect the best payday for his career. All three judges scored it 117-111 for Mayweather. Although I scored the bout 117–112 (8-3-1) for Mayweather, the match was not as close as the score suggested. Cotto may have won only a few rounds, but the rounds he won were more decisive, and he did bloody Mayweather's nose. The final pay-per-view numbers for Mayweather-Guerrero were disputed. Showtime claimed the bout did over a million buys. However, several boxing sources and websites claimed the real number was closer to 870,000.

CHAPTER 23
Canelo

Saul Canelo Alvarez a freckled-faced, red-haired Mexican had proven himself to be a major network attraction. Many believed that this son of an ice-cream parlor owner was destined to be the future cash cow of the sport. Alvarez had smashed HBO "After Dark" rating records, and Golden Boy Promotions meticulously promoted, molded, and mentored Alvarez to climb the throne of superstardom. Golden Boy was careful in selecting his opponents to make sure his undefeated record would remain unblemished until he was put in a mega fight. Alvarez was nicknamed "Canelo," meaning "cinnamon" in Spanish. Due to his light complexion, Alvarez would often get picked on by other kids. As a kid Alvarez had to learn to fight in order to get respect from bullies. Like Danny "Red" Lopez, Canelo was a fighter of Mexican blood that was redheaded. Lopez was a former featherweight champion who was notorious for generating great power from a tall, skinny frame (like Thomas Hearns). The major difference between Lopez and Alvarez was that although Lopez had some Mexican blood, he mainly promoted himself and was identified as Native American. Lopez lived in a Ute Native American reservation in Utah, and his most popular picture featured him sporting a Native American headdress on the cover of *Sports Illustrated*. When Lopez would lose his featherweight title to Salvador Sanchez, he would give Sanchez a headdress as a gift.

BOXING'S QUINTUPLE CHAMPIONS

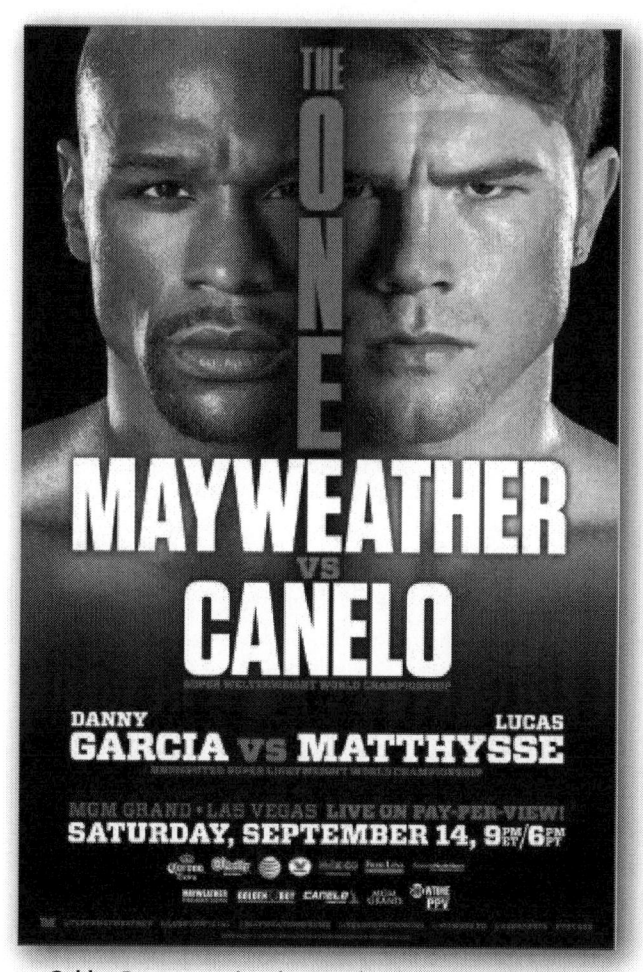

Golden Boy promotional poster for the Mayweather and Alvarez fight, which was billed as the "one."

Alvarez would start as an amateur at an early age, and by the age of nineteen, he had thirty-two professional wins. Canelo would win his first title against Matthew Hatton for the vacant WBC light middleweight title. The fact that Alvarez won a vacant title had many cynics feeling that he was simply a "paper champion" created by the WBC that wanted another Mexican phenom to hold a world title. This happened around the same time as Julio Cesar Chavez Jr. was given a shot at a fight for a world title against Sebastian Zbik after the WBC had stripped Sergio Martinez for not fighting the German fighter. Canelo

237

would gradually prove naysayers wrong by defeating former champions such as Baldomir, Cintron, Mosley, and Austin Trout.

Alvarez's biggest win was Austin Trout. Although I felt the match was a draw, Canelo did showcase how far he had progressed as a fighter. Alvarez had developed into a clever fighter with his counterpunching and slipping ability, coupled with his solid power. The bout with Trout was held in the San Antonio Alamodome in front of nearly forty thousand spectators. The audience was a clear indicator that Alvarez was the largest Mexican American attraction in the sport since the heyday of guys like De La Hoya and Chavez Sr.

Although it initially appeared that Mayweather wasn't interested in fighting Canelo, the fact remained that both sides were aggressively trying to get a deal done. Ultimately, both sides agreed to a September 14, 2013, date with a 152-pound catchweight. Critics who recollected Mayweather claiming that Miguel Cotto was undefeated since Margarito had "cheated" and fought Pacquiao in a "catchweight" were now calling Mayweather a hypocrite. Mayweather advisor Leonard Ellerbe would respond by stating that Canelo's "idiot manager" (Chepo Reynoses) was the one foolish enough to offer the catchweight, and they simply took advantage of it. Canelo would call the allegation a lie and state to the media, through his translator, "They asked me to come to 147, to fight at welterweight. I told them, 'No way, those days are over for me.' Then they said, 'Let's do the fight at 150.' I said I couldn't do that, and then 151, and finally we agreed on 152." The deal guaranteed Mayweather $41.5 million and Alvarez $12 million, with both expected to make more from the pay-per-view revenues. The tickets would go on sale on June 25, 2013, and would sell out within twenty-four hours. The record-setting MGM Grand live gate would be a shade over $20.7 million from 16,146 seats. It was fully expected and anticipated that the pay-per-view sales would be over two million purchases. Alvarez would make the contracted weight of 152 pounds, and Maywather would come in at 150.5 in the official weigh-in. However, the day of the bout Alvarez would rehydrate to 165 pounds while Mayweather would lose a half pound and come in at 150.

The opening round had Canelo on his back foot trying to box with Mayweather and counterpunch. Despite both fighters making each other miss, there were few notable shots landed in response. Canelo would score with a left jab to the body and follow it with a right hook. Perhaps the left hook to Mayweather's upper body (2:35)—that actually lifted Mayweather off his feet—gave Canelo the close round.

The second round was a bit of a feinting contest as both fighters tried to make the other overcommit. Canelo would score with a jab followed by a right hook (1:05) to Mayweather's body. Mayweather would respond with an inside left hook. The final notable connect was a Canelo left hook (2:45) that possibly gave him the round.

The third would be the first clear Mayweather round as he started to be more effective with his right hand. A pair of right crosses (1:51 and 1:53) would be the most solid Mayweather connects up to that point.

In the fourth, Mayweather would continue to keep his right glove high and left glove wrapped around the body as he came forward, which meant he was going to be aggressive. Canelo was having most of his shots blocked, while he would get punished with an overhand right (0:55) as both fighters engaged in the center of the ring. Referee Kenny Bayless would warn Canelo for a low blow. When action resumed Mayweather offered his left glove to show sportsmanship, which was promptly ignored by Canelo. The Mexican fighter had learned from watching the Victor Ortiz and Gatti fights not to foolishly allow his guard down and decided to protect himself at all times. Mayweather would punish Canelo with a right hook to the body and avoid the return fire with his elusive defensive skills. It was easily the second consecutive round on the Mayweather column.

The Mayweather's hand-speed advantage became more apparent in the fifth as he was able to land his lead right while using his mongoose reflexes to avoid the return fire. Canelo's face swelling was increasing and so was his frustration. A left hook (1:23) would score for Alvarez, yet the Mayweather chin withstood the blow well. The sixth saw a much more aggressive Canelo cut off the ring and take the fight to Mayweather. A tenacious Canelo would have his best shots eluded by an agile Mayweather who was able to slip three consecutive haymakers in the waning seconds. It was another close round that could have been scored evenly.

The seventh was another Mayweather-dominated round as he utilized his left jab, feints, and slipping ability to control the round. A right uppercut (2:06) would be, possibly, the best punch Mayweater landed in the entire bout. Ironically, it was Mayweather walking down the bigger man and punishing him on the ropes. Canelo would do better in the eighth by landing a few decent body shots and closing the distance. Mayweather would be pinned to the ropes several times and manage to leave unscathed, despite taking heavy shots. The eighth was possibly the most convincing Canelo round. Mayweather would answer back in the ninth as he blocked most of Canelo's shots and scored with a vicious lead right (1:56). Canelo's punishment would continue in the tenth as Mayweather would jab to the body and score with lead right shots in the middle of the round. Canelo's left eye was almost reduced to a slit as he often stayed on the ropes to get rest. The round would end with a stare down by both combatants, who were separated by referee Kenny Bayless.

Mayweather's dominance continued in the eleventh as a lead right (1:00) would land flush on Canelo's head. The Mayweather dominance continued, as he would tee off on Canelo with his left hook and lead right while meticulously navigating the ring. The only suspense in the round was when Mayweather would check the ring ropes after Canelo missed a colossal shot.

Canelo won the final round essentially by default as Mayweather got on his toes and circled the ring; he understood the fight was in the bag and that there was no need to get caught with something. Canelo would land a few glancing blows to earn the last round. The only mystery after the bout was by how many points Mayweather earned the win. As nothing shocks anyone in the sport of boxing, the first score announced by Jimmy Lennon Jr. was 114–114 from judge C. J. Ross. Ross was one of the two judges who had Timothy Bradley defeating Manny Pacquiao in that scoring controversy. The camera would pan to Mayweather who had just put on his hat that read "TBE" (The Best Ever), and his lips would say, "What the **** is this?" The other two judges, Dave Moretti (116–113) and Greg Metcalfe (117–111), would both have it for Mayweather to give him the majority decision. I felt Mayweather won 116–113 (7-4-1).

Mayweather would credit Canelo as being a "tough competitor" and felt if he had been more aggressive he may have been able to stop the young fighter.

Canelo would concede that Mayweather's defense and elusive style made it difficult to connect with his best shots. The fight would generate $150 million from the confirmed 2.2 million viewers. The $150 million, along with the money from the gate, would both be records. However, the 2.4 million purchases from De La Hoya-Mayweather would still be the most PPV purchases ever for a boxing match. Furthermore, if inflation were factored in, then the De La Hoya-Mayweather 2007 match would do more than the $150 million. Nonetheless, Mayweather-Alvarez was a resounding success and a major rebound after the disappointing Mayweather-Guerrrero numbers. Moreover, Mayweather-Alvarez made millions from sponsors, international television, and merchandising. Mayweather would earn a record purse of over $80 million after getting his share of pay-per-view revenue. The numbers ensured that Mayweather was the top-paid athlete, despite not having the luxury of lucrative endorsement deals that many other top-paid athletes historically have had. Unfortunately, the economic success of Mayweather-Alvarez couldn't prevent the violent aftermath of the match. An Irving Texas man named Eliseo Lopez was shot and killed in Dallas trying to stop an argument stemming from the Mayweather-Alvarez match. This occurrence was reminiscent of another death that happened after the Mayweather-Cotto fight back in May 2012. Francisco Suarez, a young man from Arizona, was shot outside of a liquor store after arguing about Mayweather-Cotto. When Suarez came back to his car with a friend, he was shot down and killed. Fortunately, the violence never escalated to the race riots that followed the Jack Johnson-James Jeffries match of 1910.

CHAPTER 24

El Chino

When the choice of the next Mayweather opponent was up for grabs, the consensus was that Amir Khan was the clear front-runner. Golden Boy promoted Khan and he was actually in the undercard of Mayweather-Alvarez, fighting former welterweight champion Luis Collazo. After Khan won, it was expected that Mayweather would choose Khan. However, many fans weren't receptive to the proposed match as the knockout loss that Khan suffered to Danny Garcia in 2012 was still fresh in their minds. However, Amir Khan would win a Mayweather-sponsored Twitter poll for fans to determine the next Mayweather opponent. The poll, created in February 2014, had Khan winning with 20,105 votes, compared to 15,474 for Marcos Maidana. Khan would use this fact as ammunition to try to secure the lucrative payday against Mayweather. An immediate detriment to the bout was that Mayweather wanted to fight in September—a month in which Khan would be required to fast in religious observance of Ramadan. Khan would charge, "Maybe my fasting gives Floyd the excuse he has been looking for not to fight me. Even with the fans' poll over who he should fight went in my favor, he still didn't fight me."

Despite the poll, many boxing fans preferred Maidana over Khan simply because Maidana won the WBA welterweight title by soundly defeating Adrian Bronner—a loquacious and ostentatious fighter who was reminiscent of Mayweather in more ways than one. Besides the self-aggrandizing personality that both Mayweather and Bronner shared, both fighters utilized the shoulder roll defense, which received increasing popularity due to noted practicer Floyd Mayweather. It was a public responsibility per Maidana (a five-to-one underdog) to "shut Bronner's mouth." It was thought that Maidana's unorthdox style and heavy punching ability could perhaps give Mayweather some trouble. Khan, who had suffered recent defeats to both Lamont Peterson and Danny Garcia, was considered by many to be the safer opponent. Although Maidana had three losses, only his defeat to Devon Alexander was considered a convincing win. The other Maidana losses were a split decision loss to Andriy Kotelnik and a narrow unanimous decision to Amir Khan. The Khan fight saw Maidana nearly get knocked out in the first round by a body shot and be able to rally in the later rounds to make it a close contest. I actually felt Maidana did enough in the second half of the bout to earn a draw. There were still questions if Maidana, who was an Argentine fighter without mainstream recognition, could prove himself to be a solid pay-per-view commodity. Despite any calls for concern, Marcos Maidana would officially be named the next Mayweather opponent on February 24, 2014, which happened to coinside with his birthday. Marcos Maidana, who had an official purse of $1.5 million, was expected to earn more after final PPV revenues were factored in—which couldn't come at a better time as he had a newborn daughter on the way. Mayweather, who was entering his third fight of the Showtime contract, was guaranteed $32 million after earning $115 million for the first two. The Mayweather-Maidana live gate would do $14.9 million a few weeks before the event, illustrating that there was solid public interest for the bout that was billed as the "Moment."

The fighter known as "El Chino" would be the next in line to attempt to become the first fighter to give Mayweather a loss. Maidana got the nickname "El Chino," which means "Chinese man," due to his distinct Asian appearance. Trainer Robert Garcia, who helped perfect the strategy that gave Bronner his first official defeat, relished the opportunity to devise a plan to shatter the nearly immaculate Mayweather defense. For Mayweather it was yet another opportunity to prove that, at the age of thirty-seven, he was on top of his game and also a shot in getting some revenge for Adrian Bronner (who viewed Mayweather as an older brother).

Mayweather had some out-of-the-ring distractions as his well-publicized four-year relationship with fiancée, Shantel Jackson, was officially over. The Grand Rapids fighter was now more mature and had gone through prison and wouldn't allow events outside of the ring to disturb preparation for the bout.

In fact, as Mayweather declared he was "still enjoying the flyest bitches, cars, and properties." Maidana reminded many of former Mayweather opponent Carlos Baldomir who was also from Santa Fe, Argentina. The two fighters were unorthodox and rugged while being rough on the inside. The major difference was that Maidana had much better hand-and-foot speed and a vastly superior boxing résumé.

As there isn't always smooth sailing the day before a fight, there was controversy the day before the bout. Mayweather's camp objected to the gloves that Maidana was going to wear for the fight as they felt that the Maidana Everlast gloves that sported the Argentina flag's colors didn't have enough padding around the knuckles. Maidana trainer Robert Garcia protested as he claimed they were the same gloves that Mayweather had used against Miguel Cotto. After a collective breath held for hours, the Maidana camp relented and agreed to use gloves that were both accepted by the Mayweather camp and NSAC. There is always the possibility that these prefight incidents can distract a fighter before the main event. Mayweather grabbing Ortiz's throat and then Leonard Ellerbe making Ortiz rewrap his hands may have unsettled some Ortiz butterflies and nerves before the main event. Despite being told that the hand wraps would be given to the WBC for tests, Ellerbe wanted the entire protocol done again. Did these tactics "ice the kicker"? It's difficult to say, but it can't hurt.

If there were any nerves, Maidana would show them early, and he never did. Mayweather would enter the ring wearing black trunks with the Mexican stripe colors of green, red, and white. The Mayweather gesture may have seemed odd as he was fighting an Argentinean not a Mexican. However, it appeared Mayweather was paying homage to Mexican fans since it was the eve of the Cinco de Mayo festival. While Mayweather would hydrate to 148 pounds, Maidana would come in the ring weighing 165 pounds.

The opening round saw Maidana fight like a disciplined Ricardo Mayorga as he fired lunging punches and overhand chopping rights without taking any colossal counterpunches. Maidana, unlike Mayorga, actually kept his guard up and moved his head while displaying decent boxing defensive skill. Maidana didn't land much, but his rough tactics dictated the pace of the opening round. In addition, Maidana also landed several effective body shots as he had Mayweather on the ropes. Mayweather would fight back on the ropes with some decent blows of his own. Referee Kevin Weeks would warn Maidana for a low blow before the closing bell.

Mayweather countered Maidana in the middle of the ring while working the body with his jab in the second round. It was a very close round, yet Mayweather's cleaner punches could have given him the round. The first Mayweather one-two combination would score (0:51) in the third round, which didn't seem to deter his challenger. Maidana responded to the Mayweather shots by punishing Mayweather on the ropes again and throwing his off-balance and awkward shots, cemented by a solid right uppercut. While Mayweather fought back, the final minute saw Maidana once again do effective work, which conceivably gave him at least two of the first three rounds.

In the opening minute of the fourth, Mayweather would complain to referee Tony Weeks for some of the holding and elbows Maidana would do on the inside. Weeks would warn Maidana on his rough tactics. Things got worse for Mayweather as an inadvertent head-butt woud cut his right eye. Maidana, an opportunist, took advantage and banged Mayweather up on the ropes as the champion started to flee on his back foot. "I can't see," Mayweather would tell his corner in between rounds. "Keep your hands up," Floyd Sr. would respond. This was the most difficult situation in which Mayweather had found himself—in possibly more than a decade. Things got bleaker in the fifth as Maidana actually started to jab effectively and even landed a combination to the head and body.

The fact that Kevin Weeks was a referee known to let fighters fight seemed to help Maidana as he tangled Mayweather and wasn't separated immediately by Weeks. This trend continued in the sixth as Maidana was able to fight on the inside. Mayweather would respond by landing his best uppercut (1:35) in the bout. Mayweather would also score a pull counter (2:24) and rallied with a few decent scores in the waning seconds to possibly steal a crucial sixth round. Although Maidana had more volume, Mayweather landed the cleaner shots in the sixth.

Mayweather would take control in the seventh by using his agility and ring generalship to punish Maidana in the center of the ring. Another brilliant pull counter (0:35) landed flush on Maidana's face. Even during the brief moments that Mayweather was near the ropes, he used his hand speed to land combinations that gave him a convincing round.

Maidana would get warned for a low blow again (0:58) in the eighth round. This time a point could have been deducted, as it was flagrant. Maidana would fight better in the eighth by using his jab; however, Mayweather had again landed the cleaner shots to mitigate the Maidana improvement. The round could have been scored evenly.

The Mayweather dominance continued in the ninth and tenth rounds as he landed thundering counter shots and combinations in the center of the ring. It could be argued that Mayweather had swept the last five rounds. Mayweather appeared the fresher fighter in the eleventh, as he was the aggressor chasing Maidana down. The clean Mayweather right hands scored abundantly while Maidana's final-minute aggression didn't produce any major damage. Maidana continued with his rough tactics, which included almost pushing Mayweather outside of the ropes. If someone like Vic Drakulich had been officiating, Maidana likely would have had at least two points deducted by now. The final round was another round that Mayweather narrowly won with his right hand, as he landed the cleaner shots. I had Mayweather win the bout 116–113 (7-4-1). Mayweather would win via majority decision with official scores of 114–114 (Michael Pernick), 116–112 (Dave Moretti), and 117-111 (Burt A. Clements). The punch stats reflected Mayweather landing 230 of 426 and Maidana 221 of 858. It was interesting that two judges, Moretti and Clements, would give Mayweather three of the first four rounds while Pernick would give Maidana four of the first five rounds. Mayweather would concede it was a "tough fight" and was open to the possibility of a rematch. "I gave fans an exciting fight. He put pressure on me, and I stood there and fought him. He's a good fighter. I take nothing away from him," Mayweather would state in his postfight interview.

Maidana would declare himself the winner after the bout and felt that, as he was the winner, it was his decision whether to give Mayweather the rematch.

Mayweather didn't make Maidana pay for missing as much as I had anticipated. Mayweather's great reflexes and panther-like counterpunching ability weren't utilized consistently until the second half of the bout. Was this bout the most competitive Mayweather match since Mayweather-Castillo 1? I thought the matches with De La Hoya and Judah were similarly competitive even if the scores varied. In many ways the Maidana match was reminiscent to the Judah match in which Zab had won the early rounds and faded in the later rounds. I had the Judah match for Mayweather 116–112 and the Maidana match at 116–113. If a knockdown that should have been scored would have been factored, then Judah would have lost by only three points on my card.

CHAPTER 25

Rematch with Maidana

Although I thought Maidana had won four of the first six rounds against Mayweather, I didn't see him win another round decisively in the second half of their first bout. At best, I thought Maidana had just earned one even round in the second half of the bout. However, there were many who felt Maidana did enough to earn a rematch, despite the fact that no major boxing publication or website thought Maidana had won the bout. If the last six rounds of the first contest would repeat themselves, then Maidana would be in for a long night. The result was too close for comfort in the eyes of many boxing fans; so on July 10, 2014, on his Twitter account, Mayweather would officially announce the rematch for September 13.

In the first press conference promoting the event, which would be held in Times Square in New York City, Mayweather would declare, "I wanted to give the fans what they wanted to see. They wanted to see Mayweather-Maidana part two, so you know what? It's all about the fans." Mayweather himself didn't think he lost more than three rounds and felt that any bout in which he lost more than two rounds was closer than usual. Maidana had felt that he had won the first bout and stated that it was he who needed to give Mayweather the rematch, as he felt that he was the winner. If Maidana had any chance in the rematch, he would need to improve his defense in the middle of the ring as Mayweather countered him often in the second half of the bout.

This time around Mayweather was guaranteed $32 million and Maidana $3 million with both expected to earn more from the final pay-per-view revenue. The winner would lay claim to both a portion of the welterweight and junior middleweight titles. A major complaint from both fans and boxing media was the undercard—or lack of it. Major Golden Boy fighters such as Danny Garcia, Adrien Broner, or Saul Alvarez wouldn't be featured in the undercard. Alvarez, after his bout with Mayweather, was already an exclusive PPV star and wouldn't likely fight an undercard anytime soon. Leo Santa Cruz, a super bantamweight champion, would be the lead-up fighter to the main event. However, Cruz wouldn't be fighting a unification bout and would be defending against a relatively unknown opponent, Manuel Roman (17-2-3, 6 KOs). With a weak card, anything close to one million buys would be considered a major success for Mayweather-Maidana 2.

Most Mayweather training camps are remembered by external distractions coming into a bout, and this time would prove no exception. The Ice Bucket Challenge was becoming fashionable—a ritual that involved being doused with a bucket of ice in order to promote ALS (amyotrophic lateral sclerosis). Rapper and promoter 50 Cent would take the challenge and then offer Mayweather $750,000 to the charity of his choice if he could read one page from a Harry Potter book. 50 Cent would amend the challenge to simply reading a page of *Cat in the Hat* when he was being interviewed by Jimmy Kimmel. 50 Cent would elaborate, "We don't want to put pressure on you. We know you can't pronounce those words in that Harry Potter book, so we'll let you read *Cat in the Hat*." It was widely believed that 50 Cent was responding to Mayweather comments that labeled him, T. I., and Nelly as part of a list of washed-up rappers. There was fuel thrown into the fire when a radio station would air clips of Mayweather having difficulty reading "radio drops" that plugged a website that helped connect veterans with employment opportunities. Mayweather would respond to 50 Cent by tweeting that he would challenge him to a twelve-round match in October at the MGM for $12 million. Mayweather would also tweet copies of his last two official fight purses stating, "Read this $72,276,000. God Bless."

In a press conference call promoting Mayweather-Maidana 2, he would add, "Making fun of a person because they can't read is not funny. If I really couldn't read, it would make my accomplishments even that much more amazing." There were more jabs fired at Mayweather as Rapper Nelly called Mayweather a "high-school dropout," and Manny Pacquiao would also make comments directed at

Mayweather's academic ability by telling Jerry Izenberg of the New Jersey *Star-Ledger*, "But what I learned and heard from him, well, I realize why he is like that. I understand sometimes when the people are not educated they just talk to talk. He sets a very bad example." In a radio interview with Fox Sports 670AM in Las Vegas (when asked about 50 Cents and Manny Pacquiao labeling Mayweather as uneducated) Mayweather would reply, "My beef is with boxers; I stay on my lane. People are entitled to believe what they believe. When you get to this level, people are going to take shots every way possible. If that is the case, then that makes my story that much more interesting."

The Mayweather camp would be struck with another major distraction when former fiancée Shantell Jackson would file a lawsuit just nine days before his rematch with Marcos Maidana on September 13. The lawsuit filed in Los Angeles County alleged that Mayweather had defamed, assaulted, and imprisoned Jackson for a period prior to their breakup. Although there were allegations of physical abuse in the complaint—including twisting an arm, choking, and even being threatened with a deadly weapon—there were no previous criminal charges filed by Jackson. During Showtime's *All Access*, Mayweather had stated that Jackson had aborted their twins and that was a contributing factor to ending the relationship. In the press conference announcing the civil suit, Jackson stated that Mayweather knew about the pregnancy ending as of January 2014. However, it was ambiguous as to how the pregnancy actually came to an end. The allegations were serious as they allegedly took place after Mayweather was released from prison and could have resulted in probation violation and return to prison. The boxing world wondered if any of these distractions leading to Mayweather-Maidana II would have an impact. Mayweather would address the suit a few days later, when promoting the bout:

> "My thing is just to focus on my job, which is boxing. Jealousy and envy comes with the territory. People are always going to take shots at Floyd Mayweather. My thing is to be the best I can be in the sport of boxing and focus on my job, which is boxing. Like I've said in the past, no bumps, no bruises, no nothing. With O. J. and Nicole, you seen pictures. With Chris Brown and Rihanna, you seen pictures. With [Chad] Ochocinco and Evelyn, you seen pictures. You guys have yet to see any

pictures of a battered woman, a woman who says she was kicked and beaten (by me). So I just live my life and try to stay positive and try to become a better person each and every day."

There wasn't much trash talking between Mayweather and Maidana in the buildup. Maidana did mock Mayweather's power during an *All Access* episode by claiming that when Mayweather hit him it felt like he was "tickling." Perhaps the biggest controversy generated in *All Access* was when Mayweather set up sparring matches with "doghouse rules" where both combatants continued to box until one retired. This was reminiscent to some of the early bare-knuckle days of the sport where there were no round limits and fights could go on for hours. However, one must also consider that the sparring match participants had both headgear and boxing gloves. The Nevada State Athletic Commission would later order Mayweather to present himself to inquire about the sparring matches and some alleged depiction of marijuana use during the *All Access* program. Mayweather would tell the committee essentially that both incidents were staged to help promote the event. Both the commission and Mayweather would get criticized as the commission failed to take the testimony under oath, which could result in pejury charges, and Mayweather would take heat since he was a producer for the show and possibly staged an alleged reality TV show. If we had a dollar for every staged reality-TV show incident, then there would be enough to feed possibly half of the world's hungry children. However, both Hasim Rahman Jr. and his brother, Sharif Rahman—who were amateur fighters who fought Donovan Cameron in the Mayweather Boxing Club—disputed the testimony. Both Rahman brothers would later file a suit against Mayweather alleging false imprisonment, tortuous assault, and negligence in both supervision and training.

The day before weigh-in had Mayweather come in at 146.5 pounds and Maidana at 146 pounds. Maidana had come in lighter expecting to be faster and have more stamina in the latter rounds. After hydrating Maidana came in at 157 pounds, and Mayweather didn't climb on the scales for the same day weigh-in. Mayweather displayed much more mobility in the opening two rounds as he made to sure to evade the ropes while targeting Maidana with jabs to the body. Mayweather would also score with his right, both as a counter and lead shot. Maidana would bounce back in the third by working his jab, which at one point (2:27) would jerk Mayweather's head back. A straight Maidana right that landed a tad after the closing bell rang would temporarily wobble Mayweather. The two effective Maidana shots may have earned him an even round and possibly persuaded judges to give him the close round. The fourth would be the first clear Maidana round. In the fourth, Maidana would finally do damage to Mayweather's body as he finally got him in the ropes and punished him with solid hooks to the body. Maidana's sense of urgency may have been motivated from seeing Mayweather stagger to his corner at the end of the third. The next two rounds had Mayweather displaying his great defense by slipping wild, lumbering shots while making Maidana pay with pull counters and straight rights. The audience at the MGM started to voice some displeasure as Mayweather increasingly got on his bike, while many felt that referee Kenny Bayless was separating the combatants too fast during clinches. The perception was that Mayweather was initiating the clinches to disrupt Maidana.

The seventh saw Maidana jab better, while Mayweather still controlled the center of the ring. Mayweather's superior hand speed scored with combinations, and then he would clinch Maidana when he sensed danger. Maidana's unorthodox shots were mainly catching air as Mayweather slipped the blows. The next round would end in controversy, as both fighters would be holding each other, and Maidana would allegedly bite Mayweather's left hand. Mayweather would complain to Kenny Bayless who would separate the fighters and have the ring physician examine Mayweather. There were no deductions as there was no way to prove if, in fact, Maidana had bitten Mayweather. The actual round was quite close and could have been scored evenly. Mayweather was backpedaling but scoring as Maidana came in with short counter shots. This continued in the ninth a round that was more decisively a Mayweather round.

The tenth saw Maidana get a point deduction for allegedly pushing Mayweather down in order to break up a clinch. After the point deduction, Maidana came back and cut off the ring and landed some of his best shots on Mayweather until Bayless would break up the fighters, once again prematurely. Maidana would pin Mayweather in the ropes in the final twenty second and win the round. However, due to the point deduction, at best it would be a 9–9 round for Maidana if he was given the round. Maidana would take a needed rest after a low blow in the eleventh. Mayweather would later claim it was really a body shot, and Maidana took the time to recuperate. The blow did appear to be south of the border. Mayweather still controlled most of the action in the eleventh and would fire a counter right (1:55) when Maidana threw a lazy left jab.

The final round was essentially a Maidana round by default. Mayweather would conspicuously get on his bike and not do much in the final stanza. The final punch stats had Mayweather land 166 of 326 and Maidana 128 of 572. Judges Dave Moretti and John Mckale had it 116–111 for Mayweather, while judge Guido Cavalleri had it 115–112 for Mayweather. I had it 117–111 for Mayweather. The contest was possibly the least entertaining Mayweather match since his bout with Juan Manuel Marquez in his 2009 return. Mayweather would explain what happened after the eighth round: "After the eighth round, my hand was numb, and I really couldn't use my left hand." He also denied that he deliberately tried to prevent Maidana from breathing by putting his glove on his face. "We were just tangled up in the center of the ring, and he bit my left hand."

Despite the lack of star power in the undercard, the Mayweather-Maidana II pay-per-view numbers were 925,000 purchases, which all things considered was better than many anticipated. The live gate per the NSAC would generate nearly $14.9 million from 14,859 tickets sold. There was still plenty of "Money" left in the Floyd Mayweather name moniker. The immediate question was who the next Mayweather opponent would be. My best guess was Danny Garcia since he would generate solid PPV numbers with the loyal Puerto Rican boxing audience. Moreover, Garcia was undefeated on paper and that could help generate interest from the casual boxing fan. However, there were recent shake-ups in both Golden Boy Promotions and Mayweather Promotions. De La Hoya had officially broken up his long-standing business relationship with former Golden Boy CEO Richard Schaefer. De La Hoya would tell Showtime simply, "I had one agenda and he had another agenda and we just didn't agree on it...and my agenda is to make sure the fans are happy." It was widely believed that the source of the two terminating ties was that De La Hoya wanted to do business with Top Rank again while Schaefer didn't want to do business with Bob Arum again. There were also many in the industry who felt that Schaefer's strong connection to Al Haymon was causing friction with Golden Boy as many Haymon-managed fighters were being featured at Golden Boy events.

It was also unclear if Leonard Ellerbee would still be the CEO of Mayweather Promotions, as Mayweather told Fighthype.com, "We're outgrowing each other." Mayweather alluded to some issues with the Maidana fight that he wasn't pleased with, as both his junior middleweight and welterweight titles were on the line, and the ticket arrangement had his daughter not sitting next to her mother. As Richard Schafer was ringside for the Maidana rematch, it appeared that Mayweather may have had him in mind to help run Mayweather Promotions. In fact, Mayweather has a solid working relationship with Richard Schaefer and considers him a friend. Yet, despite any rumors that he would help in running Mayweather Promotions, there was a legal battle between Golden Boy and Schaefer. Golden Boy Promotions sought $50 million as they alleged breach of contract when Schaefer left Golden Boy, claiming that he was still under contract for them until March 2018. The suit (which went to arbitration) was expected to dissuade Schaefer from joining Mayweather Promotions or any other boxing-related business until the conclusion of arbitration.

CHAPTER 26

Securing Both Legacy and Greatest Payday

I, like many other boxing fans, felt Mayweather did need to fight Pacquiao at least once to secure his legacy. Even if he lost, I felt that, if he put in a great effort and pleased the fans, the overall boxing media and fans would at minimum give him the added respect he deserved. In the last few years leading up to Pacquiao, the Grand Rapids–born fighter faced off with Mosley, Cotto, and Canelo, which added some key names to his legacy. Of course, some cynics will say the latter two should have been fought a few years ago. Nonetheless, the fact remained that when Mayweather fought these opponents they were all coming from major wins on the upside, not on the downside. Mosley and Cotto had both defeated Margarito, while Canelo had earned a close win over Austin Trout. However, there was still the Pacquiao name missing on the Mayweather résumé, and the waiting could pay off big time.

Still, the fight had to be officially signed before Mayweather got the chance to silence his critics and secure his legacy. Getting a fight of this magnitude done required both persistence and luck. Two major strokes of fortune—perhaps given by the boxing gods—helped secure the biggest match of this young century. The first came in the form of Gabriel Salvador, an actor and part-time waiter, who happened to serve CBS President and CEO Leslie Moonves at Craig's Restaurant. Salvador and Moonves would occasionally talk about boxing. Salvador's teenage son had worked with Freddie Roach, and Salvador came up with the idea of introducing Roach to Moonves in the hope of them getting the wheels in motion for the Mayweather-Pacquiao superbout. A meeting was arranged in the Beverly Hills Hotel in June. Roach then arranged for Bob Arum and Les Moonves to meet and further discuss the possibility of the match in Arum's Beverly Hills mansion. The two felt the meeting was constructive, and Moonves then hosted a meeting between Mayweather advisor Al Haymon and Bob Arum. There were still many obstacles to overcome, but having the head of CBS/Showtime, Bob Arum, and Al Haymon all actively involved signaled that this time the match would finally take place.

Mayweather himself told Showtime: "I would love to fight Manny Pacquiao. He is now in a very tight situation; his PPV numbers are low. I wanted the fight in the past; I wanted random blood and urine testing. I offered $40 million; I'm just waiting on them. The fight needs to happen on Showtime. I'm not ducking or dodging; Bob Arum is stopping the fight. The fans have been fooled. We want the fight; we are ready. Let's make it happen May second—let's do it." By January 2015, several media outlets had prematurely announced that the bout was going to take place on May 2, 2015. Once the Super Bowl passed without any official announcement, it appeared that the match wouldn't take place after all. Perhaps it was just luck or divine intervention through bad weather, but Manny Pacquiao delayed his trip out of Miami to stay and watch a Miami Heats game. It so happened that Floyd Mayweather was aslo court side for the same game. Despite the fact that both had shared the boxing stage together in 2001 when Pacquiao fought in the undercard to Mayweather-Chavez, the two had never met in person. Pacquiao advisor Michael Koncz arranged for both to meet during half time for the first time. Prior to the half-time meeting, the American Airlines jumbotron juxtaposed live images of both combatants with the question, "Coming in 2015?"

As they met it was obvious that their body language indicated they wanted to speak further, and Pacquiao appeared to save Mayweather's number on his phone. The two met again that same night as Mayweather visited Pacquiao in his hotel suite. A video later surfaced of Mayweather talking as Pacquiao sat in the background, purportedly to show the world he did in fact want the fight. Despite many feeling that the entire meeting was staged, it was in fact a coincidence that both met during the game. However, the two rival networks would need to negotiate the complicated issues in doing a dual, live, pay-per-view telecast in what was expected to be the richest fight in boxing history.

Mayweather officially announced the date of May 2 on Feburary 20 through Shots, a social network in which Mayweather is an investor. Mayweather declared, "Boxing fans and sports fans around the world will witness greatness on May 2. I am the best ever, TBE, and this fight will be another opportunity to showcase my skills and do what I do best, which is win. Manny is going to try to do what 47 before him failed to do, but he won't be successful. He will be number 48."

The fact that there were only two and a half months to prepare for the bout meant there was a condensed promotional plan. There wasn't a multicity promotional tour around the world or even within the United States. There were only two press conferences and no customary face-off prior to the event. There wasn't a *24/7* or a *Fight Camp 360*, but both HBO and Showtime were allowed to air documentaries of their contracted fighters in order to help promote the event. The guaranteed prize money—$120 million for Mayweather and $80 million for Pacquiao—was unheard of. With the added incentative of pay-per-view, it was expected that Mayweather would make over $200 million and Pacquiao well over a $100 million. Perhaps only the prize money earned by Gene Tunney and Jack Dempsey back in 1927 came close to this fight's shock value. Gene Tunney earned $990,225 (receiving $1 million by paying the difference to promoter Tex Rickard), and Jack Dempsey got $447,500 in their rematch. However, even when adjusted with inflation, those prizes don't come close to the unprecedented amount that both Mayweather and Pacquiao were set to make. There is no way that both fighters would have earned a nine-figure payday from the fight five years ago.

The first conference was held in Los Angeles on March 11 in the Nokia Theater. The face-off at the press conference was respectful, with both fighters keeping a proper distance and not pulling any stunts or exchanging trash talk. There were prearranged foot markers, which both fighters stood on top of for about one minute in the stare down. Both had on designer suits that emphasized the professional atmosphere everyone wanted to convey to the international media present. An event of this magnitude didn't require any stunts or trash talk to sell. Even the rival networks and promoters seemed to be cordial and respectful. Perhaps the only minor acrimony was when Bob Arum differed with Showtime Vice President Stephen Espinoza regarding the reason the fight took five years to happen. Arum, with a facetious smirk, replied, "Well, Steve and everybody has their own opinions." The press conference was also a major turning point for Mayweather Promotions, as the company demonstrated they could co-promote an event of this magnitude without any assistance from Golden Boy Promotions. It also dispelled any rumors that Mayweather had terminated his relationship with Leonard Ellerbe, as he promoted the event as CEO of Mayweather Promotions. The actual bout was available in 175 nations, demonstrating the international appeal of the event. This was the closest thing that boxing could offer in comparison to a World Cup or a Super Bowl.

Mayweather trained in his own gym and resorted to work such as chopping wood as he prepared for the match. Old nemesis southpaw Zab Judah was also brought into camp for sparring. Judah told ESPN's *Friday Night Fights*, when asked about trying to mimic Pacquiao in sparring sessions, "In the long run I can never mimic another fighter; I can come in there and give Floyd the southpaw look, fast hands, good power, and good angles. Personally I think it will be great fight. Like I tell everybody over an over, I think the defense will be the difference. I think Floyd will come out victorious that night." Not sparing any expense in training, Mayweather even had a high-priced diet, using Chef Q, which cost him approximately one thousand dollars a plate, carrying a price tag of four thousand dollars for four meals a day. TMZ reported that the total expense was estimated to be $184,000.

Mayweather, in the final press conference on April 29, proclaimed, "This has been a truly amazing event and amazing turnout. Training camp has went remarkable. My dad done a tremendous job working with my uncle Roger. We had a great chemistry throughout training camp. I want to thank all the sponsors that's covering this event. I want to thank the MGM Grand, I want to thank Al Haymon, Mayweather Promotions, Top Rank Promotions, Freddie Roach—your team and our team have done a tremendous job. It's time to fight now; you guys came out here to see excitement, you guys came to see a great event and that's what both competitors bring to the table, excitement. The biggest fight in boxing history and I'm a part of it. I'm just truly blessed to be where I am at. I feel good, I feel strong."

The weigh-in saw both combatants come in with sharply contrasting facial expressions. Mayweather appeared stoic with a stone-faced, serious "it's business time" poker face. Pacquiao appeared jubilant as he did the customary face-off at the weigh-in. While Pacquiao sported a T-shirt declaring "All glory goes to God," Mayweather had on a TMT (The Mayweather Team) hat and shirt. Pacquiao came in at 145 pounds and Mayweather at 146.

A gala of celebrities and aficionados, including Michael Jordan, Magic Johnson, Robert De Niro, Donald Trump, Andre Agassi, Steffi Graf, Mike Tyson, and Clint Eastwood, were in attendance. The national anthems of both the Philippines and the United States were played, along with the Mexican national anthem. Many wondered why the Mexican national anthem was played, since no Mexican fighter was featured in the main event. The act was homage to Mexico as the country that put millions of dollars in advertising into the event through sponsors such as Tecate beer.

Still, one major criticism of the event was the undercard (or lack of)—the event featured Vasyl Lomachenko and Leo Santa Cruz, both of whom were challenging relatively obscure opponents. For such a high-priced event, most people expected better appetizers leading up to the main fight. However, the Santa Cruz bout ended up being surprisingly competitive and more entertaining than anticipated.

When the time came, HBO's Michael Buffer introduced Pacquiao, who took a selfie while doing the ring walk. Mayweather was introduced by Showtime's Jimmy Lennon Jr. Kenny Bayless's instructions made a point to keep a fight of this magnitude clean. As the opening bell rang, many around the world must have been wondering if this was really happening after five years. The action commenced with both fighters touching gloves again at the opening bell. Mayweather landed a short, ineffective right hook (0:10). Both fighters feinted and exercised upper-body movement. Pacquiao scored with a straight left (0:25) to Mayweather's body. Mayweather tried to work the jab, but most were blocked by Pacquiao's gloves. A solid straight right (1:05) landed for Mayweather. A straight left to Pacquiao's body and another sizzling straight right connected for Mayweather in the final minute, giving him a mainly cautious opening round. All three judges also scored it for Mayweather. Freddie Roach told Pacquiao to "give me more head movement." It was obvious that Roach wanted Pacquiao to avoid those right hands.

As Pacquiao cornered Mayweather on the ropes, he got stung by another straight right (0:21). The crowd would boo in the opening minute as Mayweather clinched Pacquiao. Unlike Maidana, Pacquiao wouldn't throw inside short uppercuts to discourage Mayweather from holding. The middle of the round saw Pacquiao score with a couple of left hooks on the ropes, which were immediately negated by Mayweather clinching. Mayweather's straight rights (1:56, 2:25) carried the round again. Pacquiao connected with his left (2:35), which possibly gave him the confidence for the next two rounds. All three judges gave the round to Mayweather, as I did.

A left hand connects for Mayweather in the fight of the century. AP Photo/Isaac Brekken.

The opening thirty seconds of the third round saw Pacquiao land a two-punch combination on a backpedaling Mayweather. Mayweather got a warning for a low blow on a borderline body shot. Pacquiao easily landed his best shot up to that point, a straight right (0:55). The middle of the round saw a short Pacquiao flurry on the ropes, which was stopped by a Mayweather clinch. Mayweather scored with another straight right (1:41) that Pacquiao seemed to handle well. A crushing right hand (2:53) by Pacquiao sealed the round for him on my card. All three judges differed and gave it to Mayweather.

The fourth was easily Pacquiao's best round up to that point. Pacquiao was able to cut off the ring well and had several flurries in the opening minute. Mayweather fired his jab in the middle of the round, which Pacquiao waived on. This set up a counter left (1:35), which momentarily staggered Mayweather onto the ropes. Pacquiao unleashed combinations as Mayweather kept an armadillo guard as he took the punishment. Mysteriously, Pacquiao did let up, possibly to avoid a counter or due to a later-disclosed injury. An overhand right hand (2:05) also punished Mayweather, which gave Pacquiao his most convincing round. All three judges agreed and gave the round to Pacquiao. The result of the round saw Mayweather Sr. scold his son: "You fighting like you scared. Go take care of your business." Mayweather Sr. understood his son would lose the bout if he got too tentative or complacent. There was no need to give technical advice to his son, who had two decades' worth of experience. It was more a pep talk to get active instead of going into a shell, which would mean losing future rounds by default.

The fifth saw Mayweather utilize a straight left stiff jab (0:35). Two additional straight rights (1:08) connected as Mayweather controlled the distance, and Pacquiao felt content in boxing him. Mayweather took control of the round by his customary potshots, firing one punch at a time. Pacquiao missed with his vintage straight left (2:28), which demonstrated that Mayweather still retained excellent reflexes. All three judges concurred with me and gave the round to Mayweather.

Mayweather opened the sixth by landing his straight right (0:11). Pacquiao came out much more aggressively in the sixth and was able to put constant pressure on Mayweather. The key moment was when Pacquiao connected with a left hook near Mayweather's right ear (1:43). The punch momentarily stunned Mayweather, who received further punishment on the ropes. The fact that

Mayweather could handle the shot without going down was another example of Mayweather's underrated durability in taking shots. The ear helps maintain equilibrium, and it was remarkable that Mayweather maintained his balance. Mayweather audibly said, "No," and shook his head (indicating he wasn't hurt), as he took shots on the ropes. He fought back and landed a few good shots, but they were not enough to carry the round. After six rounds, I had this contest even. All three judges also gave the round to Pacquiao.

Possibly sensing the fight was getting closer on the cards, Mayweather came out with urgency in the seventh. Mayweather's best right hand (0:20) landed in the seventh round. Mayweather temporarily put Pacquiao on his back foot with the excellent timing of his jab and straight right. In fact, Mayweather was so confident, he had his gloves down and head facing forward, almost as if inviting Pacquiao to fire shots at him. All three judges gave the round to Mayweather.

Mayweather slipped in two power shots as Pacquiao came out aggressively in the opening thirty seconds of the eighth. The opening minute belonged to Pacquiao as he dictated the pace. Mayweather came back to land his own left hooks and jabs. The round was actually close, and I gave it narrowly to Mayweather. However, Mayweather was noticeably bleeding from his mouth. All three judges gave it to Mayweather as well.

The ninth saw Mayweather maintain the distance as Pacquiao connected with partial blows. Pacquiao missed with wild lefts (1:12, 1:41). Mayweather landed a counter left (1:19) over Pacquiao's guard. Pacquiao scored with a straight left (1:22). Mayweather landed another bruising straight right (2:52) to close the round. It was just enough to give Mayweather the round, but two of the three judges ended up giving the round to Pacquiao.

Pacquiao, sensing he was behind, did better in the tenth. A sensational straight left to the body (0:28) was designed to take the air out of Mayweather's lungs. If he had done this earlier, it may have paid dividends down the stretch. The middle of the round saw Pacquiao take Mayweather to the ropes and dictate the pace while scoring with both hands. A three-punch combination (2:18) gave Pacquiao his best round since the sixth. The end of the round saw Pacquiao a bit frustrated, as he knew he could have possibly done a bit more damage. Two of the three judges also gave the round to Pacquiao.

Only four seconds into the eleventh, Mayweather landed a punishing right. He followed it up with a two-punch combination to Pacquiao's head. An uppercut on the inside (0:48) also connected for Mayweather. Pacquiao was reduced to chasing Mayweather around the ring, without landing anything of substance. A counter left also scored for Mayweather. Mayweather and Pacquiao both banged their gloves during the round. It was another round for Mayweather in my books, and all three judges also gave the round to Mayweather.

Mayweather, who had been expected to get on his bike to avoid the possibility of a knockout, actually stayed in the pocket for a portion of the final round. Even Roberto Duran, known for his machismo, was actually idle on the final round against Leonard in their first contest—and that was a much closer fight. Pacquiao, however, did get in a straight left (1:07). Mayweather fired his pistol jab, but most were blocked. The final minute saw Mayweather get on his jets and land a final right hand (2:22) to level the round. There was no clear winner in the final round, and I scored it an even 10–10. Judges Burt A. Clements and Glenn Feldman both had it 116–112, while judge Dave Moretti had it by a wide score of 118–110. My final score was 116–113 (7-4-1) for Mayweather. Mayweather landed 148 out of 435 shots, while Pacquiao landed 81 out of 429. It's interesting to note that Pacquiao threw 68 more power shots (63–236), while Mayweather landed 81 out of 168. Mayweather ultimately told Pacquiao, "Your hell of a fighter…your tough as a (expletive)."

Pacquiao was hit by straight hands and was fighting Mayweather at a distance that made connecting an arduous task. Pacquiao himself stated in the postfight interview that "Mayweather moved a lot," and that was the reason he threw less punches; he wasn't a stationary target as Margarito and Clottey were. Pacquiao needed to be at Mayweather's chest and come from different angles. On the clinches Pacquiao never once fired an inside uppercut as had Marcos Maidana, who was able to punish Mayweather on the inside in their first contest. Moreover, Maidana was able to establish his jab in the center of the ring. Mayweather both kept distance and also got very low at times to make himself a smaller target for the smaller fighter. If Mayweather had stood erect and stationary, he would have suffered similar fates as had De La Hoya and Margarito against Pacquiao.

Mayweather responded to Pacquiao's disclosure of a shoulder injury (further discussed in Pacquiao's section), saying, "I had injuries also going to this fight. If he had came out victorious the only thing I come out and show respect and just say he was the better man if he beat me. Both of my arms were injured and both of my hands injured but like I said before I will always find a way to win."

The total pay-per-view (PPV) sales were over 4.4 million purchases, which easily shattered the record for most purchases and money generated. The final PPV tally was expected to increase after all the numbers were tabulated. Combined with a live gate of over $72 million, added with merchandising, television rights, and sponsorships, the total revenue was expected to exceed $600 million. Mayweather was expected to earn more than $220 million after receiving his portion of the PPV revenue. Despite the record-breaking revenue generated, the public disappointment and Mayweather expecting to retire soon would make a rematch unlikely, but not impossible.

The win was important for Mayweather as he disproved cynics who thought he was too afraid to fight Pacquiao, and it also debunked the theory that his old legs would lead to his own demise in the bout. However, Mayweather's celebratory mode was once again distracted with another lawsuit. This time Mayweather was sued for $20 million by Josie Harris for an interview he conducted with Katie Couric, in which he stated, "Did I restrain a woman that was on drugs? Yes, I did. So if they say that its domestic violence, then you know what, I'm guilty of restraining a person." The Harris defamation suit sought $20 million in damages for false and defamatory statements. Many in the media were putting domestic abuse front and center, especially after the infamous Ray Rice scandal in the NFL. As Mayweather's name continued to be in the limelight, the lawsuit became an issue that he was expected to address. But after the contest Mayweather told Showtime's Jim Grey that he should be doing "that Disney commercial." Mayweather was alluding to the commercial in which a famous athlete would say, "I'm going to Disneyworld," usually after winning a championship. The fact that boxing hasn't always been a favorite of Madison Avenue coupled with the domestic abuse cloud made it improbable that Mayweather would get "that Disney commercial." Perhaps Barry

Bonds of baseball is the only athlete to come close to rivaling Mayweather's magnitude while still being shunned by many endorsement opportunities.

Mayweather was expected to do one more fight in September, with the possible opponent being Amir Khan (31–3, 19 KOs). There were also two undefeated fighters that were being considered, Kell Brook (35–0, 24 KOs) and Danny Garcia (30–0, 17 KOs). Hard-hitting Keith Thurman (25–0, 21 KOs) was eliminated when he agreed to fight Luis Collazo in July. Personally, I would have preferred Mayweather to cross the Atlantic for the first time and fight the undefeated Kell Brook in England. Brook, who held the WBO welterweight title name value was still growing, but his ability and skill gave him the worthiness of any of the other welterweights. It would have been interesting to see how Mayweather would fight outside of Las Vegas, which many consider his comfort zone. However, Andre Berto would be officially announced as the next Mayweather opponent with the bout scheduled on September 12, 2015. Mayweather would defeat Berto via unanimous decision with scores of 120-108, 118-110, and 117-111. The question many have is if Mayweather is going to be satisfied with 49–0 or if he will try to break the Rocky Marciano mark by going for 50–0. Those milestones alone would keep the public interested whenever Mayweather exits from the sport. The fact that Mayweather will be heavily involved with boxing promotions through Mayweather Promotions also should guarantee that the Mayweather brand will remain a major force in the boxing industry.

Mayweather is a fighter who came from the hip-hop generation in which youth tried to break free from the shackles of how a previous generation defined them. In a capitalistic society where advertising lionizes money, luxury cars, and material things, it is expected that some of those who obtain it will flaunt it. Floyd Mayweather makes no apologies for obtaining wealth and then flaunting it. He makes no apologies for not facing opponents who some felt boxing legacy mandated. As he proclaimed, "Legacy don't pay bills." Floyd Mayweather is a character and persona full of contradictions: a man who unabashedly flaunts material possessions but concedes that it all will come off when coming to the kingdom of God; a man who gives to the needy, while also burning money away (real or fake); a boxer who verbally chastises opponents and then later lavishes praise on the fallen victim. It is fully expected that such a manic, contradictory personality would evoke a polarizing reaction. That positive and negative energy that fuels a battery is what has fed the Mayweather marketing strategy. The lovers and haters are equally interested in what Mayweather is doing, even if their motivating purpose varies. For someone like Floyd Mayweather, the fact that he participated in some of the biggest money fights, surpassed Oscar De La Hoya as the greatest prize earner in boxing history (with over $600 million as reported by *Forbes* magazine), while enjoying the fruits of his labor and still retaining his faculties means he got the job done.

IBHOF Members Defeated (2): Arturo Gatti, Oscar De La Hoya
Probable IBHOF Members Defeated (4): Shane Mosley, Juan Manuel Marquez, Miguel Cotto, Manny Pacquiao.
Possible IBHOF Members Defeated (3): Genaro Hernandez, Diego Corrales, Saul Alvarez.

Professional Boxing Record
(49-0, 26 KOs)

1996

October 11	Roberto Apodaca WTKO 2, Texas Station Casino, Las Vegas, NV
Nov 30	Reggie Sanders WUD 4, Tingley Coliseum, Albuquerque, NM

1997

January 18	Jerry Cooper, WTKO 1, Thomas & Mack Center, Las Vegas, NV
Feb 1	Edgar Ayala WTKO 2, Swiss Park Hall, Chula Vista, CA
March 12	Kino Rodriquez WTKO 1, Stadium Arena, Grand Rapids, MI
April 12	Bobby Giepert WKO 1, Thomas & Mack Center, Las Vegas, NV
May 9	Tony Duran WTKO 1, Orleans Hotel & Casino, Las Vegas, NV
June 14	Larry O'Shields WUD 6, Alamodome, San Antonio, TX
July 12	Jesus Chavez WTKO 5, Grand Casino, Biloxi, MS
Sept 6	Louie Lejia WTKO 2, County Coliseum, El Paso, TX
October 14	Felipe Garcia WKO 6, Bank of America Centre, Boise, ID
Nov 20	Angel Nunez WTKO 3, Olympic Auditorium, Los Angeles, CA

1998

January 9	Hector Arroyo WTKO 5, Grand Casino, Biloxi, MS
Feb 28	Sam Girard WKO 2, Atlantic City, NJ
March 23	Miguel Melo WTKO 3, Foxwoods Resort, Mashantucket, CT
April 18	Gustavo Fabian Cuello WUD 10, Olympic Auditorium, Los Angeles, CA
June 14	Tony Pep WUD 10, Trump Taj Mahal, Atlantic City, NJ
October 3	Genaro Hernandez WTKO 8, Las Vegas Hilton, Las Vegas, NV
	WBC World super featherweight title
December 19	Angel Manfredy WTKO 2, Miccosukee Indian Gaming Resort, Miami, FL
	WBC World super featherweight title

1999

Feb 17	Carlos Alberto Ramon Rios WUD 12, Van Andel Arena, Grand Rapids, MI **WBC World super featherweight title**
May 22	Justin Juuko WKO 9 Mandalay Bay Resort and Casino, Las Vegas, NV **WBC World super featherweight title**
Sept 11	Carlos Gerena WTKO 7 Mandalay Bay Resort and Casino, Las Vegas, NV **WBC World super featherweight title**

2000

March 18	Gregorio Vargas WUD 12, MGM Grand, Las Vegas, NV **WBC World super featherweight title**
October 21	Emmanuel Augustus WTKO 9, Cobo Hall, Detroit, MI **WBC World super featherweight title**

2001

January 20	Diego Corrales WTKO 10, MGM Grand, Las Vegas, NV **WBC World super featherweight title**
May 26	Carlos Hernandez WUD 12, Van Andel Arena, Grand Rapids, MI **WBC World super featherweight title**
Nov 10	Jesus Chavez WTKO 9, Bill Graham Civic Auditorium, San Francisco, CA **WBC World super featherweight title**

2002

April 20	Jose Luis Castillo WUD 12, MGM Grand, Las Vegas, NV **WBC World lightweight title**

December 7	Jose Luis Castillo WUD 12, Mandalay Bay Resort and Casino, Las Vegas, NV
	WBC World lightweight title

2003

April 19	Victoriano Sosa WUD 12, Selland Arena, Fresno, CA
	WBC World lightweight title
Nov 1	Phillip Ndou WTKO 7, Van Andel Arena, Grand Rapids, MI
	WBC World lightweight title

2004

May 22	Demarcus Corley WUD 12, Boardwalk Hall, Atlantic City, NJ

2005

January 22	Henry Bruseles WTKO 8, American Airlines Arena, Miami, FL
June 25	Arturo Gatti WTKO 6, Boardwalk Hall, Atlantic City, NJ
	WBC World light welterweight title
Nov 19	Shamba Mitchell WTKO 6, Rose Garden, Portland, OR

2006

April 8	Zab Judah WUD 12, Thomas & Mack Center, Las Vegas, NV
	IBF World welterweight title
Nov 4	Carlos Baldomir WUD 12, Mandalay Bay Resort and Casino, Las Vegas, NV
	WBC World welterweight title

2007

May 5	Oscar De La Hoya WSD 12, MGM Grand, Las Vegas, NV
	WBC World light middleweight title
December 8	Ricky Hatton WTKO 10, MGM Grand, Las Vegas, NV
	WBC World welterweight title

2009

Sept 19   Juan Manuel Marquez WUD 12, MGM Grand, Las Vegas, NV

2010

May 1   Shane Mosley WUD 12, MGM Grand, Las Vegas, NV

2011

Sept 17   Victor Ortiz WKO 4, MGM Grand, Las Vegas, NV
WBC World welterweight title

2012

May 5   Miguel Cotto WUD 12, MGM Grand, Las Vegas, NV
WBA Super World light middleweight title

2013

May 4   Robert Guerrero WUD 12, MGM Grand, Las Vegas, NV
WBC World welterweight title

Sept 14   Saul Alvarez WMD 12, MGM Grand, Las Vegas, NV
WBA Super and WBC World light middleweight titles

2014

May 3   Marcos Rene Maidana WMD 12, MGM Grand, Las Vegas, NV
WBA Super and WBC World welterweight titles

Sept 13   Marcos Rene Maidana WUD 12, MGM Grand, Las Vegas, NV
WBC World welterweight title
WBA Super World welterweight title
WBC World Super welterweight title

2015

May 2   Manny Pacquiao WUD 12, MGM Grand, Las Vegas, NV
           WBO World welterweight title
           WBA Super welterweight title
           WBC World welterweight title
Sept 12   Andre Berto WUD 12, MGM Grand, Las Vegas, NV
           WBA Super welterweight title
           WBC World welterweight title

BIBLIOGRAPHY

Ames, Jonathan. "Floyd Mayweather Jr." *Interview Magazine*. Web. Fall 2009.

Badenhausen, Kurt. "Floyd Mayweather Heads 2014 List Of The Worlds Highest Paid Athletes." *Forbes Magazine*. Web. 11 June 2014.

Bishop, Greg. "Behind the Scenes, Haymon is Shaking Up the Fight Game." *New York Times*. 11 December 2011.

Juipe, Dean. "Rancor in the Ring." *Las Vegas Sun*. 7 December 2000.

Lois Ricardo. "USADA Chief Tygart says Xylocaine okay for Mayweather." *Examiner.com*. Web, 23 May 2010.

McCable, Francis, Haynes, Brian, and Carp Steve. "Police Called To Another Dispute Between Mayweather and a Woman." *Las Vegas Review-Journal*. Web, 18 September 2012.

Rogers, Martin. Life with Floyd Mayweather: 'I was a Battered Woman.' *USA Today*. 18 November 2014.

Wertheim, Jon. "Pride and Punishment." *Sports Illustrated*. Web 10 October 2005.

Front Cover Mayweather Photo Credit: AP Photo/Eric Jamison.

Manny Pacquiao

Lifespan (1978–Present)

Active: 1995–Present (57-6-2, 38 KOs)

Titles Held: WBC Flyweight, IBF Super Bantamweight, WBC Jr. Lightweight, WBC Lightweight, WBO Welterweight, WBC Jr. Middleweight

CHAPTER 1
Discipline and Strength through Struggle

Emmanuel Dapidran Pacquiao was born on December 17, 1978, in Kibawe, Bukidnon, Philippines. Bukidnon is a regional province located on the island of Mindanao. Pacquiao was born to Dionesia Dapidron-Pacquiao and Rosalio Pacquiao. His mother often worked doing housework for clients who could afford such luxuries. Pacquiao's biological father would work as an agricultural laborer on farms. His parents would separate when Pacquiao was twelve years old. This would make the family economic situation dire. Pacquiao would drop out of school out of necessity to help his family.

Pacquiao was the fourth of six children. While he was still an infant, Pacquiao's family would move to the town of Tango in the Sarangani province. Tango is a mountainous area that is located in the municipality of Glan. The region is rich in agricultural products such as bananas, coconuts, fish, mangoes, sugarcane, and pineapples. This provided an immediate food source that could help sustain living. A young Pacquiao would develop his calf muscles by carrying buckets of water, rice, and flour through the strenuous terrain. He also worked his legs by spending time with local fishermen carrying heavy nets of fish. His compensation was fish and getting instilled with the understanding of a strong work ethic. Despite his efforts, Pacquiao has stated there were periods when he went hungry, as food was rationed and not plentiful. Pacquiao's family would move again, this time to General Santos City. The city was the home of former super featherweight champion Rolando Navarette who became a world champion in 1981. The large city was a major acclimation for Pacquiao who essentially went from the forest to a metropolis. This, however, would provide him the opportunity to see his uncle Sardo Mejia who followed the sport of boxing. Meeting Uncle Mejia would prove to be a catalyst for Pacquiao's seeking pugilistic dreams. The move to General Santos City would be a blessing in disguise.

At the age of twelve, Pacquiao would watch the Tyson-Douglas fight with his uncle. He states that the fight changed him forever when he saw that a heavily favored fighter could lose to a Cinderella. This inspired Pacquiao to feel that great odds in life can be overcome. At the time, Tyson was an undefeated fighter, and the loss to Douglas is considered by many as one of the greatest sports upsets—along with the Jets beating the Colts in Super Bowl III and the 1980 US Miracle on Ice in the Winter Olympics.

Pacquiao's mother wanted her son to become a priest. Unfortunately, this was not practical since his family didn't have the money to pay for the education. Most importantly, his family needed immediate relief for their dire economic situation. Selling peanuts, fish, and bread in the streets didn't have the potential of big paydays that a professional boxer did.

The Philippines already had a rich boxing tradition that stretched to the beginning of the twentieth century. The first Filipino champion was Francisco Guilledo, known mainly as "Pancho Villa," who captured the flyweight title against fighter Jimmy Welsh in 1923. Villa would become a major star in the American northeast (in part due to being promoted by Tex Rickard) as he fought in New York, Pennsylvania, New Jersey, and Massachusetts. Villa would die a few weeks short of his twenty-fourth birthday due to Ludwig's angina. The ailment was caused by a tooth infection that spread after he had three teeth extracted. There would be future Filipino champions who would follow, such as Cerefino Garcia, Flash Elorde, Ben Villaflor, Bernabe Villamcopo, and more recently Gerry Penalosa. Five out of nine medals won by Filipino athletes in the Summer Olympics have been in the boxing category. It is believed that if there was better equipment and funding for Olympic programs that the medal tally would be much higher.

Uncle Sardo Mejia would devote his time to help his nephew learn the sport at the age of twelve. Pacquiao would finally get a proper punching bag and gloves to train at his uncle's house. There were no formal boxing gyms in the immediate vicinity for Pacquiao to practice in. A local basketball court would be converted to a gym, which allowed Pacquiao to spar and train with local kids. Immediately, it was evident that Pacquiao's boxing progression was accelerating to the point that he defeated every local kid. A fourteen-year-old Pacquiao would go to Digos City where he joined a group of fighters who traveled and fought as amateurs. This group was part of the Philippine national boxing team. Pacquiao would become friends with fourteen-year-old Abner Cordero, a young boxer who was also part of the team. Abner's dad, Dizon Cordero, was a local trainer and guided Pacquiao with basic boxing techniques. Per Dizon, Pacquiao won all thirty fights under his tutelage before Pacquiao left for Manila in search of a professional career. Some sources report that Pacquiao had a 60–4 record as an amateur during this period. Pacquiao grew up admiring fighters such as Julio Cesar Chavez, Sugar Ray Leonard, and Oscar De La Hoya.

CHAPTER 2

Making the Dream Happen

A promoter from Manila spotted Pacquiao's ring exploits and gave the teenager an invitation to box as a professional in the nation's capital. Part of the deal was that Pacquiao would need to come up with the transportation expenses to make the five-hundred-mile trip. For Pacquiao it was to time to turn professional and take the risk for both the sake of his family and himself. Since Pacquiao didn't have the transportation money, he would sneak into a boat to make the journey. Feeling that his mother would not have approved of his new destination, he decided to keep the trip secret from his family. Although Pacquiao's actions were surreptitious in nature, he felt the meaning and purpose of the trip overruled any sense of guilt. For millions of Filipinos, this story resonates with the exodus of fellow countrymen who travel distances in order to help their families. There are no entitlement programs such as social security, unemployment benefits, and food stamps; this means families often need to fend for themselves. Each year more than one million Filipino workers find work abroad that helps stabilize their families who remain on the island. In 2013, more than $25 billion was received in the Philippines in the form of remittance according to the country's central bank. Per the World Bank, the figure is approximately 10 percent of the nation's gross domestic product.

Often elderly Filipino parents require their children to take care of their economic and health requirements. Eldest children are often required to pay educational expenses for their younger siblings. The support system within the family unit is not just a Filipino cultural custom, but it is a common practice in many Asian countries.

Pacquiao's mother would get news of his trip to Manila and support the decision. Pacquiao would train at the former L&M Gym in Manila in hopes of a successful boxing career.

Manny Pacquiao was still a frail teenager and actually weighed less than the 106 pounds when he officially recorded in his professional debut. Pacquiao reportedly had to put a few weights in his pockets to make the minimum weight. Not only did Pacquiao need to gain weight to become a full strawweight, he still needed to learn more of the technical side of the sport. When a fighter has a limited amateur career, he usually has to put his time in both the gym and ring to pick up things. In other words, it's either sink or swim, and Pacquiao decided to swim. Boxing is prizefighting, so fighters understand that oftentimes if they win they can eat; if they lose they go hungry. This prospect couldn't be more real for the teenage Pacquiao who was far from his family's province. Pacquiao did have ingredients that would make him stand out despite his lack of technical training. Pacquiao had determination, power, and he was a southpaw. When you are facing fighters who also lack experience, it is difficult for them to adjust to a boxing stance they have rarely seen.

Ben Delgado would be Pacquiao's new trainer in Manila. Odd jobs like construction, gardening, and tailoring helped pay for Pacquiao's expenses, while providing him the opportunity to send pesos to his mother in the province. At one point Pacquiao was able to send his mother three hundred pesos on a regular basis. As Pacquiao trained he often would sleep in the gym in a small room or on the ring canvas. Despite the hardships, Pacquiao felt optimistic about turning professional and felt his faith in God would see him through. At the age of sixteen, Pacquiao would win his first three professional fights by decision against Edmund Enting Ignacio, Pinoy Montejo, and Rocky Palma. However, Pacquiao gave his age as eighteen, which allowed him to compete.

Pacquiao made one hundred pesos for his first professional bout, which he sent to his mother. His first two bouts were in Mindoro Occidental, and his third was in Cavite. The majority of his bouts for the next two years would be fought in the Metro Manila area. Pacquiao would wear white trunks with his name in red lettering. He had yellow stars on the side of each trunk. His early fights were often held in local basketball gyms with local audiences. Pacquiao would get more exposure when his fourth professional fight would be telecast by a local boxing show entitled *Blow by Blow*. The program would cover some of Pacquiao's early bouts. In his television debut, a long-haired Pacqiuao didn't suffer from impaired vision as he kept firing a measured left to Dele Desierto's face. The commentators would point out how low Pacquiao kept his right arm, which made him vulnerable to a left hook, but it seemed that Pacquiao was not much concerned about getting hit. He seemed to expect it and enjoyed the exchanges. With all the talk about Pacquiao being mainly a left-handed puncher, it was interesting to note that it was a right shot to the body at 2:39 in the second round that would knock out Desierto. Desierto turned his back to Pacquiao, which compelled the referee to stop the fight. (Unfortunately, referees haven't always followed this precedent as the Arguello-Mancini fight in 1981 highlighted.)

Pacquiao's next opponent was a more durable Acasio Simbajon who effectively fought Pacquiao on the inside. A sharp left uppercut in the second round would momentarily stagger Simbajon. Pacquiao would get stunned in the fifth by a straight right and then would take a low blow. The referee afforded him some recovery time. Both combatants came out firing in the sixth, sensing the decision was in the balance. Pacquiao would land his trademark right pawning jab and straight-left combination to take the final round and win by a six-round unanimous decision.

Pacquiao would next defeat Armando Rocil by a third-round knockout and would then defeat Lolito Laroa by an eight-round decision. Pacquiao was now 7-0 with only two of those wins coming by the way of knockout. There was still a maturity process for Pacquiao to establish his power. Pacquiao needed to get more leverage on the punches and not just fling arm punches. People often assume if the power is there, it automatically produces results. Pacquiao still didn't work the body, and he still didn't set up his shots as a seasoned professional would. The early Pacquiao would beat down opponents by attrition as he winged shots and outworked them with sheer volume. He would still need to learn much more about combination punching and defensive skills like blocking, slipping, and rolling with punches. The teenage fighter was still winning over audiences with his style and relentless drive to win. The entertainment value of performances was something that Pacquiao felt was just as important as winning. Pacquiao felt that, despite winning, if you were perceived as monotonous and mundane, then your product value (in a commodity sense) would depreciate. Pacquiao explained, "I could not imagine disappointing my fans because, to me, that would be worse than losing."

Pacquiao would get his third knockout victory after literally throwing the kitchen sink at Renato Mendones in Puerto Princesa City, Palawan. Mendones bled so much that some of the blood would actually fall on Pacquiao's left shoulder. Pacquiao would win his next three bouts to improve to 11-0 with 4 KOs. His last bout with Lito Torrejos was officially a technical decision due to an accidental head-butt, but it appeared that the cut from Torrejos's left eye was a result of a punch. Pacquiao would get the decision instead of getting credit for a TKO. This period also saw Pacquiao suffer a profound loss as his friend Eugene Barutag would collapse in the ring in an undercard match with Randy Andaga. He would later be transported to a local hospital only to be dead on arrival. Pacquiao would still go on and win his match against Toyogon.

Pacquiao would soon face a different form of adversity who went by the name of Rustico Torrecampo. Pacquiao would face the boxer from Davao City on February 9, 1996. As a penalty Pacquiao would be given heavier gloves due to failing to make the stipulated weight agreement of 112 pounds. Ironically, in boxing sometimes the best thing that can happen to a fighter is to suffer their first defeat because it makes them more mature as both a person and fighter. Being undefeated, Pacquiao was becoming more complacent and still had some defensive liabilities. Pacquiao would often pawn his right hand as a measuring stick or jab and then follow it up with his more powerful straight left. Torrecampo got underneath the left hand and countered with a straight right to the body. Pacquiao would go down only seventeen seconds into the third round. He wouldn't beat the count and suffered the first loss of his professional career. Pacquiao almost had Torrecampo finished in the second round but failed to finish him. This happens often in the sport; a fighter fails to finish an opponent, and it comes back to haunt him. As the years have gone by, some observers have classified it as a low blow, but the punch was on the beltline, and Pacquiao never made any complaints about the loss. In fact, he credits the defeat as helping him become a better fighter. Pacquiao would be forced into a ten-round slugfest with Marlon Carillo, an experienced fighter, in his next contest. Pacquiao would win the ten-round decision, which proved (along with his decision win over Rolondo Toyogon) that Pacquiao had the stamina to go ten rounds.

A knockout win over John Medina would set up his first match in his local town of General Santos City. Pacquiao was better conditioned and actually got up to 116 pounds for his fight with Batiller. The pesos earned from fighting were allowing him to eat better and to have better nutrition as he went through puberty. Pacquiao would knock out Batiller in four rounds. The trip to General Santos City was a momentous occasion for Pacquiao as he was able to see his mother in person for the first time in years. The trip to General Santos City would also result in a chance encounter with his old friend Buboy Fernandez. Pacquiao would decide to give Fernandez work and bring him back to Manila to train with him.

The next test would be the experienced Indonesian flyweight Ippo Gala, who was credited as being 31-6-4 with 10 KOs at the time he fought Pacquiao. Some other sources had him as really 1-11-1. It was apparent that Pacquiao was finally able to work the body more consistently by digging in hooks to the rib cage. Gala would go down by accumulative punches one minute into the second round. Gala would complain that one of the punches was in back of his head, but Pacquiao would unleash a barrage of blows as Gala would cover his face with both gloves on top of the ropes, which prompted the referee to stop the contest. Pacquiao was now 15-1, 8 KOs.

Pacquiao would get more exposure, as he would fight on ESPN's *Asia Fight Nights* against Korean Seung-You Lee. San Miguel Beer sponsored the event. It was eighteen-year-old Pacquiao's a favorite drink, and he was now legally allowed to drink. Lee was an opponent who kept a low stance and tried to pressure Pacquiao on the ropes with nonstop aggression. Pacquiao didn't mind brawling and would bloody Lee's nose and force the stoppage two minutes into the second round. It may have been a premature stoppage as Lee was still on his feet, but there was no complaining from Lee. Pacquiao would embrace his opponent after the fight for his valiant effort. The commentators were still concerned about Pacquiao's lack of defense and exclaimed, "This boy has a lot of talent, but he needs to be guided, and if you put any halfway decent flyweight, he will get knocked out because his defense is hardly there, and he is all offense-type fighter." The challenge for Pacquiao would be to remain an offensive fighter while balancing proper defensive approach. There have been plenty of offensive-minded fighters who succeeded in the sport—such as Harry Greb, Aaron Pryor, and Joe Frazier—who did it with proper technique.

A crack at the OPBF flyweight title would be Pacquiao's first real test and would make him a legitimate international flyweight contender if he won. Before getting a shot at the OPBF title, Pacquiao would dispatch Mike Luna with a straight left in the southwestern corner ropes to earn a first-round knockout. A left hook to Wook-Ki-Lee's body would earn him a second straight first-round knockout victory. A six-round knockout win over Ariel Austria, and now Pacquiao was ready to fight for the OPBF title.

Thai fighter Chokchai Chockvivat (34-2, 16 KOs) had defended his Oriental Pacific Boxing Federation title eight times and was ranked number five by the WBC prior to facing Pacquiao. The fact that the bout would be in Metro Manila and in front of his fellow countrymen would add pressure for the young fighter. But that didn't matter to Pacquiao who saw it as an opportunity at an international title. It would be only Chockvivat's second time fighting outside of Thailand. Pacquiao would actually use his right jab in the contest instead of just pawning it, as he had in the past, to measure his straight left. As Ronnie Nathanielsz would exclaim, "This was the acid test for Pacquiao against critics who claimed he was given only patsy opponents." Chockvivat, possibly hearing about the body-shot loss to Torrecampo, would fire a few straight rights to Pacquiao's body, but Pacquiao was not going down this time. Pacquiao possibly started a bit cautiously to test how much power the Thai fighter had. Chockvivat again piled another straight right to Pacquiao's body in the opening of the second round. Pacquiao would get more aggressive and land a straight left to the champion's chin. This was a direct result of Chockvivat's desire to keep going to the body, which left him open upstairs. Pacquiao would rally toward the end of the round, throwing more power shots as Chock stood patiently taking the shots. Both fighters would exchange tremendous hooks to the body in the middle of the ring in the third round. It was obvious that Pacquiao's conditioning had improved significantly to withstand all the body shots. The improved footwork and new angles of punches would prevent Pacquiao from being a stationary target. A compact short left hook to Chockvivat's head at 2:21 of the fifth round would KO him and make Pacquiao the new OPBF champion.

Pacquiao would get a game challenge from fellow Filipino Melvin Magramo in Cebu City, Cebu. The contest would not be for Pacquiao's new OPBF title as the match was held over the 112-pound limit. Magramo was a very experienced fighter who resided at San Jose City, Philippines. He knew how to counter a southpaw. Magramo had thirty-seven professional fights, including opponents such as Chocvivat and an early version of the great Thai fighter Veeraprol Sapharom. Both fighters would trade their best shots and still remain standing. Pacquiao would reportedly go to the wrong corner due to the punishment he received. Magramo himself would later win the OPBF title, a testament to the fact that he was not a tune-up fight before Pacquiao's first OPBF defense. Despite winning a contested decision against Magramo, the question was raised, "How far could Pacquiao go by taking so many blows?" Magramo had stopped Pacquiao's knockout streak at eight. However, Pacquiao was a flyweight titleholder and would successfully defend his OPBF title with two consecutive first-round knockouts.

The first knockout was against Thai fighter Panomdej Ohyuthanakom, who would get pressured from the opening bell and forced into the ropes until a devastating left hook to the body would KO him at 1:38 of the first round. The bout against Ohyuthanakom was once again in General Santos City and allowed Pacquiao to spend more time with his family. The second consecutive first-round knockout would come five months later in Tokyo against Shin Terao. Pacquiao would drop Terao three times. The actual third knockdown would be a result of a head collision that would crumple Terao to the canvas.

Upon returning to the Philippines, Pacquiao would be introduced to his future wife, Maria Geraldine Capeña Jamora (Jinkee) by a friend. She was employed at the General Santos City mall at a beauty shop. Pacquiao would instantly fall in love and court Jinkee. They would get married a year later and have a total of four children. After the Terao win, Pacquiao would have his longest ring hiatus up to that point. He was away from the ring for nearly seven months. As the saying goes, good things come for those who wait. His next match would be for the WBC flyweight title.

CHAPTER 3

Becoming the People's Champion

December 4, 1998, would be the date that Pacquiao would fight for his major international title. Pacquiao would go to Thailand and face Chatchai Sasakul (33-1, 24 KOs). Sasakul was far from a paper champion of the modern variety. Sasakul was a crafty boxer who had excellent ring generalship and counterpunching ability. His only loss (to Russian-born Yuri Abarchakov) would be avenged in Japan where Abarchakov made his adopted home. Pacquiao (23-1, 13 KOs) was facing an opponent who understood how to exploit defensive mistakes and weaknesses.

There was some evolution to be seen in Pacquiao's style; he would keep his guard high with some bobbing and weaving. Pacquiao would also have his hair trimmer in the front so that it wouldn't impede his vision or cause extra perspiration to irritate his eyes. Yet there were still enough defensive liabilities for a crafty Sasakul to take advantage of. Sasakul was one of the few early Pacquiao opponents who circled away from the powerful Pacquiao left and would fire a straight left when Pacquiao's right hand was low. Sasakul would often use quick two-punch combinations that consisted of a straight left to the head followed by a right to the body. Sasakul would score with a strong left hook to Pacquiao's head in the first round, as the challenger got careless coming up after bending down.

Sasakul was able to use his feet to create distance in the second round and dig straight lefts to Pacquiao's body. Pacquiao would eat a heavy-handed right hand to the face that made him grimace. Sasakul understood that Pacquiao was looking for one measured left shot, and by keeping on the move, that wouldn't happen. Pacquiao would lunge a wild right, but Sasakul would move his torso back to avoid the shot. Despite losing the second round, Pacquiao was a bit more confident as he took the best shots from his opponent and remained standing while finally landing two solid lefts: one to the body and one to the head.

The third round saw Sasakul again confusing Pacquiao with feints and movements. A three-punch combination tapped off with a left hook to the chin would ice the round for Sasakul. Pacquiao would finally be able to score with an overhand right and a two-punch combination before the round ended. However, Pacquiao surely understood that he was likely down three rounds in the scorecards and fighting a world champion in his own backyard; things looked bleak for the challenger. One positive sign was that, despite getting hit often, Pacquiao was able to walk through those punches. Most importantly, Sasakul was starting to actually trade with Pacquiao as he sought out his own offensive opportunities.

The fourth would be the first round that Pacquiao really cut off the ring and closed the distance with Sasakul. A short left hook would land squarely on Sasakul's chin and make the champion take a few backward steps. The local Thai outdoor arena would get more to cheer about as Sasakul would counter Pacquiao for missing in the fifth, and he avoided any powerful Pacquiao lefts. After being hit, Pacquiao would not only notoriously bang his gloves, but he would also pounce his head with his gloves—an act reminiscent of fighters like Vinnie Paz and Marvin Hagler. As good as Sasakul's ability as a boxer was, he failed to slow down Pacquiao's pressure. Often boxers clinch and slow a heavy-handed puncher's pace down to take seconds off the clock. Moreover, it gives them a little more rest time so they can go back to their bike. This is like a defensive football team running the football against a high-powered offense to keep the score low. Sasakul never really slowed the match or clinched much, and by the sixth Sasakul was becoming more flat-footed as the Thai sun was increasingly radiating the ring. The Thai champion would work the body more often with double rights, and Pacquiao protested—claiming they were low blows, which prompted the referee to warn Sasakul.

The seventh round would be the best Pacquiao round since the fourth round. The straight left was finally hitting the mark. Early in the round, Pacquiao landed two straight lefts after measuring with a right. Moments later, a short compact left hook landed on the button. Sasakul was still hanging, but unless he changed strategy, he was putting himself in serious risk. The champion would instead remain flat-footed to try to get his own shots in. As a result, Sasakul would get hit with a fourth powerful left in the seventh round. Sasakul would be hurt by a straight left in the middle of the ring in round eight. His nose was bloodied, and he would retreat to the northeastern corner ropes where Pacquiao would finish him off with a left hook to Sasakul's chin. Sasakul would crawl around during the count and get up, only to fall again, which prompted referee Malcolm Bulner to stop the contest. Despite being down 64–69, 65–68, and 64–70 in the cards, Pacquiao became the new WBC Flyweight champion of the world with one punch. Sasakul could have lost the last five rounds in the cards and still remained champion with a split-decision draw. But on that sunny Thai afternoon, the fighter from General Santos City wouldn't be denied. Pacquiao would cross himself in the middle of the ring and pray in the ring post. He had defied the incredible odds and joined Rolando Navarrete as another world champion from General Santos City. Pacquiao was greeted home as a local hero and felt a sense of accomplishment due to the hard work and sacrifices bearing their fruit.

BOXING'S QUINTUPLE CHAMPIONS

Pacquiao takes on Chatchai Sasakul, whom he defeated to capture the WBC Flyweight title.

CHAPTER 4

Weight Issues

Pacquiao would not immediately defend his new WBC title after getting a homecoming celebration in the Philippines. He would fight an Australian fighter, Todd Makelim, trained by Hall of Famer Jeff Fenech. Fenech, known as the "Marrickville Mauler," had won titles in three weight classes and was on the verge of a fourth (all while undefeated) until receiving a dubious draw in his first fight with Azumah Nelson. Perhaps Fenech's greatest example of his pound-per-pound ability came outside of the ring as, in a club scuffle, he reportedly knocked out a NYC bouncer who outweighed him by more than one hundred pounds.

Pacquiao would weigh 116 pounds and Makelim came in at exactly 115 on February 20, 1999, in the contest held at Kidapawan City, Cotabato (del Norte), Philippines. Bobby Pacquiao, Manny's younger brother, would also fight in the undercard against Primo Erasan and would win by a fourth-round KO. Pacquiao would punish Makelim with combinations as the Australian lay on the ropes in the first two rounds. Makelim would be forced to take a knee at 2:25 of the second round due to body shots. The actual count may have been delayed since Pacquiao was slow to go to the neutral corner. Seventeen seconds elapsed between Makelim going down and the action resuming. Makelim would fight back in the third round and land an overhand right on Pacquiao's head, yet the new champion wouldn't blink an eye. Pacquiao would send a barrage of hooks to Makelim's body that crumpled the Australian; however, he wouldn't go down, which forced his corner to throw the towel to stop the blitzkrieg. What was impressive was that Pacquiao finally worked the body as a seasoned pro and was much better at connecting with precise combination punching. Those extra four pounds also seemed to add power to each of his blows. However, Pacquiao was the flyweight champion and needed to drop four pounds in order make his first defense.

After the fight Fenech would tell the local commentators why he threw the towel. "Pacquiao is a great champion and a hard puncher, and we had only ten days to prepare for this, and Todd was not going to learn by getting knocked out." When assessing Pacquiao's style, Fenech would observe: "He throws punches in bunches, which is good, but he needs to be careful when his hands are down when he is punching, and if he fights one of those little Mexicans who have a good punch, he could be knocked down or knocked out."

Pacquiao would get his first crack against a Mexican fighter in his next match.

Gabriel Mira would be that first Mexican that would test Pacquiao. Some of the press labeled it "The Fight." It was well publicized in the Philippines, and American referee Richard Steele would go to the Philippines to officiate. Steele would tell the press, "Everything I hear about the two of them will make it a great fight, full of action." The fight would be known as "Demolition at the Dome," and both fighters would attend press conferences and meet the Philippine president, Joseph Estrada. Pacquiao would weigh 111.75 pounds, and Mira would come in at 110.5 pounds. In attendance would be Pacquiao's soon-to-be wife, Jinkee. The bout would officially take place on April 24, 1999, in the Araneta Coliseum, Quezon City, Metro Manila.

Mira would start out well by landing short combinations to the body and head. The five-feet-two-inch fighter wouldn't be an easy target, until Pacquiao landed a flush left to Mira's chin. Mira's plan was to land left hooks to the body to try to slow Pacquiao down. After winning the first round, Mira would get more aggressive and would actually hurt Pacquiao in the second round with combination punching. A straight right to the body in the second round (1:02) would have Pacquiao wincing. For one of the few times early in Pacquiao's career, he would get on his bike. The champion would jab with his right as he bought time to fully recover. Mira would back Pacquiao to the ropes and land a four-punch combination. The champion would come back to drop the challenger with his own three-punch combination. Pacquiao would drop Mira a second time, but the punch was ruled after the bell, so it wouldn't count. Mira would drop to the floor several times in the third round mainly due to rubbery legs, and Steele wouldn't count them as knockdowns. At least one of the Mira falls seemed to be a result of a punch.

Steele would finally count a knockdown when Mira would take a knee as a result of a punch in the third. Pacquiao would have two consecutive 10–8 rounds after an inauspicious start. A straight left to the head would send Mira down in the middle of the fourth round. Mira would get up only to be knocked down again by a left hook. Mira would go down as a warrior and not as a patsy. He would score with a solid uppercut and hook in the center of the ring—until a final left would drop him again, and Richard Steele would wave off the fight. The fact that the 111-pound Pacquiao was hurt and backpedaling could have been an indication that he was drained as a flyweight.

The question of whether or not Pacquiao was weight drained would soon be answered in his next bout. Pacquiao would again fly to Thailand—this time as a champion and not as a challenger. Medgeon Singurat, also known as "3K Battery," would challenge Pacquiao on September 17, 1999, at the Pakpanag Metroplian Stadium, Nakhon Si Thammarat, Thailand. The issue of weight would once again be a major factor prior to this fight. Pacquiao essentially lost his title on the scales when he came in at 113 pounds. On paper, Pacquiao was a flyweight, but physically, he was closer to a bantamweight or super bantamweight.

Medgeon Singurat (18-0) came in to this fight with confidence, as he was undefeated and fighting in his home country. Pacquiao was coming back to the country of his greatest triumph. The first round of the fight saw Pacquiao standing erect with little head movement and shooting the right jab that Singurat mainly caught on the gloves in the sunny, outdoor arena. Interestingly, Pacquiao almost fell down after losing his balance in the first while slipping a Singurat left hand. Perhaps the unsteadiness was a result of rubbery legs. The rest of the round was mainly a jab contest without any major artillery being landed—until the closing moments when Singurat got Pacquiao to the southeastern ropes and landed a few straight hands that seemed to stun the champion. Pacquiao would bang his gloves but not return much fire. The second saw Pacquiao being more active with his jab, but he seemed a bit lethargic, and he was not throwing punches in bunches. Singurat, sensing a weak opponent, came after Pacquiao with a fury, landing combinations and actually pinning the champion on the ropes. Pacquiao's accuracy, power, and legs did not seem to be in the fight. The champion felt content to just go for one-two combinations while going on his bike. In the third round, Pacquiao did land a solid straight left, but Singurat took the punch well. Singurat held a tight guard over his head as he came in to pressure the champion. Eventually, after missing a few shots, he would get Pacquiao near the southwestern part of the ropes and deliver a devastating straight right to the body. Pacquiao, wincing in pain, wouldn't beat the count and would suffer his second knockout loss. The new Thai champion was raised in the air and celebrated with crowd whistles and jubilation.

It was obvious that Pacquiao had a weight problem. Although many felt the loss to Singurat was due to weight, other observers were a bit critical of Pacquiao, feeling that he had abandoned a lot of the skills he had recently implemented and instead reverted to his very early bouts where he was more of a brawler.

CHAPTER 5

The Super Bantamweight Risk

Manager Rod Nazario would take a major risk by moving Pacquiao up three weight classes, but his wisdom would pay off big time. Instead of going up to super flyweight or even bantamweight, the decision was made to have Pacquiao fight next as a super bantamweight. Although there would no longer be an issue of being weight drained, the question would arise of whether the former flyweight champion could handle the power of the new division. The other question raised was whether Pacquiao could carry his power to three divisions north. The biggest risk was the weight issue; going up three weight classes in only three months was also a gamble. Often fighters move up, and the power doesn't come up since they are there with naturally bigger opponents. Roberto Duran still had power in the higher weights but not that one-punch-knockout power he had as a lightweight or at lower weights. There would be no slow period of acclimation, climbing the divisions one by one; instead Pacquiao would face Reynante Jamili for the WBC International super bantamweight title on December 18, 1999.

Reynante Jamili (41–5) would be a bit of gamble for the Pacquiao camp after the knockout loss in Thailand. Jamili would not be classified as a safe tune-up fight. Jamili was a former OPBF champion who had won twenty-one consecutive fights, until getting knocked out in six by Erik Morales. In that fight Jamili would be stopped in the final seconds of the sixth round by a powerful lead right. After being dropped by the right hand, Jamili would actually beat the count, but his failure to walk toward referee Marty Denkin would prompt the stoppage. Pacquiao would be fighting Jamili for the WBC International title.

Pacquiao would pass the Jamili test with flying colors. The fighters started out cautiously in a feeling-out process. Jamili would land a few short punches as he put his left glove on Pacquiao's shoulder while connecting with the right. Any questions about Pacquiao's power at the higher weight were answered when he seriously hurt Jamili with a straight left that resulted in him being down in the canvas spread eagle. Jamili would go down by another left, this time on one knee. The fight would end due to the three-knockdown rule when Pacquiao would unload another straight left that knocked Jamili down for a third time. Instead of clinching and getting on his bike, Jamili would land a hook to the body and a solid right until he received the final blow. A very disappointed Jamili had gotten up, but his own corner had thrown the towel despite the three-knockdown rule having officially ended it. The victory was a career-saving win. If Pacquiao had lost a second consecutive fight, this time to a domestic fighter, it would have made it very difficult to climb up the ranks and command the public's attention.

Arnel Barotilo was regarded as another good contender before Pacquiao would fight for another major world title. Barotilo, a native Filipino, had moved to Australia and was known mainly for going the distance with Lehlo Ledwaba, the future IBF champion and future Pacquiao opponent. He was an aggressive fighter who had solid power in both hands. The match would take place on March 4, 2000, at the Ninoy Aquino Stadium, Manila, for the WBC International super bantamweight title. In the first round, he came after Pacquiao with overhand rights and straight lefts. He had Pacquiao on the ropes and went after the body, but Pacquiao was able to elude danger and escape the round without much damage. Although Barotillo landed some powerful shots that moved Pacquiao's head back, it was obvious he was not going to go down as he had in the Singurat fight. Pacquiao's calves were stronger in this weight, and his body was more durable. The second round would see both fighters exchanging willingly in the center of the ring; it seemed the tide was going to Barotillo when he landed shots that would move Pacquiao's head back. There was more brawling than boxing in the early going as both fighters were obviously trying to knock the other one out. Barotillo would eventually start to miss shots as he went after the head instead of the body. However, Barotillo did land a powerful straight hand in the second round.

The third would see Pacquiao take over the fight with powerful left-hand leads that started to slow Barotillo down. The more Barotillo clinched, the more determined Pacquiao would come in for the finish. Pacquiao's accuracy would get better as Barotillo's punches would get both wider and wilder. It would be a right hand to Barotillo's ear that would send him down. This could have been a result of losing balance by taking a blow to the place that controls equilibrium. Barotillo would get saved by the bell after the referee Bruce McTavish finished his count. Unfortunately for Barotillo, it couldn't stop the inevitable fate when the fourth round began. After taking punishment to the body, it was only a matter of time before Barotillo would go down. To his credit, Barotillo kept fighting on to the bitter end. Pacquiao would end the contest with a stunning overhand right (1:50) in the fourth round that produced a delayed reaction. Barotillo would go down, and there was no need for a count as he was knocked out cold. The scene was scary for moments. Pacquiao probably had flashbacks of his friend Barutag who died in the ring near the end of 1995. The victory showed again that Pacquiao could knock out an opponent not only with his left but also with his right hand.

The next opponent would be Seung-Kon Chae (23-0, 18 KOs), a fighter not well known outside of his native South Korea. He was undefeated but never fought for a world title, and his biggest win was a Korean Featherweight title. Chae had fought as high as a super featherweight; he was now fighting as a super bantamweight. Obviously, fighting for the WBC International super bantamweight title was Chae's biggest opportunity at that point. The actual match would last only less than two minutes as Chae came in very aggressive and left himself open for a short left hook. Chae got back on his feet, but he didn't seem to have fully recovered, and the referee, Bruce Mctavish, stopped the fight.

CHAPTER 6

The Disputed Count

Most boxing careers usually contain a few controversies. Perhaps Pacquiao's most controversial win was the fight with Nedal Hussein. The fight was foul infested and perhaps among the most criticized fights of the official Carlos Padilla's illustrious career. Padilla was well known for his work on the Leonard-Duran 1 fight and Ali-Frazier 3 fight, also known as the "Thrilla in Manilla." Nedal Hussein's record was 19-0, 11 KOs when he would meet Pacquiao on October 14, 2000, at the Ynares Sports Center, Antipolo City, Rizal. The fight did produce good action—despite the controversial long count and fouls. Hussein, a Lebanese-born Australian citizen, was trained by three-divisional world champion Jeff Fenech. Fenech already knew Manny Pacquiao well as he had been to the Philippines as Todd Makelim's trainer. At that time Pacquiao was flyweight champion, and now he was making a run as a super bantamweight. Fenech likely studied any flaws in Pacquiao's game. On the flip side of the coin, this Pacquiao version was more advanced than the mainly offensive fighter of nearly two years before. There was a lot more bobbing and weaving, lateral movement, and overall physical maturity. Pacquiao's assistant trainer, Buboy Fernandez, had felt that Hussein would pose a serious challenge to Pacquiao. This was no tune-up fight for a possible world title down the road.

- The first stanza of the contest would have Pacquiao frantically attacking Hussein's body with hooks downstairs. Padilla would give Hussein stern warning for a flagrant elbow or push-off early in the round. It was an easy round to score for Pacquiao, but interestingly, Hussein would score with a few left jabs that would foreshadow what would happen later in the fight. The second saw a lot of the same action. This time Pacquiao would counter with his right, often over Hussein's left glove. Hussein would get another warning after he shoved Pacquiao to the ropes while they were holding. There was more rough stuff in the third with Hussein forcing Pacquiao against the ropes. There would be no point deductions until that point. All three opening rounds would appear to go to the Pacquiao column. The fourth round would go down as the most controversial round in Pacquiao's history. It is perhaps not as discussed as the final round of Chavez-Taylor 1 or the seventh round between Tunney-Dempsey 2, but it is still getting more publicity as Pacquiao's fame continues to grow.

Hussein would drop Pacquiao forty-six seconds into the fourth with the same laser left jab that he had used earlier in the fight. Pacquiao would start to get up at 2:23 of the round, but Padilla would still give instructions and seemingly continue to count. When the action resumed, over twenty seconds had passed, and Pacquiao was still hurt. Hussein would stagger Pacquiao with some hooks to the body and straight rights, but Pacquiao would intelligently hold on. When Padilla couldn't separate the fighters, Hussein threw another elbow to get Pacquiao off. Padilla would take a point away from Hussein, and his warning incensed Jeff Fenech who felt it was giving Pacquiao more recovery time. The rest of the round would include more rough stuff, but Pacquiao's legs had recovered. The cameras would pan to Pacquiao's wife, Jinkee, who was five months pregnant and was in tears due to what had transpired. The preoccupation would end after Pacquiao survived the round.

It was apparent that Pacquiao had his legs back, and Hussein would resume with holding and hitting in the fifth. The tide had shifted to Pacquiao as he landed straight hands and left hooks. Hussein was still in the fight as he scored a few good rights himself. In the sixth, Hussein would score with a solid right to the chin thirty-four seconds into the round and a powerful left at 1:41 of the round, but Pacquiao had his legs back. Pacquiao would land a powerful right at 2:17 of the round and possibly steal a close round. Pacquiao would use his legs to create more distance and space with Hussein in the seventh, which would create more angles to score with his right hand. There would be another infraction when Hussein would use his shoulder to throw Pacquiao to the canvas sixty-one seconds into the round. Many in the arena and broadcast team felt there were already grounds for a disqualification. The broadcast team would echo "Never have I seen a fighter as dirty as Nedal Hussein,"—perhaps a bit of a stretch if they saw footage of the Norris-Santana and Bowe-Golota bouts. Perhaps a little bit of Fenech had gotten into Hussein—who was known to be a bit rough at times, as his rugby tackle of Azumah Nelson in their first fight could attest.

Hussein would not get another major opportunity to win. In the eighth round, he landed a powerful left hook to Pacquiao's face forty-four seconds into the round, but it didn't do much damage. Both fighters would exchange flurries in the closing seconds, but no fighter would go down. There would be some seesaw action in the ninth round with both fighters trying to end the fight. However, a major gash in Hussein's left eye was bleeding profusely. Hussein would hit Pacquiao immediately after the break in another flagrant foul. It was obvious that between the fourth-round knockdown and this incident that this was not Carlos Padilla's best officiating. Perhaps many Australian fans watching the fight would say the same thing after watching the fourth round during the controversial count and point deduction. The ringside physician would eventually stop the fight in the tenth at 1:38. The foul-infested and controversial affair was over. The Hussein corner was angry as they felt it was a premature stoppage, and they were still livid due to the events of the fourth round. Nedal Hussein was barking at the officials and felt that the entire event was hometown cooking. After all the postfight bickering, Hussein and Pacquiao did briefly embrace when things calm down.

Despite the entire controversy, there was no immediate rematch for anytime down the road. Interestingly, both fighters would share the same ring when they both fought in the undercard of the Tyson-Lewis fight in the Pyramid in Memphis, Tennessee. Hussein would go on to win seventeen consecutive fights until he would lose to Oscar Larios for the WBC super bantamweight title in 2004. Hussein's next shot for a world title was in 2005 when he would lose to Scott Harrison for the WBO super featherweight title.

Before fighting for the world super bantamweight title, Pacquiao had two more fights that served as solid preparation for his world-title ambitions. Both fights would be held in the Philippines. Pacquiao would face Tatsura Senrima (19-4-3) who, like former WBC super-flyweight champion Masamori Tokuyama, fought out of Japan but was of North Korean descent. The bout also took place at the Ynares Sports Center on February 24, 2001. The fight would last only five rounds, but it was an action-packed affair. Pacquiao would wear his blond highlights for the first time and sport his nation's flag on his trunks. Senrima took a lot of punishment but showed bravado to the end. He tried to go to the body early on against Pacquiao but could never pin him down as Pacquiao was like a buzz saw throughout the fight. Pacquiao looked like a sonic blur in the fight with his speed and accuracy. Senrima would land a solid counter left early on, and Pacquiao replied by banging his gloves and coming back stronger. Senrima would wave to Pacquiao to come in during the second round in contempt of Pacquiao's power and would later show further indignation after taking shots in the fourth round by sticking out his chin to show he could eat the punches. Unfortunately for the challenger, sometimes a fighter can be too brave for his own good, and by the fifth round, Senrima was bleeding from his nose and mouth. After additional pummeling the referee stopped the fight. Senrima threw his arms in frustration as he wanted to continue, but it seemed a futile affair. To his credit Senrima never went down, but the punishment was excessive, and stoppage was appropriate. Like the Energizer Bunny, it appeared Pacquiao would never punch himself out and was able to finish his opponent in the fifth round.

Pacquiao would take another step closer to championship level when he fought Wethya Sakmuangklang (41–3) on April 28, 2001, in Kidapawan City. The Thai fighter was a good technical fighter. He would pepper Pacquiao with his jab and use solid lateral movement to avoid getting countered. Pacquiao didn't just go out and blitz the Thai fighter as he did with Senrima. This was a slower, tactical affair. Patience would be a virtue in this fight as it was with the Sasakul fight. It was just a matter of time where opportunities would present themselves. Sakmuangklang continued bobbing and weaving while keeping his guard high. He was obviously not ignorant enough to think he was going to win a slugfest with Pacquiao. Sakmuangklang would land straight right jabs to both the head and body in the first two rounds. Sakmuangklang would score with a looping counter right at 2:01 of the first round that snapped Pacquiao's head back. The action would speed up in the second round with the Thai challenger now connecting with both short right and left hooks while remaining on his bike.

Pacquiao would cut off the ring and land several combinations that partially connected. The fight would tilt to the Pacquiao direction when he would score with hooks to the body in the closing seconds of the round. Sakmuangklang would revert to boxing using his right jab and following it up with a straight left, which he landed cleanly with about a minute left in the round. Sakmuangklang would be warned for a low blow in the fourth round that resulted in Pacquiao going down on the canvas. Throughout the early part of the fight, both fighters were accusing each other of low blows. In many ways similar to the Sasakaul fight, after Sakmuangklang tasted some strong Pacquiao left hooks, the Thai fighter decided to start to engage Pacquiao more aggressively. This would produce nonstop action in the fifth. Sakmuangklang would start the sixth with his head tilted low and come in as the aggressor, which would prove to be his own demise. After a furious combination on the ropes, Sakmuangklang would tumble down to the canvas. Reminiscent of Tyson-Berbick, he would get up only to fall back down on the canvas again. Like the Sasakul fight, despite being outboxed early on, Pacquiao would find the knockout victory. Pacquiao was now ready to make his big splash in the United States. Although never winning a major world title other than the OPBF, Sakmuangklang would go on to win his next thirty-seven fights.

CHAPTER 7

Making a Name in Sin City

As fate would have it, IBF super bantamweight champion Lehlohonolo Lewbada needed an opponent in short notice for a bout scheduled on June 23, 2001, at the MGM Las Vegas, Nevada. The match would be telecast on HBO as part of the De La Hoya-Castillejo undercard. Pacquiao would be given only two weeks' notice, and his management immediately accepted the offer. The $25,000 payday would be the most Pacquiao had received up to that point. Most importantly, Pacquiao would travel to Los Angeles and meet his future trainer, Freddie Roach, at the Wild Card Gym. Pacquiao's manager, Rod Nazario, would introduce the men to each other. Roach agreed to work the mitts with Pacquiao to test him. Almost immediately both men realized there was chemistry, and working together was a foregone conclusion.

Roach—a noted fighter who had shared the ring with the likes of Bobby Chacon, Greg Haugen, and Hector Camacho—was now a world-class trainer. Some of his biggest clients included Mike Tyson, James Toney, and Michael Moorer. Roach himself was trained by the legendary Eddie Futch, who is easily among the most influential trainers in the history of the sport. Roach would need to have a crash-course training session with Pacquiao as he had a brief period to get Pacquiao ready for the world-title bout. Roach was quite impressed by the young fighter although he had never heard of him. Murad Muhammad would also be Pacquiao's first American promoter and he tried to help him get spotlight in the United States. Pacquiao would sign a promotional contract with M & M Sports Inc., headed by Murad Muhammad, on June 19, 2001. With both a new trainer and promoter, the fighter from General Santos City was ready to conquer the North American market. The hope was for Pacquiao's appeal to go beyond the large Filipino population in the United States. With each fight there would be more exposure to North American and European fight fans who would get their first glimpse of Pacquiao.

Working the corner with Roach would be notable trainer and cut man Ben Delgado. The fight would be the first fight that a North American audience would see Pacquiao. Pacquiao, who was always linking boxing to business, wanted to impress this new audience. Before the bell rang, Pacquiao's eyes spoke of determination, and his body language showed exuberance and anxiety to start. In fact, the referee Joe Cortez had to tell Pacquiao to stay in his neutral corner before the bell was rung. Larry Merchant would even tell the audience that if "Pacquiao is near the talent of the late Flash Elorde, then expect to have a great fight."

The opening round started off as a jabbing contest with both fighters using their jab while bobbing and weaving on their bike. Pacquiao was able to land a solid left to the body (1:33). Ledwaba was able to answer back with a straight left to the head with a right hook to the body. The final thirty seconds saw Pacquiao blitz Ledwaba with lead lefts and straight rights. There was no point in Pacquiao trying to box Ledwaba; he needed to fight him. Some of the shots seemed to stagger the champion. The first round punch stats had Pacquiao landing 32 of 82 while Ledwaba landed 9 of 28. The second round saw Pacquiao take control of the fight with his great speed. He would counter Ledwaba with straight rights over the left jab and connect with a left hook to the head. Pacquiao would score a knockdown in the second round mainly due to a delayed reaction from a straight left. Bleeding from the nose and mouth, the champion was able to beat the count but took more punishment in the remaining two minutes of the round. The champion, being very hurt, would now abandon his boxing skill and try to slug it out with Pacquiao. Ledwaba would land a few good body shots and stiff left jabs, but the pendulum was swinging to the challenger's direction.

The third round increasingly became a Pacquiao whitewash. He continued to land power shots with both hands, and the amount of blood coming out of Ledwaba was enough to help a Red Cross blood drive. Ledwaba did land a few stiff left jabs, but it was apparent that he didn't have the power to hurt Pacquiao or the durability to handle the punishment dished out against him. At the corner Freddie Roach said, "Straight left hand followed up with the right hook." Pacquiao would see his powerful straight left hit the mark on Ledwaba's chin in the fourth round. At 1:14 of the fourth, Pacquiao would land a left hook to the body that would have knocked out a lesser opponent. Ledwaba would score with a solid straight left (1:24), but it didn't faze Pacquiao at all. Larry Merchant would observe in the fifth round "Ledwaba is said to have hands of stone, but Pacquiao is the one who seems to have rocks in his hands."

The fifth round was more of a dancing contest, as both fighters would be displaying more lateral movement and body movement. Ledwaba landed the most significant blow at 2:19 of the fifth round. Pacquiao would bang his gloves hard, which meant the right hook to the body did seem to hurt him. However, at the closing bell, Pacquiao would score with a powerful lead left. With only thirty-one seconds into the sixth round, Pacquiao would land a straight left to Ledwaba's chin that would send the champion to the canvas for the second time. He would beat the count, but after being knocked down again with a short left hook, the referee Joe Cortez would mercifully stop the contest. Manny Pacquiao was now the new IBF super bantamweight champion of the world. Most importantly, he had made his name in the United States with only two weeks' notice. With a new promoter and a new trainer, the young fighter was now on the route to superstardom.

Pacquiao shares a photo with Lehlo Ledwaba after defeating him to capture the IBF Super Bantamweight title. AP Photo/ Laura Rauch.

Manny Pacquiao would fight in the states again shortly after the tragic events of September 11, 2001. Agapito Sanchez (33-7-1, 20 KOs), who was the WBO champion like Pacquiao, was also a southpaw. Sanchez came to the bout sporting a black "America United" cap in reaction to the events of 9/11. Sanchez was a Dominican fighter with strong lateral movement and hand speed, but he did have seven losses coming into the fight. He also suffered a disqualification for low blows in the past. Like Pacquiao, he was making his first defense of his title. The announcer Michael Buffert did not introduce Pacquiao as "Pacman" but actually as "Manny the Destroyer" Pacquiao. Ironically, the fight was an undercard for Floyd Mayweather-Jesus Chavez. Eventually, the "Destroyer" moniker would be replaced simply with "Pacman," due to the violent connotation. Freddie Roach would once again lead Pacquiao's corner with Ben Delgado as the second assistant and Ruben Gomez as the cut man.

Sanchez was the shorter opponent and commenced the action by shooting a straight left jab with success. He followed that up with solid right-and-left hook upstairs with additional combinations downstairs. Pacquiao would throw his arms up in protest claiming some were low blows. Sanchez would further score with an overhand left that landed effectively at 1:25 of the first round. Sanchez's shorter height—added to his footwork and speed—gave Pacquiao problems in the opening round. Often shorter opponents give problems since they are less of a target for the taller opponents. Sanchez had an effective round by landing his one-twos and even doubling up on the jab. Sanchez had thrown eighty-four punches compared to forty-two for Pacquiao in the first round.

The second saw both fighters do the sign of the cross before the action began. An accidental head-butt caused blood to spurt out below Pacquiao's right eyebrow. The ring physician examined the cut and felt it could be contained and allowed the fight to resume. Sanchez continued his aggression and landed a perfect left hook through Pacquiao's guard at 1:13 of the second round. Sanchez continued to go after the cut eye without relenting and seemed to have won both opening rounds. After two rounds Sanchez had out landed Pacquiao 35–19 and had thrown sixty-four more punches (140–76). The cut man Ruben Gomez frantically tried to stop the bleeding in between rounds. A low blow warning would be issued to Pacquiao in the beginning of the round. Pacquiao finally scored with several lead lefts as Sanchez got more aggressive but left himself open. Sanchez would get a point deduction for pushing Pacquiao's head back during the break. The point deduction and increased activity resulted in a 10–8 Pacquiao round on my scorecard. The fourth once again saw Sanchez get a deduction of another point due to a low blow. This time referee Marty Dickens gave Pacquiao five minutes to recover, as he went down on the canvas grimacing in pain. This was a close round that could have gone in Sanchez's favor, but the deduction eliminated that. The final thirty seconds saw back-and-forth action with possibly another low blow by Sanchez. The Sanchez corner admonished him to avoid low blows since he could get disqualified.

Sanchez continued to attack the body in the fifth round with borderline shots. Dickens could have disqualified Sanchez, but it seemed Pacquiao preferred to fight on despite wincing in pain. The fifth round was quite close and could have gone to either fighter. Pacquiao was landing more accurately in the opening moments of the sixth round. Another head-butt (1:20) in the sixth round effectively ended the bout. Pacquiao's right eye was not in any condition to continue, and the ringside physician stopped it. As a result it went to the scorecards by rule, with the following judges' scores: Raul Caiz (57–55) for Sanchez, Rio Bays (58–54) for Pacquiao, and Marshall Walker having it (56–56) a draw. The result was a technical draw with both fighters retaining their titles. I scored the fight (57–56) for Pacquiao and thought the flurry in the sixth round gave him the victory. However, the final punch stats were almost even with Pacquiao landing 74 of 247 and Sanchez landing 73 of 349.

Pacquiao did win over more boxing fans as he could have used the head-butt as an excuse to get a no contest early on, but he decided to fight on. It was essential to Pacquiao's marketability to soldier on regardless of circumstances. As a result it was a Pacquiao moral victory despite getting a draw and dealing with all the fouls inflicted during the contest.

Pacquiao would have a seven-month hiatus before he returned to the ring again. Several things would change in the Pacquiao camp. Pacquiao would bring back his longtime friend Buboy Fernandez and also get a new cut man (Jimmy Glenn) as well. This would also be the biggest stage in his career, as he would be fighting in the Lewis-Tyson undercard. This bout would be many boxing fans' introduction to Pacquiao. My first impression was that Pacquiao reminded me of Filipino American southpaw Andy Ganigan, a fighter who was known as the "Hawaiian Punch" who knocked down Alexis Arguello in the first round of their lightweight title match in 1982.

Pacquiao had stated many times that he was inspired to be a boxer after watching the Tyson-Douglas fight. He understood that fighting on the Tyson undercard was an ideal situation to make an impression on millions of boxing fans around the world.

Opponent Jorge Julio (44-3, 32 KOs) would be the second consecutive Dominican fighter Pacquiao would face. Julio was a former two-time bantamweight champion. Perhaps due to the magnitude of the event, we saw a very aggressive Pacquiao. He came in with his lead left and attacked the body with short rights. Julio was able to land a strong left counter in the middle of the round, but Pacquiao ate the punch. Roach advised Pacquiao to come in with the double-right jab and then follow it up with the left. Pacquiao would land his left hand indiscriminately on Julio. Julio was too much of a stationary target, and thirteen seconds into the second round, Pacquiao would land a powerful straight left that floored Julio. Pacquiao would knock him down again with a straight left and then not show any mercy to his opponent; he would pummel him until the referee Bill Clancy stopped the fight at 1:09 of the second.

After the Julio fight, there were rumors that Pacquiao would fight one of the big names at featherweight, such as Prince Nazeem, Erik Morales, or Derrick Ganier. However, Pacquiao took on the obscure Fahprakorb Rakkiatgym in the Philippines. On paper, Rakkiatgym seemed a decent opponent with a 37-2, 25 KOs record. In reality, he had faced limited opposition, and his last two opponents prior to Pacquiao included one who had never won and another who had dozens of losses. As a result there was no major suspense when Pacquiao knocked out Rakkiatgym in one round at the Rizal Memorial College in Davao City, Philippines. In fairness, when fighters face lesser opposition, it is imperative to make quick work of them, and this is precisely what Pacquiao did when he knocked Rakkiatgym down four times in the first round and finished him off.

The next Pacquiao fight against Kazak fighter Serikzhan Yeshmagambetov would be more of a challenge. The match would take place on March 15, 2003, at Luna Park, Metro Manila. It would be the first time that Pacquiao would fight as a featherweight, and he would also suffer a knockdown. It would also be featured once again in his native Philippines. Yeshmagambetov started the contest by pawing with the left jab and then trying to follow it up with a straight right. Pacquiao's left finally started to penetrate the Kazak's poor guard later in the round, which eventually resulted in a knockdown at 2:07 of the first round. Yeshmagambetov would get more cautious and would never really have a sustained effort in the following rounds, as he would spring forward with the lazy jab and try a few rights and then go out of range quickly. With less than forty seconds in the third round, there were a few decent shots landed by Yeshmagambetov but no real damage. On the other hand, Pacquiao had already damaged the challenger's left eye to nearly a slit. Within a minute of the fourth round, Pacquiao would go down to the canvas due to walking in to a straight right. This time he was not as hurt as the Hussein fight; it was more of a flash knockdown. Despite being pressured and having his back on the ropes, Pacquiao was able to fully recover due to the inaccuracy of his opponent and his excellent conditioning. Perhaps feeling a sense of urgency due to being knocked down, Pacquiao threw many more punches in the fifth. He would sometimes miss and be off-balance, but his opponent didn't have the skills to capitalize on those opportunities. A looping left hook at 1:30 would have Yeshmagambetov down for a second time. Pacquiao wouldn't waste any time and would land another vicious left that almost had Yeshmagambetov falling out of the ring. He did get up, but the referee Silvestre Abainza stopped the fight without even doing a count. It was a bit of a premature stoppage, but it was unlikely that the fight would have gone much further.

The fourth defense of Pacquiao's IBF super bantamweight crown would be against Emmanuel Lucero. This would have Pacquiao return back to the United States in a card held at the Olympic Auditorium on July 26, 2003. Lucero was a very awkward fighter, reminiscent of Edwin Viruet, due to having a very low stance while his head pointed down with both his gloves tucked in tight as he bobbed and weaved. Fighting this style can sometimes be like a predator trying to crack a turtle's shell or like taking down a porcupine without getting a quill stuck in you. While there was some difficulty in figuring out Lucero, there would also really be no major offense to worry about since Lucero was way too low to counter fast enough, and that stance with tight gloves impaired his vision on the inside. Lucero connected 5 of 41 punches in the first round while Pacquiao landed 16 of 64. Pacquiao was able to finally end the fight forty-nine seconds into the third round with a short left hook that had Lucero stumble and then turn his back to his opponent. The referee Jose Cobian wisely stopped the fight as Lucero was defenseless and could have been in serious danger if Pacquiao had been allowed to load up with power shots. It was now time for Pacquiao to test the best featherweights out there and get a shot at another world title.

CHAPTER 8

Halting the Baby-Faced Assassin

Pacquiao was now going to step into the serious prime time when he announced that he was going to fight Marco Antonio Barrera, also known as the "Baby-Faced Assassin." Barrera had to leave his training camp early due to California fires that forced evacuation of Big Bear. Although Barrera didn't own a featherweight title from the four major sanctioning bodies, he was still both the lineal and ring champion. As a result, if Pacquiao defeated Barrera, he would be considered a triple-weight champion by some of the boxing publications and media.

The odds would be stacked against Pacquiao in coming out with a victory against Marco Antonio Barrera (57-3, 40 KOs), as the fight was scheduled for November 15, 2003, in the Alamodome in San Antonio, Texas—literally the backyard for any Mexican or Mexican American fighter. On paper both fighters were foreigners in the states. But even an American fighter would be an outsider fighting in San Antonio against a Mexican fighter. We just need to look no further than the preposterous Whitaker-Chavez draw in 1993. Pacquiao must have been thinking that he surely needed a knockout to get the win. Barrera was considered by many to be the best featherweight, after his schooling of Naseem Hamed in 2001. Barrera also had two classic ring wars with Erik Morales that saw him losing the first by split decision and winning the second by majority decision. It was widely believed that Barrera should have won the first contest with Morales and that the second fight was a makeup decision for the first, as it appeared he lost the rematch.

Pacquiao, a big NBA fan, would sport a local San Antonio Spurs jersey as he entered the Alamodome arena. Despite Pacquiao appeasing the local crowd with his attire, all the cheering was reserved for Marco Antonio Barrera.

Things must have seemed a bit strange to Pacquiao when he would receive a count for a phantom knockdown in the first round (0:26). Lawrence Cole would start the count while Pacquiao would hold both his gloves up in disbelief that it wasn't ruled a slip. What actually happened was that Pacquiao had tripped on Barrera's left foot. Both fighters would come out firing to the body, and there would also be several jabs exchanged. Barrera was more offensive oriented, which was contrary to his cautious boxing style early on. Freddie Roach would ask Pacquiao to use the "double jab" before the start of the second round. However, it would be Barrera who would be scoring with the jab in the second round. Barrera would block most of Pacquiao's right jabs. The change would come when the fight would break out in the last minute of the round, and Pacquiao started to land his combinations.

Pacquiao would drop Barrera with a straight left in the third round (0:30). Barrera, after shooting his left jab, would keep his right guard down and would pay for the mistake. Despite getting up, Barrera really didn't fully recover from the shot, and Pacquiao would punish him for the last two minutes of the round searching for a knockout. Barrera would fight bravely, out of instinct, but his legs were gone.

Barrera found in Pacquiao an opponent with power, speed, and both head and lateral movement. He needed to slow the fight down to his pace. Barrera had to circle away from Pacquiao's left and capitalize with counterpunches in combinations in order to repel the challenger. Pacquiao saw that he was the younger and faster fighter and needed to keep taking the fight to the champion. After four rounds Pacquiao had landed eighty-nine power punches on Barrera, and sooner or later those shots would take their toll on Barrera. Perhaps Barrera was naïve and thought that Pacquiao would punch himself out with all the volume shots. Barrera would make a brief stand in the middle of the sixth round where he landed two dazzling right hooks. Pacquiao would raise both arms to show that he wasn't hurt. There would be, arguably, another knockdown scored for Pacquiao when Barrera would fall again due to a short left hook (2:48). It would be ruled a slip due to a wet spot, but when a punch lands and a fighter later slips, it is usually scored a knockdown. In a close fight, sometimes subjective calls like that make a difference.

The seventh round would have an accidental head-butt resulting in a gash over Barrera's left eye. The fight would resume and would see both fighters have moments. Barrera would fire combinations as he had Pacquiao on the ropes but fail to do any damage as Pacquiao put both arms in the air. The crowd would try to rally Barrera with "sí, se puede" (yes, it can be done) in the eighth round. The picture still looked grim for Barrera as he was getting pummeled and didn't have much of a solution. After eight rounds the punch stats had Barrera 87 of 185 and Pacquiao 185 of 407. Pacquiao seem bothered with some ailment in the start of the ninth round, as he put his glove on his nose. Previously, in between corners, we saw him coughing in between rounds. Barrera would sense an opportunity and would land an overhand right followed by a left uppercut on the ropes. Pacquiao would come in with another batch of flurries to the body. These shots landed with pinpoint accuracy. A frustrated Barrera would punch during the break and get a point deduction from Lawrence Cole. At the end of the ninth round, Pacquiao would look at Barrera and know his opponent was nearly done. If the Barrera corner had thrown the towel, no one would have complained. To his credit Barrera never quit and, like a champion, wanted to lose on his feet. Pacquiao had tripled Barrera's connect total (39–13) in the ninth round.

The end for Barrera would come in the final minute of the eleventh round. A pair of solid left-right hooks (2:00) to Barrera's chin near the ropes had him hurt and trying to hold. One more short left hook had Barrera take a knee (2:05). Pacquiao would leave his neutral corner before the action resumed with the intention of finishing the contest once and for all. Pacquiao's promoter, Murad Muhammad, would signal to Pacquiao to keep coming and attacking. Barrera would consume more combinations as he lay on the ropes until his corner would step into the ring to stop the fight. Pacquiao would win the ring and lineal featherweight title. Pacquiao would land 309 of 838, while Barrera would land 172 of 547.

This is still, in my opinion, the greatest win in Pacquiao's career. There were no excuses about being weight drained, past prime, or a hand-picked opponent. Barrera had won thirteen of his last fourteen contests, and the only defeat was a disputed split-decision loss to Erik Morales. Moreover, the fact that Barrera would still have future impressive wins clearly indicates that he was still a relevant fighter. Barrera would blame the loss to a training camp cut short at Big Bear due to fires. There was a rematch clause, but it wasn't exercised. Pacquiao didn't just beat a champion but a future Hall of Famer. The win also made history as Pacquiao, by winning the ring title, could claim that he was the first Asian boxer to become a triple champion. That was an achievement that Japanese boxer Fighting Harada should have claimed, if not a controversial loss to Johnny Famechon for the featherweight title in 1969 in Famechon's backyard of Australia. Harada not only dropped Famechon three times, but to many observers he won the majority of the rounds. The American referee Willie Pep had initially scored it a draw but then later changed it to a win for local fighter Famechon. The decision was so egregious that even the Australian crowd in attendance booed the decision and cheered for the foreign fighter.

CHAPTER 9
El Dinamita

Juan Manuel Marquez (42-2, 33 KOs) was both the WBA and IBF featherweight champion of the world and a very experience counterpuncher. Trainer Nacho Beristain slowly brought the Mexican City fighter up the ranks. Legendary Mexican trainer Nacho Beristain trained Marquez. Beristain had worked with Mexican boxers since the early 1960s, shortly after he retired from the sport at the age of twenty (due to an eye injury). He would gain national prominence after working with the Mexican Olympic team in 1968. In all, Beristain would train nineteen boxing champions. His most notable Mexican champions were Ricardo Lopez, Chiquita Gonzalez, and Daniel Zaragoza. Beristain would instill Marquez with a boxing stance of gloves high, chin down, and the proper leg stance for balance and power. Marquez, by having the proper stance, was in good position to counterpunch.

There was a grit and determination instilled in Marquez that allowed him to recover from a spine injury that delayed his boxing career for nearly two years. The injury was a result of an eighteen-year-old Marquez falling off a tree. Marquez even considered going into accounting after getting an accounting certificate in a Mexican trade college since he was uncertain if he could resume his boxing career. Eventually, Marquez would work as an accountant for the Mexican government while balancing a boxing career. Hence, the nickname the "Fighting Accountant" was sometimes used instead of "Dinamita."

Marquez—who grew up around drugs, gangs, and crime—would not easily give up in the sport that his father once practiced and that his brother, Rafael, was learning.

Things got off to an inauspicious start when Marquez would get disqualified in his professional debut in 1993 against Javier Duran. Marquez would later claim that he was disqualified for a head-butt because Duran was associated with the Mexican boxing commission. Marquez had dropped Duran twice and was in route to a knockout until the ring physician bailed Duran out with a DQ win. The loss wouldn't discourage Marquez who would win his next twenty-nine professional bouts. Marquez would wear his customary black trunks and red trimmings for most of his early bouts instead of the green, white, and red often exhibited by Mexican fighters.

There were a few stumbles on the way, such as his bout with Julian "The Dealer" Wheeler. Marquez was fortunate that the referee Larry Rozadilla stopped the bout with five seconds left for excessive holding as two of the three judges' scorecards had Wheeler ahead. Marquez and Wheeler both scored knockdowns that the referee, Rozadilla, failed to score. Wheeler was hurt a few times during the match, but Marquez failed to finish him. The match was close, and I had it even if it had gone to the cards.

Despite having a few one-punch knockouts, mainly via body shots, there were several times where Marquez failed to finish an opponent. In an early bout with Julio Sanchez Leon, he also had Leon hurt early but failed to finish him. Rodrigo Valenzuela, who was totally outclassed by Marquez, would quit on his stool in the eighth after being almost done in the second. There was also the match with Darryl Pinckney in which Marquez dropped Pinckney with a triple-left hook in the fifth round and a straight right in the ninth but couldn't finish him. However, Marquez would show his championship heart by getting up after being dropped by a counter left hook in the seventh in that same match. Although Pinckney's win-loss record didn't suggest championship caliber—the fact remained that Pinckney did knock out notable names such as Junior Jones and Guty Espadas. As Marquez moved up the ranks, he was fighting under the shadow of both Marco Antonio Barrera and Erik Morales who—despite their good boxing skill—would be willing to brawl and go for the finish when necessary. Marquez didn't have the charisma, swagger, and attitude that his two Mexican counterparts had, but his ring intelligence, humility, and discipline would eventually lead him to arguably greater heights. Unlike both Barrera and Morales, this Mexican fighter can brag, "I've never been knocked out."

Marquez's ability to assimilate to style and adjust was demonstrated when he captured the WBO-NABO featherweight title against Cedric Mingo. Nacho Beristain was told that Mingo was an orthodox fighter, and they trained as such. However, when they got in the ring Marquez realized that he was fighting a southpaw for the first time, and he dominated the opponent who quit on his stool after ten.

As Marquez moved up the ranks, notable charismatic champion Prince Naseem Hamed ducked him. Hamed's trainer, Emmanuel Steward, would years later admit that he told his management to avoid Marquez. The scenario would change years later when Marquez blamed a hand injury to avoid a fight with Hamed. Marquez would suffer a second loss to southpaw Freddie Norwood for a title shot that could have easily gone the other way. Referee Joe Cortez failed to score a knockdown when Marquez dropped Norwood with a short left hook that had the St. Louis champion touch the canvas with his right glove. Both fighters would trade knockdowns as Marquez was dropped in the second and Norwood in the ninth. Norwood was an elusive southpaw who made Marquez miss often and look bad. However, Marquez was the aggressor and appeared to win three of the last four rounds. HBO's Harold Lederman would give the nod to Marquez 115–111. I had Marquez winning (114–113), but it would have been 115–111 in my card if the eighth-round knockdown would have been scored, as it would have switched a 10–9 Norwood round to a 10–8 Marquez tally. The final punch stats had Norwood landing 73 of 290 and Marquez 89 of 445.

Marquez would wait more than three years before he fought for another major world title in 2003. This time Marquez would win by a seven-round stoppage over Manuel Medina for the vacant IBF featherweight title. Marquez dropped Medina in the second round and dominated most of the action. Marquez would unify the title by adding the WBA strap with a seventh-round technical decision over a noncombative Derrick Gainer. Marquez was expected to fight Marco Antonio Barrera, but Pacquiao put a stop to it by scoring the upset win. The Barrera win was the catalyst to set up the Pacquiao-Marquez match. The dedicated Filipino boxing fans had probably heard of Marquez since he had knocked out Filipino fighters Reynante Jamili and Baby Lorona Jr. in recent contests. Jamili and Agapito Sanchez were the only common opponents for both fighters. The match between Pacquiao and Marquez was scheduled for May 8, 2004, in the MGM Grand, Las Vegas, Nevada, in front of a crowd of more than seven thousand spectators.

Few would know that what would be regarded as among the greatest recent boxing rivalries almost didn't get past one round. When the match started, Marquez controlled the first half of the first round with solid rights (0:42 and 1:11). The straight right was always the weapon of choice against a southpaw. Pacquiao would respond back with a feint and then a straight left (1:29) that would floor Marquez. The proud Mexican would come back and try to trade only to be floored again (1:52) by another left. A third knockdown would occur near the ropes due to a one-two combination. Marquez's prospects looked dim to escape the round. Yet somehow, after taking three additional power left shots, he would survive the first round. Marquez would be bleeding profusely from his nose, and that would make it difficult for him to breathe through it the rest of the fight. The scoring of the round would be an ageless debate. Judge Burt A. Clements incorrectly scored it a 10–7 round instead of 10–6. The plausible argument that Marquez was actually winning the first half of the round before the three knockdowns would allow for a 10–7 score instead of a 10–6 if a judge wanted to do so. However, protocol usually would follow the 10–6 score—which is how I would have scored it. Since Marquez was down four points after only one round, he would need to win at least eight of the last eleven rounds to win the fight. Would he be able to do that?

Marquez would open up, landing a double-right uppercut in the second round. He saw an opening underneath Pacquiao's guard. Pacquiao was pawing with his right hand to set up his powerful left. Pacquiao would get a solid left body shot (0:57) while he maintained his head movement. Marquez was able to work his counter combinations, as he was able to both better time Pacquiao and get his legs back. As Pacquiao came in, Marquez would nail him with a straight left then block the left while coming back with two more counters. Pacquiao was still able to get the more powerful left shots and, arguably, pulled out the second round. The punch stats had Pacquiao landing 18 of 77 and Marquez 8 of 45 in the second round. The third saw Marquez able to get a left hook body shot (0:50) as he started to pick apart the Pacquiao defense. Joe Cortez would give Marquez a warning for low blows. As Marquez was picking up the Pacquiao left more effectively, Pacquiao would try to jab more, but Marquez would be able to block most of them. The third round was possibly the first round to be scored for Marquez.

Pacquiao would leave himself off-balance when he leaned after throwing punches in the fourth round. This would give Marquez opportunities to land counter shots (1:05). Cortez would give Marquez another warning for low blows in the middle of the fourth. The Marquez jab would nick him his second straight round on my card. Freddie Roach would tell Pacquiao, "Throw the hook with the uppercut behind it…more than one shot." Roach wanted to make sure Pacquiao wouldn't resort to just one punch at a time. The fifth round would be very tactical with both fighters doing an excellent job in catching and blocking each other's shots. It would be the third round where Cortez would warn Marquez for low blows. The shots weren't egregious or flagrant, but a point deduction is usually anticipated after two warnings. The best punch of the round would be a double right (1:43) that would whip Pacquiao's head backward. There would be some solid Pacquiao lefts as well. The fact that Pacquiao was on the ropes and had a cut right eye would possibly tilt the close round to Marquez's direction. After possibly being down five points, Marquez had possibly won three straight rounds.

A perfectly executed right hook (1:14) to Pacquiao's chin would be the highlight of the sixth round. The fact that Pacquiao was able to take such a punch was a credit to his conditioning and strong legs. Marquez would follow up as he pressed Pacquiao to the ropes. The problem was that Pacquiao didn't keep moving his head as he had in the early rounds. Roach had admonished him earlier to keep the head movements. In addition, Pacquiao had stopped using the feints, which actually were the catalyst for the first knockdown. A crushing left hook that was designed to take the air out of Pacquiao's lungs would also land for Marquez (2:24).

After six rounds the trainer Nacho Beristain would tell Marquez that he had won every single round after the knockdowns. Beristain's pep talk was to encourage Marquez to stay aggressive in an attempt to win the bout in the cards. There have been instances where fighters have won despite suffering three knockdowns; some of the bouts where this occurred were Benitez-Curry 1, W. Klitschko-Peter 1, Famechon-Harada 1, Peter-McCline, and Mesi-Jirov. Of course, not everyone agreed with all those decisions. The recent Jirov-Mesi match was one of the more miraculous wins as Mesi won despite being knocked down three times in a ten-round match. This same thing goes for Wilfred Benitez when he got the controversial nod over Curry.

Marquez would score again with the overhand right (0:39) in the seventh round. As Marquez would circle away from Pacquiao's left, it was imperative that Pacquiao avoid Marquez's right hand. Pacquiao would have his best round since the second by having better head movement and finding angles for his straight left. Marquez would get in a solid punch—a straight right (2:48)—and Pacquiao would get a solid straight left in the closing bell. The eighth round was another close round that may have gone to the Marquez column after Pacquiao would slip in the final thirty seconds and get peppered with shots as he retreated to the ropes off-balance. Through eight rounds the punch stats revealed a close fight: Pacquiao 91 of 432 and Marquez 104 of 337. The looping right hand (0:51) would partially score for Marquez in the ninth round. Pacquiao would be reticent to fire much and just kept up with the upper-body movement. Marquez would score with short left uppercuts and a right to the body in the first half of the round. A resounding left (1:45) would land squarely on Marquez. Pacquiao would land the more solid blows in the round.

Pacquiao was starting to find the range again and would take control of the final minute of the tenth round. The tenth round was another close round that could have gone either way, but I felt the more telling punches were Pacquiao's, giving him the second consecutive round on my card. Marquez established his left jab and right cross in the eleventh round. The jab was fired at Pacquiao's body. Two more solid rights on the inside (1:49) would get in for Marquez as he tried to win the final two rounds of the fight. Marquez would win the round with his counterpunching and jab. Pacquiao would cross himself and look up for divine intervention to seal a fight in which he possibly had a five-point lead after two rounds. Marquez would score again with an overhand right-left uppercut combo (0:33) and the double-left jab (0:40) in the final round. Pacquiao would stalk and throw straight lefts that partially connected. Pacquiao would land a solid left (2:08) that buckled Marquez. A final overhand right-left upper combo (2:48) would get in for Marquez in the closing seconds. Both would trade in the final seconds in a fight that wasn't expected to last long after the three knockdowns. They both would raise their arms in the center of the ring and embrace.

This is a fight that could have been scored either way due to the number of close rounds. If you had Pacquiao winning five rounds with all the knockdowns, he should have won. If you felt Marquez won eight of the last eleven rounds, then you would think Marquez won. Judge John Stewart had it 115–110 for Pacquiao, while judge Guy Jutras had it 115–110 for Maquez, and the third judge, Burt A. Clements, had it 113–113, which made it an official draw. I had it 113–113 (7-4-1), which was a draw. However, I do think there should have been, at minimum, a point taken away from Marquez for low blows that should have given Pacquiao a one-point victory. It would seem to be an excessive point deduction, perhaps, since Marquez was already down several points after the first round, but there were three warnings for low blows. The punch stats had Pacquiao landing 148 of 639 and Marquez 158 of 547, which highlighted how close the fight was. The power punches were Pacquiao 100 of 231 and Marquez 122 of 339. Pacquiao had nursed a foot injury before the fight and stated that the injured foot bothered him in the third and fourth round, but nonetheless, he felt he did enough to win the fight.

Marquez claimed the decision was erroneous feeling that, after the first round, Pacquiao won perhaps one more round. It was obvious there was still some unsettled business between these two adversaries. Pacquiao's team would file an official protest with the commission due to the judge scoring. Judge Bill Clements would concede, "I feel badly because I dropped the ball, plainly and simply. You can make a lot of arguments that it was a very close fight, but that's immaterial. The fact is, I dropped the ball."

Pacquiao and Marquez both raise their arms, proclaiming victory in their first contest, which ended in a disputed draw.
AP Photo/Joe Cavaretta.

Marc Ratner, the executive director of the Nevada State Athletic Commission, ruled that Clements's admission was no grounds for a protest. The argument is similar to a baseball game in which an umpire scores balls and strikes; it is a judgment call. Essentially, the commission wouldn't overturn the decision, as judges' scoring is subjective. The rematch with Marquez wouldn't happen until four years later. It was widely expected that both combatants were going to meet in early 2005. In fact, when Marquez fought Orlando Salido in the Hopkins-De La Hoya undercard on September 18, 2004, Manny Pacquiao was at the MGM ringside watching the match. Unfortunately, the match never took place. The Marquez team would reject a reported $750,000 as they wanted $1.5 million. Marquez would later fight Chris John for $30,000 after rejecting the offer.

The Marquez draw was not something that sat well with Pacquiao, and it made him hungrier. He wouldn't get back in the ring until seven months later back in the Philippines. This time he would face another Thai fighter who used the "3K" moniker. The 3K Battery Company is a major automobile and motorcycle sponsor that often uses boxers to endorse its product. Fashan 3K Battery was a former IBF Pan Pacific super bantamweight and intercontinental bantamweight champion. He had never been knocked out in a professional contest when he met Pacquiao on December 11, 2004. Battery was a southpaw but had a decent right hand, which was exhibited when he landed a solid straight right in the opening minute of the first round. Battery would miss a wild left and fall on the canvas in the process. It was conspicuous that the Thai fighter was not interested in trying to win a decision in the Philippines but was trying to score a knockout. Unfortunately for Battery, these types of dog fights are what Pacquiao loved and excelled at. What was also obvious was that Pacquiao was becoming a more efficient inside fighter by landing short uppers and hooks in close range. He didn't just load up for those big outside shots as he had in the past. The right jab was also peppering Battery's face. An overhand left would drop Battery in the northeastern corner ropes in the first minute of the second round. Battery was getting out of danger but committed boxing suicide by circling the wrong way against a fellow southpaw. Battery needed to circle away from Pacquiao's left instead of going toward it. A second knockdown would be scored in the third round as Battery would fall prey again to the straight right-overhand-left combination that plagued him the whole fight. Battery would get up again only to be dropped again by a left uppercut. The final knockdown would be another left uppercut that landed squarely under the chin in the fourth round, compelling stoppage at 1:26. It was an excellent exhibition and helped take the emphasis off the disputed Marquez draw.

CHAPTER 10

El Terrible

Erik Morales (47-2, 34 KOs) had known the art of war. Morales had fought Barrera three times, Wayne McCullough, Junior Jones, Daniel Zaragoza, and Kevin Kelly. The fighter, who was literally born in a boxing gym to a boxing dad, lived and breathed the sport.

When Erik Morales would challenge for his first world title against Daniel Zaragoza, the legendary trainer Nacho Beristain would tell Zaragoza, "Este es un novato." Essentially, Beristain reduced Morales to a novice or a rookie and felt his Hall-of-Fame fighter was giving him too much respect. The "novato," also known as Morales, would take the indignation with a grain of salt and would go on to produce one of the greatest résumés in Mexican boxing history. Morales would go undefeated for his first forty-one professional bouts. Many believe that the first encounter with Barrera on February 19, 2000, could have gone the either way. To some, there was poetic justice when the second bout between the rival Mexicans would go Barrera's way, while many felt that this time Morales should have won.

The negotiations between Pacquiao-Morales would be conducted by Top Rank and M & M Inc., which was headed by Murad Muhammad. In order to finalize the contract, M & M would agree to the Morales stipulation of ten-ounce gloves. The irony was that Morales, a Mexican fighter, preferred ten-ounce Japanese Winning gloves while Pacquiao, a Filipino fighter, customarily wore the eight-ounce Mexican Reyes gloves. This was the same arrangement that Morales had for his third fight with Barrera (in which he lost). After the bout Barrera, who was irked by the gloves, would state, "We wanted to prove that we were better than both Top Rank and their gloves."

The Pacquiao-Morales bout would be scheduled for March 19, 1995. Pacquiao would have a blood test the day before the fight. This was because the medical facility lost his original blood-test results. There would be a full-capacity crowd at the MGM with 14,623 in attendance. This was a significant figure proving that super featherweight fighters could attract a large audience. The sport of boxing, which was mainly carried by the illustrious heavyweight division, was now being carried by smaller fighters after a declining interest in the heavyweight division. Pacquiao would be going up to his eighth divisional weight class as he fought as a super featherweight. Both fighters would be trading jabs in the first minute of the round. There would be plenty of talk of Pacquiao not fully developing his right hand. Yet he was jabbing from that right hand in the first round. Pacquiao would land a one-two combination of straight hands (1:08) in the first round. The Pacquiao left hand would land with authority (1:38) as his offense started to open up. Morales would respond with a stiff left jab and a flurry (1:45) that had Pacquiao on the ropes. A solid Pacquiao right hand (2:20) and several body shots in the final thirty seconds would give Pacquiao the close round.

Both fighters would be flat-footed but would exercise upper-body movement in the second round. Morales would come in stalking with his stiff left jab and did some work momentarily, as he had Pacquiao in the northwestern corner ropes. The middle of the round saw Morales counter Pacquiao as he got himself out of position after coming with his left. Morales would use his reach advantage and defense to avoid a good portion of the Pacquiao leads. In the third, Morales would continue to work the right hand (1:07) followed by the stiff left jab (1:11) as weapons of choice for the Mexican veteran. Pacquiao was still working his left to the body (1:16) designed to slow Morales down for the later rounds. After an exchange, both fighters would raise their arms claiming they weren't hurt from the punches. Morales would occasionally push Pacquiao down and put his weight on him. This is an old-school technique used by bigger fighters to try to slow down smaller opponents. Morales likely got the round on the judges' scorecards. Freddie Roach would tell Pacquiao, "When you hurt him on the ropes, you need to take advantage of it."

In the fourth, Morales would work Pacquiao's body with straight rights. At 1:12, Morales would raise his arms and look up after another brutal exchange. The Morales message was that he was coming forward with more ammunition. The fact that Morales would back up Pacquiao to the ropes would give the impression that he was the one dictating the fight, even if all the punches weren't landing. Despite losing the round, Pacquiao still would get in a right hook (2:38) to Morales's body. The Pacquiao hope was that repeated body shots would slow down the older fighter for the later rounds. Pacquiao would also work upstairs as he landed a solid straight left (0:49) at Morales's chin in the fifth.

Morales wouldn't take anything for granted and would continue to be aggressive and land a right uppercut (1:25) in the fifth round. Morales would land hooks from both hands that would change the complexity of the fight in the middle of the fifth round. Pacquiao would be cut severely near his right eye due to the fighters' collision of heads; it was ruled as the result of a punch, but it was a head-butt. The ringside physician would look at it and allow the fight to continue. Lenny Dejesus would work on the cut to control the bleeding in between rounds. Pacquiao would get inspired by the chants of "Manny," understanding that he needed to step up the action. The Pacquiao corner would keep telling him to back up Morales and not to wait on him. After six rounds, Morales would out jab Pacquiao 51–8. Pacquiao's hand speed would be the difference in the seventh round, as he would pop Morales with flurries underneath. The head movement that Pacquiao used brilliantly in the Barrera fight was missing in this fight. This allowed Morales to solidly land a straight right (2:18) in the seventh round. Morales would rally in the last thirty seconds in an attempt to steal the round.

Pacquiao showed a lack of footwork, and perhaps he felt he needed to stay flat-footed to trade with Morales. This left Pacquiao open for some power straight right hands in the middle of the eighth round, such as the solid right (2:16) that Morales connected. Pacquiao looked a bit lethargic compared to his other fights; however, this still didn't prevent him from landing a pair of straight hands (2:30). Pacquiao would continue to try to break Morales down in the body. Morales would be momentarily staggered by a combination (1:50) in the ninth round. In fact, Freddie Roach felt confident in between rounds that if Pacquiao would pressure Morales for three minutes that he would "quit on him."

It would now be a test for Morales to see if he could withstand the Pacquiao onslaught that would come in the final rounds. Morales would get in a strong right hook (2:24) to Pacquiao's body in the tenth round. Both combatants would trade shots in the middle of the tenth round; Morales would continue to fire the lead right in hopes of finishing off Pacquiao. A stiff left jab (1:50) by Morales would knock Pacquiao's mouthpiece off. There were so many fireworks that it would take Joe Cortez thirty additional seconds to call time out for Pacquiao to get his mouthpiece back on. Morales still had fresh legs in the eleventh round and would work inside shots on the Pacquiao defense. Morales's father would tell him "the fight is in the bag, but don't get overconfident." Morales would ignore his father's admonition and switch southpaw for more toe-to-toe action with Pacquiao in the final round. This enabled Pacquiao to land his best left in the fight (1:42). The final round was clearly a Pacquiao round as he rocked Morales several times. I had Morales winning 116–113 (7-4-1); the judges all had it 115–113 for Morales. The final punch stats had Morales landing 265 of 714 and Pacquiao 217 of 894. Morales would out jab Pacquiao 96–34.

In the postfight interview, Morales would say that "Pacquiao was tough and strong but not as big of a knockout artist as people said...Without necessity I still would trade shots in the final round because that is what the public wants." Pacquiao would complain about not using the eight-ounce Reyes gloves for the fight. He felt that if he had his usual gloves, he would have knocked Morales out. Freddie Roach would create an uncomfortable situation as he essentially called out promoter Murad Muhammad, who was right next to him, for having the ten-ounce winning gloves as part of the contract. This was the same Roach who had said, "We are going to walk through this guy; he has nothing left."

Murad Muhammad would later fire back at Roach and Shelley Finkel, who joined Pacquiao's management team. He felt the criticism aimed at him was "a smokescreen to hide his own failures just like the issue of the gloves. Speed and timing is key to a knockout, and if Morales had used eight-ounce gloves, then Pacquiao may have been knocked out." Murad had alluded to two occasions in which Pacquiao was hurt. Murad also called out Roach for claiming he didn't advise Pacquiao to keep going to the body and not allowing the cut man Lenny Dejesus to sit on the stool and work on a major cut instead of leaning over

Buboy Fernandez. It was Murad's opinion that the failure to control the cut and work on Morales's body was more to blame than the gloves.

The entire acrimony between Roach, Murad, and Pacquiao would lead to class action claim against M & M Sports Inc. and Murad Muhammad individually. The complaint filed on April 27, 2005, alleged that M & M failed to withhold 30 percent of his purse to pay the Internal Revenue Service. The money that was supposed to be held for taxes was instead diverted to a Shell LLC, which Pacquiao's managers oversaw. It was alleged that Pacquiao's managers kept over 50 percent of his purse by violating 26 USC 1441 and 15 USC 6307e (Ali act). The Ali act requires specific revenue disclosures that the complaint claimed that M & M and Murad Muhammad failed to adhere to. Pacquiao's suit would seek $5 million in damages with an additional $20 million in punitive damages. Pacquiao would state in a released statement, "I intend to see this suit to the bitter end so that I can recover every dollar that was stolen from me, as well as help protect other fighters from being taken advantage of by Mr. Muhammad." Murad in a press release would say, "The case was settled amicably. I decided there is no need to fight. Manny will go his way; we will go our way. I wish Manny all the luck. May God be with him."

The suit would later be settled and both sides would execute a stipulation of discontinuance. Due to a nondisclosure agreement, the terms of the settlement would never be revealed. The fact that both parties seem to be mute about their past association likely meant that there was a nondisparagement clause as part of the general releases. Pacquiao would call the settlement a "triumph for all of boxing." Pacquiao was now essentially a free agent by being released from his contract with M & M. Pacquiao would also turn to new business advisors Eric Pineda and Jayke Joson to manage his business affairs. In addition, he would also seek the assistance of the attorney Jeng Gackal to help manage his legal matters. Gary Shaw would briefly promote Pacquiao as they signed an agreement on August 23, 2005. This was only a few weeks before Pacquiao was scheduled to challenge Hector Velazquez.

For Pacquiao, as in the Torrecampo fight, having a loss was another learning lesson. The match was quite close, and certainly, a different strategy would be utilized if he fought Morales again. The plan Morales implemented—using counterpunching, jabs, and his reach advantage—was the difference in the bout. Obviously, the major cut on Pacquiao's face didn't help him. However, he needed to get to Morales's body and stop headhunting on a guy that had one of the best chins in boxing. Pacquiao would also feel that the blood taken before the bout did have an adverse impact. It would later be revealed that the NSAC had ordered Pacquiao to take two blood-test samples forty-eight hours before the scheduled bout. In a television interview, Pacquiao stated that the commission had lost the medical records of the blood tests he had given about a month prior to the contest. Pacquiao, speaking in the interview, would claim he felt weakened by the blood drawn and felt suspicious about the medical tests being lost since he was notified that the hospital kept the records computerized.

CHAPTER 11

Return to Glory

The two fighters Pacquiao and Morales would fight the same day on September 10, 2005, in the Staples center. The city of Los Angeles—with both a large Mexican and Filipino audience—would be an ideal setting to showcase both of these two cultural icons. Filipino American Brian Villoria would also be part of the undercard, as he would win the WBC light flyweight title with a first round (2:59) TKO over Eric Ortiz.

For Pacquiao and Morales it was quite simple; both fighters win, and both would face each other in a rematch. Often in life things are easier said than done. Pacquiao would take six rounds to dispatch Velasquez. Velasquez kept a low head while coming with straight lefts and following with right hooks; he did well in the early action. Velasquez would land a sizzling right hook to Pacquiao's body at 1:25 of the first round. The Mexican fighter would also land solid combinations to both the head and body. Freddie Roach would tell Pacquiao, "You are too stationary; move your head, and be the first to get off." Pacquiao would nail Velazquez with a left hook at 1:53 of the second round and change the momentum of the contest. Pacquiao resorted more to boxing and even, at one point, walked away from Velasquez prompting the Mexican to put his gloves down in frustration. Velasquez was actually making a mistake by getting too confident. He needed to box more behind his jab instead of trying to land a Hail Mary. Even the Velazquez corner would urge him to keep up the pace. "All he has is quick hands, but he can't fight." The corner was foolish to believe this.

I felt the second round was a draw, possibly giving Velazquez a lead (20–19) after two rounds. Pacquiao would land a right uppercut at 1:45 of the third round from a bizarre angle. This was because Pacquiao spotted the opening due to Velasquez's wide and high guard. A few more Pacquiao left hooks would give him the round convincingly. Pacquiao would out land Velasquez 23–9 in the third. Referee Lou Moret would warn both fighters for holding and hitting. Velazquez held Pacquiao's head with his left hand and then hit him with the right. Pacquiao would retaliate with his own shot, prompting Moret to warn them. Roach would tell Pacquiao to work the body, and Pacquiao would do that in the fifth round by landing left hooks to the body. The ending of the contest would be set up with a perfect right hook by Pacquiao when Velazquez put his left glove down at 2:11 in the sixth round. A staggering Velazquez would go to the ropes only to receive more punishment until he held on. A barrage of Pacquiao left hooks and straight rights with Velasquez pressed on the ropes would force him to take a knee in the waning seconds of the sixth round. Velázquez would beat the count, but Lou Moret would waive off the fight. Pacquiao would embrace Velasquez and would prepare to watch the Morales-Raheem fight.

Pacquiao was very well aware of Zahir Raheem's ability, as he had knocked out Lusito Espinosa—a seven-time defending Filipino featherweight champion. Raheem would box circles around Morales and win the unanimous decision. It is very possible that the recent bout with Pacquiao and the accumulative ring wars had taken something out of Morales. The HBO camera would pan to the Pacquiao team, who looked somber as they saw the Morales match on television. It appeared that the lucrative rematch and opportunity for revenge was now out of the question. However, while a dejected Morales would get interviewed and asked about a rematch with Pacquiao, an irate Bob Arum would interrupt the interview and answer the question for Morales. "Yes, the match with Pacquiao would still go on." So it was written, and so it was done that there would still be a rematch. It would have been a difficult sale to get a bout between Zahir Raheem and Pacquiao. Most importantly, Raheem was fighting as a lightweight and fought Morales above the super featherweight limit. The WBC International super featherweight title was still on the line, so there was still a selling point there.

The rematch between Pacquiao and Morales was scheduled for January 21, 2006, at the Thomas & Mack Center, Las Vegas, Nevada. Having watched the fight, Freddie Roach understood that Morales could be outboxed. The blueprint was there to defeat Morales. However, Pacquiao had been a fighter who demanded action-packed fights to please the audience. As a result, it was unlikely that Pacquiao would use his speed and footwork to try to win a technical match with Morales. There needed to be some combative exchanges to make it a trademark Pacquiao fight. Pacquiao always wanted to keep the audience satisfied. In that very audience, there would be Floyd Mayweather Jr. who seemingly appeared to be cheering for Pacquiao at times during the match. Perhaps Mayweather had put some money on Pacquiao to win.

This time Morales would wear his ten-ounce Winning gloves, while Pacquiao would wear his eight-ounce Reyes gloves. Morales would continue the same scenario as the first fight by landing that straight right (2:06) in the first round. Roach would tell Pacquiao "to move to the side after throwing combinations." Devastating straight lefts (1:34 and 1:39) would pulverize Morales in the second round. This time around, the speed difference between the fighters was more noticeable. A short Pacquiao left hook (2:11) would almost floor Morales as he grabbed the ropes with his right glove to keep his balance when his feet took several steps back. Morales would keep himself up and would throw both his gloves down in a gesture to acknowledge that this would be a war tonight. After two rounds Morales must have second-guessed his wisdom in wearing the Winning gloves. He really couldn't even block the best Pacquiao left shots because he was not keeping the guard tight up the middle. The extra-padded gloves are ideal to protect brittle hands and to block shots. However, it appeared Morales was not blocking much and was getting return fire from eight-ounce gloves.

The opening minute of the third round saw Pacquiao taking Morales straight rights up the middle. Pacquiao would land flurries to Morales's body and would follow by a lead left (2:19). Morales would stand straight up with his gloves down and would gesture with both hands to suggest, "Is that the best you can do?" It would be a silly mistake, as that wouldn't discourage Pacquiao's morale as he would continue attacking. Yet, Morales was still doing well in the early going. He would land the stiff left jab followed by the right lead in the fourth round. It was possible that some of the scorecards would have Morales winning three of the first four rounds. The left-jab right-hook combo (0:32) would get in solidly for Morales in the fifth round. Pacquiao would set up his power left (0:49) by pawing with his right. What was interesting was that Morales would be controlling the fight in the middle of the ring despite being the slower fighter. Morales would out land Pacquiao 28–17 in the fifth round while throwing three fewer punches (59–62).

The sixth round was the comeback round that Pacquiao needed. He started to tattoo Morales with his speed and combinations. Morales would start to pay for staying in the middle of the ring. The ending of the round saw Morales fall backward and land on Kenny Bayless, who possibly saved him from a last-second knockdown. It would be the second time in the fight when Morales was almost knocked down. Pacquiao would out land Morales 32–8, and Morales's hawklike nose was starting to get rearranged. The sixth round could have been easily scored a 10–8 round for Pacquiao, even without a knockdown.

In the seesaw battle, things would change again when Morales would catch Pacquiao with a left hook (0:36) in the seventh round. Pacquiao would retreat to the ropes and cover up well while slipping punches. The Filipino fighter would even hit his own head to show that he wasn't hurt. The right hooks to Morales's body were possibly taking their effect, as the Mexican fighter started to slow down. The body shots were landing with both precision and accuracy. Morales had to clinch and slow down the pace in order to disrupt Pacquiao's rhythm. Pacquiao had to keep going to the body, as that would take Morales legs away. The plan was working as Pacquiao would continue to take command of the fight, and even when Morales would land a counter, Pacquiao would walk through the punches. Morales stood on rubbery legs and needed to gain his second wind. Pacquiao would win his third consecutive round in the eighth.

A solid right uppercut (1:32) in the ninth round by Morales couldn't hurt Pacquiao as he was too conditioned and had strong legs. Pacquiao was using his right hand more effectively, but it was the odd angles (2:41) that would give Morales trouble picking them up. Morales would be on the ropes and circling away in the closing seconds of the ninth round. Pacquiao would deliberately keep enticing Morales to put his guard high by feinting high with the right and then immediately going for the exposed body (0:58) in the tenth round. A lead left would connect (1:50) for Pacquiao that would even get approval from spectator Floyd Mayweather, who would wave him to continue the pressure. Morales would fight back out of instinct but would fall to the canvas (2:06) due to both a short left hook and exhaustion. Another flurry would drop Morales a second time (2:30), which prompted Kenny Bayless to stop the contest. Pacquiao would land 196 of 795 and Morales 184 of 644. Pacquiao would land 171 power shots compared to 107 for Morales. It would be the first time Morales would be stopped, and it was his second consecutive loss.

It was one of Pacquiao's biggest wins of his career, along with the Sasakul and Barrera fights. In some ways this win was more important as it avenged a loss, and—like the second Leonard-Duran fight—it was a make-or-break deal. It would be difficult for a fighter's career to recover from a second loss to the same fighter. The fight would also do over 350,000 pay-per-view sales, which were excellent numbers for a bout under the welterweight limit. Pacquiao would go back to the Philippines to a hero's welcome. As a token of appreciation to his local fans, Pacquiao would have his next contest in the Philippines. Pacquiao would face Oscar Larios on July 2, 2006, at the Araneta Coliseum in Metro Manila. Larios (56-4-1, 36 KOs) was naturally a bigger opponent. Larios started with plenty of movement of head and side-to-side movement. He appeared more interested in boxing than brawling with Pacquiao. The middle of the first round saw Larios throw wild rights that Pacquiao mainly blocked or dodged. Larios would score with a double-straight right (2:31). Seeing all of Larios's moving around inspired Pacquiao to do his version of the Ali shuffle (2:47). Pacquiao tried to measure Larios for his lead left but couldn't find the mark in the first round.

Both fighters would start out aggressively in the second round by firing their best artillery. There would be many exchanges but not many clean punches since both fighters were very mobile. Triple-left shots by Pacquiao would possibly give him the close round. A collective breath would be held at the Araneta Coliseum in the opening seconds of the third round. Larios would stagger Pacquiao with a short right hook to the top of the head, forcing Pacman to retreat to the ropes. Another battery of right hands and a flush left hook would have Pacquiao almost out on his feet. It was easily the most hurt Pacquiao had been since the fourth round of the Hussein fight. It was one of those telling moments in a fighter's career. There was over two minutes left in the round. How would Pacquiao survive the round? After taking seventeen unanswered blows, Pacquiao would simply bang his gloves and come forward. Larios didn't work the body, and Pacquiao's strong legs would keep him up. Pacquiao would rally back and fire left hooks to back up Larios to the ropes. Larios would get in some jabs in the closing minute of the round, but he suffered a cut.

The use of the right hand, which was important in the last two Morales fights, would be used with right hooks to the body. So would the double-straight left (1:12) in the fourth round. The fight that started out as a boxing match was now becoming a brawl. Larios himself would be banging his gloves after taking Pacquiao shots. The problem for Larios was that he was taking shots from different angles and also right hooks to the body (2:09) in the fifth round. The combinations and flurries were starting to score for Pacquiao in the sixth round. Pacquiao was employing the strategy of hitting then quickly stepping to the side. It was designed to confuse slower-footed fighters. Larios would get floored by a straight right to the body-left hook to chin combination. Larios took a knee in the middle of the canvas in the opening minute of the seventh round. The Mexican warrior would come back still firing some heavy shots, but most didn't land cleanly.

Pacquiao would almost slip on the wet canvas in the eighth round but would regain his footing, which would prompt Larios to touch gloves in sportsmanship. Larios would get Pacquiao to the northwestern corner ropes and pelt him with right hands. Then Pacquiao would turn the tables and get Larios on the ropes and fire his own right-hook straight-left-hook combinations. Larios really couldn't sustain an offense full of combinations as Marquez did in his 2004 fight. The final rounds saw both fighters mainly lunging and winging shots. Larios, looking for the big knockout shot, would often unload with a big right that Pacquiao would be able to elude with head movement. Even when the right cross would land (1:16) in the eleventh round, Pacquiao's strong legs would keep him up. Pacquiao would get an added insurance policy when he dropped Larios again with a lead-left-straight-right combination (2:13) in the final round. Pacquiao would win in all scorecards with scores of 118–108, 120–106, and 117–110. Pacquiao had improved his record to (42-3-2, 32 KOs). The entire boxing world was taking notice of Pacquiao who now, along with Floyd Mayweather Jr., was considered among the top two pound-per-pound fighters in the game.

As Pacquiao signed to have a rubber match with Morales on November 18, 2006, it wasn't surprising what happened when Pacquiao arrived back to Los Angeles in the fall of 2006. Oscar De La Hoya would be waiting at the airport with a stretched limo. De La Hoya took Pacquiao to a steakhouse to propose a contract to officially sign him as a Golden Boy fighter. There would be a $500,000 signing bonus with half of it in cash and the other half by certified-fund check. It was obvious that De La Hoya had done his homework and knew that Pacquiao preferred cash in business transactions. Pacquiao would take the suitcase filled with money and sign the contract with Golden Boy Promotion, even if he was fully aware that Top Rank was going to dispute the Golden Boy deal. Pacquiao felt that he made the best decision and that the best promoter would win the legal battle that would ensue.

Pacquiao would go on with his training at the Wild Card Gym with Freddie Roach for his fight with Morales. This time both fighters would agree to wear the eight-ounce Reyes gloves for the rubber match. Pacquiao was the two-to-one favorite coming into the match on November 18, 2006, at the Thomas & Mack Center, Las Vegas, Nevada.

Morales and Pacquiao would trade solid body shots early, but there was more cautious tactical posturing in the opening half of the first round. Pacquiao would do more in the second half with a straight left hand to the body and also an overhand right (2:00) that hurt Morales. Morales looked lethargic and slow; he would land one solid left uppercut that would get answered with more body shots. It was one of the few times that we saw the "Terrible" Morales retreating and not initiating action. This would change in the second round as Morales would take Pacquiao to the ropes but would land nothing of significance, while Pacquiao would use his feet to turn the table with his own combinations against Morales. Pacquiao is always going to come back after being hit, and if an opponent is unwilling to clinch, expect him to absorb punishment. Morales would still march on and get in a short left hook and take Pacquiao to the ropes again with his best combination. Pacquiao would bang his gloves to show he still had plenty of game left.

Morales would pay the price when he would get dropped by a left hand that Pacquiao had cocked and waiting to be released on the right temple. Pacquiao would just take a step back, and Morales would still come back and be able to land a few rights as both fighters would exchange in a furious pace near the ropes and the center of the ring. Pacquiao was able to elude and block most of the shots, but the Mexican legend was not going out without a fight. Morales would again dig into the Pacquiao body to slow him down and would follow it up with an overhand shot. Morales would get dropped a second time (1:36) in the third round by a straight left after taking a barrage of shots previously. Morales would get up only to have a rabid Pacquiao coming in for the finish. Miraculously, even without his legs, Morales would make a final stand, landing some stiff straight rights and one solid left that snapped Pacquiao's head back. Pacquiao wasn't hurt from the flurry and came back and landed furious combinations to both head and body and eventually finished Morales with a straight left in the closing seconds of the round. Morales would look at his corner and decide not to continue the contest. It only lasted three rounds, but like Hagler-Hearns it was more action than many twelve-round contests. The win over Morales would officially end the year (3-0, 2 KOs) for Pacquiao. Pacquiao would go on to win *Ring's* Fighter of the Year for 2006. The only other serious contender for the award was Bernard Hopkins who had scored two impressive wins over Antonio Tarver and Ronald "Winky" Wright. ESPN and the Boxing Writer's Association of America would also award Pacquiao Fighter of the Year. By the end of 2006, *Ring* considered Pacquiao to be the number-two ranked pound-per-pound fighter behind Floyd Mayweather Jr.

CHAPTER 12

Politics and Rematch with Baby Face

With the start of 2007 came the possibility of Pacquiao's entering the political arena. The first district of South Cotabato and General Santos City was up for election in May 2007. Darlene Magnolia Antonino-Custodio, who belonged to the Nationalist People's Coalition, occupied this seat. Custodio was a seasoned veteran who was a third-generation politician. Pacquiao would run as part of the Liberal party, and the odds were heavily stacked against him.

Before Election Day, Pacquiao had other business at hand, by the name of Javier Solis (34-0-2, 25 KOs). Pacquiao would face Solis on April 14, 2007, at the Alamodome, San Antonio, Texas. The bout would be only a few weeks before election night. The date in Texas would include an undercard that would showcase both Filipino and Mexican fighters, such as Julio Cesar Chavez Jr., Brian Viloria, Jorge Arce, and Bernabe Concepcion. It was becoming increasingly clear that both the Mexican and Filipino market were becoming important target markets in boxing. Solis was an undefeated fighter, and it was unclear how he would do against Pacquiao. Solis didn't have experience with someone like Pacquiao, but he had decent technical skills and had the size advantage. The only major name Solis had fought was Humberto Soto in a bout that was declared a no contest.

The first round saw both opponents go to the body and fail to consistently land. Pacquiao had the slight advantage due to the combinations landed near the ropes. The pawing of the jab was something that Pacquiao and Solis continued to do in the second round to try to set up their power shots. There was plenty of head movement that caused both combatants to miss shots and have their timing be off. Solis would land a three-punch combination in the closing seconds to even out the round. Pacquiao focused more on the body in the third round by landing straight lefts and hooks to slow Solis down. Moreover, the left was increasingly finding the mark Solis's face. Solis would get warned for hitting Pacquiao on the hip in the fourth round. It caused a delay in the round. Solis was making a mistake by not fighting behind his jab and using his legs. Many fighters fall into the trap thinking they can physically dominate a smaller opponent. This often proved to be the demise of Pacquiao opponents who felt they could impose their size on him. Solis had both the reach and height advantage and, instead of boxing, thought he could get Pacquiao out of there.

Pacquiao wound increasingly go to the body with straight lefts and hooks that were followed with punches upstairs. Solis would answer back with his best power right hand and a few combinations with Pacquiao pressed on the ropes. Pacquiao wouldn't be hurt and seemed happy to take some rest on the ropes. The biggest scare for the Pacman was when he would clash heads with Solis in the sixth round when he was charging in. The cut over the left eye was manageable and wouldn't be a big factor. Solis never really worked the eye with his jab, as a more skillful fighter would have tried to do. Pacquiao would floor Solis with a straight left while the Mexican was checking if he was cut—but it would be scored as a push. The fireworks would explode as both fighters would trade punches around the ring. Most of the best shots came from Pacquiao who finally started to score with his combinations. Solis would eat some clean left hooks to the chin that would have sent a lesser opponent out of the match. Finally, after throwing everything except the kitchen sink, Pacquiao would knock Solis down with a short left hook at 0:41 of the eighth round. Solis got up, only to be floored by another left. This time Vic Drakulich would count Solis out. Pacquiao would land 140 of 516 punches and Solis 63 of 351. "He was hard to fight because of his low arms, head movement, and height," Pacquiao would tell Wallace Matthews after the contest.

A few weeks after the Solis win, Pacquiao would lose the congressional election in disappointing fashion. The final vote count had Custodio with 139,061 votes (64.5 percent) and Pacquiao with 75,908 votes (35.5 percent). To some, the result was indicative of a public that didn't want Pacquiao to join the world of corrupt politics but to simply stay in the ring. However, for Pacquiao the loss was difficult, as he had an idealistic view of how politicians should serve the public. He felt that he could help the working poor and also spearhead a new culture in politics where altruistic deeds could permeate the perception of political corruption. Pacquiao felt part of the reason he lost was lack of organization and preparation. He vowed not to quit and to seek political office in the future.

On March 17, 2007, two old Pacquiao nemeses would square off in the ring. Juan Manual Marquez would capture the WBC super featherweight title by defeating Marco Antonio Barrera by unanimous decision. Marquez would be a possible opponent for Pacquiao if he tried to win a world title at the super featherweight title. There was also a rising Venezuelan star named Edwin Valero (22-0, 22 KOs) who held the WBA title, Joan Guzman (27-0, 17 KOs) who had the WBO strap, and Mzonke Fana (26-3, 9 KOs) who was the IBF champion. Valero, despite his great power, was still a bit green, and due to difficulty getting a boxing license in the states because of a head injury, he was not considered a serious opponent in the short term. Guzman had the hand speed to rival Pacquiao, but he was Dominican and was not as marketable as a Mexican fighter. Fana had already lost to Barrera, and there was no way that bout could be marketed as a pay-per-view event. Ultimately, the final choice would be a rematch with Marco Antonio Barrera. This was made possible by Daniel Weinstein's June 29, 2007, mediation ruling that settled the Top Rank and Golden Boy legal battle and reportedly gave Golden Boy a 25 percent vested interest of Pacquiao promotional revenue. Pacquiao wanted Barrera again since Barrera had made excuses about the fires in Big Bear hurting his training for their first contest. The bout would be scheduled for October 6, 2007, at the Mandalay Bay Resort and Casino.

Pacquiao would rehydrate to 144 pounds after making the 130-pound weight limit. Barrera would rehydrate to 138 pounds after making the 130-pound limit. Barrera would look strong in the first round with his jab and upper-body movement. There was a more determined look this time around. He would also come into the ring drier this time. Pacquiao would also have the upper-body movement while coming in. Pacquiao would score with straight lefts (1:39 and 2:16). The right jab connects would give Pacquiao the close round. Barrera was much more vigilant of Pacquiao's left in this rematch, opposed to the first fight. Despite the round suiting Barrera's tactical pace, it was Pacquiao who connected with the more solid blows—likely giving him the first two rounds.

Pacquiao would continue to be the aggressor in the third round by pressuring Barrera into the ropes with an overhand right followed by a left to the body. Barrera would rough up Pacquiao on the inside with an overhand right (1:27). It could have been the first round scored for Barrera; however, his delusional corner would tell him he was ahead three rounds to zero on the cards. Barrera would fight very cautiously, and his poor output would give Pacquiao the fourth round. Perhaps Barrera realized that if he fought "mano a mano" he would risk KO. Pacquiao would out land Barrera 26–5 in the fourth round.

Barrera would try to rally with a three-punch combination (0:48) in the fifth round of the fight, but his power couldn't do much damage on a 144-pound Pacquiao. In the middle of the fifth, Barrera would land pawning jabs in the round that weren't stiff enough to do much damage. Moreover, none were landing on the body. The fireworks would come in the final minute of the round when both fighters would exchange some solid right hands. The round was close enough to be scored evenly. Barrera would again utilize the left jab followed by straight right (1:02) in the sixth round. The problem for Barrera was that Pacquiao was landing the more solid blows, such as a lunging left (1:07). Barrera would land his best shot (2:17)—a counter right to the chin—that would turn Pacquiao's face to the right. It would be discouraging for Barrera to see that Pacquiao would take the punch well. Barrera would box well, but Pacquiao was still finding holes and capitalizing on those opportunities. Barrera's head movement, which was lacking in the first fight, prevented Pacquiao from landing those big combinations, and that would help ensure that Barrera would last the entire fight. Conversely, Pacquiao's head movement and catching of gloves would decrease the connect percentage of the Barrera jab. The eighth round would probably be the best round for Barrera. He would get a solid right (0:22) and one-two combination (0:55). The Barrera boxing skills missing in the first fight were more evident in this rematch; however, the inconsistent and lack of sustained work output cost him several rounds.

Pacquiao would get Barrera on the ropes in the middle of the ninth round and take command of the fight again. Barrera would fight in spurts but didn't feel he could engage in a gung ho, toe-to-toe match with Pacquiao. Freddie Roach would tell Pacquiao, "Stop fooling around." (His attention appeared to be drawn to the ring card girl in between rounds.) This would be another indication that Pacquiao was loose and relaxed, while Barrera was the one who appeared tense. In fact, the Barrera corner would give the usual pep talk spiel about winning the fight for his family. The contest was mainly mundane as not much fire was coming from the combatants due to the boxing style implemented. The end of the tenth round saw Roach once again tell Pacquiao, "Stop fooling around; this fight is too close." The added sense of urgency would give us some of the best action with both fighters connecting with power punches. Failing to do damage would possibly frustrate Barrera enough to commit a deliberate foul in the eleventh round. He would hit Pacquiao with a vicious right cross while they were on the break, which would result in a point deduction. Barrera would have a nasty cut over his right eye. There would be no knockout in the final round. Pacquiao had proven he could win a technical boxing match with his speed and work rate. The judges' scored it 118–109, 115–112, and 118–109 for Pacquiao. I had it 8-2-2 (117–111) for Pacquiao. One of the even rounds was the eleventh due to the point deduction. Pacquiao was now making a run at a fourth-divisional title. Barrera would promise retirement but didn't live up to his word. There was still "unfinished business" with Juan Manuel Marquez.

CHAPTER 13

Fighter of the Year 2008

It would take four years for Pacquiao and Marquez to match up again. This time it was for the WBC super featherweight title that Marquez owned. It would take place at the Mandalay Bay Resort and Casino, Las Vegas, Nevada, on March 15, 2008. The match would be dubbed as "Unfinished Business." The WBC super featherweight title that belonged to Marquez would be on the line. Pacquiao would hire new strength-and-conditioning coach Alex Ariza. Ariza was known for his work with Diego Corrales and would be in Corrales's corner the day he was stopped by Mayweather in 2001. Ariza used a new training method that varied muscle movement instead of using repetitive drills. Swimming was also added to the Pacquiao training scheme. There were also drills to improve speed and power as Pacquiao increased his weight. Soon Pacquiao would know if it paid dividends when he faced Marquez.

The match commenced with both fighters trying to land their jab. There would be upper-body movement and feints in attempts to take each other off rhythm. Pacquiao would block an overhand right (0:41) in the first round that was thrown by Marquez. Marquez would land an accurate straight right (1:53) that would get Pacquiao to bang both of his gloves in acknowledgment. Marquez would get a warning for low blows. Pacquiao would get in a good combination in the final minute. Marquez would get in an overhand left (1:23) that got Pacquiao's attention. A straight Pacquiao left (1:49) would buckle Marquez in the second round. Marquez would land his best punch in the fight—a full-extend left hook that was precipitated by a right cross. This punch would momentarily stagger Pacquiao in the closing seconds. After two rounds you could have had the fight even, giving either any of the first two rounds. Pacquiao would follow Roach's instruction of doubling up on the right jab then following it with his straight left as the third round began. Marquez would score with his straight right (0:53) as he came forward.

Marquez was controlling the third round with his counterpunching and measured pace. A fighter like Pacquiao can change things with one punch. In the final minute, the action started to open up in the center of the ring. Pacquiao would set up Marquez and land a solid left (2:27) that would hurt him. A short left hook (2:39) would drop Marquez spread eagle on the canvas. The angle of the shot was a difficult one as few fighters could generate such power from such a trajectory. Marquez really never had his legs back from the previous left and now had twenty seconds to survive the round. He would get up and stay near the ropes where he took a few more flush shots that almost dropped him again.

A rejuvenated Pacquiao would come in determined in the fourth round after Marquez. Marquez would land a combination that drove Pacquiao to the ropes at the one-minute mark of the round. Pacquiao would bang his head with his gloves, almost inviting Marquez to come in to set up a trap. Marquez would work the body with hooks, but Pacquiao was not going to take a step backward. The straight left (1:45) would land for Pacquiao again. An enraged Marquez would fire combinations on Pacquiao near the southeastern corner ropes in retaliation. Pacquiao would bob and weave his head in exaggerated fashion to play along. More importantly, Pacquiao would land another solid lead left (2:09). It pretty much stamped another round for Pacquiao. The pressure was on Marquez since he was likely behind in the cards after the first third of the fight. Marquez would get his legs back and score with precise combinations on the inside in the middle of the fifth round. He would also continue to lunge in with his left hook to the body. A right hook (2:12) would also punctuate a rebound round for Marquez. After five rounds Pacquiao landed 43 of 115 and Marquez 42 of 107. This demonstrated how even the punch stats were almost a dead heat.

Pacquiao's lack of head movement would get him caught with lead rights (0:30, 0:53, and 2:57) in the sixth round. A left hook (1:45) would get in on the inside for Marquez as well. The slower tactical pace was suiting Marquez very well. Pacquiao would need to make the fight a faster pace, which would give Marquez difficulty in anticipating shots. Marquez would work with his straight left (0:24) in the seventh round. What was working for Marquez was catching the Pacquiao punches and then countering immediately. Pacquiao was also catching Marquez's jab with his right glove. In the middle of the round, there would be an accidental head-butt that would cause a gash on Marquez's right eye. Referee Kenny Bayless would have the ringside physician examine it and then resume the action. There would be no trepidation from Marquez who landed a three-punch combination (1:52) shortly afterward. Both fighters would then have vicious exchanges, and when they reached their stools, both corners would work on the cuts feverishly to control the blood.

The early stages of the eighth saw Marquez throw a left upper designed to get Pacquiao to put his right glove down. This would give Marquez the opening for a straight right that landed flush on Pacquiao's right eye and made him blink his right eye rapidly. Blood would gush out of Pacquiao's eye similarly to something out of a slasher-horror flick. Interestingly, the referee Kenny Bayless wouldn't have the ringside physician examine the cut as he had Marquez do in the previous round. If there was an opportunity for Marquez to blitz and go for the finish, it would be now. A prime Barrera and Morales would have come out like a rabid dog after that eye. However, Marquez would be cautious, throwing mainly one punch at a time. Pacquiao was laughing openly (1:00) at Marquez after taking shots downstairs and upstairs. Of course, Marquez had to be worried about running into a punch that could hurt him, but his lack of confidence with a wounded Pacquiao was mysterious. What was more bizarre was that he was going after the body when there was a cut eye that had impaired vision. Fighters understand you go after the handicap and try to go for the finish. We remember Roberto Duran as he went after the wounded Davey Moore and later, the same year, he did the same thing against Marvin Hagler in the twelfth round.

At 1:58 Marquez would score with four punches as he had Pacquiao in the northeastern corner ropes. Again, not even one punch was thrown at that injured eye. Then the light bulb popped on in Marquez's head, and he fired a two-punch straight left-right on that eye. It was an easy round to score for Marquez. However, if he had stepped up and pressed the action, it could have been a 10–8 round—or possibly even a stoppage win. The stoppage win could have been possible since the cut was a result of a punch, and it wouldn't go to the scorecards as a technical decision. The final punch stats had Marquez out landing Pacquiao 21–5 in the eighth round. Ironically, Joe Chavez, a cut man of Mexican heritage, would be the one working on Pacquiao's cut in an attempt to control the bleeding. Pacquiao's eye would be much better in the ninth round. The blood had stopped completely, which was a tribute to Joe Chavez's skills as a cut man. The sands of time had run out for Marquez with each blood drop in the eighth. There was a window of opportunity that closed shut for Marquez in the eighth.

Marquez would still get in his straight rights in the ninth (1:25 and 1:28). Pacquiao scored with a straight left (1:38) that Marquez took well. Kenny Bayless would send Marquez again to examine his cut (2:37). Pacquiao would finally cork his overhand left (0:16) that buckled Marquez. Marquez, being a veteran, knew to stay near the ropes to hold him up as he got his bearings back and fought back despite being hurt. Pacquiao would do a much better job blocking that Marquez lead right by keeping his gloves high on lock. It was the first clear Pacquiao round since the fourth round.

Marquez would open the tenth round with a left hook-straight combo that pushed Pacquiao's head back again (1:31). Pacquiao would loosen up and throw his wide rights. Marquez would get a warning for a low blow that would halt the action temporarily in the opening minute. Marquez would score with a combination ending with his left again (2:32). The final round saw Marquez cleanly land a straight right (0:31) again as he came forward. Pacquiao would partially block some short uppercuts that Marquez would throw (0:43). A right hook (2:06) would reel Pacquiao to the ropes, and Marquez followed it with a solid right uppercut (2:09). Marquez would skillfully bring his head down every time Pacquiao came forward with an onslaught. The judges had it a split decision: 115–112 (Duane Ford) for Pacquiao, 114–113 (Tom Miller) for Pacquiao, and 115–112 (Jerry Roth) for Marquez. The final punch stats had Pacquiao landing 157 of 619 and Marquez 172 of 511. On the official cards, the knockdown would be the one-point difference in the Pacquiao win. I had it 7-4-1 (115–113) for Marquez. Marquez landed 130 of 310 power shots, while Pacquiao landed 114 of 305.

Pacquiao would concede that he couldn't see the Marquez right hand due to the cut. What was a bit perplexing was that Pacquiao really didn't work the body as he had done in the Morales rematch. This may have been because he feared counterpunches upstairs. Yet, with his speed and footwork, you would have expected Pacquiao to at least jab at the body. The decision is a game changer in a career. If Marquez had gotten the decision, it would have possibly elevated him higher than Morales and Barrera in the great Mexican all-time list. The Mount Rushmore of Mexican pugilists are Julio Cesar Chavez, Salvador Sanchez, Ricardo Lopez, and Ruben Olivares. All three—Barrera, Morales, and Marquez—were vying to be that fifth head in that pantheon. Marquez, in particular, was trying to get past the shadows of both Barrera and Morales.

The boxing media was equally divided in the opinion of the winner. Those who felt Marquez won included Yahoo Sports, ESPN, Associated Press, *Ring Magazine*, and *Philippine Daily Inquirer*. Filipino-born fighter Nonito Donaire had Marquez winning 114–113. There were several, such as Larry Merchant, Marco Antonio Barrera, and Dougie Fischer, who felt it was a draw. Those who felt Pacquiao won included HBO's Harold Lederman, Lance Pugmire (*LA Times*), Bill Dwyer (*LA Times*), and Lee Groves (Maxboxing). It was obvious there was still more unfinished business between both combatants.

Despite the controversial loss, Marquez would only get hungrier and more determined. Having lost questionable decisions to both Chris John and Freddie Norwood, he was accustomed to bouncing back. Marquez would win five of his next six decisions before he would face Pacquiao again in November 2011. Marquez's only loss would be a shutout loss to Floyd Mayweather in 2009. Regardless of the opinion of the outcome, there was no denying that the bout was a success as it had over 400,000 pay-per-view purchases, which generated over $20 million. Pacquiao's win would now open the door to both higher weights and bigger paydays.

There would be no rematch with Juan Manuel Marquez—despite a $6 million guarantee by Golden Boy Promotions. Pacquiao had come in at 145 pounds the day of the fight against Marquez, which signaled the next option to fight for a lightweight title (something that was very well within his body frame). Alex Ariza would assist Pacquiao in essentially climbing three weight divisions in less than one calendar year. When training boxers, Ariza has felt that balanced muscle distribution is important to a fighter. His work with Pacquiao would develop the powerful calf muscles that allowed Pacquiao to keep his balance and generate more power. Ariza would add swimming in both the pool and the sea as important ring-simulation exercise. There would also be lateral drills, hill climbing, and customary strength-and-conditioning gym exercises. The nutrition regimen would include special shakes that would provide vital protein and carbohydrates. Ariza would also prepare recovery shakes after strenuous workouts.

The first test for Pacquiao as he moved up to the lightweight division was Chicago fighter David Diaz. It would be scheduled for June 28, 2008, at the Mandalay Bay Resort and Casino, Las Vegas, Nevada. The fight with David Diaz would have rallies and a publicity tour called "Lethal Combination." Diaz was the WBC lightweight champion. Diaz won the interim title from Jose Armando Santa Cruz and obtained the full title when he defeated Erik Morales. The choice of Diaz did receive its fair share of criticism by some in the boxing press. Besides a rematch with Marquez, there were two other viable opponents for Pacquiao. The fighter Nate Campbell held the WBA, WBO, and IBF lightweight titles. Campbell had just defeated Juan Diaz by split decision the same month that Pacquiao won a split decision against Marquez. There was also Dominican fighter Joan Guzman who was the WBO super featherweight champion and could have offered a unification bout if Pacquiao had decided to stay a super featherweight. Guzman had among the fastest hands in boxing, and it could have been a great match.

However, David Diaz was seen as the most marketable fight with a fighter who had the style to make it entertaining. Diaz was not going to use speed and technical skill like a Campbell or Guzman. He was going to pretty much brawl and slug it out, which is the style in which Pacquiao has been the most proficient. Perhaps this entertainment aspect—along with Diaz's Mexican heritage, which added to the marketability—made him the next Pacquiao opponent. Most importantly, the added incentive of picking up an additional title with Diaz sealed the deal. Pacquiao would hydrate to 147 pounds the day of the fight after coming in at 134.5 pounds for the official weigh-in.

The actual contest saw Pacquiao comfortably fighting Diaz in the middle of the ring using his superior footwork and hand speed. Diaz would try to make it a brawl with the hope of imposing his size and strength. In reality, Diaz was sticking to his style, as he didn't have the technical skill to try to outbox Pacquiao. Pacquiao was able to use the right jab as a deterrent when Diaz would come straight in. The right hand was increasingly becoming a major arsenal in the Pacquiao repertoire. Diaz would essentially be target practice due to lack of head and lateral movement. The Chicago fighter had decent blocking ability, but it would be impossible to block the sheer volume of Pacquiao punches without anything landing. It's logical to move your head and utilize lateral movement when you fight an offensive fighter like Pacman. Pacquiao would find the holes in the Diaz defense and exploit them (for example landing a short left uppercut between the guard at 0:40 of the second round). Diaz would score his own left hook at 0:54 of the round. Pacquiao would outclass Diaz with combinations scoring from different angles and already have Diaz bleeding with a cut on top of his nose after only two rounds. Diaz would take a plethora of right hands because he kept his left guard down and stood too erect.

Pacquiao would be motivated to use his right hand since he was fighting a fellow southpaw. Diaz would do much better in the fourth round as he would have better movement and use his own right hand to score with hooks to the body. Diaz would suffer a gash over the right eye at 0:57 in the fourth round. The ringside physician would examine it and let the fight continue. All the momentum Diaz had would be squandered away as Pacquiao took control with his speed in the middle of the ring. Lead rights and hooks to the body were slowly taking their toll on Diaz who had two cuts to worry about on his nose and eye. Having impaired vision and not the greatest reflexes and speed would have Diaz eat more combinations downstairs and upstairs in the fifth round.

At 1:41 of the sixth, Diaz would take a solid overhand left after pawing his right hand. Diaz would answer as he demonstrated heart and determination, and he kept burrowing himself forward. However, this couldn't stop the inevitable outcome. The ringside physician would again check the cut at 2:42 and let the fight continue. This would only allow Diaz to get pummeled for the next two rounds without much return fire. A left hook at 2:21 of the ninth round would finally send the former champion—headfirst—down to the canvas. Referee Vic

Drakulich wouldn't bother to count and stopped the contest. Diaz had scars and swelling in both eyes. Diaz would more than earn his $800,000 guaranteed payday. The win would be Pacquiao's fifth divisional world title and would make him a quintuple champion, if you included the lineal featherweight title. Some publications would still consider him a quadruple champion, as they wouldn't include the ring lineal title as a featherweight since it wasn't from one of the four major sanctioning bodies.

Pacquiao would get honored with his win by becoming the flag bearer for the Philippines in the 2008 Beijing Summer Olympics, despite not being a competitor in the games. The symbolic gesture was to confirm that Pacquiao was the biggest athlete in his country. Pacquiao's reach in the Philippines was not limited to being an athlete. He also got involved in entrepreneurial measures: he owned a basketball team, stakes in hotels, and other recreational businesses. There was still a window of opportunity to become a bigger international star and that was to fight the man who, along with Floyd Mayweather Jr., broke the pay-per-view record.

CHAPTER 14
Mega Stardom

Larry Merchant had once toyed with the idea of a mega fight between De La Hoya and Pacquiao. There appeared to be too many hurdles to clear (such as the discrepancy of weight) to make it a reality. The last De La Hoya bout was at 150, and the last Pacquiao contest was at 135. If they could meet at around halfway, then it could be a possibility. It was expected that De La Hoya would face the winner of Margarito-Cotto after his win over Steve Forbes in 2008. De La Hoya would instead turn his eye to Pacquiao. Many, including Pacquiao, felt that De La Hoya still held a grudge due to the contested contract he had signed with Golden Boy in 2006.

Pacquiao would be guaranteed $6 million and De La Hoya $20 million for the bout scheduled December 6, 2008, at the MGM Grand, Las Vegas, Nevada. It was expected that after the pay-per-view revenues would be added, both would make millions more. De La Hoya would get the favorable two-thirds of the PPV split. Pacquiao was on the heels of his thirtieth birthday, and his handlers felt that the moment was now to enter a new stratosphere of notoriety. As Pacquiao was preparing for De La Hoya, his wife Jinkee was pregnant with his daughter, Queen Elizabeth, which would be another source of motivation. "This is my biggest moment in my boxing career," Pacquiao would say in the press conferences and interviews leading up to the fight. Having Freddie Roach would help Pacquiao, as Roach had seen De La Hoya slip away, firsthand, in the last four rounds of the Mayweather fight. De La Hoya would claim, "Roach had the wrong game plan." Pacquiao couldn't have helped seeing the lack of legs in the last rounds against Mayweather. In addition, Pacquiao realized De La Hoya was fighting at his lowest weight in about a decade. He didn't need to knock out De La Hoya; he just needed to break him down little by little. Like Leonard, who would go down two weight classes and get pummeled by Terry Norris, De La Hoya was risking the same fate. Freddie Roach would boast, "De La Hoya couldn't pull the trigger anymore."

De La Hoya's official weight would be 145 pounds, his lowest weight in nearly twelve years. Pacquiao weighed in at 142 pounds and then hydrated to 148.5 pounds on fight night. Freddie Roach will later declare that he knew De La Hoya was badly drained in HBO's 24/7 series for the Ricky Hatton fight. Roach described his observation. "I see the IV marks in his arms…I see the fresh blood…I say to myself, 'They hydrated him after they weighed him in the dressing room…wrong thing to do, way too late.' I told Manny, 'Jump on him right away.'" Pacquiao would do precisely what Roach ordered as he used a combination of head movement and foot work to take away De La Hoya's jab. His smaller height combined with the head-and-foot movement made it hard for De La Hoya to establish a jab. Pacquiao would land some solid straight lefts while using his feet to avoid most of De La Hoya's counters. De La Hoya's guard was not tight, and it allowed Pacquiao to land in between the gloves. There would also be some body shots landed in the second round as Pacquiao created angles to land them.

De La Hoya didn't have the head and footwork necessary to avoid the incoming shots. Emanuel Steward would observe, "Oscar was just a taller fighter but not bigger; he picked up no weight." At 1:28 in the third round, De La Hoya landed a solid left hook to Pacquiao's body, but Pacquiao was not going to crumple as many felt he would. There were still people who read too much into the body-shot knockouts in the Torrecampo and Singuarat fights. Pacquiao was much better conditioned and a far superior fighter at this point in his career. The third round saw Pacquiao routinely land his lead left—similar to a thread thrown through the eye of a needle—against the De La Hoya guard. Moreover, by spinning De La Hoya with his footwork, he was able to make it difficult for

De La Hoya to set up his offense. There would be no cross-arms or armadillo defense to cover the holes that Pacquiao was exploiting.

Despite De La Hoya's jab finally seeing some improvement in the fourth round, it didn't make much of a dent, as Pacquiao was able to weave off and take the sting off the punches. After four rounds De La Hoya was already bruised and had plenty of swelling in both eyes. The fifth round saw nearly total annihilation of the Golden Boy with punch after punch landing with accuracy on both the face and body. De La Hoya would get in a few shots but did not make much impression. Due to the punishment De La Hoya received, the judges could have scored the fifth 10–8 for Pacquiao without a knockdown.

The straight left up the middle consistently found the mark in the sixth round for Pacquiao. De la Hoya would take fewer power shots than in the previous rounds, yet he didn't look like he belonged in the ring. Pacquiao looked both fresher and stronger. Pacquiao would start to put the finishing touches on De La Hoya in the seventh round. Fighters are taught to protect themselves at all times. Sometimes they clinch or use their feet to escape danger. De La Hoya had no strength to clinch and no legs to move; he was slowing down and retreated to the ropes in the middle of the round. This pretty much gave Pacquiao the green light to throw his combinations. Pacquiao would pummel a helpless De La Hoya who didn't have the legs to get out of the ropes. Experienced trainer Nacho Beristain could have mercifully stopped the contest after seven without anybody complaining; however, De La Hoya would come back in the eighth and be a recipient of more punishment. A glimmer of hope for De La Hoya was a decent combination downstairs and upstairs that the conditioned Pacquiao withstood. The Filipino fighter would raise his arms as an invite to get more in; however, Pacquiao would respond with more combinations at the southwestern corner ropes that would spell the end for De La Hoya. De La Hoya would get out of his stool in between rounds and stop the bout.

Ironically, what De La Hoya had done to Chavez a decade earlier, the younger fighter did to him—in a more dominant fashion. Pacquiao landed 244 of 650 punches compared to 114 of 311 for De La Hoya. The win was easily the biggest name on Pacquiao's résumé and introduced him to a mainstream international audience. Pacquiao was now on the top of the pound-per-pound list. Ironically, by losing to Pacquiao, the Golden Boy had made Pacquiao a superstar fighter that he still had a vested interest in. Pacquiao would win 2008 Fighter of the Year accolades from Ring TV, BWAA, and ESPN—for a second time.

CHAPTER 15
The Icarus of Weight Divisions

Since Pacquiao had won a title in five different weight classes, he could have gone down to 140 in an attempt to be a sextuple champion. There were several options at the junior welterweight limit as there were several champions: Andreas Kotelnik (WBA), Paulie Malignaggi (IBF), Timothy Bradley (WBC), and Kendall Holt (WBO). Bradley and Holt were scheduled to fight each other in April 2009, so those options were eliminated. In addition, at the time those names didn't have the commercial appeal of the final choice, which was *Ring Magazine* lineal champion Ricky Hatton. Hatton actually called out Pacquiao after he defeated De La Hoya. The Manchester native felt his career was rejuvenated after winning two consecutive matches after losing to Mayweather by knockout in December 2007. Hatton had replaced longtime trainer Billy Graham with Floyd Mayweather Sr. in his last contest against Paulie Malignaggi. The Hatton fan base was easily the biggest among the available opponents for a title at the division. As a result, it was the most economically feasible match to make as a pay-per-view event. Despite not holding any of the four major titles, Hatton did have the lineal title and had never lost a match in the junior welterweight division.

Pacquiao was attempting to become the fourth Filipino boxer to become a junior welterweight champion, joining Roberto Cruz, Pedro Adigue, and

Morris East. A Pacquiao win would also tie De La Hoya, and Pacquiao would become only the second fighter to be a sextuplet champion.

Initially, there were some negotiating hurdles that needed to be cleared to make the Pacquiao-Hatton match for May 2, 2009. Hatton wanted an even 50–50 split of all the PPV revenues and Pacquiao wanted 60–40. By January 2009 it appeared the fight was off, with Bob Arum of Top Rank stating, "The fight is off." However, cooler heads prevailed, and ultimately Pacquiao got a guaranteed $12 million and 52 percent of the pay-per-view revenues. The bout was officially signed on January 23, 2009. The match would be promoted as "The Battle of East and West."

The Hatton camp felt convinced that they were going to win. Hatton boasted, "Put some money into the fight, and you will win big." The odds were two-to-one against Hatton—much closer than the five-to-one odds in the Tszyu bout. I myself concluded that Hatton had a real chance if he could neutralize Pacquiao's speed by forcing him into the ropes and keeping him there (similar to what Hatton did to Kostya Tszyu). However, it wouldn't be an easy proposition since Pacquiao had the legs to get out of the ropes. Hatton's goal was to make it an ugly fight with more inside fighting and wrestling. Theoretically, the idea was to take Pacquiao off his game. Floyd Mayweather Sr., who would train Hatton, felt that Pacquiao was vulnerable to the body. Perhaps Mayweather Sr. was reading too much into Pacquiao's past two knockouts, which happened ten and thirteen years ago. It would be like a trainer looking into Henry Armstrong's and Alexis Arguello's early losses and expecting to be facing the same fighter. They were not facing a weight-drained or green version of Pacquiao; this was a different Pacquiao that Hatton was facing. In fairness, Hatton could be lethal to the body as evidenced in his one-punch KO of Jose Luis Castillo. Roach and Pacquiao felt confident that Hatton's defensive shield could be penetrable, as evidenced by the Collazo and Mayweather fights. The logic was that if southpaw Collazo could seriously hurt Hatton, then what was Pacquiao going to do?

Both fighters would participate in the HBO 24/7 series again. The loquacious and poetic Floyd Mayweather Sr. would use the program to lash out at both Pacquiao and Roach. There was possibly some tongue-in-cheek in the comments in order to publicize the fight. However, Freddie Roach was irked at being called "Freddie the Joke Coach Roach" and having his fighter being reduced to one of "amateur skills." Roach would fire back that Hatton was the more one-dimensional fighter and, while observing film, didn't think Mayweather really helped Hatton much. Pacquiao would add former heavyweight and light-heavyweight-champion Michael Moorer as a second trainer. Moorer, like Pacquiao, was a natural southpaw who also trained under Roach. The addition of Moorer was designed to alleviate some of Roach's strenuous workload since Roach was battling Parkinson's disease. Moorer would advise Pacquiao, "When you get your punch off, get out of there; you will be safer as he is going to try to wrestle you."

Pacquiao and Hatton would actually play a game of darts that the "Hitman" won. Despite both combatants having access to some local pubs, there wouldn't be a drink binge contest. Perhaps since Pacquiao was a San Miguel drinker and Hatton preferred Guinness beer it would have been a difficult arrangement to make.

After all the press-related shenanigans were over, there would be the main event at the MGM Grand, Las Vegas, in front of a capacity crowd of 16, 262. Pacquiao would officially weigh in at 138 pounds, and Hatton would come in at the 140-pound limit. Pacquiao would hydrate to 148 pounds, which again demonstrated that he was fully comfortable going back to welterweight if needed. Ricky's younger brother, Matthew Hatton, would also fight the same day and win the unanimous decision over Ernesto Zepeda in an undercard match.

Pacquiao commenced the match by using his feet to create angles and find openings in Hatton. There was no need for Pacquiao to stay flat-footed and brawl. The De La Hoya fight was an exhibition of getting into the pocket and scoring then getting out of danger. Hatton wanted to pin Pacquiao to the ropes and work the body. Pacquiao would land an overhand right hook (0:27) in the first. Hatton bum-rushed Pacquiao and momentarily got him in the ropes and scored with a right hook to the body. Pacquiao would use his feet to get out of danger and would throw both his arms in the air to convey that he wasn't hurt from the shot. Pacquiao would land another short right at 1:13, demonstrating how effective he was with the right as well. Hatton would have Pacquiao on the ropes but would get separated by Kenny Bayless. This is where Pacquiao would score with his first solid straight left. Hatton was hurt and held on. Hatton would take a three-punch combination to the chin in the ropes and then get dropped by an overhand left. Intelligently, Hatton would take a knee and full count to try to get himself together. The only way Hatton could survive like Marquez did in his first fight with Pacquiao was to resort to boxing, yet Hatton often abandoned boxing for brawling when he came forward. As a result, it was a recipe for disaster unless he could land that one big shot. Hatton never fully recovered and took a barrage of punches that included another measured straight left that dropped him again with eight seconds left in the round. After one round Hatton was down 10–7.

Hatton would start the second round better by landing a short right hook (0:23) that made Pacquiao take a couple steps back, but Pacquiao was not going down. Pacquiao would tattoo Hatton with straight rights and left hooks in the center of the ring. Hatton would land a short right on the clinch that didn't last long as Pacquiao got out. With less than ten seconds, Pacquiao anticipated Hatton dropping his right hand and countered with a fully loaded left hook that put all his leverage to Hatton's chin. Hatton would raise his arms and then go down and lie motionless. It was one of those knockouts that brought back memories of Tyson-Spinks, Hearns-Duran, and Benitez-Hope. Kenny Bayless didn't need much time to wave off the fight. Hatton remained motionless for some time before getting his wits back. Pacquiao now claimed a sixth divisional title. The knockout would be voted as Knockout of the Year by *Ring Magazine*. For Hatton it was one of those knockouts that was difficult to recover from. He would retire from the sport until making a one-fight comeback in December 2012. The win solidified Pacquiao as the pound-for-pound king of the sport. Perhaps it would not be a coincidence that Floyd Mayweather Jr. would announce his return to the ring on May 2, 2009.

CHAPTER 16

Welterweight Division and Political Triumph

Pacquiao would finish work on the movie *Wapakman* after the Hatton win. The film would eventually be released on December 25, 2009. The tabloid media would have a field day—not because of the film but due to an alleged fling Pacquiao had with costar Krista Ranillo. The actual film would be a box-office disaster as it did only P750,000 (roughly $15,000 US dollars at the time) on opening day. Pacquiao had previously done some minor television and film work. Due to his increasing international notoriety, he would be given opportunities for nonboxing endeavors. In 2006 he had released an album entitled *Laban Nating Lahat Ito* (this is our fight). The following year he would release *Pac-Man Punch*. Although some did praise Pacquiao for branching out to other mediums, there were others who felt he should simply stay focused on what he did best, which was the ring. The one passion that Pacquiao still felt outside of the ring was the world of politics. Pacquiao was a fierce competitor, and the 2007 congressional loss to Representative Darlene Antonino-Custodio was still lingering in his mind.

In June 2009 Pacquiao would be awarded Fighter of the Year for 2008. He would attend the award ceremony in New York and watch the WBO welterweight match between Miguel Cotto and Joshua Clottey in Madison Square Garden with great interest.

After the win over Ricky Hatton, Manny Pacquiao would have many options available. He could have simply stayed as a junior welter and tried to clean out the division, or he could have gone up to welterweight and tried to capture a seventh divisional title. Miguel Cotto always appeared as the front-runner to be the next Pacquiao opponent. Bob Arum totally realized that due to both the Filipino and Puerto Rican fan base that Pacquiao-Cotto was a lucrative fight to make. In addition the fact that both fighters fought for Top Rank meant that the same promotional company could retain all the promotional revenues and the WBO strap. It was a win-win situation for Top Rank.

Cotto, after winning a split decision over Clottey, was the next logical opponent for Pacquiao. At welterweight the only other major name with a title was Shane Mosley who won the WBA title from Antonio Margarito in January 2009. However, Golden Boy promoted Mosley at the time, and the tumultuous relationship with Top Rank made a Pacquiao-Mosley bout improbable.

Miguel Cotto was 34-1, 27 KOs at the time, and his only loss (to Antonio Margarito) was under suspicion due to the illegal hand wraps the CSAC discovered before the Margarito-Mosley fight. I always felt Cotto was a solid boxer and one of the best body punchers in the game. However, many felt his chin was a bit suspect, and he had a propensity to cut. There wasn't a big Cotto size advantage as some made it out to be. The fact was Cotto's height and reach were almost identical to Pacquiao's. Cotto's body was just naturally bigger and wider than Pacquiao, but, like Pacquiao, Cotto also fought in light divisions as an amateur when he was a teenager. In fact, Cotto once fought fellow Puerto Rican Ivan Calderon as a light flyweight amateur.

Miguel Cotto was arguably the biggest name in Puerto Rican boxing since the heyday of Felix Trinidad. Cotto was a devastating body puncher as a junior welterweight and had some ambidextrous ability as he could fight either orthodox or southpaw if needed.

The Pacquiao-Cotto fight would be officially announced to take place on November 14, 2009. The agreed contract would essentially have Pacquiao getting two-thirds of the PPV revenue and a 145-pound catchweight. The fight would be promoted as "Firepower."

Cotto would make it clear in the promotional tour leading up to the fight that "he was no Ricky Hatton or Oscar De La Hoya." It was important to convince the audience that they were not going to waste their money in another one-sided demolition.

Despite the thousands of miles that separate the Puerto Rican island and Filipino archipelago there is some shared history. Both Puerto Rico and the Philippines were colonies of Spain and still carried some of that influence not only in culture and language but also in architecture. Having visited both Puerto Rico and the Philippines, I can attest that going through Old San Juan and El Murro is reminiscent of walking through Intramuros. While Puerto Ricans speak Spanish that includes indigenous Taino influences, the official Filipino Tagalog language carries some mixture of Spanish influence with its own indigenous dialects. The two combatants had national followings that would guarantee a lucrative bout.

Coming into the Cotto fight, Pacquiao had to juggle stardom with domestic family issues. Pacquiao would meet his dad for the first time in nearly two decades. Not only did Pacquiao have some resentment because his father abandoned his family, but he also ate his pet dog. Pacquiao has stated that he has reconciled and forgiven his father. This was part of being consistent with the Christian doctrine of forgiving others in order for God to forgive you for your transgressions. Pacquiao's father would be brought to watch the fight live for the first time in his life. The media would again try to highlight one of Pacquiao's alleged transgressions. When fight night occurred, the media would report that Jinkee Pacquiao was conspicuously absent from the MGM. They would report rumors that she felt betrayed by the reported fling that Pacquiao had with actress Krista Ranillo. There would be widespread footage later showing Jinkee crying during a church service. It was not the first time the media focused on Pacquiao's alleged extracurricular personal affairs. There was also a paternity suit filed by a Joanna Rose Bascoa in 2006. Pacquiao has stated that he has taken responsibility for both his actions and his children. This time the media attention would be difficult to escape, as he was now an internationally known celebrity. The media's increased scrutiny was expected as Pacquiao had now reached an international level, and his life outside the ring was going to get coverage.

Although there were distractions, Pacquiao was confident in training and preparation for the bout. Freddie Roach even made a first-round knockout prediction that later would be revised. The Pacquiao-Cotto terms stipulated that there would be a 145-pound catchweight for Cotto's WBO title. The fact that Cotto had weighed in 146 pounds for his previous fight with Joshua Clottey suggested to some that one pound less was not going to be a major hindrance. Moreover, the fact that fighters rehydrate one day after the weigh-in makes actual ring weight and weigh-in two distinct things. The fact that a camp would want a stipulated catchweight does suggest that it does count for something. However, losing the extra two pounds means more work before the fight. However, Cotto may have wanted to come in lighter as he was fighting the quicker opponent.

The Cotto camp was confident that trainer Joe Santiago, who replaced uncle and former Cotto trainer Evangelista Cotto after a notorious split, would devise a plan to neutralize Pacquiao's speed with both timing and counterpunching. Legendary trainer Emmanuel Steward even tried to volunteer his services. "If I train Cotto, he will knock out Pacquiao." Due to the major cuts suffered in past fights with Torres, Mosley, Judah, Margarito, and Clottey, there was a major possibility that Cotto would lose via TKO due to a cut stoppage.

Freddy Roach and the Pacquiao camp actually felt that Cotto made many of the same mistakes that Ricky Hatton did. Roach predicted a first-round knockout as he felt that if Cotto was hurt in the first round, then Pacquiao would finish him. Pacquiao would get some excellent sparring with future IBF welterweight champion Shawn Porter. Although there were reports that Porter had actually dropped Pacquiao during training, Freddy Roach would respond by saying that Porter did get a solid shot against Pacquiao but that it would be Porter who would actually fall on the canvas.

The Pacquiao-Cotto fight was well publicized thanks again to HBO's 24/7 series and also to both fighters' solid fan bases. Pacquiao would also attend the Jimmy Kimmel late-night program to publicize the fight. Kimmel would have Pacquiao as a guest several more times in the following years. Pacquiao was the clear favorite, but some did feel that Cotto was the first true welterweight that

Pacquiao had faced, and his bodywork would stop Pacquiao. The bout would take place in front of 15,930 spectators at the Grand MGM arena in Las Vegas.

The first round of the fight surprised some as Cotto actually used his left jab and timing to win the round. There was a bit of a feeling-out process as Pacquiao wanted to test Cotto's power before going to heavy offense. Cotto also countered Pacquiao with a two-punch combination at 1:45 and would follow it up with a solid left hook at 2:28. Cotto's lateral and head movement made Pacquiao miss some shots. It was obvious that this fight wouldn't be an easy two-round demolition as the Hatton fight had been.

The second round belonged to Cotto early on with his ring generalship. Cotto kept jabbing and even scored with a left hook to Pacquiao's body. However, things would change when Pacquiao broke Cotto's defense by scoring with a left uppercut between the gloves at 1:22 of the round. Pacquiao's precise and accurate punching would be crucial in this fight. Pacquiao has the ability to capitalize on even the smallest of openings in a standard guard defense. There would be no crab-like or cross-arms defense that would cover up those holes against Pacquiao. Cotto didn't slow the fight down by clinching after scoring either. Cotto still tried to win the round by scoring with a good left hook at 1:41, but Pacquiao took the shot well. Pacquiao would get momentum when he scored with a straight left to the body at 2:23, and he would flurry in the last thirty seconds of the round.

Pacquiao continued the momentum of the second round by landing a short right hook at 0:47 of the third on Cotto's chin, which resulted in a knockdown as both of Cotto's gloves touched the canvas. Cotto would switch southpaw, something he had done often in the past but usually only briefly. At 2:38 Cotto would land a combination that was highlighted by a powerful left uppercut. Despite the Cotto rally, it was still a 10–8 round for Pacquiao.

The fourth round was a major turning point in the fight. The final minute of the fourth was the moment Cotto realized he couldn't hurt Pacquiao. Cotto was able to get Pacquiao on the ropes with only a minute left in the round; he scored with hooks to the body and straight punches to the chin while Pacquiao kept his gloves high and urged Cotto to hit him. After a noticeable, collective scare for Pacquiao supporters, Pacquiao was able to get out of the ropes and even knock down Cotto for a second time with a left hook that landed on the jaw that Cotto didn't see. Cotto looked like he had temporarily punched himself out after Pacquiao escaped the ropes. The result was another 10–8 round for Pacquiao and the possibility of Cotto being down as many as five points on the cards with eight rounds left.

Cotto came back to win the fifth, but to his frustration he couldn't really hurt Pacquiao. He landed the stiff left jab, like he did at 0:38. Pacquiao took another left uppercut and even a shot to the ear at 2:26 that often results in knockdowns due to lost balance, as the ear helps maintain equilibrium. Despite doing better, Cotto must have been demoralized that he didn't at least slow down Pacquiao.

In the sixth round, Cotto was able to land the left-overhand punch twice, yet Pacquiao took control of the fight again. Cotto's face was becoming increasingly more bloodied and swollen. A powerful left hook at 2:08, followed with more flurries showing both great speed and accuracy, had Pacquiao erasing any momentum Cotto had won in the fifth. Pacquiao had Cotto in retreat in the seventh round as the champion was reduced to fighting only in flurries as he picked his shots to fight. Cotto tried to rally by fighting off his left jab and even jolted Pacquiao's head back at 1:03.

At 1:40 of the eighth, we could hear Cotto's corner scream "metele" (hit him) as Pacquiao followed Cotto with his gloves up and Cotto responded with shots to the head and body and Pacquiao banged his gloves. All of that work would come in vain as Pacquiao was able to load up with possibly his best shots of the fight and had Cotto staggered on the ropes. Freddie Roach's eighth-round TKO prediction almost came true. (His other first-round TKO prediction was already eliminated by the wayside.)

The fight was essentially over after the eighth round. The only question was if Cotto would last the distance. When Pacquiao pressed the action, it was obvious that Cotto was going to retreat and just try to land a few shots. Pacquiao was able to dominate both the ninth and eleventh, while we could have charitably given the tenth to Cotto for landing his jab and due to Pacquiao taking a rest. At 0:53 of the twelfth, Kenny Bayless finally stopped the fight after Pacquiao loaded and landed a powerful straight left. Pacquiao was now regarded as a champion in a seventh weight class. To some, the fight should have been stopped—possibly as early as the ninth or, at the latest, in the eleventh. Economically the bout was a major success having done more than 1.2 million PPV sales, which grossed over $70 million. The live gate would earn nearly $9 million with an attendance of nearly 16,000 at the MGM. Pacquiao reportedly earned $22 million and Cotto $12 million.

The end of the year would bring a third Fighter of the Year award from *Ring TV*. Pacquiao would join only Joe Louis, Rocky Marciano, Joe Frazier, Muhammad Ali, and Evander Holyfield as fighters who had won the award three or more times. ESPN and the BWAA would also name Pacquiao Fighter of the Year for 2009. The Boxing Writers Association of America would also give Pacquiao fighter of the decade for the 2000s. Pacquiao beat out notable fighters such as Floyd Mayweather Jr. and Bernard Hopkins for the decade accolade.

Two major items away from the ring would consume the months leading to the next Pacquiao bout. The first, which was covered in the Mayweather chapter of this book, was the failed negotiations to make a super fight between Pacquiao and Mayweather.

The second item away from the ring was that Pacquiao would again file his candidacy for political office. This time he would seek office in his wife's backyard of Sarangani province. There would be a vacant congressional seat left by Rep. Erwin Chiongbian. Chiongbian's family had a political reign that ran for nearly four decades. His brother Roy Chiongbian, a local businessman, would seek the seat running in the Sarangani Reconciliation and Reformation Organization. The Lakas-Christian Muslim Democrat Party would endorse the party. Pacquiao would make his announcement in November 2009. This time he ran under own his party, the People's Champ Movement (PCM). He understood that organization and a good ground game was essential. This time he set up a better turf system in which his and his wife's associates would spread through different areas to reach different voters. This time Pacquiao would be a more effective communicator, understanding how to inspire people to vote and listen to their needs. Two years after his loss in 2007 saw the Pacman reach a new stratosphere in public recognition, and he was now more mature at the age of thirty. He was now a full five years beyond the twenty-five-year-old age requirement. There was also a bigger war chest as Pacquiao could shell out millions of his own money to finance his own political aspirations. Pacquiao also enlisted the help of advisor Michael Koncz and promoter Bob Arum. Arum, who helped make the "Thrilla in Manila" back in 1975, was happy to get involved in a political campaign. Pacquiao would have a two-room headquarters in General Santos City nicknamed the "Pentagon." There would be security measures taken to keep his workers safe in the "Pentagon," as the Philippines has had approximately 1,200 political assassinations in the last decade.

In response to Mayweather's allegations of performance-enhancement drugs, there would be a defamation suit filed against Mayweather on December 30, 2009. The complaint was filed by the firm O'Melveny and Myers. Pacquiao attorney Daniel Petrocelli would tell Fanhouse, "We filed a defamation of character lawsuit in the federal court in Las Vegas, Nevada, against the Mayweathers, Oscar De La Hoya, and Richard Schaefer based on their false and defamatory statements about Manny Pacquiao—specifically their public statements that Pacquiao was taking steroids or other illegal drugs to enhance his performance, knowing that there is absolutely no basis for any such assertions."

Pacquiao would add, "I view using steroids, synthetic growth hormone, or any illegal or banned substance as cheating—plain and simple. I would never cheat this sport that I love. I would never cheat the legacies of the great champions I have been blessed to challenge." The lawsuit would eventually settle in September 2012 for an undisclosed amount. However, it was reported that Mayweather would have to pay $114,000 in legal costs and expenses due to failing to attend the scheduled deposition. With the lawsuit behind both fighters, it was widely expected that this would open the door to a future match between them.

As Pacquiao prepared to fight for political office, he was also scheduled to fight in the ring on March 3, 2010, against Ghanaian fighter Joshua Clottey. The time between bouts was used to help victims of Typhoon Onday that had hit the southeast Pacific weeks before his match with Miguel Cotto. He also continued with his work on local public-work projects in education and health.

As I wrote in an article in the buildup for the fight, Joshua Clottey actually deserved the match. I felt he deserved—at minimum—a draw against Cotto, and he did have the durability to go the distance with Pacquiao. Pacquiao himself felt Clottey won the close fight with Cotto. Bob Arum would ally himself with Cowboys' Jerry Jones and would have the bout held at the Cowboys Stadium at Arlington. The capacity crowd could easily accommodate over 40,000 and bring a live gate of over $6 million. This wouldn't be the Pacquiao-Mayweather showdown that most of the public demanded, but on paper I felt Clottey was a respectable opponent compared to some of the future opponents he would face.

Pacquiao would weigh 145.75 the highest he had ever weighed before rehydrating. Clottey (35-3, 21 KOs) would come in at the full welter limit of 147. As Clottey entered the ring, he would be greeted by one of the Filipino flag bearers who would give the infamous slash throat gesture. Clottey was not intimidated and still danced around the ring. Pacquiao would come into the ring to Survivor's "Eye of the Tiger."

Clottey would keep his arms up with elbows pinned to his ribs in an armadillo defense. Pacquiao spotted a few openings in the lower body and was able to score a few straight lefts, but most of the shots upstairs were either fully or partially blocked. Clottey would pawn with his jab on occasion but was not doing much. Pacquiao would land a counter right at 1:59 of the first round that had Clottey lose his footing temporarily; it was the best punch in the round and a reminder of how solid the right hand was for Pacquiao at this stage of his career. It was difficult to figure the Clottey strategy for victory. He did land a clean straight left at 0:41 of the second round, but he was being outworked. Perhaps Clottey thought Pacquiao would punch himself out and start to fade in the second half of the fight. Roach had instructed Pacquiao to keep working the body. This is what the champion would do with short right hooks and straight lefts to the body. Pacquiao would land five unanswered punches that would have Clottey doing a mock spaghetti-legs dance with about a minute left in the round. Pacquiao would throw ninety-six punches in the second round—an astonishing number of punches considering a good portion were power shots and not jabs.

The third round would be a much better round for the Ghana challenger. He would land a solid left uppercut and a solid straight right at 1:51 that would be his best punches up to that point. Pacquiao would rally with combinations and make it possibly an even round. The combinations would continue in the fourth round, which included a two-handed punch that would get a warning from the referee Rafael Ramos. There was perhaps an attempt at humor with the punch, as it was never seen before in a Pacquiao fight.

After five rounds Clottey had landed 47 of 151 and Pacquiao 84 of 495. The lopsided stats would continue in the sixth and seventh round where Clottey would stay in his shell both blocking and taking punches without returning much fire. Clottey would receive a fierce combination of blurring hand speed in the middle of the seventh round and would then fire a straight left-overhand-right combo but not follow up with much. Clottey would get a warning for a low blow in the middle of the eighth round, and Pacquiao would be given time to recuperate. Clottey stood idly taking shots in a turtle shell, and in order to lighten up the one-sided, mundane contest, the commentator Jim Lampley would have an infamous, over-the-top episode in the broadcast in which he repeated "bang! bang!" sixteen times to end the eighth round. Clottey would land some clean shots and combos in the ninth and tenth round, but Pacquiao would answer those shots with combinations.

Clottey never clinched Pacquiao to stop the shots; he used the turtle shell until the final bell. The eleventh round was the best round of the fight. Clottey would land several solid uppercuts and straight rights. The round could have been charitably given to Clottey, but Pacquiao more than answered every punch with combinations downstairs and upstairs. The twelfth round may have been the only round that could have narrowly been given to Clottey. Clottey came in much more aggressively for the full three minutes and landed some effective hooks and a solid uppercut. I had the fight 10-1-1 or 119–110 for Pacquiao. The judges had it 120–108, 119–109, and 119–109, all for Pacquiao.

Pacquiao threw 1,231 punches—an incredible amount for any fighter. He landed 246 of those punches for a 20 percent connect percentage. Clottey landed 108 of 399 for a 27 percent connect rate. Both fighters would have visible swelling and scars. Pacquiao would call Clottey a "strong fighter" and conceded he felt some of his power. "This is the first time I lost a fight; I didn't think I lost the three other times," Clottey would proclaim. Many critics were very hard on Clottey for not throwing more punches. Yet the truth was that Clottey did land some good shots on Pacquiao, and the champion was able to take them. More credit needs to be given to Pacquiao for being able to handle the power and not gassing out after all those punches thrown. The final pay-per-view numbers were a bit disappointing as it registered over 700,000 buys, well short of what the Cotto bout did. Some felt it was a result of some backlash from boxing fans who wanted the Mayweather bout, while others felt there needed to be a stronger undercard featuring other stars.

After the Clottey win, Pacquiao had to turn his attention to the upcoming May election. On May 13, 2010, Pacquiao would win a resounding victory by getting 120,052 votes (66.4 percent) against Chiongbian who received 60,899 (33.7 percent) of the votes. Essentially, Pacquiao had turned the margin of defeat in his last election to the margin of victory in this election. As Pacquiao was officially a congressman elect, he needed to balance his life both inside and outside of the ring. This included balancing the roles of fighter, congressman, husband, and father.

CHAPTER 17

Mayweather Time Clock and Tornado Tijuana

Some were still optimistic that a Pacquiao-Mayweather bout could be arranged for the fall of 2010. Mayweather had defeated Shane Mosley in May, and there was still interest in the bout. Pacquiao himself felt that a motivating factor was his eldest son, who wanted him to retire shortly but wanted his father to defeat Mayweather before retirement.

Top Rank would actually have an offer on the table with a proposed time clock for Mayweather to respond with a July 16, 2010, deadline. Bob Arum would have a headline attached to the clock "Money Time: Mayweather's Decision." There would be no response to the twelve o'clock deadline as Mayweather was "on vacation." The Mayweather camp would deny negotiations ever took place. Top Rank would fire back stating that negotiations did take place with HBO president Ross Greenburg acting as an intermediary. Greenburg would claim he did try to make the fight happen. The bottom line of whether negotiations did or didn't take place was trivial, as there was no super fight. At the time I wrote an article titled "Mayweather vs. Pacquiao: It's Now or Never" and predicted that the Mayweather and Pacquiao bout would never take place. Despite all the negative and hateful things said about members of both teams and their fan bases, Pacquiao and Mayweather were more similar than many of them would admit.

On the surface, Pacquiao and Mayweather seem on the opposite side of the spectrum in almost every facet. While Mayweather is perceived as arrogant and ostentatious and Pacquiao as modest and humble, these two pugilists do have a few things in common: 1) They both had estranged and difficult relationships with their fathers; 2) They are often in the company of large entourages; 3) They both have a passion for basketball; 4) They both have a reputation for high-stakes gambling.

A match between the two combatants wouldn't be easy to predict. Pacquiao could give Mayweather problems for several reasons. The three most noted are his southpaw stance, power, and speed; the fourth—and possibly the riskiest—are the angles. The angles of the shots could still penetrate the shoulder-roll defense utilized by Mayweather. This is why the Mayweather version that fought Diego Corrales that utilized getting on the bike and lateral movement—would be the best strategy, while using the reach advantage. The question is "Does a thirty-plus-year-old fighter have the same legs he had in his prime?" In addition, Pacquiao's foot speed is excellent in cutting off the ring, so it would be an interesting chess match.

Mayweather would also give Pacquiao difficulties for several reasons. Mayweather's lead right hand would likely be able to get through Pacquiao's defense. Mayweather's speed and counterpunching ability far exceeds Marquez's, an opponent who gave Pacquiao difficulty in four bouts. Mayweather has an underrated chin, and his exceptional condition combined with his ring intelligence could allow him to escape danger. If Mayweather needed to use his legs or clinch, he would do that. Unfortunately, it appeared the only way the bout would take place would be in video games or possibly as a computerized version a la Ali-Marciano in 1969.

Without Mayweather, Top Rank's plan-B fight was Antonio Margarito. A possible bout between Pacquiao-Margarito would be highly criticized for numerous reasons. It was felt that Margarito was being rewarded with a license by the state of Texas. Margarito beat an unknown challenger (Robert Garcia) for a WBC International junior middleweight title. He was now rewarded at a shot at the vacant WBC junior middleweight title. The payday and a catchweight of 150 pounds raised questions about how this fight was made. Pacquiao had never fought as a junior middleweight, and Margarito had only one recent win over an obscure opponent to get a chance at the title. Nonetheless, fans of boxing had the opportunity of serious action as both fighters had an entertaining come-forward style. The fact that both fighters fought for the same promotional umbrella, had the interest of both the Filipino and Mexican market, and gave Pacquiao a shot at an eighth divisional title would prove to be the catalyst in making Pacquiao-Margarito a reality. As Margarito still couldn't get a license to fight in the state of Nevada, as they honored the CSAC suspension, the state of Texas would be the second consecutive Pacquiao match held there.

Pacquiao would get a guarantee of $25 million for the bout. The bout would be scheduled for November 13, 2010, at Cowboys Stadium, Arlington, Texas, as the Clottey bout had been. In HBO's 24/7 Pacquiao would state that he felt Margarito deserved a second chance despite the hand-wraps scandal. However, Pacquiao would find Margarito's excuse (that he didn't know) laughable and exclaim, "Of course he knew; this is common sense." There would be other controversy besides dealing with the entire Margarito hand-wrapping scandal. A taped video by FanHouse prior to the bout would appear to show both Antonio Margarito and a young Mexican American fighter (Brandon Rios) appearing to mock Freddie Roach's Parkinson's disease. In the video Margarito can be seen with trembling hands and head and muttering "*Fre-die Roaaach.*" Trainer Robert Garcia would then point to Rios and say "that is Freddie Roach," and then the camera would pan to Rios who had his eyes closed and face trembling and stuttered "Ma-nny Pac-quiao." Margarito would immediately issue a public apology and state that one of his aunts has Parkinson's and that he wouldn't trivialize the disease. There was some trash talking and exchanges between both camps as Roach felt that Margarito's camp was hurting the sport by making fun of "attempted murder" while joking about loaded gloves.

On the night of the fight, Pacquiao would weigh in at 148 pounds after the initial weight of 144.6 pounds. Margarito would hydrate up to 165 pounds after officially weighing in at 150 pounds. This meant Pacquiao would have to engage an opponent that had a four-and-a-half-inch and seventeen-pound advantage. The action would be slow to start as both fighters engaged in a jabbing contest in the first round. Pacquiao used a double-right jab followed by a straight left on the taller opponent. The straight left was aimed specifically at the pit of Margarito's stomach. At 2:06 Pacquiao landed a straight upper right on Margarito's chin. The unusual angle was not easy to pick up for a fighter like Margarito. It was apparent that Pacman's use of odd angles would give Margarito problems. Margarito came in straight while dragging his right left and ignoring lateral movement, which is essential with an offensive-whirlwind fighter such as Pacquiao.

Within the first thirty seconds of the second round, Margarito would land a straight right jab-left hook combination that was partially blocked by Pacquiao's left glove. Margarito was successful in landing some looping shots on top of the head and almost had Pacquiao on the ropes. However, Pacquiao's feet were swift enough to elude any traps on the ropes. Margarito would get in two solid uppercuts, but the use of speed and angles aided Pacquiao in slowly taking Margarito apart. At 1:51 of the third round, Margarito would again score with a right hook but failed to keep Pacquiao on the ropes. Pacquiao's feet would get him out of danger, and then he would come back to score combinations. Margarito would laugh off the punches, but they were slowly having an adverse effect. Pacquiao figured out how to work Margarito's body by throwing a high straight right to get Margarito's guard high and then following it with a straight left downstairs.

In the fourth round, Pacquiao noticed Margarito kept his hands low and punished him with overhand lefts. Margarito was becoming a stationary target with little head and lateral movement. Margarito's eye would become a slit as those shots came in with more frequency and precision. There would be a red mouse under Margarito's right eye. A solid right to Margarito's body at 1:42 staggered the Tijuana fighter, as his knees buckled, until he got air back in his lungs. The maligned fighter's character would be demonstrated by taking incredible punishment and coming back with his own uppercut at 2:31. However, this was almost a 10–8 Pacquiao round without a knockdown. Pacquiao would out land Margarito 43–10 in power punches in the fourth.

In the opening minute of the fifth round, Margarito had Pacquiao on the ropes—this time for a longer duration. He would score with short body punches and an uppercut that would get Pacquiao to pounce his gloves. Most of the round would be Pacquiao fighting in the center of the ring and peppering

Margarito with combinations upstairs and downstairs. Robert Garcia would tell Margarito, "Don't throw your punches from so far; throw them close inside." The reason was that those punches thrown from far were allowing him to get countered.

The biggest suspense of the night would come when Margarito would land four solid hooks to Pacquiao at 2:30–2:34 of the sixth round. Pacquiao would be momentarily hurt for the first time since the second round of the Oscar Larios fight. Pacquiao would be able to escape with his feet after dominating most of that round.

The Pacman version of the Ali shuffle would be in full display at 1:10 of the seventh round as he felt more in control of the fight. Pacquiao would also spin Margarito and run circles around him to not allow him to set his feet to throw his best shots. Pacquiao realized he could still easily land without standing in front of him. As a result, Pacquiao gave new angles but different directions. Margarito's next best moments were between 1:03 and 1:13 of the eighth round when he again had Pacquiao against the ropes, and he tried to work the body. This time Pacquiao did a better job in blocking the punches and would get out of the ropes to punish Margarito again. Margarito would take Pacquiao momentarily again and land his best left uppercut at 1:59. In an incredible display of durability, Pacquiao was able to take the punches from a fighter who came in as a super middleweight.

"He is not breaking Pacquiao up like Miguel Cotto; draw your own conclusions," Jim Lampley would observe. Margarito received so much punishment by the end of nine rounds that it would prompt the referee Lawrence Cole to have Margarito tell him how many fingers he was holding up. It was odd since often the referee will simply have the ringside physician check the fighter to determine if the action should continue. Cole would ask, "Cuantos?" (How many?), and Margarito would say "dos" (two), which would allow the action to continue. Unfortunately for Margarito, he would take an additional, incredible amount of punishment. Pacquiao would land fifty-seven power shots in the tenth round, compared to nine for Margarito. The tenth round was possibly a second 10–8 round for Pacquiao. Pacquiao himself would seem to ease it down in the last two rounds, hoping that the referee would mercifully stop the fight by looking at him on several occasions to stop it.

At 0:58 of the eleventh round, Pacquiao would look at Cole to wonder why it wasn't stopped. At 1:46 of the eleventh, Cole would comically again put up his fingers and ask how many fingers, and Margarito would say "uno." When the bell would ring for the end of eleventh, Pacquiao would look at Margarito's face and gasp in horror at what he saw. The best makeup for a *Rocky* movie couldn't reenact the blood and swelling of the face. What happened to Margarito opponents Cotto and Luje was now staring back at him in the mirror. The fight should have been stopped, as it was impossible to know if any serious hemorrhage damage was done.

Pacquiao would get on his bike and mainly pawn with his jab in the final round, as he possibly feared a repeat of Eugene Barutag. The scores of 118–110, 119–109, and 120–108 didn't tell the full story of the contest. Pacquiao landed 474 of 1,069 punches. Most importantly, 411 of the punches Pacquiao landed were power punches. Margarito would land 228 of 817, which is the most any opponent would land on Pacquiao since punch-stats numbers were recorded. "He is really strong, and I got hurt," Pacquiao would say after the fight. Margarito would immediately go to the hospital after the bout where it would be discovered that he had suffered a broken orbital bone due to the fight and required surgery.

Despite all the negative publicity Margarito received due to the hand-wraps scandal, his warrior heart couldn't be denied. The win gave Pacquiao a claim to an eighth divisional title, and, hence, he became the first octuple champion. This feat was accomplished while skipping both the super-flyweight and bantamweight divisions. The Pacquiao-Margarito pay-per-view would do 1.1 million purchases, which was a major improvement from the Clottey bout.

CHAPTER 18

Sugar Shane

There were many who clamored for Pacquiao to even move up again and challenge Sergio Martinez for the WBC middleweight title, as Martinez had a recent sensational knockout of Paul Williams and had captured the middleweight title earlier in the year by defeating Kelly Pavlik. Pacquiao held titles in both the junior middleweight and welterweight divisions, and there were several names that held titles. Champions who held titles in the welterweight and junior middleweight division included names such as Cornelius Bundrage, Sergiy Dzinziruk, and Andre Berto. There was also Timothy Bradley, who called out Pacquiao after his welterweight match with Luis Carlos Abregu on July 7, 2010. Bradley was willing to put aside the light welterweight unification match with Devon Alexander if he could get the bigger payday with Pacquiao.

What would follow was a bit perplexing and shocking, as Shane Mosley became the leading contender for the next Pacquiao bout. Mayweather dominated Shane Mosley for the last ten rounds of their contest, and nobody expected Shane Mosley would ever get a chance at Manny Pacquiao. After he had a lackluster draw with Sergio Mora, it became more improbable. Bob Arum himself would shoot down any possibility of such a contest with Mosley. He would comment about Mosley's performance against Mora in *Sports Illustrated*. "I heard them saying Mosley was huffing and puffing for air in the fourth or fifth round," Arum said. "To me, that is the real tip-off for an aging fighter. Even Big George Foreman did that in his forties, but he always had that big, big punch like in the [Michael] Moorer fight. What I've read is not very supportive to make any Mosley-Pacquiao bout. Look, he's going to be forty, and he's in the lighter weights where speed is so important. He's on a show with guys—example, twenty-year-old Saul Canelo Alvarez—old enough to be his son. I guess Shane needs the money due to his matrimonial situation (a divorce under harsh California community-property rules)," Arum said. "I've always considered Shane to be a nice guy, but this is what happens to fighters when they age." Nonetheless, Shane Mosley would be selected as Pacquiao's next opponent.

Mosley was a fighter who Roach had eliminated as a Pacquiao opponent in the past. Roach would state, "Shane came to the gym twice to ask me to let him fight Manny. I told him no both times, and both times for the same two reasons: First, there isn't enough money there, and second, you're too good a fighter." What had changed were two things. First, Mosley was a free agent after his departure from Golden Boy, and secondly, this was not the same Mosley who had dismantled Antonio Margarito in January 2009. Mosley would have been an ideal opponent in early 2010, but after the Mayweather loss, his name lost stock value. However, despite his age, Mosley still had three ingredients that would make him a dangerous opponent if Pacquiao took him lightly; Mosley had speed, power, and was a durable fighter who was never knocked out.

The fight would take place on May 7, 2011, at the MGM Grand, Las Vegas, Nevada. In order to boost sales, the undercard featured Jorge Arce and Wilfredo Vasquez Jr. to appeal to the Mexican-Puerto Rican rivalry. Former middleweight champion Kelly Pavlik would also be part of the undercard as he faced Alphonso Lopez. Pacquiao was guaranteed $20 million, and Mosley was guaranteed $5 million. Pacquiao was expected to make millions more, contingent upon the final pay-per-view revenue numbers. This time the bout would air on Showtime PPV instead of HBO. Ross Greenburg, the President of HBO sports, was understandably not thrilled with the Pacquiao-Mosley bout.

Shane Mosley's trainer, Nazeem Richardson, would tell Showtime during the fighter meetings aired by *Fight Camp 360*, "Pacquiao is very fast and very dangerous, but like I said so is a bully. But if a bully misses by two inches, then it's no longer dangerous...Anything that Shane Mosley hits at 147 pounds, he is going to hurt it." Mosley would state in the same meeting, "In my heart and mind, I know I can beat him." Pacquiao's own assessment, as he would tell Showtime during the meeting, was that "if you train hard, then you become confident. I am trying to get better and better." Freddie Roach would claim the style of the fighters would make the fight compelling. "Manny Pacquiao is going to attack this guy, and that is what Shane wants…This is why Manny is in the best shape ever."

The actual fight was more of a staccato-pace chess match than the fireworks that were expected. Mosley actually tried to fight behind his flickering left jab during most of the fight. He actually gave Pacquiao some trouble by making it difficult for him to be pinned down because of his circling around the ring. Unfortunately for Mosley, he simply didn't let his right hand go, and Pacquiao never really landed his great combinations. Pacquiao still got the better of Mosley in most rounds by simply outworking him. Mosley would land a left jab to the head followed by a straight right to the body at 1:52 of the first round. Mosley would also score with another straight right at 2:29 to possibly give him the opening round. The tactical style would help Mosley as he slowed down the pace and was able to land another two-punch combination in the middle of the second round. Pacquiao would answer back with an even more solid two-punch combination of his own. Both fighters would clash heads, but fortunately no blood or cuts would result. Another combination to end the round would give Pacquiao the second round.

Mosley, having one of the best chins in boxing, would be tested in the third round. Pacquiao was landing his straight left consistently. At 1:42 Mosley would get dropped—for the first time since facing Vernon Forrest—time with a straight left. The shot landed near Mosley's left ear, which can explain why he lost his equilibrium. The knockdown was not of the flash variety; he was hurt. Mosley would be on rubbery legs but got his balance back.

Mosley was more cautious in the fourth, but he did land a counter right hand at 1:19 and a three-punch combination at 2:38. Yet Pacquiao controlled most of the round with his straight left. After four rounds Pacquiao had landed fifty-six punches, which was the lowest total in recent fights. This was because he had an opponent who was able to move and slow down the pace. Pacquiao still clearly outworked Mosley—although with less activity. He would feint with the right and then land the lead left at 2:21 of the fifth round.

Mosley was a shadow of his former self, as Bob Arum himself had predicted with his comments to *Sports Illustrated*. When Pacquiao initiated, he would backpedal instead of his customary style of fighting back (as happened in the sixth and seventh round). Mosley surely felt he would get knocked out if he went "toe to toe." However, in order to get the glory, he needed to take the risk. Mosley was never knocked out and surely wanted to keep that record intact. Yet this was a major PPV event, and people paid money both at the MGM and at home to see the action promised. They didn't pay to see two fighters pawn at each other and mainly trade jabs while circling around the ring. This can help explain why the audience in the arena was jeering constantly. The ninth round saw Pacquiao starting to increasingly find the mark with the straight left and right hook. At 2:08 a straight left would land bull's-eye between the eyes and hurt Mosley. He would continue to stalk Mosley in the tenth round until Kenny Bayless would count a push as a knockdown. What actually happened was that what appeared as a glancing punch was actually a push that sent Pacquiao to the canvas. The indignant champion, angered by the bad call, would come in for the knockout. Mosley would be in retreat for the first time in his career by clinching and retreating. It was the first time we saw Mosley, a true warrior, refuse to engage, but this was the present Mosley who had lost the last ten rounds to Mayweather and had a recent draw with Sergio Mora.

Pacquiao threw less than half what he did against Margarito and Clottey. It shows how styles make fights. Mosley did land a few straight blows to the body, and Pacquiao threw his gloves up to say "keep them up." There were also plenty of Bayless warnings to both fighters about the head-butts. Pacquiao's accurate punches would find the mark on Mosley's head, but he would often get tied up to prevent further attack. Both fighters would repeatedly touch gloves during fouls and at the beginning of rounds, which seemed to irk some of the audience and commentators. Mosley was able to block punches well and actually made Pacquiao miss, but he never made him pay. He appeared content with trying to keep his record clean of any knockouts. In fact, barring any right hand or shoulder injury, it is difficult to understand why Mosley was so gun-shy. Boxers need to take risks. Freddie Roach would tell Pacquiao before the twelfth, "He is done; you can be the first to finish this guy." Mosley wouldn't get finished and would survive the final round.

It would later be revealed in the Showtime epilogue of *Fight Camp 360* that Mosley's trainer Nazeem Richardson talked him out of quitting on his stool. Richardson told him, "You're cut from a different cloth…Dig down and fight." The actual fight scores showed the that judges seemed to have disregarded the errant knockdown in the tenth and had the dominating scores of 119–108, 120–108, and 120–107 all for Pacquiao. The final punch stats were 182 of 552 for Pacquiao and 82 of 260 for Mosley.

After the fight Pacquiao said, "It wasn't my best performance, but I did my best. My leg tightened up in the middle rounds, and I couldn't move. This is the same problem I had when I fought [Juan Manuel] Marquez, so we are going to have to work on this."

Mosley said, "Manny is an exceptional fighter with good speed and power, power that I have never felt before…Early in the fight, I was surprised by his punching power. I fought my best, and I came up a little short. We will go back to the drawing board." It would later be revealed that the PPV event would do more than 1.3 million buys, which generated more than $75 million PPV revenue. The live gate did nearly $9 million and had sold out. These numbers were also helped by the undercards, which included Mexican and Puerto Rican fighters. Overall, it was a major victory for Top Rank and Showtime who were criticized for giving Mosley a chance at fighting Pacquiao.

CHAPTER 19

Deuce with Dinamita and Desert Storm

The hopes of a Mayweather fight off the horizon made the possibility of a Marquez fight. On paper, it was a difficult prospect for Marquez. Marquez was now a natural lightweight and looked both flabby and slow in his only welterweight match in 2009 against Floyd Mayweather. Marquez had told the boxing world that he had defeated Pacquiao twice and was trying to solicit a third match. Pacquiao wanted to knock out Marquez to end any controversy. However, Pacquiao was fighting two divisions north of Marquez, and it appeared unlikely they would meet again. If there would be a catchweight, one would think that junior welterweight made the most sense. Pacquiao wanted to extinguish Dinamita once and for all.

Pacquiao-Marquez 3 was officially announced on May 17, 2011, to take place on November 12, 2011, at the MGM Grand, Garden Arena. There would be a catchweight of 144 pounds for Pacquiao's WBO welterweight title. Pacquiao would be guaranteed $22 million and Marquez $5 million, and both would get an added percentage from the pay-per-view sales. The press tour would include stops in both Manila and Mexico City. Marquez would wear a T-shirt claiming he had won both prior matches and would further antagonize Pacquiao by claiming that many Filipinos had told him he had won his matches against Pacquiao. Pacquiao felt he had dropped Marquez four times in two matches and had done enough to come out victorious in two previous matches. Marquez would learn his lesson from the Mayweather bout and added noted strength conditioning coach Angel "Memo" Heredia to help make the welterweight division while retaining both his muscle build and speed. Heredia's dad was a chemistry professor, and Heredia—also a chemist—would work with notable track-and-field Olympic athletes. In 2002 the infamous Balco scandal and investigation had its eye on Heredia after allegedly finding damaging evidence. Heredia would cooperate with authorities and implicate others instead of facing possible prosecution. While some dismissed Heredia as a snitch who did everything to spare himself, he would respond that many of those very people had a chance to come clean and cooperate but chose not to follow suit. Despite rumors, there wouldn't be any random drug testing for the bout, and it would follow the usual Nevada drug-testing guidelines. Both fighters were very motivated to dispel the controversy of the first two contests.

Pacquiao would come in at 143 pounds at the weigh-in and Marquez at 142. The prefight weight saw Marquez balloon up to 150 and Pacquiao up to 148. Unlike the Mayweather fight, this time Marquez carried chiseled and defined muscle mass. Pacquiao's weight would be his lowest weight since the Hatton bout three years earlier. Marquez was back to the 142 he weighed in his lopsided loss to Mayweather.

The first round saw little action as both fighters were feeling each other out. Pacquiao would score with a solid straight left in the middle of the round. Marquez would land a few decent body shots in combo; however, Pacquiao would still win the round as he had the more telling blow. Marquez looked a bit tentative and uncertain how to attack early on. Pacquiao's constant head movement made it difficult for Marquez to establish his jab in the second round. Pacquiao's lead right jab would get in a few times in the second round, but there was still plenty of trepidation shown by both fighters, who wanted to avoid counterpunches. The lack of action insinuated that Marquez's three-punch combination (2:05) and a partial right connect (2:17) may have given him the close round. Judge Dave Moreti scored it for Marquez, while both judges Hoyle and Trowbridge gave it to Pacquiao. The CompuBox numbers had Pacquiao landing 9 of 42 and Marquez 8 of 30. The continuous pattern of Marquez landing that left uppercut in between Pacquiao's wide opening would commence again at 0:31 of the third round. It was a shot that Marquez had used in the previous two fights. Marquez would land that same left uppercut in the middle of the round and follow it with a straight right. Pacquiao would score with a solid right connection (2:51); unlike the previous fights, Marquez wouldn't buckle or go down.

Pacquiao continued his success with solid straight lefts in the opening minute of the fourth round. Marquez would fire combinations, but most missed the mark against the agile fighter, for most of the round. Pacquiao made him pay for that miss with counter lefts. There would be a little success downstairs for the Mexican challenger. Marquez would have a rally in the waning seconds of the round that included his best overhand right hook that made Pacquiao take a couple of steps back. All three judges gave the fourth round to Marquez; this could have been because two of those three judges had already given Pacquiao the first three rounds, while two of those first three rounds were close. There would be little action in the opening minute of the fifth round until Pacquiao would bang his gloves, and Marquez would respond with a left uppercut again. Marquez would have his best round as he repeatedly countered Pacquiao with three-punch combinations. A sizzling straight right (2:15) would seal the round for Marquez. It would be the second time in the fight that a Marquez blow would make Pacquiao take a couple of steps backward. Marquez would land a few body shots that Pacquiao complained were below the waist.

Pacquiao and Marquez trade shots in the third installment of their fight series. AP Photo/ Jae C. Hong.

The sixth round was another close round that could have gone to either fighter. A three-punch combination in the middle of the round near the ropes could have tilted the round to Pacquiao's direction. Marquez would answer back in the seventh with a powerful overhand right (0:40) that failed to make Pacquiao flinch. Yet, the momentum of the bout was starting to swing to Marquez's favor. As Pacquiao came forward, he would be greeted with a straight Marquez left. Marquez would finish the round with a solid right uppercut. This was a clear Marquez round. Freddie Roach would admonish Pacquiao in the corner after the seventh round, "We are falling behind, and we are falling behind." More importantly, Pacquiao was bleeding profusely from the mouth. Marquez would land underneath shots in the middle of the eighth round. Marquez's counterpunching ability was starting to take control again. However, only judge Robert Hoyle would give Marquez the eighth.

There was no change of strategy for Pacquiao in the ninth round. He was pawing too much with his punches and leaving himself off-balance. Marquez was more active with his jab and connected with his trademark three-punch combination (1:02). This is about the time of the bout that Pacquiao complained about cramping in his legs. His whirlwind offense was conspicuously gone between rounds seven and nine. A few haymakers fired by Pacquiao would miss the mark in the ninth. The final minute of the round would see the best action of the bout, as both fighters would trade some of their best shots. This was reminiscent of the some of the action we saw in the first two bouts. Roach would tell Pacquiao, "We need to knock this guy out, and go after him." Unfortunately for Roach, this would not happen in the final three rounds of the bout. Marquez would still get in that straight right (1:10) in the tenth round cleanly. There would be more exchanges in the middle of the round with both fighters not taking a backward step. Pacquiao would complain about a head-butt in the middle of the tenth round. Two of the three judges would give the round to Pacquiao. Pacquiao now had a bad gash on his right eyebrow. Perhaps this gave him a sense of urgency, as he would land his best shots since the sixth round. He was able to land his left hand with more authority. Marquez was not able to get in more than one solid combination in the round.

Going to the eleventh round, Judge Robert Hoyle had Marquez ahead by one point, Dave Moreti had Pacquiao ahead by one point, and Glenn Trowbridge had Pacquiao ahead by five points, in a very disparate score. Marquez had welts around his forehead and right eyebrow, while Pacquiao was bleeding from his mouth and had that gash on his right eyebrow. Without a knockout ending in the final round, a third controversial decision was inevitable. There were no major fireworks to end the bout. Marquez may have stolen the final round with a flurry (1:15–1:20) and an added minor flurry (2:30–2:33). When the final bell rang, Marquez would raise his arm and climb the ring post, and Pacquiao would pray at a corner. The final CompuBox numbers had Pacquiao landing 176 of 578 and Marquez 138 of 436. It was the first time in the three bouts that Pacquiao had landed more punches than Marquez according to CompuBox I had the bout (6-5-1) for Marquez, which would have given him a 114–113 narrow win. The official judges' scorecards gave Pacquiao a majority decision win via scores of 115–113 (Dave Moretti), 118–110 (Glenn Trowbridge), and 114–114 (Robert Hoyle). When Pacquiao would be awarded the majority decision, a good portion of the crowd jeered the decision. Some of the fans threw bottles, ice cubes, and beer from the stands. Some boxers, including Bernard Hopkins, Winky Wright, and Joe Calzaghe, would get on their Twitter account and express sentiments giving the edge to Marquez. Calzaghe, specifically, would declare that he felt Marquez won all three bouts. Boxing and media writers such as Al Bernstein, Ron Borges, Thomas Hauser, and Lance Pugmire had Marquez winning. A few—such as Tim Dahlberg (Associated Press), Kevin Iole (Yahoo Sports), and Dan Rafael (ESPN)—thought the fight should have been scored a draw. There were those who felt Pacquiao deserved the decision and cited the CompuBox stats, which favored Pacquiao. More importantly, they felt that Marquez—as the challenger—was not aggressive enough. These included Ted Sares (Boxing.com), Michael Rosenthal (Ring TV), Skip Bayless (ESPN), and Michael Woods (ESPN/Sweet Science). There were issues made about Marquez stepping on Pacquiao's foot on six occasions. However, most of it was incidental contact due to an orthodox and a southpaw fighter stepping on each other.

Marquez's trainer, Nacho Beristain, would declare it as one of the "worst robberies" in his postfight interview. *Ring Magazine* readers would vote the outcome "Robbery of the Year" for 2011. I felt that this honor belonged to the Paul Williams-Erislandy Lara match. Regardless of the opinion of who won, there was no doubt that Marquez had exceeded expectations, as it was nearly a universal consensus that Marquez would lose badly—let alone be in a position to win down the stretch. If Marquez had received the decision, he would have also been a quadruple-weight champion after skipping the light-welterweight division. Most importantly, if Marquez had gotten the decision, he would have seriously challenged Andre Ward for fighter-of-the-year honors. Pacquiao and Marquez would exchange thirty-six grueling rounds without the other being knocked out—similar to the trilogy wars between Gatti-Ward, Morales-Barrera, and Ali-Norton.

The fight would be a major PPV success by having more than 1.4 million purchases. This happened despite an era of increasing entertainment options and illegal streaming. Those numbers and the decision controversy would mandate a fourth contest.

Before Pacquiao would get in the ring, he would make a new commitment to his life outside of the ring. Pacquiao would claim a spiritual awakening and eliminate some vices that he felt explained his disappointing recent performance. Lifestyle changes would include elimination of excessive partying, alcohol, cockfighting, gambling, and a recommitment to being faithful to his wife. Freddie Roach himself felt that Pacquiao had become a changed person. Roach would point to Pacquiao selling a casino, nightclub, and a cockfighting farm as proof of a reformed man. "All the distractions caught up to Manny in his last fight." Roach would explain that Pacquiao was served with divorce papers the day before the fight. He would also allude to late nights of gambling and "girls and everything that goes with it…Now, he's back with his wife, reading the Bible every day, and he's given up basketball," Roach would tell the *LA Times*.

Some in the public speculated that perhaps Mayweather, sensing a vulnerable Pacquiao, would aggressively pursue the bout for a May 2012 showdown. Mayweather would in fact speak to Pacquiao and offer $40 million with half of it being wired within forty-eight hours. However, Pacquiao didn't think the offer was legit. Pacquiao would explain the phone conversation. "I told him I would agree with 50–50 percent sharing. Whatever you ask about blood testing is no problem with me as long it is 50–50, but he wanted only a guarantee ($40 million) and no more sharing of pay-per-view. I don't think he really wants to fight." The fact that a Pacquiao-Mayweather bout could generate as much as $200 million on pay-per-view alone would have meant Pacquiao could have forfeited millions by simply adhering to a locked guarantee. Why would the winner of the Fighter of the Decade award agree to such a one-sided contract? Cynics may say that the $40 million would be the most he ever earned; a fight with Pacquiao would also be more money than Mayweather would make in a single night.

The next Pacquiao opponent was likely realized just two months before the third Pacquiao-Marquez bout. On September 29, 2011, Timothy Bradley signed a promotional contract with Top Rank. It was no big secret that the California native's ultimate goal was a future bout with Pacquiao. Bradley called out Pacquiao after his win over Abregu. When he left Gary Shaw and had a contract dispute, the motivation was to get the "bigger fish" that he was unable to get due to the unwritten rule of promotional in-house fighting. As a result, Bradley would need to join Top Rank or possibly Golden Boy to get a shot at one of the two cash cows of the sport: Manny Pacquiao or Floyd Mayweather. Despite being undefeated, Bradley was not a proven pay-per-view commodity. He was seen as solid, but nothing stood out in terms of speed, power, or personality. What did stand out was Bradley's tenacity, great work ethic, and—yes—those frequent head-butts that seem inevitable during his matches. Being dropped twice in a bout with Kendall Holt would unfairly bring speculation of a suspect chin. However, Bradley's wins over Lamont Peterson and Devon Alexander made Bradley a definitive top-ten pound-per-pound fighter in the sport.

ARMANDO PAZ

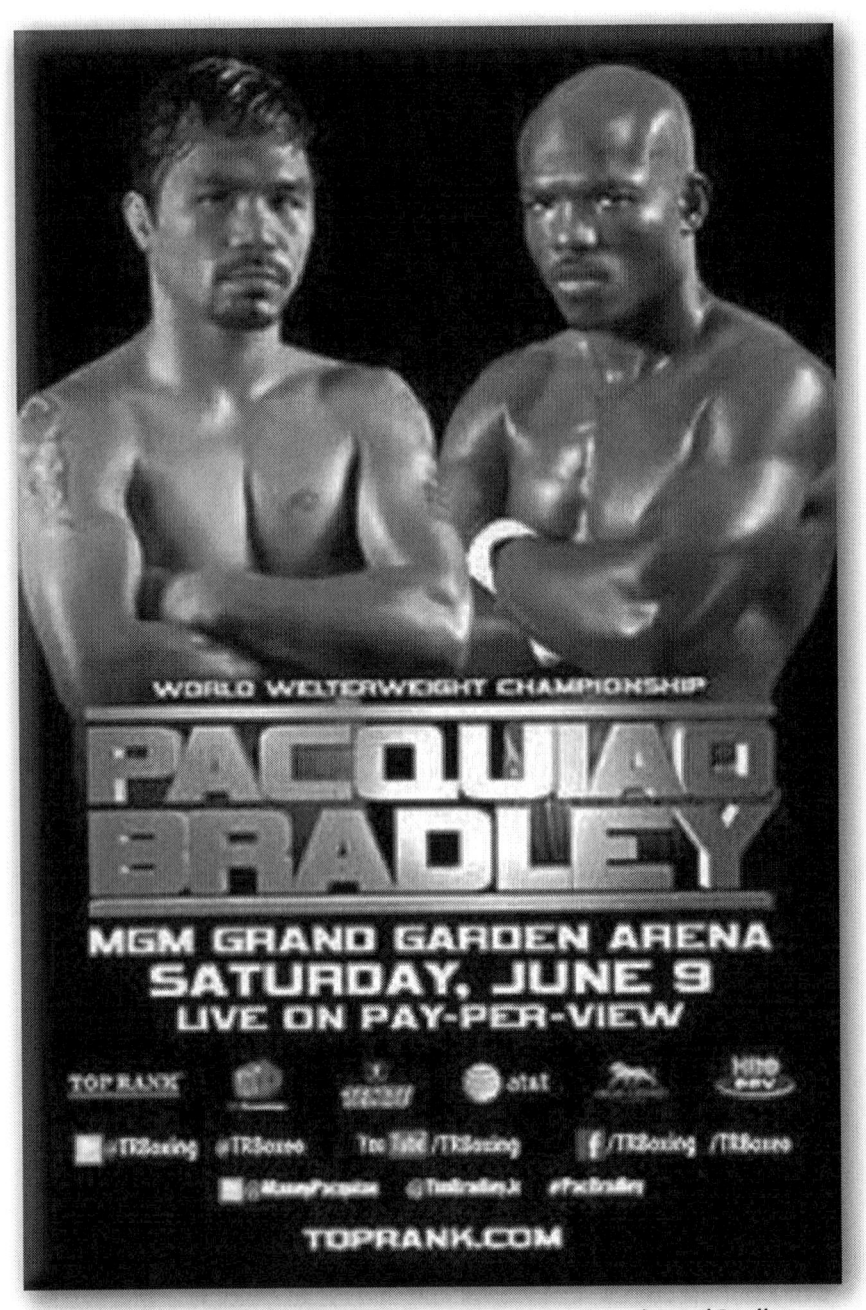

Top Rank promotional poster for the match between Pacquiao and Bradley.

There would be questions on Bradley being a viable pay-per-view commodity. He would get some PPV exposure as he fought Joel Casamayor as part of the undercard of Pacquiao-Marquez 3. Bradley would win the match against Casamayor by eighth-round stoppage. Top Rank president, Todd DuBoef, officially announced the Pac-Bradley deal on February 10, 2012. The match was scheduled for June 9, 2012, in the MGM Grand Garden Arena. Bradley was so confident he would win that he would announce November 10, 2012, as the rematch date. Pacquiao was guaranteed $26 million and Bradley $5 million, with both earning more from the proceeds of the pay-per-view. Both fighters came in excellent shape as Bradley weighed 146 pounds and Pacquiao 147 pounds. The official attendance the night of the fight had 14,206 in attendance that produced a live gate of nearly $9 million.

Bradley started the contest by flickering that left jab constantly. Pacquiao blocked a good portion, but the work rate would give him credit in the judges' eyes. He also landed a solid straight right (0:43). Pacquiao would also have most of his jabs blocked, and his straight left was a bit off the mark as he started to measure Bradley. This would change in the second as the first significant left (0:26) landed for Pacquiao. Bradley was still coming forward aggressively, but not much was landing. Pacquiao scored a significant straight left (1:15) in the third round. Bradley was not circling away from the Pacquiao left and would pay severely with two lefts (2:26), which would seal the round for Pacquiao. Both fighters would land dazzling lefts, but Bradley would get the worst of the exchange.

Bradley would come in aggressive in the fourth round trying to land on Pacquiao's body. However, Pacquiao would wobble Bradley in the final minute of the round via both the left and right hand. A left hook to the body would stagger Bradley, who had difficulty keeping his footing. Bradley would actually injure his ankle in the round. It was déjà vu in the final minute of the fifth round as a Pacquiao left (2:36) would wobble Bradley again. A round that was an even round now would be another round in the Pacquiao column; yet two judges still gave the round to Bradley.

Pacquiao would utilize short uppercuts and fire combinations as Bradley had his back to the ropes to take the sixth. Bradley demonstrated his best ring generalship in the seventh as he worked the jab, had effective aggression, and made Pacquiao miss often by slipping punches. The seventh round was possibly the first clear Bradley round since the first. Bradley started his ascension to the fight in the eighth round; he would land a brilliant left hook (0:53), and his legs seemed to have new spring. There would be a clash of heads, but no blood was drawn. After a referee break, Bradley would fire a combination that Pacquiao would partially block. Even with partial connects, the effort would get attention from the judges. This, added to the fact that there were no great Pacquiao connects, would arguably give Bradley his second consecutive round.

Bradley would continue his aggression into the ninth round with some success. Pacquiao would take back the momentum by landing a straight left and another wicked uppercut, which hurt Bradley. Bradley decided to stand in front of Pacquiao, willing to exchange punch per punch. The round was still close, and it was not beyond the realm of reality to have scored it a draw. Pacquiao would swing the momentum of the match back to his corner. Bradley would do better in the tenth, thanks to landing a few combinations with a solid overhand right (1:43).

Bradley was coasting in the eleventh round until he got caught by an excellent overhand right (2:10), which may have tilted the close round to the Pacquiao column. Bradley would come on strong to make the bout closer on my card. It was interesting to hear the various broadcasts of the bout. There would be a collective shock when a split-decision win was rendered for Bradley. The official scores were Jerry Roth 115–113 for Pacquiao, and both Duane Ford and C. J. Ross had it 115–113 for Timothy Bradley. In both the Roth and Ross scorecards, Bradley would win the last three rounds.

It was interesting that Jerry Roth (who would be the only judge to score it for Pacquiao) was the same judge who scored Pacquiao-Marquez 2 for Marquez. I felt Pacquiao won it 116–113 (7-4-1), which was a bit closer than many media outlets had the score.

The PPV numbers for Pacquiao-Bradley failed to reach one million buys. The live gate for the bout was reported as $8.9 million, but the pay-per-view purchases were just over 700,000 buys. Pacquiao was still guaranteed $26 million and Bradley $5 million, which was by far the most he had made. The PPV numbers would eliminate an immediate rematch between the combatants. Pacquiao would say, "The match was lopsided," and he didn't think there was much public demand.

Despite the official loss, it would still possibly be the best Pacquiao performance since the Cotto bout. The WBO would have an investigation, and all five judges would give the bout to Pacquiao by the scores of 117–111, 117–111, 116–112, and 118–110. Although I felt Pacquiao clearly won, the inquiry and panel of judges was a bit perplexing, as the sport didn't exercise the same internal transparency for other controversial decisions.

The sport of boxing, similar to what the federal government did with corporate bailouts, was picking winners and losers. Boxing was selectively choosing which bouts to investigate. As the major companies were deemed "too big to fail" the Pacquiao-Bradley fight "was too big" for the integrity of the sport not to have an inquiry. Questionable decisions such as Wlodarczyk versus Palacios 1, Williams versus Lara, and Cloud versus Campillo didn't get the same treatment. Months after the bout, Bradley would review the tape, as he had promised, and claim, "I saw it eight rounds to four, regardless of what anyone thinks."

After the Bradley debacle, there was some out-of-the-ring business that would be resolved. Pacquiao's defamation suit against Floyd Mayweather Jr., Roger Mayweather, and Floyd Mayweather Sr. would be settled on September 25, 2012. As in the M & M suit, there was a nondisclosure agreement that kept the terms confidential. Pacquiao, like the M & M suit, was happy with the conclusion of the matter.

The fact that Pacquiao-Bradley didn't produce over one million PPV purchases again opened up the possibility of a fourth fight between Pacquiao and Marquez. Bradley would explain to Jim Lampley why a Pacquiao rematch never happened, "I wanted to fight Pacquiao, but their part wanted to fight Marquez instead. At this level of the game, it's all about business."

Pacquiao-Marquez 4 would be a done deal in September 2012 when it was obvious that there wouldn't be a Pacquiao-Cotto 2 match, as there was no consensus in a catchweight.

Pacquiao was guaranteed $26 million and Marquez $6 million, and both were expected to make more after the tabulation of the pay-per-view revenues. As both men trained for the upcoming bout, the entire performance-enhancement-drug issue would be front and center again. Freddie Roach would openly question how Marquez was able to get such a muscular physique while putting on weight. He told *USA Today*, "[Marquez] has gotten bigger and gained weight—it throws up a red flag. If [his body] is natural, I will kiss his ass." Heredia responded by threatening a lawsuit similar to the defamation suit Pacquiao filed against Mayweather in December 2009. Interestingly, one person who also threw suspicion around Angel Heredia was Victor Conte who admitted supplying PEDs through the Balco lab. Conte, who served four months in jail, was back to training athletes who included boxers Andre Ward and Nonito Donaire. Conte would voice suspicion of Marquez's body transformation and training regiments. He told Yahoo Sports (regarding Marquez's routine of squatting and lifting heavy weights), "How many boxers do you know who are in the weight room squatting huge poundage?" You don't see that. That in and of itself would make you stiff and sore and unable to walk for two or three days unless you are using testosterone or other steroids to accelerate the healing—where instead of it taking three days to recover from that type of workout, you'd recover in one day." The Marquez camp stated they were willing to have random testing and more stringent protocol done by the Nevada State Athletic Commission. Instead both camps agreed to stay with the conventional NSAC testing. Alex Ariza, who voiced concerns about Marquez's body change in the third bout, seemed to change his tune this time. "Memo is brilliant; I don't have any suspicions. When you get someone like that who knows the science of exercise and nutrition… well, we saw a whole different fighter when he fought Manny last time."

The talk leading to the fourth encounter between the two rivals was that a knockout was going to happen. Both fighters talked about getting a knockout, and their bodies appeared to be built to get that KO win. However, a KO was not an easy task. Marquez never was knocked out, and Pacquiao hadn't suffered a KO loss since being drained against Singuarat nearly thirteen years before. The four-city press tour included stops in both Manila and Mexico City. Pacquiao-Marquez 4 would be held on December 8, 2014, in the MGM Grand Garden Arena. The official weigh-in would have Pacquiao coming in at the limit of 147 pounds and Marquez at 143 pounds.

Marquez would revert back to black and red colors for his trunks, which were customary in his old Great Western Forum days. Perhaps it would be a good luck charm.

The first two rounds saw Pacquiao doing plenty of head movement and working his feints while Marquez tried to work his left jab. Pacquiao would land the most notable blows (a straight left at 1:17 in the first round and again at 1:42 of the second round). Marquez was trying to counter, but his connects were partial connects. Despite training for speed, it appeared the muscle buildup made Marquez a tad slower, as Pacquiao was easily slipping his blows. Marquez still had excellent anticipation and slipped a lead left that was intended to take his head off thirty seconds into the third round. Pacquiao was still able to get in another left (1:04) then move to his right to avoid any counter shot. This wouldn't discourage Marquez, who set up an overhand right (1:42) that would drop Pacquiao to the canvas.

An enraged Pacquiao would pounce both his gloves as Kenny Bayless would administer the count. The overhand right was a punch that Marquez had landed in the previous bouts. Marquez wouldn't try to see how badly Pacquiao was hurt and would only engage in a small flurry at the end of the round to settle for a 10–8 round. It was likely that the knockdown leveled the score as Marquez likely dropped the first two rounds. In the corner, Roach would advise Pacquiao, "Manny you can't pull away; go under him." If Pacquiao would have moved under the punch or had his guard held higher to the head, he may have avoided the knockdown. The fourth stanza saw both combatants trade excellent clean counters in a round that could have gone to either fighter. Marquez was able to get a solid right in the waning seconds that may have persuaded the three judges to give him the round.

Pacquiao would revert back to his straight left (0:35) in the fifth round; he would follow it up and drop Marquez with the same punch (1:06). The straight left that got between the gloves was a vintage Pacquiao shot. However, the Mexican fighter—who had been floored by Pacquiao four times—was used to coming back from knockdowns. Marquez was able to beat the count and temporarily continue his sixty-one-bout, nonknockout streak. Pacquiao had other ideas, as he wanted to be the first to knock out the Mexican and end any controversy from the previous three disputed decisions. An overzealous Pacquiao who came in for the kill would be greeted by a short, compact Marquez right hand. Pacquiao would pounce both gloves in acknowledgement. After receiving another right hand, Pacquiao would land his best punch in the fight and break Marquez's nose. A sensational counter short right hook (2:15) would ironically stagger Marquez more than the left hand that had dropped him before. Despite being hurt Marquez would fight back and stay near the ropes to aid his balance. Marquez would make the stand of his life by fighting back while having his back to the ropes. Pacquiao would appear disappointed, as he badly wanted to end the bout in the closing moments of the fifth.

Marquez seemed to get his legs back in the sixth round, but his broken nose made breathing difficult, so he had to use his mouth for respiration. Marquez was still able to land a two punch consisting of a short left to the body followed by a straight right. In the waning seconds in a close round, Pacquiao would do a double feint while coming forward with a right jab that he expected to follow up with a straight left. Marquez read the play like a quarterback reads a blitz; Marquez would move to his left and plant his feet and fire a colossal straight right to the face that had Pacquiao knocked out unconscious, facedown in the canvas.

Pacquiao was out and was not going to get up to beat the count. His wife, Jinkee, who was sobbing at ringside, was trying to come up to the ring. The brutal ending was a sobering reminder of how the brutal nature of the sport can surface. The knockout would end forty-two rounds of mutual attrition in a climax. The actual punch was the same punch that Marquez had landed in the previous three bouts. It was a straight right that, this time, was aided by planting his feet and fully extending it while Pacquiao ran into the punch. It was a devastating knockout, and Pacquiao remained motionless. Paradoxically, it was set up by the overanxious Pacquiao trying to finish off Marquez, who had a broken nose that was bleeding profusely. Similarly to their first encounter, Marquez had a bloodied nose, and Pacquiao—despite dropping him three times—failed to finish him off. Going in for the kill is often the catalyst in getting caught and stopped by a counterpuncher.

Marquez's victory was satisfying since he felt that he had won the previous three bouts. It was the biggest knockout of a superstar since Roy Jones Jr. suffered a second round KO defeat to Antonio Tarver in 2004. Although Marquez is known mainly as an accumulative puncher, he had scored one-punch knockouts before against opponents such as Likar Ramos, Jose de Jesus Garcia, Johnny Walker, Hector Marquez, and Francisco Arreola. Only the Ramos knockout, which many thought was a "dive," could rival the ferocity and duration of the Pacquiao knockout. Fortunately, Pacquiao was able to recover and go to his stool after remaining motionless on the canvas for over a minute. The final punch stats had Pacquiao landing 94 of 256 and Marquez 52 of 246. Marquez, despite being badly hurt, would extend his mark to sixty-two bouts without suffering a knockout loss.

The postknockout turmoil in the ring included an incident with photographer Al Bello. Bello appeared to have a scuffle with both Michael Koncz and Buboy Fernandez as he exited the ring. The Pacquiao team wasn't happy with pictures taken of their fighter being knocked out. Ironically, in a 2009 photo that was taken after the Hatton knockout, there is a picture showing Buboy Fernandez raising his arms in celebration as a motionless Hatton is laid out in the canvas. Fernandez would later apologize for the incident, and Bello would never press any formal charges.

Juan Manuel Marquez, who was often in the shadow of Erik Morales and Marco Antonio Barrera, could now claim that he had surpassed them in the pantheon of Mexican boxing legends. Marquez could now boast that his name in Mexican boxing history belonged in the same breath as Sanchez, Chavez, Olivares, and Lopez. The aftermath in social media would vibrate around the sports world. While Floyd Mayweather wanted to see Pacquiao bounce back, Canadian singer Justin Bieber—who carried some of his belts to the Cotto match—took to Twitter to mock the Pacquiao knockout with images. This caused a major backlash in the Philippines where many called for the banning and boycott of Bieber.

The question raised was whether Pacquiao should retire. No fighter wants a career to end in a knockout loss. The fact still remained that Pacquiao's ability was far from a shot fighter. He was also winning the fight on all three cards before getting caught with the shot. All three judges had Pacquiao ahead 47–46 after five rounds. Just like what happened to Ricky Hatton in 2009, Pacquiao was knocked out with one second left in the round. This is why many boxers who feel they have won a round may take it easy in the remaining seconds to put the round in the bank. Taking it easy in a competitive match is contradictory to Pacquiao's fighting nature. However, the accumulative punishment over the years in ring wars is something that couldn't be ignored. Pacquiao had fought for seventeen years as a professional, and his combative style of taking heat to give heat was not going to change. Pacquiao was not going to change to a cautious and calculative pugilist who relied on boxing ability to win. Most importantly, when fighters get knocked out as Pacquiao did, sometimes they are the cataylst of more KO losses. Pacquiao's mother had advised him to gracefully leave the sport years before; she would point to Pacquiao's exiting the Catholic Church and abandoning the rosary as a contributing factor for the loss. Freddie Roach had repeatedly worried about Pacquiao's finances and that he might "give it all away" due to his philanthropic work and generosity. Pacquiao's fiscal philanthropy coupled with his lifestyle had many feeling that he would continue to seek big paydays longer than it was necessary.

However, it's often not money but fighters' competitive nature and love of the stage that keeps them going. There were some who felt that Pacquiao's responsibility as a member of Congress and his dreams of governorship in the province of Sarangani were a distraction. We have seen fighters who are never the same after a brutal KO loss. However, guys like Roberto Duran, Joe Louis, and Max Schmeling all rebounded after suffering devastating knockout losses. Duran would capture the middleweight title after a few years (before getting knocked out by Thomas Hearns), Joe Louis would get knocked out by Max Schmeling and avenge the loss while defending the heavyweight title twenty-five times, and Max Schmeling himself would defeat Joe Louis after being pummeled by Max Baer just three years earlier.

Pacquiao's knockout loss brought about the issue of possible neurological damage. The immediate CAT scan revealed no head injury. Both trainer Freddie Roach and promoter Bob Arum would join Pacquiao in a candid interview with Piers Morgan in 2011 as they discussed topics such as Parkinson's disease and when retirement would come. Pacquiao would tell Morgan that he felt strong and could fight a few more years. Morgan would follow up, "Do you worry you may fight too long and suffer irreparable damage?"

"I'm thinking for not to wait too long to get hurt...but my promoter, he is the one who knows." Bob Arum would comment, "I am going to do whatever I can; if Freddie or our matchmakers see any type of slippage, that is going to be it...no matter what money is out there. But right now Freddie and my matchmakers tell me he is getting better and better...but it shouldn't be more than two more years." The fact that Pacquiao had been fighting since his teenage years was a cause for the concern that he shouldn't risk fighting much longer. A fighter like Wilfred Benitez, who started to fight professionally at the age of fifteen, would later suffer dementia pugilistica. However, many boxers like Roberto Duran and Julio Cesar Chavez, who started as teenagers and netted over one hundred bouts, never suffered Parkinson's or dementia.

For Pacquiao it was simply an issue of vigilance and what his medical doctors told him. However, Dr. Rustico Jimenez—who is the president of the Private Hospitals Association of the Philippines—would tell a local radio station that he observed some symptoms that indicated that Pacquiao had the early signs of Parkinson's disease, such as stuttering and hand twitching. Through his spokesperson Pacquiao would deny the claim and emphasize that the doctor who made the observation never examined him. There would be extensive neurological and diagnostic tests that would rule out any immediate cause for concern. As Pacquiao still wanted to prove that he was an elite fighter, the medical clearance opened up the opportunity for a comeback.

CHAPTER 20

Bam Bam and Avenging Bradley

For many casual boxing fans, their introduction to Brandon "Bam Bam" Rios (31-1, 23 KOs) was an infamous video that appeared to mock Freddie Roach's Parkinson's disease by trembling his head and muttering "Ma-nny Pac-quiao." Rios would later apologize for his behavior and become WBA lightweight champion of the world by stopping Miguel Acosta after he was getting outboxed early on. Rios who grew up in Garden City, Kansas, would follow the footsteps of former sparring mate Victor Ortiz, who also became a world champion from the same town. However, there were staunch differences between the two Mexican American fighters. While Rios was known for his outlandish Three Stooges humor and his constant swearing, Ortiz was the more reserved and soft-spoken fighter. Perhaps the biggest difference between both fighters was the perception of their tolerance of pain in the ring. While some boxing media and fans labeled Ortiz as someone who succumbed to punishment—like his stoppage losses to Marcos Maidana and Josesito Lopez—Rios was otherwise known for his relentless and unstoppable ring heart that allowed him to win fights despite being outboxed.

I had a chance to see Rios when he defeated John Murry during the Margarito-Cotto undercard at Madison Square Garden. Rios, as usual, displayed tenacity and was able to impose his combative flat-footed style at Murray. Yet, the biggest news happened before the bout, as Rios had effectively lost his WBA lightweight title to the scales. The fact that Rios failed to make weight clearly demonstrated that Rios was going to fight at the higher weight classes. Rios would suffer a similar indignation as he failed to make weight in his next bout with Cuban American Richar Abril. Rios would blame his sluggish performance to being weight drained for the match. Although Rios would get the split-decision win, many observers felt Rios got the gift decision. Rios would make amends by earning a sensational seventh-round stoppage win over previously undefeated Mike Alvarado. The Rios-Alvarado bout would be regarded by many boxing fans as the fight of the year for 2012 and would actually get that honor from *Sports Illustrated*. *Ring Magazine* would bestow the fight of the year honor to Pacquiao-Marquez 4.

Rios looked forward to facing the winner of Pacquiao-Marquez 4, but this wouldn't occur as Marquez would choose to face Tim Bradley instead of Rios to seek a fifth divisional title. When Rios would lose to Alvardo in a rematch, it appeared bleak that a Pacquiao-Rios match would ever take place. However, the decision was made that Brandon Rios, instead of Mike Alvarado, would be the comeback fight for Pacquiao.

As Top Rank was also promoting Chinese flyweight Lou Shiming, it would make sense to have Shiming's third professional match in a Pacquiao undercard. Most importantly for Pacquiao, fighting in Macao would allow him to retain millions more due to the lower taxes while fighting only a two-hour flight distance from his native Philippines. The high American federal tax rate of 39.6 percent made the Macao top rate of 12 percent a very sensible decision. The combination of more money in his pocket and fighting close to home made it a win-win decision for Pacquiao. As Filipino citizens could travel to Macao with a passport, it would give many local Pacquiao fans their first chance in seven years to see Pacquiao fight live.

Promoter Bob Arum of Top Rank had always felt that Pacquiao-Rios would be an excellent pay-per-view event down the road since both fighters have an exciting, crowd-pleasing style. The match would be officially announced to the media on May 6, 2013, and be labeled the "Clash in Cotai." The bout would be scheduled for November 23, 2013, at the Cotai Arena, The Venetian, Macao, SAR. Macao, a former Portuguese colony known for high-stakes gambling and entertainment, would cater to high-stake rollers and tourists from the Far East. The emerging Chinese economy helped booster Macao into becoming the biggest gambling destination in the world. The growing Chinese middle class was also part of the motivation to sell the sport to a country with over 1.3 billion citizens.

Freddy Roach was also motivated to demonstrate that he was a superior trainer to Robert Garcia. "I want to show Robert Garcia who is the better trainer and who has the better gym." Garcia would fire back and point to the losses that Roach fighters had suffered in recent years and felt Roach should be embarrassed that a trainer fifteen years his junior was competing at his level.

There would be interesting challenges for both fighters coming into the fight. Pacquiao had to prove that both his ring reflexes and punch resistance still remained after a brutal knockout loss, and Rios wanted to prove that he was much more than a one-dimensional brawler that was easy to hit. There were other questions that would be answered, such as how Rios would do the first time he faced a southpaw professionally. There were also many wondering if Pacquiao would keep his discipline and not simply trade with Rios. How would both fighters adjust to fighting in the morning? The promotion and preparation of Pacquiao-Rios went smoothly until a notorious incident in a local Macao training gym between Freddie Roach and former Pacquiao strength-and-conditioning coach Alex Ariza. Roach felt that the gym should have been cleared by 11:00 a.m., as per the agreed scheduled time. Trainer Robert Garcia was in the middle of an interview and wanted some extra time to finish. Garcia claimed that he went a little overtime because Top Rank had him do a live interview with ESPN early the same morning.

The ugly exchange included some racial jabs; Roach referred to Rios's assistant trainer Donald Leary (actually Irish) as a "stupid Mexican" and to reporter Ellie Seckbach as an "explicit Jew." Although not the best choice of words, some in the media took it as a stretch to suggest Roach was both a racist and anti-Semitic. The Rios camp didn't fare much better when Alex Ariza would take stabs at Roach's Parkinson's disease by referring to Roach as a "stuttering prick" and tell him to "spi-spi-spi-it-out." Ariza would also kick Roach when Roach came toward him as both camps spewed out profanities and obscenities at each other.

Ariza claimed he did it in self-defense as Roach came toward him with his arm cocked. Some cynics felt the whole incident was staged to try to stir up publicity for the event.

The official weights saw Pacquiao come in at 145 pounds and Rios at 146.5 pounds. On fight night Pacquiao rehydrated to 150 and Rios to 159.

Pacquiao commenced the action with a straight left landed consistently in the first two rounds. Rios didn't circle away from the Pacquiao left hand, and Pacquiao would skillfully land his left (as he did at 2:09 of the second round) and then would step to the side to avoid a counter. Rios would do a bit better in the third as he landed a sizzling left hook solidly on Pacquiao's chin. Pacquiao would land a perfect straight left (0:41) in the fifth that whiplashed Rios's head backward. The punch was reminiscent of Pryor-Arguello 1 in which Pryor was able to take a shot that was intended to take his head off.

Pacquiao would answer any Rios punch with his own combinations and be able to anticipate most of Rios's punches and evade them by slipping or moving aside. This was crucial as it demonstrated that Pacquiao still maintained good reflexes and awareness. By the middle of the bout, it was obvious that Rios needed one major punch to change the outcome, while if Pacquiao maintained what he was doing, he could stay in cruise control.

Rios would try to work Pacquiao on the ropes and rough him up on the inside but exercised no consistent head and upper-body movement, which is crucial when fighting someone like Pacquiao. The fact that Rios was very durable kept him in a match that would have likely stopped most opponents. Despite a cut left-eye and extensive swelling, Rios would keep coming forward with relentless pressure until the closing bell. Pacquiao would have an impressive, one-sided win demonstrating that he was far from finished in the sport. The judges would have it 120–108, 118–110, and 119–109. I had it 119–110 for Pacquiao, giving Rios the third and scoring the eleventh even.

The biggest news would come after the fight when Brandon Rios would test positive for dimethylamylamine, an illegal substance that was banned by the World Anti-Doping Agency in 2010 for its reputed performance-enhancement benefits. It was speculated that Rios might have taken the drug to help him make weight. However, Rios would vehemently deny he took any illegal substance and pointed to his initial four negative test results prior to the postfight test. In addition, Rios and his camp would claim it was retaliation in response to the Macao gym altercation between Freddie Roach and Alex Ariza. That very incident that gave added publicity to the match failed to boost sales as the final pay-per-view sales had Pacquiao-Rios at approximately 475,000 purchases. Although the figure was disputed, there was no credible source that had the figure over 550,000, which was still the lowest PPV numbers for a Pacquiao event since his second match with Juan Manuel Marquez back on March 15, 2008. Nonetheless, Brandon Rios was guaranteed $4 million and Pacquiao $18 million for the contest, with Pacquiao expected to make millions more after his share of the PPV revenue. Many blamed the weak undercard, event location, and choice of opponent to explain the disappointing figure. The fact that a good portion of the promotion of the bout took place in Asia may also help explain the lower figures. This in part explained why Top Rank would announce that Pacquiao would be back at the Las Vegas MGM for his next bout in 2014.

For many, the obvious selection of the next opponent would be a fifth installment of the Pacquiao-Marquez saga. However, Marquez showed little interest in a fifth fight as he liked the ending of the fourth and felt that was the closure that he needed. Although many felt Marquez would be tempted for a fifth match if there would be a 50–50 purse split, the fact was that Marquez was actually still interested in a fifth divisional title and was more interested in a rematch with Timothy Bradley who had defeated him.

Ironically, Pacquiao still had unfinished business with Bradley, and the Bradley victory over Marquez instantly added more credibility to a Pacquiao-Bradley rematch. Bradley also had silenced many critics by surviving a previous gun-slinging slugfest with Ruslan Provodninov in a match that would later be dubbed the "Fight of the Year" by *Ring Magazine* and the BWAA for 2013. The aftermath saw Bradley suffering temporary neurological ailments and urinating blood for the first time after a match. The Pacquiao-Bradley rematch would be officially announced on January 25, 2014. Bradley wanted to prove that his win wasn't a fluke and to add credence that he had won the first 116–112 by knocking out Pacquiao (who claimed Bradley had "run" for a good portion of the first bout). Bradley would counter that he had fractured his left ankle in the second round due to not wearing socks, which lessened the cushion he had while navigating the ring. Bradley was taking a page out of the Tyson playbook. (Tyson used to wear black trunks with no socks, reminiscent of a gladiator of old.) After the first Pacquiao fight, Bradley would be wheeled out to a local hospital.

The major reason there had been no immediate rematch was the lack of sales. The hope this time was that Bradley, with his latest two wins, now had the added name recognition and respect that could see the rematch exceed one million PPV buys. A press tour would take place in both Los Angeles and New York in February to promote the match that would be known as "Vindication." Bradley would immediately assert, "Pacquiao's killer instinct is gone, and he has too much compassion." The Bradley remark would serve as motivation for Pacquiao to try to earn his first stoppage win in four-and-a-half years. Pacquiao would be guaranteed $20 million and Bradley $6 million with both getting an additional percentage from the PPV revenue. The live gate would do nearly $8 million due to 14,000 tickets being sold.

The bout would take place on April 12, 2014, at the Grand MGM in Las Vegas.

Both fighters would come in at less than the welterweight limit as Pacquiao weighed 145 and Bradley 145.5 pounds. The opening stanza saw both fighters shoot jabs while utilizing upper-body movement. Pacquiao had trouble connecting with his lead left, while Bradley did enough straight rights to narrowly capture the first round. Pacquiao would conversely capture the second with a powerful lead left that had Bradley take a few steps back. Bradley would be further tested in the third, as Pacquiao would score with combinations in the center of the ring. Bradley would respond with wild punches that often missed or partially connected. Pacquiao would flurry in the waning moments to make a final claim of the round.

The fourth saw Bradley land his best punch of the contest as a wild overhand right had Pacquiao stumble and lose his balance for a few seconds. That punch could have been enough in a close round to sway the judges, as Bradley showed improved ring generalship. The fifth saw Bradley continue to do a better job slipping punches while landing short counter right hands. The sixth was essentially an even round that saw nothing significant score as both combatants had their best shots either blocked or slipped. Pacquiao would take command in the next two rounds, as his superior hand speed would produce dazzling combinations in the middle of the ring. A valiant Bradley would wave Pacquiao to come forward but fail to score anything of significance.

As the second half of the bout progressed, Bradley looked increasingly fatigued, and by the ninth he seem to retreat—which could have been a result of both an injured leg and accumulative punishment. Pacquiao's dominance continued until the eleventh, which saw Bradley box more effectively on his bike and land a solid overhand right that could have tilted the mainly mundane round to his direction. Bradley trainer Luis Diaz would give Bradley a pep rally to come out strong in the final round, as he claimed that "many of the rounds were close." Both fighters would take nothing for granted and come out aggressively swinging wildly. Bradley would be on unsteady legs as he was still the victim of Pacquiao's left hands. An accidental head-butt would temporarily put a halt to the action in the waning moments. Overall, this proved to be a much more entertaining bout than the first. The final punch stats had Bradley connect 141 of 627 and Pacquiao 198 of 563.

My scorecard had Pacquiao winning 116–113 (7-4-1), while judges Craig Metcalfe and Michael Pernick had it for Pacquiao 116–112, and the final judge Glenn Trowbridge had it 118–110 for Pacquiao. Bradley had wanted to prove Pacquiao wrong for saying that he had to run and couldn't engage with him and trade. Pacquiao would concede that Bradley fought better the second time and had actually hurt him once.

Bradley would once again mention that an injury impeded him this time—a pulled right calf muscle. However, Bradley would make it clear it was not an excuse, and the fact that he actually moved well for many rounds after the first round (when he claimed the injury took place) was a testament to his courage and determination. The final pay-per-view numbers had between 750,000–800,000 sales. It was the second consecutive Pacquiao pay-per-view that failed to register one million buys. Many critics would point to the lack of a major Latino star either in the main event or the undercard to explain the disappointing figure. The lack of a major Mexican or Puerto Rican star could have been a factor. Nonetheless, the numbers were a major improvement from the previous Pacquiao contest. Pacquiao's win would mean that he had earned at least one official win on every single opponent he had ever faced—excluding the first two losses to Rustico Torrecampo and Medgoen Singsurat ("3K Battery").

CHAPTER 21

A Cinderella Opponent

Chris Algieri was possibly the least notable Pacquiao opponent on paper since his tune-up fight with Hectar Velasquez nearly a decade before. Algieri's biggest win was his lead-up bout in which he won the WBO light welterweight title by disputed split decision over Ruslan Provodnikov. If Provodnikov had won, it would have set up an interesting proposition as both Pacquiao and Provodnikov were former sparring mates and were both trained by Freddie Roach. Provodnikov was open to fighting Pacquiao if he felt it was the correct business move. Algieri, despite being knocked down twice in the first round and having a badly swollen eye, would utilize his boxing skills and make it a competitive bout (even if he didn't merit the decision). I felt a case could be made Algieri won up to seven of the twelve rounds to earn a 113–113 draw, which is amazing considering the damage he received in the first round. Algieri made Provodnikov miss often and exercised ring generalship with his lateral movement, jab, and hand speed that allowed him to score with several combinations. In fact, after the tenth round, Freddie Roach told Provodnikov that the fight was close and wanted a knockout to remove the necessity of it going to judges. Those who felt Provodnikov clearly won thought the heavier shots were landed by the Russian fighter, and Algieri was scoring mainly with jabs and light artillery as he ran on his bike. The final CompuBox stats—which don't always tell the whole story—did favor Algieri who landed 288 of 993 to Provodnikov's 205 of 776. Although I felt Provodnikov deserved no less than a draw and should have kept his title, no one can argue that Algieri didn't earn his six-figure payday.

Having the Provodnikov match take place was a challenge itself as Algieri's former manager, Humberto Romero, petitioned the New York Supreme Court to halt the match scheduled between Algieri and Provodnikov scheduled for June 14, 2014. Romero claimed breach of contract and claimed he had stakes of 16 percent of future prize money and 20 percent of endorsements, paid appearances, and business dealings. Judge Jeffrey Oing ruled in favor of Algieri stating that Romero should have filed his papers a year before and that he was doing this now as Algieri could lose his value as a boxing commodity if he lost to Provodnikov. Romero had alleged that Algieri had owed him over a million dollars in managerial fees and violated his contract when he broke off with Romero and signed with Joe Deguardia's Star Boxing. Algieri claimed that he left Romero since he wasn't being adequately promoted.

Algieri, at five feet ten, is a tall junior welterweight who utilizes his jab and reach advantage over the often smaller opponents. Obviously, it was expected that Algieri would use his seventy-two-inch reach to his advantage against Pacquiao. Yet, like many things in life, it's easier said than done. Algieri didn't follow the typical boxing career as he turned professional at twenty-four and holds a bachelor's degree in health-care science. Algieri also added a master's degree in clinical nutrition and took all the necessary prerequisites necessary to go to medical school. In an ESNewsReporting.com video posted by Elie Seckbach, the Oxnard gym trainer Robert Garcia openly wonders, "What the f**k is this guy doing in boxing? He is one of the few boxers that does the sport because he loves it and not because he wants to be famous or for the payday." The Long Island native of both Argentinean and Italian heritage demonstrated his proficiency in combat disciplines prior to being a boxer, as Algieri was a student of karate, kickboxing, and wrestling. As a teenager Algieri was a competitor in kickboxing amateur tournaments. In fact, Algieri won both the ISKA welterweight and WKA super welterweight titles in kickboxing. All of these combat disciplines helped transition Algieri to a boxer as he had many of the important striking and footwork skills that are essential in boxing.

Bob Arum reached out to Algieri promoter Joe Deguardia of Star Boxing and closed the deal by the middle of July. There was a collective gasp, and some boxing fans didn't think a Cinderella opponent with only twenty bouts under his belt would generate much PPV revenue. The match would be scheduled for November 22, 2014, at the Cotai Arena in the Venetian, Macao, China. Pacquiao would be guaranteed a purse of $25 million and Algieri would earn his first seven-figure payday as he was expected to earn $1.67 million. Algieri would also get a chance to travel extensively for the first time to promote a match. There wouldn't be much trash talking, as both combatants were humble and had mutual respect for each other. What was evident during their stare downs was that Algieri—along with De La Hoya and Margarito—was among the tallest opponents Pacquiao had faced. The fact that Freddie Roach saw Algieri ringside during the Provodnikov bout would undoubtedly help Pacquiao as Roach could dissect Algieri's strengths and weaknesses firsthand.

The promotion of the bout would entail an international traveling itinerary that would take both fighters to the American destinations of San Francisco, Los Angeles, Las Vegas, and New York, while the Asian destinations included Macao, Shanghai, and Singapore. All of this promotion was new to Algieri, but it also came with a great opportunity to cause a major upset.

In June, Manny Pacquiao would be hired as the head coach for the Kia Sorentos of the Philippine Basketball Association. Just two months later he would be drafted by them as the eleventh player selected in the draft. Pacquiao would actually play in a game for the Kia Sorentos on October 19. Promoter Bob Arum wasn't too keen on Pacquiao playing. He would tell the *New York Daily News*, "When I found out he was playing, before he played, I wasn't very happy. Professional basketball, no matter the country, is a rugged sport, and a player can turn an ankle very easily. These NBA players are fantastic physical specimens, and they get injured all the time, so an injury would have wreaked havoc with the fight, so I was not very pleased." To some the basketball and risk of injury was a sign that Pacquiao wasn't taking Algieri very serious. In fact, Freddie Roach may have echoed this sentiment, as he felt that some of Pacquiao's sparring partners were better than Algieri. He would claim during a prefight conference call that Pacquiao had sparred with Viktor Postel, a fighter from the Ukraine, who had both a similar jab and height to Algieri. "Postel is as talented as Algieri and has a better left hand," Roach would claim. When pressed about the sparring partners being better than Algieri, Roach replied, "Sometimes the truth hurts."

Although Roach may have sounded unabashedly blunt, the fact remained that Algieri was relatively inexperienced in fighting someone of Pacquiao's caliber. A more immediate problem for Algieri surfaced the day of the weigh-in as he failed to make weight on the first attempt. Despite going fully nude, Algieri came in at 144.2, which was 0.2 over the weight-stipulated agreement. Algieri would make weight approximately an hour before the deadline to avoid a penalty. Officially, Algieri would come in at 143.6 while Pacquiao came in at 143.8 pounds. The failure to make weight at the first attempt surprised many as Algieri is a clinical nutritionist and can tweak a diet for proper weight adjustment. Algieri would hydrate to 155 pounds and Pacquiao to 149 pounds on the day of the contest.

Both fighters would wear similarly colored light-blue trunks, which in past history has resulted in fighters getting a fine by the commission. The opening stanza saw Pacquiao exercise both upper-body and head movement as he worked his jab. Both boxers retained a high guard approach, which signaled a cautious start. A two-punch combination (0:55) scored for Pacquiao and set the tone for the rest of the round. Algieri was on his bicycle and didn't fire much and simply waited for a perfect counter opportunity that never presented itself. It was an easy round to score for Pacquiao.

Pacquiao would bang his gloves in anticipation of more action in the second. Algieri would score with a clean left hook (0:22) only to get punished in return by a couple of Pacquiao left hands. Algieri would be ruled down after taking a barrage of shots near the northeastern corner ropes. After further review it was apparent that Algieri slipped due to water accumulation in the ring. The scoring of 10–8 would prove to be academic for the rest of the bout.

Despite being outclassed Algieri did show some ring generalship in the third as he circled away from Pacquiao's left and did slip punches. However, one must make an opponent pay for missing, and Algieri didn't capitalize on these opportunities. Pacquiao was able to measure Algieri well in the third and routinely scored with both hands on a very mobile opponent. A bright spot for Algieri was when he scored with a straight right (1:52) that failed to hurt Pacquiao.

The fourth saw Algieri come out more active as he aimed for the Pacquiao body. Pacquiao would respond by raising his gloves up, feeling the shots were a bit low. The round would be the most dominating Pacquiao round up to that point. Algieri would be punished with clean solid blows that would be highlighted by a right uppercut (1:42).

The fifth may have been the only round that could have been scored for Algieri. A straight right, a short left hook, and a body shot would score for Algieri in the opening minute. Referee Genaro Rodriquez would give Algieri a warning to keep his punches higher. Pacquiao would become more aggressive in the middle of the round, but most of the shots were slipped or partial connects. Only Judge Patrick Morley would score it for Algieri, which made it the first official round given to Algieri by any of the three judges.

The sixth saw Pacquiao cut the distance and use his hand speed and accuracy to score between Algieri's guard. After getting a second warning for low blows, Algieri would get dropped (1:48) after being victimized by several left hands. Algieri's entire body would flip and roll on the canvas. Algieri would be fortunate to survive the round. Noticeable swelling could be seen in both Algieri eyes. At 2:18, a straight right would knock down Algieri again.

Algieri trainer, Tim Lane, felt that Pacquiao was expending a lot of energy and would be subject to punching himself out. After six rounds Algieri was so way behind that he likely needed a knockout to win the bout. The seventh saw a much more aggressive Algieri flickering his jab and firing haymakers. A solid right shot to the body (0:59) would score for Algieri. Pacquiao would find the mark with his straight left and punish Algieri for missing in the middle of the round. It was a close round that could have been scored an even 10–10 round.

Pacquiao would control the eighth with short shots to Algieri's head as they both navigated the ring. Algieri would complain to the referee that he had received a kidney shot, and both fighters would touch gloves in good sportsmanship. Pacquiao would be the aggressor for the remainder of the round and capitalize on the opportunities presented.

The opening minute of the ninth saw Pacquiao score with his one-two combinations to the head and body. As cotrainer Tim Lane would exclaim, "He still had his fighter in a cage and will let him out in one more round." Simultaneously, his fighter would fall violently on the canvas after getting crushed by an earth-shattering straight left (1:38). Algieri would get up but only to walk away from the referee. This should have ended the bout, yet the referee Genaro Rodriquez would allow the action to continue. After getting pummeled again, Algieri would receive another count. At 2:40 it appeared that the fight would be waved off, as the referee grabbed Pacquiao who walked away expecting the stoppage. However, the action would resume, and Algieri survived the round.

Algieri would almost get dropped again by a short left hook (1:23) in the tenth. It appeared that Algieri was fortunate to remain standing after another sizzling straight left landed (1:51). The bout was reminiscent of the punishment that Margarito received when he fought Pacquiao back in 2011. Algieri would get dropped for a sixth time in the closing seconds.

A major reason why Pacquiao would land short shots to the head was that Algieri was crouching down to fight the shorter fighter. Pacquiao obviously understood—through experience and training—how to fight taller opponents and capitalize on openings. The final two rounds saw Algieri survive on unsteady legs to finish the contest. The conclusion to the bout saw Algieri take more unnecessary, wicked shots—as in the final thirty seconds of the eleventh when Pacquiao would tattoo Algieri with overhand blows. Algieri would satisfy the Cinderella fairy tale simply by lasting the entire distance with Pacquiao, something a few Hall-of-Fame-calibar fighters failed to do against Pacquiao. The final CompuBox punch stats had Pacquiao landing 229 of 669 and Algieri 108 of 469. In postfight comments Algieri conceded, "Manny Pacquiao is the best in the world in fighting like Manny Pacquiao...His start and stop is great...He has so much experience and has perfected in fighting like Manny Pacquiao." Algieri would reiterate his belief that he felt he could hurt Pacquiao in the later rounds as he had hurt all of his previous opponents despite having eight knockouts in twenty bouts.

Pacquiao would admit that he had tried to go for a knockout, but Algieri was fast and moving, and he also didn't want to get careless or overconfident. The Mayweather question—which at this point was nauseating—would get a funny response as Pacquiao would repeat the Foot Locker commercial punch line, "He is going to fight me? Yes! Yes!"

A few days later, philstar.com reported that Pacquiao would claim, "I took pity on him [Algieri]. He is still inexperienced, yet he was already thrown into the pit. Though he has potential, he fought a veteran fighter. He still lacks experience. We're too far apart in terms of level. But he's really tough, though. He didn't want to get knocked out. He impressed me because he held on even though he was inexperienced. He tried his best."

The final pay-per-view numbers (although disputed by some sources) reported as low as 300,000 plus, while others were closer to approximately 400,000—which was what promoter Bob Arum reported. Nonetheless, it was clearly the lowest Pacquiao PPV numbers since his rematch with Juan Manuel Marquez back in 2008.

CHAPTER 22

He Is Going to Fight Me? Yes! Yes!

Besides the Mayweather never-ending saga, there were new opportunities for a Pacquiao opponent, as Golden Boy Promotions was now willing to do business with Top Rank. This meant possible opponents such as undefeated Danny Garcia and even Saul Alvarez could be on the horizon. However, Pacquiao felt a personal obligation to boxing fans around the world to help push for the superbout with Mayweather. Mayweather himself made his declaration to Showtime that he wanted the fight. A major issue was that Mayweather wanted to fight in May and that was close to what many believed would be a match between Miguel Cotto and Saúl "Canelo" Alvarez. Alvarez wanted to fight during the Cinco de Mayo time period. As that contest could be easily arranged in the future, it appeared that all parties planned to make Mayweather-Pacquiao both a priority and reality. Bob Arum communicated with CBS president, Les Monvees, and reportedly met at the promoter's Beverly Hills home via a meeting set up by trainer Freddie Roach.

Monvees perfectly understood that Showtime had invested a tremendous amount of money in Mayweather and, besides the Canelo match, there wasn't any blockbuster event for the channel in their six-fight deal with the fighter. Bob Arum seized the opportunity by alleging that Showtime was losing big on Mayweather and told TheBoxingVoice.com, "As long as Floyd has a contract with two freebies coming from Showtime, he is content with that. If I were

Showtime and I was taking losses as big as I am on Mayweather fights, I wouldn't be happy, but, who knows, maybe they have a bunch of masochists running the company." Pacquiao would also tell the Agence France-Presse (AFP) that "he has reached a dead end. He has nowhere to run but to fight me."

As the window of opportunity for getting a bout with Mayweather started to close, for the first time Manny Pacquiao aggressively called out Mayweather. The most overt attempt was through a Foot Locker commercial in which Pacquiao confused the conversation of two customers, believing it was confirmation that Mayweather wanted to fight Pacquiao. "He is going to fight me? Yes! Yes!" Pacquiao responded in jubilant fashion. Pacquiao again echoed the phrase after his bout with Chris Algieri.

The calling out continued on Twitter on January 20. Pacquiao tweeted, "If you really care about the fans, you will fight. If you care about yourself…you won't fight." Pacquiao added, "I can easily beat @FloydMayweather, I believe that." This was the closest to trash talking that Pacquiao ever engaged in to get Mayweather in the ring. It was apparent that the combined pressure of both Arum and Pacquiao was working, coupled with the Foot Locker commercial. No professional athlete with an ego could allow such a public calling out to go unchecked. *(For in-depth round-by-round coverage and prefight negotiations, see the chapter on Mayweather, "Securing Both Legacy and Biggest Payday.")*

Although many had anticipated that the match would be announced Super Bowl weekend, the failure to seal the deal appeared to take the air out of the Zeppelin-size balloon. The chance encounter at a Miami Heat game on January 27, 2015, and a subsequent visit to Pacquiao's hotel room fully convinced Pacquiao and his advisor Michael Koncz that Mayweather did in fact want the fight. The bout would be officially announced on February 20, 2015, by Mayweather on the Shots social network. Pacquiao was pleased with the news and announced, "I am very happy that Floyd Mayweather and I can give the fans the fight they wanted for so many years. They have waited long enough and they deserve it. It is an honor to be part of this historic event."

Freddie Roach went on CBS Sports Radio's "Ferrall on the Bench" and declared, "Manny's going to attack him and we're going to throw a thousand-punch combination at him, I swear. Manny just really, really knows what he wants to do in this fight. He's doing really well. The training's been great. Beating Floyd, it'll be a public service for boxing, I swear—because this guy is not a good guy."

Despite Mayweather getting all the major perks of the deal (home advantage, 60–40 split, top billing, lead promoter), to some it would be a surprise that Pacquiao was allowed his eight-ounce Reyes gloves. This was something that Pacquiao didn't get in his match with Erik Morales as a super featherweight. Pacquiao brushed aside all the advantages that Mayweather got in the contract as he thought they were akin to giving a death row inmate his final meal of his choice.

Both parties also agreed to random blood testing, which would be done by the US Anti-Doping Agency (USADA), a testing agency that Mayweather had used in the past. Pacquiao was tested by USADA just two days after the testing agency was revealed. Some critics and conspiracy theorists tried to imply that there was a Mayweather bias from the USADA, as Travis Tygart once labeled Mayweather "the clean athlete." In the past, the Pacquiao camp had voiced a preference for the World Anti-Doping Agency (WADA) to handle the drug testing. A major criticism of USADA was that testing is not done year-round. Since the fight was announced on February 20 and the bout would take place on May 2, there would be only ten weeks of possible testing. Nonetheless, the two participants did agree on the testing protocol.

The first press conference was held in Los Angeles on March 11. Freddie Roach said at the conference, "I love challenges and this is the biggest challenge of my life. I've been looking forward for this for a long, long time. I'm just going to get my fighter as ready as possible. We're in the toughest fight of our life. We're fighting the best fighter in the world. And we are going to kick his ass, I'm sorry, but Good Luck Floyd."

Pacquiao gave a sermon speech. "To the fans of boxing I believe this is what you been waiting for since five years ago. I want people to know that God can raise someone from nothing to something as he did with me." After the conference Pacquiao told *HBO Boxing* reporter Kieran Mulvaney, "He has a good defense, but I can easily break that defense."

Pacquiao's confidence during training also extended to trainer Freddie Roach. Roach told Philboxing.com, "I am confident May 2 will be celebrated for years to come as St. Manny's Day—the day he drove Mayweather out of boxing." Pacquiao during training camp sported a T-shirt of Pac-Man chopping down a dollar sign, which suggested he also anticipated a victory on May 2. As Mayweather had to prepare for Pacquiao's speed, Pacquiao had to prepare for Mayweather's speed. This wasn't going to be an opponent that was going to sit and trade. As a southpaw Pacquiao needed a plan to avoid lead right hands. To help in this endeavor, Pacquiao trained with Cuban fighter Guillermo Rigondeaux, considered among the most technical fighters in the game, to simulate Mayweather. Rigondeaux (14–0) was an undefeated fighter with an extensive amateur background that included two Olympic Gold Medals.

As an added incentive for Pacquiao to win, he was promised free food for the rest of his life. Gerry's Grill, which offers authentic Filipino delicacies in Artesia, California, offered Pacquiao, a loyal customer to the restaurant, free food for life on the condition that Pacquiao defeated Mayweather.

The final press conference was held on April 29 in the Las Vegas MGM Grand and saw Pacquiao tell the world, "Everything that I have accomplished is God who gave me the strength. I use to sleep in the streets, starving, hungry and now I can't imagine that the lord raised me this position. I can't imagine that the boy that sleeping in the streets was raised to this level of life. This fight on Saturday our goal is to give the fans enjoyment and satisfaction of our performance and entertain you guys that you will be happy on Saturday."

The weigh-in saw a very confident and jubilant Pacquiao digesting the festivities. Despite being thousands of miles away from his native home, he was greeted by the MGM audience as if he were the hometown fighter. Pacquiao stared at Mayweather, smiling from ear to ear, and then raised both his arms, feeling grateful to finally give the audience something they had wanted for over five years. Pacquiao would actually wear a T-shirt that read on the back: "All glory and honor belongs to God." Pacquiao also enjoyed Butterfinger cups as he was now an official endorser of the candy.

After five years in the making, the Mayweather-Pacquiao face-off after the weigh-in takes place. AP Photo/John Locher.

Unlike tall opponents such as Margarito and De La Hoya, Mayweather was going to use his size advantage over Pacquiao, a smaller opponent. Still, it was widely expected that Pacquiao's foot speed would be able to close the distance. The actual match had its moments, but it didn't deliver the fireworks many had hoped for. Pacquiao had a few moments in the fourth, eighth, and tenth rounds, but he didn't come close to his common thousand-punch output. Mayweather employed a strategy of distance, clinching, and lateral movement when necessary. However, another mitigating factor was revealed after the contest. Pacquiao revealed a right shoulder tear, which he explained limited the use of his right hand. Despite the injury Pacquiao after the bout stated that he felt he had won the match and thought Mayweather didn't land any major shots, doing more moving than connecting. In the postfight conference, Pacquiao added, "This training camp we were planning to postpone because for two weeks I couldn't train well. I couldn't use my right hand. We planned to file with the commission for an exemption for the shot to numb my shoulder, but we respect the decision that it's not allowed, so we didn't get a shot. One week before the fight my shoulder is getting better and better, but not one hundred percent, something wrong." Francisco Aguilar, chairman of the Nevada Athletic Commission (NSAC), fired back; he said the Pacquiao team did not disclose the injury until Saturday night, so the requests for permission to take the shot and to have a personal doctor in Pacquiao's corner were denied. "We were not aware of his injury until tonight at six thirty," said Aguilar, who made the ruling. "The medications he was taking were disclosed on his medical questionnaire, but not the actual injury...This isn't our first fight. This is our business. There is a process, and when you try to screw with the process, it's not going to work for you."

On May 4, the Pacquiao camp issued a press release that they had notified the US Anti-Doping Agency of the shoulder injury and that they had gotten approval for the anti-inflammatory drug Toradol five days before the fight. The statement further states that Pacquiao had listed the medication on his prefight medical form. Per the statement, the Nevada State Athletic Commission, despite a second attempt, refused to allow use of the drug. Pacquiao also claimed that the NSAC had deliberately withheld both his vitamins and water from the dressing room "for the first time in my boxing career." Pacquiao also told the *Manila Standard Today* that the Mayweather camp was aware of the injury. "Did you see when he was pulling my arm, because he knew. I felt like a needle was penetrating my bones. I really needed that shot because if I threw a power hook or power jab, it hurt."

Michael Koncz would reveal that the injury occurred on April 4 during sparring, when his right arm got tangled with the right arm of his sparring partner. After medical examination a tear underneath the rotator cuff in a joint was revealed. To alleviate the pain, a cortisone shot was given. The injury could have been a good reason for a rematch if the contest wasn't so lackluster. The first match between Pernell Whitaker and Buddy McGirt had a similar issue, when McGirt lost a close decision to Whitaker after complaining about an injured shoulder. However, that was a competitive and entertaining match. This match had a few moments, but it wasn't very entertaining, and demand for a rematch was uncertain.

Pacquiao was in a difficult circumstance, however; if the injury were revealed, then Mayweather becomes aware of the injury and it's tipping him off. If the fight had been postponed, then people who had waited five years would lose hope and the bout would lose interest again. Moreover, old-school fans might have pointed to injured fighters winning bouts, such as Harry Greb, Sam Langford—who won fights legally blind in one eye—and more recently Carlos

Monzon—who had lasting tissue damage due to being shot in a leg. Even more recently, guys such as Jeff Fenech and, yes, Floyd Mayweather had won fights with injured hands. If God was going to deliver Mayweather as Pacquiao promised, he had nothing to fear, even with an injured shoulder. As the saying goes for believers, "If God is with you, than who can be against you?" There was also the concern that Mayweather was retiring and, if the fight were postponed, it might never come to fruition. There was no easy way to have addressed the issue. In retrospect, revealing the injury in the questionnaire would have put adequate pressure on the NSAC to allow the shot, especially when the USADA had approved it.

Despite the disclosure of the injury and subsequent shoulder surgery, many were openly critical of Pacquiao's strategy in fighting Mayweather. Trainer Robert Garcia told ESPNNewsReporting.com, "I didn't see what I thought I would see from Pacquiao, no game plan, no instructions from the corner, maybe is time for Freddie Roach to hang it up. He is done very well for himself and go down as one of the best in history." Garcia also downplayed the injury. "Everyone has a little bit of injury, he has had leg injury, he has had cramps, and he went in there and fought. If he had an injury it was minor since he was still fighting and he could still pick up his arm. Brandon Rios has been injured in his last four fights [Garcia holding his right arm] and now when he can say he was injured against Pacquiao and now we can ask for a rematch?

To make matters worse, Pacquiao also had the distraction of pending litigation due to the disclosure of the injury. Tephane Vanel and Kami Rahbaran filed a class-action lawsuit for $5 million, claiming that if they had known about the injury, they wouldn't have placed such high bets. There were several other lawsuits filed by fans who gambled and bought the pay-per-view. In many ways the sport got another black eye just by trying to do something right. The five years of building up a fight seemed to have both more drama and duration than Wagner's ring cycle. It would only be fitting that the postfight drama would start a new act of the Mayweather-Pacquiao soap opera.

There were several options for Pacquiao after he fully recovered from the shoulder injury. Pacquiao, with the biggest payday of his career (expected to exceed $100 million after pay-per-view revenue), could retire and dedicate himself to politics, philanthropy, and his family. If you were a betting person, then expect a Pacquiao ring return, possibly in a year, as either a junior welterweight or a welterweight. A Mayweather rematch also can never be ruled out, even if it sounds unlikely at the moment.

In Manny Pacquiao we find a man who stands barely over five feet six who came from an impoverished background and did not have much formal education, and yet he would inspire millions internationally through both sport and politics. Adding both the ring achievements and the cultural influence, perhaps no other fighter has transcended boxing since the heyday of Muhammad Ali. This is also a testament to the sport of boxing that is perhaps only rivaled by football (American soccer), which can allow both economically disadvantaged and shorter athletes the opportunity for international acclaim and fortune.

IBHOF Members Defeated (1): Oscar De La Hoya.
Probable IBHOF Members Defeated (5): Marco Antonio Barrera, Miguel Cotto, Juan Manuel Marquez, Erik Morales, Shane Mosley.
Possible IBHOF Members Defeated (2): Timothy Bradley, Oscar Larios.

Professional Boxing Record
(57-6-2 38 KOs)

1995

January 25	Edmund Ignacio WUD 4, Sablayan, Mindoro Occidental, Philippines
March 18	Pinoy Montejo WUD 4, Sablayan, Mindoro Occidental, Philippines
May 1	Rocky Palma WUD 6, Imus, Cavite, Philippines
July 1	Dele Decierto WTKO 2, Mandaluyong City, Metro Manila, Philippines
August 3	Acasio Simbajan WUD 6, Mandaluyong City, Metro Manila, Philippines
Sept 16	Armando Rocil WKO 3, Mandaluyong City, Metro Manila, Philippines
Oct 7	Lolito Laroa WUD 8, Makati City, Metro Manila, Philippines
Oct 21	Renato Mendones WTKO 2, Puerto Princesa City, Palawan, Philippines
Nov 11	Rudolfo Fernandez WTKO 3, Mandaluyong City, Metro Manila, Philippines
Dec 9	Rolando Toyogon WUD 10, P. Paredes, Sampaloc, Metro Manila, Philippines

1996

Feb 9	Rustico Torrecampo LKO 3, Mandaluyong City, Metro Manila, Philippines
April 27	Marlon Carillo WUD 10, Manila Midtown Ramada Hotel-Malate Manila, Metro Manila, Philippines
May 20	John Medina WTKO 4, Malabon City, Metro Manila, Philippines
June 15	Bert Batiller WTKO 4, General Santos City, Cotabato del Sur, Philippines

July 27	Ippo Gala WTKO 2, Mandaluyong City, Metro Manila, Philippines
Dec 28	Sung-Yul Lee WTKO 2, Barangay Alabang Muntinlupa City, Metro Manila, Philippines

1997

March 8	Mike Luna WKO 1, Muntinlupa City, Metro Manila, Philippines
April 24	Wook-Ki Lee WKO 1, Ritsy's, Makati City, Philippines
May 30	Ariel Austria WTKO 6, Davao City, Davao Del Sur, Philippines
June 26	Chokchai Chockvivat WKO 5, Mandaluyong City, Metro Manila, Philippines
Sep 14	Melvin Magramo WUD 10, Cebu City, Cebu, Philippines
Dec 6	Panomdej Ohyuthanakom WKO 1, Koronadal City, Cotabato del Sur, Philippines

1998

May 18	Shin Terao WKO 1, Kurakuen Hall, Tokyo, Japan
Dec 4	Chatchai Sasakul WKO 8, Phuntamonthon, Thailand **WBC World flyweight title**

1999

Feb 20	Todd Makelin WTKO 3, Kidapawan City, Cotabato del Norte, Philippines
April 24	Gabriel Mira WTKO 4, Quezon City, Metro Manila, Philippines **WBC World flyweight title**
Sept 17	Medgoen Singsurat LTKO 3, Nakhon Si Thammarat, Thailand **WBC World flyweight title**
Dec 18	Raynante Jamili WTKO 2, Paranque City, Metro Manila, Philippines

2000

March 4	Arnel Barotillo WTKO 4, Ninoy Aquino Stadium, Metro Manila, Philippines
June 28	Seung-Kon Chae WTKO 1, Araneta Coliseum, Quezon City, Philippines
Oct 14	Nedal Hussein WTKO 10, Ynares Sports Center, Antipolo City, Philippines

2001

Feb 24	Tetsutora Senrima WTKO 5, Ynares Sports Center, Antipolo City, Philippines
April 28	Wethya Sakmuangklang WKO 6, Kidapawan City, Philippines
June 23	Lehlo Ledwaba WTKO 6, MGM Grand, Las Vegas, NV **IBF World super bantamweight title**
Nov 10	Agapitho Sanchez D 12, Bill Graham Civic Auditorium, San Francisco, CA **IBF, WBO World super bantamweight titles**

2002

June 8	Jorge Eliecer Julio WTKO 2, The Pyramid, Memphis, TN **IBF World super bantamweight title**
Oct 26	Fahprakorb Rakkiatgym WTKO 1, RMC Gym, Davao City, Philippines **IBF World super bantamweight title**

2003

March 15	Serikzhan Yeshmagambetov, WTKO 5, Luna Park Quirino Grandstand, Metro Manila, Philippines
July 26	Emmanuel Lucero WTKO 3, Olympic Auditorium, Los Angeles, CA
Nov 15	Marco Antonio Barrera WTKO 11, Alamodome, San Antonio, TX

2004

May 8	Juan Manuel Marquez D 12, MGM Grand, Las Vegas, NV
	IBF, Super WBA World featherweight titles
Dec 11	Fahsan 3K Battery WTKO 4, Taguig City, Metro Manila, Philippines

2005

| March 19 | Erik Morales LUD 12, MGM Grand, Las Vegas, NV |
| Sept 10 | Hector Velazquez WTKO 6, Staples Center, Los Angeles, CA |

2006

January 21	Erik Morales WTKO 10, Thomas & Mack Center, Las Vegas, NV
July 2	Oscar Larios WUD 12, Araneta Coliseum, Quezon City, Philippines
Nov 18	Erik Morales WKO 3, Thomas & Mack Center, Las Vegas, NV

2007

| April 14 | Jorge Solis WKO 8, Alamodome, San Antonio, TX |
| Oct 6 | Marco A. Barrera WUD 12, Mandalay Bay Hotel and Casino, Las Vegas, NV |

2008

March 15	Juan Manuel Marquez WSD 12, Mandalay Bay Resort and Casino, Las Vegas, NV
	WBC World super featherweight title
June 28	David Diaz WTKO 9, Mandalay Bay Hotel and Casino, Las Vegas, NV
	WBC World lightweight title
Dec 6	Oscar De La Hoya WTKO 8, MGM Grand, Las Vegas, NV

2009

May 2	Ricky Hatton WKO 2, MGM Grand, Las Vegas, NV
Nov 14	Miguel Cotto WTKO 12, MGM Grand, Las Vegas, NV
	WBO World welterweight title

2010

March 13	Joshua Clottey WUD 12, Cowboys Stadium, Arlington, TX
	WBO World welterweight title
Nov 13	Antonio Margarito WUD 12, Cowboys Stadium, Arlington, TX
	vacant WBC World light middleweight title

2011

May 7	Shane Mosley WUD 12, MGM Grand, Las Vegas, NV
	WBO World welterweight title
Nov 12	Juan Manuel Marquez WMD 12, MGM Grand, Las Vegas, NV
	WBO World welterweight title

2012

June 9	Timothy Bradley LSD 12, MGM Grand, Las Vegas, NV
	WBO World welterweight title
Dec 8	Juan Manuel Marquez LKO 6, MGM Grand, Las Vegas, NV

2013

Nov 24	Brandon Rios WUD 12, Cotai Arena, Macao, China

2014

April 12	Timothy Bradley WUD 12, MGM Grand, Las Vegas, NV
	WBO World welterweight title

Nov 22   Chris Algieri WUD 12, Cotai Arena, Macao, China
                  WBO World welterweight title

2015

May 2   Floyd Mayweather LUD 12, MGM Grand, Las Vegas, NV
                  WBO, WBC, WBA super World welterweight titles

BIBLIOGRAPHY

Boxing Press. "Shaw to Promote Pacquiao." *Saddoboxing.com,* web, 23 August 2005.

Hartwell, Darren. "Restaurant Offers Manny Pacquiao Free Food for Life If He Beats Floyd Mayweather." *Nesn.com,* web, 17 March 2015.

Lagumbay, Salven L. "Pacquiao, Murad Settle Out of Court." *Philippine Day Inquirer,* 30 June 2005.

Marley, Michael. "Arum: Mosley Not Likely to Fight Pacquiao." *Sports Illustrated.com,* web, 20 September 2010.

Nathanielsz, Ronnie. "Murad Muhammad Strikes Back at Roach and Finkel." *Boxingscene.com,* web, 24 March 2005.

Pugmire, Lance. "Manny Pacquiao, Trainer Say Boxer Was Distracted before Last Fight." *Los Angeles Times,* 10 May 2010.

San Diego Jr., Bayana. "Pac-Man Flick Knocked Out First Day." *Philippine Day Inquirer,* 26 December 2009.

Trinidad, Chino. "The Dangers of Boxing." *Gmanetwork.com,* web, 26 January 2010.

Yap, Karl Lester M., Yap, Cecilia. "Philippine Diaspora Rushing Storm Aid Shows Remittance Reliance." *Bloomberg.com,* web, 25 November 2013.

Front Cover Pacquiao Photo Credit: AP Photo/ Vincent Wu.

Printed in Poland
by Amazon Fulfillment
Poland Sp. z o.o., Wrocław